Handbook of Youth Ministry

Contributors

James A. Davies

Ronald L. Koteskey

Gary L. Sapp

Jerry Aldridge

Kenneth E. Hyde

Blake J. Neff

Bonnidell Clouse

James Michael Lee

Anthony Campolo

Donald Ratcliff

James F. Engel

Handbook of Youth Ministry

edited by

**DONALD RATCLIFF
and JAMES A. DAVIES**

**R.E.P. Books
Birmingham, Alabama**

Library of Congress Cataloging-in-Publication Data

Handbook of youth ministry / edited by Donald Ratcliff and James A. Davies.
    Includes bibliographical references and indexes.
    ISBN 0-89135-079-9
    1. Church work with youth.   2. Church work with young adults.
  I. Ratcliff, Donald.   II. Davies, James A. (James Alan), 1948-   .
  BV4447.H2946   1991   91-10394
   259'.23—dc20   CIP

R.E.P. Books
5316 Meadow Brook Road
Birmingham, Alabama 35242
10 9 8 7 6 5 4 3 2

Contents

Introduction

The *Handbook of Youth Ministry* is a comprehensive resource, authored by top specialists in the area of adolescent development and religious education. Like the predecessor handbooks in this series, it provides concise and informative summaries of the most important topics in religious education. In contrast with other kinds of youth books, it attempts to give a research-based foundation for quality religious education.

Adolescence is defined as individuals between the ages of thirteen and eighteen, basically the teenage years. Younger and older individuals will at times be considered for the purpose of comparing and contrasting abilities, interests, and other characteristics. A major exception to the designated age span is chapter four which considers in detail the "almost adolescent," the pre-teen.

Overview

Chapter one describes adolescent subculture. This phenomenon is analyzed in terms of its major norms and values, the sense of in-group solidarity and distinctive aspects of the subculture. Fads, fashions, media influences, and hero worship are also examined. Current research on the subculture is included, but the primary emphasis is upon the purposes of specific activities of teenagers.

In chapter two the author examines how adolescence developed, a topic he has previously considered at the popular level, but here for the first time in scholarly detail. He posits adolescence to be a cultural innovation that had its genesis in the nineteenth century, a creation nonexistent previously in history. In nearly every non-Western culture the adolescent normally would be defined as an adult, or a beginning adult, rather than being a distinctive stage separate from both childhood and adulthood. The implications for parenting, as well as religious education, constitute a major section of the chapter.

Adolescent thinking is considered in chapter three. This survey of developmental theory and research emphasizes cognitive development, in which the young person moves from concrete operational thinking, to an immature formal operational ability, and finally to mature formal operations. Other topics include the ideal-

1

ism of adolescence, the self-concept, and the development of personal religion.

Preadolescence, which occurs during the eleventh and twelfth years of life, has become a prominent topic in child development. Religious education of pre-teenagers is emphasized by Merton Strommen and other major researchers as particularly crucial, thus a separate chapter is given to this topic. The long-standing practice of treating these youngsters as children in most churches separates them from teenagers and adults, while the media encourages adolescent roles for them (such as falling in love and dressing maturely). As David Elkind has so well documented, this produces a tension between being a child and becoming a teenager. The chapter includes an analysis of what religious educators should do as a result of this double message.

Chapter five considers the wealth of research on adolescence and religion. Many studies on this topic are summarized, including a number from other areas of the Western world to provide cross-cultural comparisons. Aspects of affective, cognitive, attitudinal, and lifestyle dimensions are considered. Topics include attitudes about religion, religious experiences of adolescents, religious beliefs, adolescent concepts of God, parental influences, and the effects of religious schools.

Communication and relationships constitute the topics of chapter six. Two issues predominate: the relationship between the religious educator and parents (churched or nonchurched), and how one can foster good relationships between teenagers and their parents. Religious education that expedites communication between parents and their adolescent offspring is crucial in church ministry.

Moral development and sexuality are the topics of the following chapter. It opens with a research review of moral development in adolescence, concentrating upon Kohlberg's theory and related research. Other theories are cited as contrasts to Kohlberg. The second half of the chapter gives an overview of the sexual behavior and attitudes of teenagers today, including a comparison of churched and nonchurched youngsters. The stages of sexual intimacy are briefly examined, including the implications of the stages for adolescent dating and courtship. Guidelines for helping youngsters develop healthy sexual attitudes and behavior are provided.

Chapter eight is a comprehensive survey of the methods of religious education, written by the leading proponent of the social-science theory of religious education. A variety of methods of learning and teaching are included, both traditional and modern, and the effectiveness of each is examined. The chapter opens with a survey of general instructional procedures, then moves to a more detailed analysis of specific procedures. It concludes with a brief section on how to improve teaching practices. Religious education involves more than verbal, cognitive, didactic teaching in a formal classroom. It includes any procedure in any setting that deliberately facilitates any kind of learning outcome.

A well-known speaker, writer, and sociologist concentrates upon the importance of an activist youth ministry in chapter nine. Using Richard Niebuhr's famous paradigm of Christ and culture, the various types of youth ministry are compared and contrasted. While those who work with youth probably will use some combination of approaches, an important component should be social, political, and cross-cultural activism by church young people. Learning by doing, rather than just listening, is central to the chapter, although telling stories about one's experiences is important in influencing others to become involved.

The handbook concludes with a chapter on research in the local church. While the entire research and development process is outlined, the emphasis is upon conducting a needs analysis to determine the most crucial needs of adolescents in a particular religious education context. The needs analysis is most likely to involve a survey or interview, thus the chapter concentrates upon how the religious educator can design an appropriate measurement instrument, implement the needs analysis, and interpret the results. These results then serve as a basis for educational objectives and program development to help meet the needs. This chapter helps open the door to practical research strategies so that virtually any church can provide religious education that is based upon the greatest needs among its youth.

Youth Ministry Today

While demographic data suggest that the number of youth in the United States has been in decline for several years, the trend should bottom out in this decade, followed by sustained growth for the foreseeable future. Yet it must be acknowledged that many churches are ill-prepared to minister to the youth they now have, let alone additional numbers in the future.

The writers of this book maintain that youth ministry is vital to the future of the church. This ministry should be based upon researched understandings of young people and usage of research-proven methodologies. Many young people (some sources claim the majority) leave the church sometime in their teen years, and a large number of them never return. The church that fails to understand and minister to young people may eventually be forced to close its doors. Great potential is available to the church that effectively reaches teenagers.

Youth ministry is a central factor in church growth. One survey conducted by Group (a Colorado youth ministry) in 1989 indicated that 80 percent of families see the presence of youth ministry as an important consideration in attending and joining a specific church. The American Institute for Church Growth reports that ministry to youth was the second most important reason people join a church (preaching was number one).

In some respects young people are quite religious, in other respects they are irreligious. One Canadian survey found that 84 percent of youths believe in God and 81 percent believe in the divinity of Christ. Yet only one in ten stated that God influenced his or her life a great deal. Only one in two hundred looked to religious leaders for advice or help, although 30 percent felt a need to be accepted by God (reported in *Canada's Youth* by R. Bibby and B. Posterski).

While the family is clearly the most important religious influence upon adolescents, a Search Institute study reveals that 42 percent of families never talk about religion and another 32 percent speak of their faith just once or twice a month. Only 13 percent discuss religion once a week. Another indication of the lack of adequate religious education is that, according to Gallup polls, 30 percent of teenagers do not understand the significance of Easter. This figure only decreases to 20 percent if they attend Sunday school regularly! The need is obvious for effective ministry with adolescents today.

In one of the largest studies of mainline churches ever undertaken, Search Institute found that religious education is strongly related to maturity in faith. From surveys and firsthand observations in six major denominations from 1986 to 1990, it was found that families can particularly influence faith during the adolescent years. Thus churches should not only conduct youth ministry but also help parents develop skills in facilitating faith development. The Search Institute concluded that religious education is far more important than church leaders have usually thought.

Faith as a Personal Construction

I spoke recently with a youth director who felt his teens really wanted to learn, but they were turned off by traditional approaches to religious education. They told him, "We don't want Bible stories, and all we hear about is sex, drugs, and rock music." They had plenty of questions but were hesitant to ask them because they had long heard, "You just ought to believe it" and "It's the right thing to do." (How's that for short-circuiting formal reasoning abilities?)

He decided to take a different approach. He raised provocative questions in youth meetings, such as, "Why go to church?" and, "What purpose is there in religious faith?" He tolerated teenagers who responded, "I don't believe that" and, "Aw, come on now." He once initiated a discussion of what the church youth did *not* believe, concluding they should "believe what you can now and keep an open mind about the rest"; he did not require immediate absolute belief in all the church's doctrines.

He was not afraid to go into controversial areas. He spoke of the responsibility parents have in the spiritual nurture of their children, which prompted one teenager to talk with his father about this idea. A long discussion between father and son resulted in setting aside a regular devotional time together.

This youth minister apparently realized that faith is a construction. We are given the various components of religion in bits and pieces by the church, parents, and others. But these components require personalization to be ultimately meaningful. Personalizing occurs when we reflect upon our religious heritage so that our perspective of the world and our behavior in the world are shaped by religious faith. This constructing is through an act of the will, an affirming (or denial) of what we have been taught. Just as important is the building and developing of faith through ongoing recommitment.

Curiously, doubt and questioning can help initiate faith construction. Unless we consider an alternative, faith tends to be immature, borrowed from others. To use biblical language, we drink milk instead of eating meat. The adolescent, in part because of new mental abilities and in part because of social influences, often challenges the religious content that he or she has been given. Out of this crucible can come affirmation of faith, a faith full of wonder and mystery, a stronger more mature faith, a faith that is personalized and individualized, a faith that can mature further with time, a faith that is constructed within one's worldview yet can transcend that worldview. Doubt can create a quality of faith that childish capitulation to belief may never accomplish.

Long ago Socrates commented that "the unexamined life is not worth living." The critical examination of the religious ideas passed down to them is crucial for adolescent spiritual development. It may not be easy for parents and religious educators, but it can be productive in the long run. The following account underscores how questioning and doubting helped lead to a more mature faith in the life of one of the editors.

When I was seventeen, I became very disillusioned with the church my family attended. I spoke with my parents about the problems I saw in the church and told them I saw no value in attending. My parents were amazingly sympathetic to my criticisms and agreed that the church had plenty of faults.

Instead of my abandoning church, they suggested, why not try a creative alternative? If my family's church was not adequate, why not attend several churches to see if I could find one I could appreciate?

I readily agreed with their suggestion and soon drew up a protocol of questions and guidelines to be used as I visited various churches. I began the next week by attending three different churches. My project took me to over a hundred churches in the next year. One Sunday morning I attended a Catholic Mass, followed by a sermon on hell, fire, and brimstone at a fundamentalist church. That evening I observed a "dance in the aisles" Pentecostal church. The next week I attended a more subdued Methodist service. I tried to visit as many different denominations as possible and included a variety of ethnic groups as well.

I guess this story should end by my returning to my home church more fully committed to it. It did not quite work out that way. But I learned a great deal about the Body of Christ during that year of "research." I grew to appreciate religious diversity and the value of multiple perspectives on faith. I saw strengths and weaknesses in nearly every group I attended. Today, more than twenty years later, I find it difficult to align myself exclusively with any one denomination because my spiritual identity is broader than a single religious group (although I do not fault those who have a strong denominational identity). I have come to enjoy formality and ritual as well as informality and exuberance. I grew a lot from that one year of experience.

Dedications

I dedicate this book to my parents, Clarence and Lois Ratcliff, for their insightful suggestion at a crucial point in my life. They helped turn my questions into a quest, my doubts into development. I will always be thankful for their positive influence.

Donald Ratcliff
Toccoa Falls, Georgia

As this book is being completed, my family is going through tremendous changes. I wonder why my thirteen-year-old son, who has previously shown no interest in fads and styles, now wants his hair spiked. The telephone rings more than a dozen times every night. Inevitably the calls are for my oldest son, now fourteen. He receives five times more calls than his mother and I. My daughter's friends invade our home for supper on a regular basis (usually without a prearranged invitation), and doing "sleepovers" every weekend is becoming her norm. These and many other factors indicate my offspring have entered adolescence.

They still practice their faith and they still seek out my wife, Sherry, and me for advice. I pray it will still be so when they complete the teenage years. It is to Jamie, Jeff, and Jenni, the trio who are teaching me many lessons about youth, that I dedicate this book.

James A. Davies
Regina, Saskatchewan, Canada

Chapter One

Adolescent Subculture

JAMES A. DAVIES

I didn't know what to do, yet there was the note tucked in a typewriter at Shawnee Mission North High School in Mission, Kansas. It was after normal school hours and, as a part-time janitor working my way through college, I'd stumbled across the document. I read it again:

> What's the sense to all this we call life?
> I mean there used to be answers to it, didn't there?
> I'm so confused. Nothing makes sense anymore.
> The pieces just don't seem to fit.
> Why are we here? Is this all there is?
> Can't anyone help me? Please?

Was the writing a teenage prank, carefully worded to tease someone into answering? Was it a psychology class experiment? Did it represent the cry of a young person trying to find answers in a disordered world? I didn't know.

During break I came back to the room, typed a carefully worded response and left it in the typewriter for the next day's classes. I don't remember what I said. The next evening there was a second note left in the same typewriter. It interacted with my comments and asked additional questions.

We wrote back and forth in this way for four months. Her name was Betty. Barely out of the teenage years myself, I tried to guide her as best I could through some issues with which she was struggling. We never met. When the school term was ending and I was going back home for the summer, she wrote a long "thank you" note saying how much our "talking together" had meant to her. There are thousands of Bettys in today's teen world.

Is There a Youth Subculture?

This topic assumes that teenage subculture is a reality. Empirical evidence generally confirms the existence, to some degree, of an adolescent subculture. Limits of space do not permit a full-scale debate as to whether there is in fact a youth subculture separate from that experienced by adults. The argument of proponents can be summed up by three related tenets: The typical adolescent is characterized by "storm and stress" stemming primarily from an uncertain position in the social structure; teenage subculture exists and is powerful and widespread; and affiliation with peers provides a structured social environment and a degree of personal identity. The argument was originally set forth over forty years ago by Parsons (1950). It was further enhanced by Coleman's (1963) large-scale surveys in the late 1950s, and by Williams (1960). In 1968 Green maintained a subculture unique to teens existed, calling it a "world of irresponsibility, specialized lingo, dating, athleticism, and the like, which rather sharply cuts off adolescent experience from that of the child and from that of the adult" (1968, 113).

Opponents of the youth subculture theory also have a rich history. They have completed various studies—mostly on a small scale—and concluded that the difference in values between youth and adults is not large enough to warrant a separate subcultural system. Much of this research is based on highly specific and nongeneralizable samples. For example, Elkin and Westley (1955), in a widely publicized and often quoted dissent from the teen subculture theory, found teenagers in a Montreal suburb more integrated in the adult society, its customs, norms, and values, than was commonly thought. Generalizing the results of this study to the total teenage population is difficult, however, due to the small size, ethnic distinctiveness of the French-English community and socio-economic uniformity (it was confined to a well-to-do suburb). The teenager described in Elkin and Westley's study may well be a different type than ones found throughout most of this hemisphere. Other advocates of nondifferentiated youth-adult culture include Douvan and Adelson (1966), Hill and Aldous (1969), Bandura (1972), and Offer, Ostrov, and Howard (1981). The latter maintain that parents have invented the teen subculture and use it as a scapegoat for the complaints they have about their kids. Several of these studies appear to be reliable, although allowances must be made for researcher bias and faulty methodology. However, their generalization to all North American teens is unwarranted. They are either nonrepresentative, or too specific.

What Is Meant by Youth Subculture?

This chapter overviews the general teen subculture from theoretical, historical, and descriptive research. Since "culture" refers to a blueprint of behavior for an entire society, "subculture" refers to the blueprint for behavior of a smaller group within the society (Yinger, 1960; Gordon, 1974). The focus of the chapter is on North American teenagers as a whole, not on any particular adolescent subgroup specifically. It must be recognized however that there is no uniform culture for all teenagers. Adolescent behavior is highly diversified. A wide variety of subcultures often exist side by side, each with its own language, value system, and worldview. These differences form what Campolo calls the "kaleidoscope of teen subcultures" (1987, 39).

Some who research youth would deplore the blanket application of the concept "youth subculture" because it implies a monolithic membership group for all teens. There is some justification in this criticism. Important differences in behavior patterns do exist. They include such variables as age, ethnicity, socioeconomic class, peer group, and rural or urban residence. For example, a black innercity teenager living in the slums exhibits different values, has a different outlook on life, and belongs to a different peer subculture than a white middle-class teen growing up in suburbia.

Delinquent adolescent gang subculture is one distinct variation which has received much attention in America. Stratton (1985) suggests the delinquency model has evolved because of the commodity-orientedness of North American teens, while in Britain the Marxist-structuralist and semiotic models have greater cultural specificity for youth. Each of these models of adolescent subculture has received much attention both in the media and in research. It is likely these types have received such a focus because they have such clearly discernible and sometimes spectacular patterns of behavior. But not all teenage subcultures are deviant in nature. Many of them rally around relatively harmless recreational styles, such as subcultures for surfers, bikers, backpackers, and athletes.

The general function of the youth subculture is to compensate for the failure of the main culture to provide a definite status, a feeling of acceptance, and need-satisfactions unique to adolescents. Such collective stirrings of modern youth are largely a consequence of the adolescent crisis in postindustrial society. The formation of a teenage subculture compensates for this crisis. It provides temporary security and a collective bonding mechanism.

A majority of the research relating to youth examines one aspect of teen behavior for one adolescent peer-group only and makes no attempt to place its findings within the larger youth subculture. In order to bring a workable schemata to the immense amount of material available from the overall teen scene, some kind of theoretical framework is necessary. The methodological paradigm followed, in part, throughout this chapter is the one proposed by sociologist Hans Sebald (1975, 1984). This approach provides an overarching structure for holistically describing the various dimensions of the contemporary youth subculture. Seven major dimensions delineate the most significant aspects of adolescent subculture. The dimensions are: in-group values and norms, unique language, channels of mass communication, fads and styles, sense of solidarity, "hero" worship, and activism-radicalism.

In addition to the need for systematic structure, this format is followed for three other reasons. It provides a tool that, if consistently applied, can promote compatibility of different research findings—a key consideration. Second, it promotes greater reliability in following the fluctuations of a subculture. Third, the multidimensional aspect of this model allows for measurement in terms of degree of subculture quality. Qualities always exist in terms of degree, and attempts to summarize the research must be responsive to this fact.

Norms and Values

This section examines the in-group standards of popularity, status, friendship, peer influence, dating, and sexuality. Attitudes toward parents and religion, the influence of significant others and value commitments complete this section.

Young people have derived from their interactions norms and values that no longer consist of child standards nor are they part of the adult world. Teen groups hold values that, though not always different from those of the adult community, at least reflect a unique accent. Several teen in-group standards are highlighted by the research. These include the areas of popularity, status, friendship, peer influence, dating, and sexuality.

Popularity. Researchers have repeatedly noted that popularity is the dominant value among teens. Coleman (1963), in his famous survey of American high schools, found this desire was more intense among girls (60 percent) than boys (56 percent). Remmers and Radler (1962) and Douvan and Adelson (1966) confirmed that a desire to be popular was a consistent preoccupation for girls from middle-class backgrounds. One of the few longitudinal studies addressing popularity shows the significance attached to being popular in high school has changed only slightly over the past two decades (Sebald, 1984). Affirmative responses to the question "How important is it to be liked and accepted by other teenagers?" decreased from 98 to 95 percent between 1960 to 1982. Respondents in this study also chose very similar criteria for determining popularity: first was the "conformity principle" of doing things "our" way; second, having a desirable personality; third was individualism or the importance of being yourself; fourth was taking an interest in others and helping them. The rank order of these criteria has remained unchanged for almost twenty years.

The main price of popularity, for either sex, still seems to be conformity. Several studies and research summaries have corroborated this and discovered a consistent age correlation (Brownstone and Willis, 1971; Strommen, 1974; Selye, 1976; McCoy, 1982; Cauce, 1986). While conformity is not particularly characteristic of children below seven to nine years of age, it increases thereafter, reaches its peak during early adolescence (around thirteen), and then declines. Young teens are more vulnerable to the conformity influence of peers than older adolescents.

Status. Faded blue jeans are not just clothing, they are a symbol of belonging and status. Flaunting the possession of the latest popular hit does not necessarily mean the teenager finds the music personally meaningful, but it is a means of letting others know she is up on the latest production. The aforementioned are examples of status criteria, or the fine art of gaining and maintaining prestige. Status criteria differ from peer group to peer group and depend heavily on the teenager's orientation. The process of status attribution is complex and varies greatly within any given adolescent culture.

However, certain items are used throughout most, if not all, groups to assess a teenager's standing. One of them is clothing and appearance. Research indicates that adolescent girls in urban settings use "first impression" labeling based on clothing and appearance to decide whether the new girl qualifies as a friend and as a group member, even before the new girl's personality and friendliness are known. The consequences that follow this type of status behavior are of considerable significance. Such labeling perpetuates the status quo, contributes to socio-economic isolations of lower-class youth, and reinforces moral reasoning on a low level (Eicher, 1974). In contrast to the first impression behavior of girls, boys' status behavior consists primarily of drinking and dating practices through which "manhood" was tested and proved (Schwartz and Merten, 1967; Easterlin and Crimmins, 1988).

Studies seem to indicate that young people perceive status to be a set of ranked, slightly ambiguous prestige categories that are internally differentiated. There is a horizontal dimension determined by each group's dress, speech, interpersonal demeanor, and prestige in the community; and there is a vertical dimension within each group, by which the members are assessed and status-ranked. The horizontal dimension is qualitative, while the vertical is quantitatively designated (Herzog and Bachman, 1982; Benson, Yeager, Wood, Guerra, and Manno, 1986; Hare, 1988).

Friendship. In addition to popularity, friendship is an in-group concern supported by significant amounts of research. Gaining friends is the adolescent's way of broadening his or her social base. In this manner they can become integrated into a larger group without necessarily breaking from their parents.

Adolescent peer relationships generally fall into three broad categories: the "crowd," the "clique," and dyads, or "individual friendships" (Mussen, 1979). The most inclusive of these categories is the crowd. It is also the least personal. The members meet on the basis of mutual activities, interests, likes, or social ideals, not because of mutual attraction for one another (Hurlock, 1967; Norman and Harris, 1981). Crowds provide a reservoir of acceptable associates who can be drawn upon to the extent required by any social activity. Cliques and crowds are different in both size and function. The clique, smaller in size (with a limit of nine members according to Norman and Harris, 1981), permits and encourages a far higher degree of intimacy and group cohesion than the larger crowd. Some researchers suggest that the clique's similarity in size to the family provides an alternative center of security for teenagers (Dunphy, 1963; Coleman, 1980).

Others have noted the centrality of "talking" especially on the telephone or at their favorite hangout. Such conversations center on the preparation of "crowd" activities, dissemination of information about such, and evaluation after "crowd" activities are over (Savin-Williams, 1980; Youniss, 1980).

Among the peer relationships of adolescents, friends hold a special place. Friendships typically are more intimate, involve more intense feelings, and are more honest and open and less concerned with self-conscious attempts at role-playing to gain acceptance. Significantly, relationships of this kind can involve reproving each other without condemning each other (Douvan and Adelson, 1966; Konopka, 1976). In what is perhaps a testimony to the degree of loneliness and alienation felt by many adolescents in postindustrial society, Levinson (1978) observes that a majority of participants he interviewed did not have a close friend that they recalled from youth. This lack of close friendships significantly contributes to failure in developing higher levels of personal self-consciousness and results in intensified loneliness (Franzoi and Davis, 1985).

Peer friendships are, thus, extremely important. Bibby and Posterski's study (1985) of 3,600 Canadian high-school students found that the highest value was placed on the importance of friendships. Similarly, religiously oriented youth in grades five through nine respond that they "very much" want to have friends. There is some sex differentiation in that girls are more concerned than boys about establishing friendships, although a vast majority of all teenagers—75 percent—show concern in this area (Benson, Johnson, Wood, Williams, and Mills, 1984).

Peer influence. For many teens increased self-identity is a dominant value derived from interaction with friends. Peer acceptance has been found to be crucial for the maintenance of positive self-esteem (Eskilson, Wiley, Muehlbauer, and Dodder, 1986), for self-evaluation (Street, 1985), and for providing mutual emotional support (Hunter, 1985; Cauce, 1986). This positive peer influence has been validated in many different ethnic or racial settings. When such support is lacking, emotional deprivation may result.

When examining other possible results of peer influence, a less clear picture emerges. Many parents will be comforted to know that, in some instances, peer influence encourages misconduct less than other types of behavior (Brown, Lohr, and McClenahan, 1986). For many teens, pressures to conform to peer norms diminish as perceived pressures toward misconduct increase across grade levels (Clasen and Brown, 1985). Peer influence is, for most teens, a curvilinear pattern which seems largely to peak in early adolescence and decline in the later teen years (Morgan and Grube, 1989). In a study examining the peer influence of young, latchkey adolescents, Steinberg (1986) found that those who were removed from adult supervision were more susceptible to peer influence and engage in more antisocial activity. But, latchkey youths whose parents knew their whereabouts and were raised authoritatively were less susceptible to peer influence. Peer pressure is a very powerful force, however. It had a stronger effect on teens than personal biological maturation in one longitudinal sample of

335 young adolescents (Peterson and Crockett, 1985).

Peer influence can be either positive or negative. Several recent studies have examined the impact of peer influence on either adolescent drug use or abstinence (Johnson, 1986; Swadi and Zeitlin, 1988; Morgan and Grube, 1989). The same pattern of mixed results is shown from studies of adolescent sexual activity. In some instances, when best friends of the individual were sexually experienced, results were "almost certain that the subject will have sexual intercourse within two years of the study" (Billy and Udry, 1985, 31). Other inquiries have found discrepant results. When best friends' sexual involvement was related to low levels of personal sexual drive the adolescent female was less likely to become involved sexually, irrespective of the sexual involvement of her friends (Smith, Udry, and Morris, 1985). A third study suggests it is not what friends actually do but what the teenager believes they do which impacts behavior (Bauman and Fisher, 1986). The lack of consistent results can likely be attributed to the multidimensionality of peer pressure and to a number of differences in each study, including variance in teen subcultures, personality, familial structures and support, degree of religiosity, and research design variation and flaws.

Youth subculture exhibits many in-group concerns, among them are desire to be popular and achieve status, increased involvement with friends, and peer influence. For most teens the transition from childhood into adolescence is marked more by a lessening of dependency on parents and an increasing dependency on peers, rather than straightforward and unidimensional growth in autonomy. Peer influence is a transient factor which must be encountered in pursuit of healthy personal well-being. Youniss (1980) has observed that interaction with peers is the crucible in which children develop, partly by trial and error, the rules and principles of responsible human behavior.

Dating. Dating is an in-group concern that is not necessarily in conflict with adult norms and institutions. It defines the culturally accepted meeting ground for young men and women and patterns much of their interaction. In many youth subgroups there is tremendous pressure to date, inspite of the fact that it is quite normal not to date a great deal during grades 7-12 (around one-third of teens have had less than five dates when they graduate from high school).

Evidence to support the benefits of early dating is minimal. The increased stressful effects are becoming known (Elkind, 1981, 1984). Rome (1985), while primarily addressing the subject of frank disclosure of sexual information, contends that the emotional and behavioral price of hurrying young adolescents into activities, such as dating, deserves more serious study. At least one study has found a direct relationship between the age at which a girl's first date occurs and the initiation of sexual intercourse before high-school graduation (Miller and Olsen, 1986).

The findings of Roscoe, Diana, and Brooks (1987) indicate that early and middle adolescents perceive dating from an egocentric, immediate gratification orientation. Young teens tended to weigh the date's superficial features and

AGE AT START OF DATING	PERCENT OF GIRLS WHO HAVE SEX BEFORE GRADUATION
12	91%
13	56%
14	53%
15	40%
16	20%
17	7%

Source: Miller and Olsen, (1986).

their approval by others. For early adolescents, attracting dates means greater emphasis on physical appearance. Kephart (1981) refers to this as the "era of good looks." He points out that those who lack attractive faces and proper body builds will find themselves excluded from the dating game. With maturity, however, late adolescents place greater emphasis on reciprocity in a relationship (Roscoe, Diana, and Brooks, 1987). They become more realistic and independent in their perceptions of dating partners.

The subject of steady dating has received relatively little attention in recent research. In one large study of Israeli eighth, tenth, and twelfth graders, steady dating was found to be significantly more important to males than to females. Those who had steady dates were perceived by their peers as possessing higher self-esteem, self-perception, and gender identity (Samet and Kelly, 1987).

Violence and rape within dating relationships have recently come to the attention of researchers. There is little support for predicting dating behaviors based upon family structure, race, or socio-economic status (Coleman, Ganong, and Ellis, 1985; O'Keeffe, Brockopp, and Chew, 1986). The strongest relationship appears to be between date violence and violence in the precipitator's family, with parents, fathers, or brothers being the primary perpetrators (Roscoe and Callahan, 1985; O'Keeffe, Brockopp, and Chew, 1986).

Studies vary concerning the amounts of violence that occur on dates. This appears to be due to differing definitions for the term. O'Keeffe, Brockopp, and Chew (1986) report that 35.5 percent of the subjects experienced violence in a dating relationship, with violence between boys and girls being reciprocal. Lane and Givartney-Gibbs (1985) indicate similar findings. They found 36 percent of both males and females had been pushed, grabbed, or shoved by a dating partner; 29 percent of females and 26 percent of males reported being slapped, kicked, or punched; 13 percent of females said physical force had been used to force them into kissing, petting, or intercourse; and 5 percent reported being raped by a date.

Sexual behavior. One of the most striking bones of contention between younger and older generations is in the area of sexual experience. This area is addressed more specifically in chapter seven. Only a brief summary is included at this point. North American society presents a picture of schizoid values and a notoriously confused blueprint concerning sex. Sex and "love" are eulogized and longed for, while, simultaneously, furtive and guilt-ridden apprehensiveness continues to grow. Intensifying this dual impasse, movies and literature invite teenagers to participate in a type of love that magnifies the erotic and exploitative. Sex has become part of the American "fun" concept, although law, religious traditions, and public opinion condemn premarital sex. The ubiquitous fact is, however, that the modern adult's world is preoccupied with sex. This has saturated the adolescent's environment with images that encourage sexual activities.

One of the chief tasks of adolescence is to develop responsible sexual maturity. Much of the current research continues to support widespread teenage ignorance about sexuality. Goldman and Goldman (1984) interviewed one thousand subjects from intact nuclear families in Australia, England, Sweden, and North America. They found misunderstandings were common concerning bodily changes, contraception, procreation, and venereal diseases. This misinformation, when combined with various sources of social influence (parents, peers, media, schools, race, social class, and religion) leads to gender role development that is characterized primarily by role strain and confusion (Harrison and Pennell, 1989).

Experimentation with sex often fails to yield the expected results. On the basis of books, movies, rumors, and pseudo-academic promises, many adolescents are faced with sexually superhuman expectations that sooner or later lead to frustration and disappointment. The failure of sex to be as glamorous as expected tends to downgrade the value of human sexuality. The disillusionment becomes crucial when it is combined with the failure to establish a secure relationship. Inexperienced teenage lovers who try sex as a cure for alienation and loneliness are often left deeply disillusioned (Goldman and Goldman, 1984).

It should be noted that researcher bias, design flaws, and exaggeration or misinterpretation of data may skew findings regarding teenage sexual experience. Sebald (1984) maintains that, to some extent, academians who are overimpressed by the immediacy and vociferousness of students may have helped fabricate the adolescent sexual revolution. Many researchers have been guilty of equating verbal statements about behavior with actual behavior. Other social scientists are not certain whether actual sexual activities of this generation have really been drastically different from previous cohorts or if the current generation's outspokenness and matter-of-fact attitude toward sex is what has changed (Reiss, 1966). An example of possible misinterpretation of data is the high premarital pregnancy rate, which is commonly attributed to a higher premarital coitus rate. While premarital sexual experience may have increased, the higher premarital pregnancy rate may merely indicate that fewer young people feel obligated to marry because of pregnancy. For some teen subcultures this lack of pressure is quite significant. In a study of unwed prospective black teenage fathers, for instance, 57 percent did not want to get married, care for the mate's health, or interact with and make plans for the expected infant (Westney, Cole, and Munford, 1986).

A more holistic approach to the study of adolescent sexuality is being called for in some of the research. This is particularly important for church-sponsored sex education programs. At least one ecclesiastically oriented program that focused on both clarity of knowledge and personal sexual values has shown positive short-term results (Powell and Jorgensen, 1985). *Values and Choices* and *Yes You Can!*, both from Search Institute and HealthStart, Inc. (St. Paul), have been shown to be effective in promoting sexual abstinence among young teenagers (*Christianity Today,* Oct. 6, 1989, p. 40). Churchworkers and parents should welcome and promote this emphasis on values when educating youth about their sexuality.

Attitudes toward parents. The widely held notion that young people reject the influence of their parents at about age twelve is not supported by longitudinal stud-ies or current major adolescent research. Instead, many teens continue to seek out their parents for counsel, not only through the junior high years, but also in senior high. It is true that, in gradual yearly steps, the percentages of those who do so diminish. However, even in twelfth grade, many teenagers say they go to their parents for advice or help (Sebald, 1984).

Sebald (1986) has examined changes in the orientation of young people toward parents and peers over the last three decades. In 1963, 1976, and 1982, 570 identical questionnaires were administered to comparable samples of teenagers. Data formed a curvilinear pattern over time, reflecting the decline of parental influence during the counterculture movement of the 1960s and 1970s and its partial recovery during the early 1980s. More recently, Benson, Williams, and Johnson (1987) supply data which indicate that parental influ-ence is once again the single strongest source of help for young adolescents.

Influence is often reciprocal for parents and teens. Adolescents can be effec-tive agents in shaping their parents' attitudes and behavior in such topics as politics, sports, leisure, minority groups, and religion (Peters, 1985). Parents and peers, on the other hand, exert strong influences on teenage self-esteem (Walker and Greene, 1986; Levinson, Powell, and Stellman, 1986) and behav-ior (Chassin, 1986).

Significant others. Few studies have, to date, examined the importance of significant others. In one report, two studies of comparative research on "refer-ent others" was examined. (One study compared subjects in four Western coun-tries—Australia, France, Norway, and the U. S.—and the other compared teen groups from Australia, Malaysia, and India.) When data were analyzed adoles-cents ranked parents first in importance, followed by friends, referent adults, and then siblings (Keats, 1983). Peers do not take up where parents leave off on matters of drug use. The majority of teenagers, when they stop consulting parents, continue to choose adults for advice. About half of those surveyed by Benson, Williams, and Johnson (1987) named some other adult as a preferred source of advice. Some chose a relative, but almost a third chose a category called "Adult Friend (not a relative)." Now, as always, young people crave adult friends. They need and seek access to the experience, wisdom, and the sympathetic ears and minds of adults accessible to them: neighbors, relatives, and leaders of youth organizations. But there are also large numbers without such a support network. Many live in large cities. Though they may not recognize it, this lack of adult support is a genuine deprivation. Adolescents need, and continue to search for, trusted adult friends.

Religious attitudes. Between childhood and adulthood profound changes occur in the realm of religion (see chapter five). What happens during this period is a crucial prelude to the shape of religious belief and commitment in adult life. The simplest and most common ways to measure adolescent religiousness are the level of interest/importance the teenager attaches to religion and the frequency of attendance at worship. It is important to remember that these two propositions are not the same. One is an attitude toward God and matters of faith; the other is an attitude toward the activities of a particular congregation.

In general, girls are more likely than boys, in middle adolescence, to maintain a high level of religious interest and activity. Almost every study that includes measures of religiosity reports the same finding: a decline for boys (some say sharp, others say slight), especially in worship attendance and prayer.

Recent research, while not providing conclusive answers for this sex differentiatedness, has helped in understanding the nature of religious belief during the teenage years. Young adolescent boys tend to maintain an extrinsic religious perspective that highlights belief as a means to an end. They see religion as a set of rules and guidelines by which to live. Girls show a greater tendency toward belief as an end in itself. This intrinsic religion provides, for girls, a clearer sense of freedom and a greater sense of connection with God and other people through their faith (Benson, Williams, and Johnson, 1987).

A curious mixture appears in the research when examining religion-related differences between adolescents of different races. Intrinsic religion is found to be markedly more important to blacks than whites. Hispanic students show similarly high interest, but, like blacks, have a lower record of regular attendance at worship (Greenman and Heeter, 1983; Hare, 1988).

Adolescents appear to have maintained the same degree of interest in religion over the last fifteen years. The Survey Research Center of the University of Michigan annually questions 16,000 high-school seniors. One topic routinely included is participation in worship and attitudes toward religion. High-school seniors' participation in worship has, according to these surveys, both risen and fallen from year to year since 1976, but the net effect is not dramatic. On a ten-year average, the number of teens having "no religious preference" is about 10 percent ; 30 percent see religion as "very important"; while almost 40 percent "attend weekly" services. Additionally, Search Institute has completed several major studies of junior and senior high-school young people. Most of their studies have shown a slight to substantial decline in interest in religion from early to late adolescence (Benson, Williams, and Johnson, 1987). Gallup reports that their studies across the age range of thirteen-to-eighteen-year-olds show a relatively stable level of interest in religion across the last fifteen years (as cited in Benson, Donahue, and Erickson, 1989).

Parents who make the financial sacrifice involved in sending a child to a parochial school should realize such schooling is not without effect. In one Catholic high school the religious attitudes for both boys and girls, when compared with Catholic students in public high schools, indicated more frequent church attendance, higher contributions to the church, and rated religion as being higher in importance (Benson, Donahue, and Guerra, 1989). Other religious schools show no influence upon student behavior, as noted in chapter five.

Perhaps the most unusual development in adolescent religiosity is the new religious-philosophical syncretism. This new form of adolescent religion has evolved over the past twenty to twenty-five years and blends elements of Christianity, Hinduism, Buddhism, and various aspects of the occult into a new pan-mysticism. Theodore Roszak emphasizes in his book, *The Making of a Counter Culture,* that the infusion of Oriental philosophy and religion is *"the unique benchmark* of the twentieth-century counterculture" (emphasis mine; Roszak, 1969; p. 124). One of the outcomes of the new religious synthesis is that teenagers who think of themselves as Christian now innocuously add belief in reincarnation, karma, and other Oriental or occult notions to their personal belief system. The resultant religious credo, while promoting a new mystic consciousness, is neither Christian nor Oriental. The young synthetic believers, given the historical ignorance of most of them, fail to be aware of the disparate religious origins of those beliefs. Workers with teens need to address these new religious attitudes, clarify their origins, and guide teenagers to a consistent, biblical faith.

Value commitment. Three clusters of value orientations have been selected in an attempt to document the values of today's adolescents: values of conduct, compassion, and commitment. In all three value areas, there may be reason to be concerned.

The orientation of *conduct* refers to upholding certain traditional cultural values regarding personal self-restraint. This includes injunctions against cheating, stealing, lying, destruction of property, aggression, and excessive pleasure seeking which harms self or others. There is mounting evidence that a significant number of teenagers are rejecting basic cultural standards of self-discipline. Consider, for example: 1) The California Department of Education recently published a study showing that three-fourths of high-school students admit to cheating on tests and say that most of their classmates accept cheating as a general practice. 2) About three out of ten American high-school seniors report shoplifting "during the last twelve months" (Johnson, O'Malley, and Bachman,

1985). 3) A large percentage of ninth graders admit to vandalism "during the last twelve months"—42 percent for boys and 22 percent for girls. 4) When defining being drunk as having six or more consecutive drinks, four out of ten high-school seniors report getting drunk once or more "during the last two weeks" (Benson, Johnson, and Williams, 1984). 5) The *Chronicle of Higher Education* (July 16, 1986) reports findings that 30 percent of all college students have tried cocaine by the end of their senior year. 6) Two-thirds of all high-school seniors in the class of 1984 have tried at least one illicit drug. National experts estimate American youth to "have the highest levels of illicit drug involvement to be found in any developed country in the world" (Johnson, O'Malley, and Bachman, 1985; p. 15).

The orientation of *compassion* refers to caring about the welfare of other persons (see Sapp, 1991, for a detailed, scholarly analysis of religious compassion). Compassionate values include kindness, altruism, generosity, equality, social justice, and peace. National studies of high-school seniors conducted by the Survey Research Center of the University of Michigan show that the value placed on making a contribution to society and working to correct social and economic inequalities trails far behind financial and occupational goals (approximately 60 percent to 13 percent). From 1975 to 1984 the importance adolescents place on prestige and money increased while the value placed on helping people decreased (Bachman, Johnson, and O'Malley, 1985). Data collected from high-school seniors and college freshmen in 1976 and 1986 on their personal goals indicate those surveyed more recently place more importance on wealth, having a job with good earning potential, status, opportunity for advancement, and having time for personal pursuits (Easterlin and Crimmins, 1988). In terms of actual behavior, fewer adolescents are becoming involved in people-helping activities. Only one out of four young teens donate one hour a week or more to giving help to other people. The rate falls to less than 10 percent for high-school seniors (Benson, Johnson, Wood, Williams, and Mills, 1984); this may be partially explained by the fact that about 40 percent of all high schoolers have part-time jobs (Wynne and Hess, 1986).

It would be incorrect, however, to assume that teenagers are not significantly involved in activities which show positive orientation to the values of compassion and commitment as Strommen (1988) seems to imply. Consider, for instance, *student volunteerism*. This manifests itself in civic concern, political interests, and various social services all across North America. The commitments include a wide range of voluntary public service programs: tutoring disadvantaged children, assisting with tax returns, entertaining and nursing patients in hospitals, renovating slums, cleaning up ecological disasters, and offering health care for the underprivileged. Many adolescent volunteers work through such organizations as Candy Stripers, 4-H Clubs, Boys' Clubs of America, Scout and Camp Fire groups, student governments, and religious organizations. Federal programs such as the Peace Corps, VISTA, and Youth Conservation

Corps have drawn thousands of young Americans who seek fellowship and the experience of serving others. The American Red Cross attracted over four million unpaid youth volunteers during the early 1980s. Young people work longer hours, have more energy, and were more willing to take physical risks to help people in need ("Youth on the Move," 1981). It may be a minority phenomenon, but nevertheless thousands of young people chose volunteerism as an expression of their philosophy and curiosity.

For teens who participate in volunteerism, the results may be significant. The benefits go far beyond simple goal achievement. Consider these byproducts: 1) Integration into society—volunteerism bonds youth to society; it helps alleviate youth's feelings of alienation and shows them a side of society with which they can identify. 2) Self-testing—it provides simultaneous opportunity to assess one's own resources, capabilities, and interests and thereby apply a valid test to one's identity. 3) Independence—volunteerism offers meaningful service in a constructive expression of independence from parents; helps young individuals achieve social maturity more quickly. And 4) solidification of values—those who focus on humanitarian concerns are able to test their chosen values through service projects. The outcome of such experimentation often reinforces the concerns. Additionally, the person achieves greater certainty and self-assurance (Sebald, 1984).

The orientation of *commitment* has to do with ultimate loyalty. In a sense, commitment is one's reason for living. Commitment gives an overall direction and purpose to life. There is a danger that adolescents may have adopted the faulty premise that a life of seeking to please and enhance the self gives meaning, direction, and hope. In a study of adolescents in Canadian culture, Ban (1986) discovered a mixed bag of egocentric and nonegocentric values. The dominant focus of life was to "be happy," while the values of love, friendship, freedom, cleanliness, hard work, and music were predominant. Self-interest without commitment to some ideal or purpose larger than self does not provide the kind of anchor needed to survive the challenges of adulthood. Many contemporary teenagers need to rediscover that true meaning and purpose require abandoning the pursuit of individualistic goals and pursue instead a course where one lives by moral conviction (Bellah, Madsen, Sullivan, Swidler, and Tipton, 1985).

Values of personal conduct, compassion, and commitment are not being effectively communicated to all teens. It is not clear, however, if this trend is part of a cyclic phase of adolescence which naturally evolves into relatively normative values in late adolescence. In other words, will today's teenager follow the liberality-disillusionment-conservativism pattern of many counterculture adolescents of the 1960s? With increased experience in life situations, will older teens return to traditional values of personal conduct? Krau (1987) finds support for such a spiral pattern for value development from his research on work values of adolescents. A second interpretation of the shifting of adolescent values is offered by Thornburg, Thornburg, and Ellis (1984). They discovered that adolescents ranked highest those values that could be experienced to some extent, but social values—which seemed abstract or impersonal—were ranked lower. Religious education practitioners who favor this interpretation will place high emphasis on involving adolescents in service projects which expose teens to human need. (See chapter nine for more detail on social involvement.)

It is possible that teens are mimicking values that are now omnipresent in society at large, embodied in social institutions, modeled by significant adults, and reinforced by the print and broadcast media. Adolescents may be simply reflecting a society that has shifted dramatically to an individualism motif (Yankelovitch, 1981; Bellah, Madsen, Sullivan, Swidler, and Tipton, 1985). In addition North American society no longer presents a coherent value system from family and community, and adolescents are being cast adrift to make hit-and-miss choices from among a variety of known value systems. At present, significant numbers of teenagers appear to be making moral decisions based more on expediency, pleasure, and self-fulfillment than traditional Judeo-Christian standards of right or good. During the last five to eight years there has been some moderation in this long-term trend of deterioration (Wynne and Hess, 1986). However, the overall picture is one of normlessness.

This first section has examined adolescent in-group norms and values. Another major area in which a distinct youth subculture is apparent is in language.

Teen Language

Argot is a "special language" reflecting the idiom of a particular group or social class. Many professional groups have argot unique to them. Lawyers, miners, medical doctors, the military, and ecclesiastics all employ specialized language. The common function of an argot is adapting communication to the particular needs of each group.

Acquisition of an argot means something more than just learning a new vocabulary. It signifies membership in the subculture to which the lingo is indigenous. In addition, argot acquisition promotes group cohesiveness and insures privacy (Opie and Opie, 1959). It may also stand for new knowledge and insights, both cognitive and affective.

Teen lingo is a special argot. Every adolescent lives in the bidialectism of two cultures, his in-group and his family (Shapiro, 1985). The reason why teenage argots constantly evolve and are tenaciously maintained must be sought in their functions. At least six functions can be discerned:

1) *Shorthand device.* It is designed to save time when referring to complex processes in which teens are involved. For example, to spell out the fine details and connotations of what is meant when referring to a person or event as "cool" would take considerable time and unduly hamper expedient discourse. The word evokes a clear concept for teenagers, saves time and effort, and preserves the unique style of in-group communication. More important, it prompts them

toward expected subculture emotions, and sometimes actions. Danesi (1989), in an interesting study of adolescent language, discovered three basic speech-programing categories: emotive, connotative, and socially coded language. He concludes that the verbal behavior of adolescents depends on the socio-affective organization. The usage of in-group teen lingo, then, provides significant emotive reinforcement for the teenager.

2) *Precise reference.* Teenagers have different experiences and perceive human relations from a different angle than adults, thus they develop a correspondingly different set of words. Teenage lingo can be vivid and clever. Many play their lingo like virtuosos, skillfully hitting just the right nuance of pronunciation and accompanying it with appropriate body language.

3) *Status criterion.* Ardent and masterly use of argot functions as a prestige gauge among peers. It is sufficient, many times, to determine leader and follower status. Rule bending (i.e., Harman's, 1985, "acceptable deviance") is allowed provided the message stays within the predefined in-group. Greater status is provided to the group member who is the first to use the term in a novel manner without violating the in-group propriety code.

4) *Group solidarity.* The use of lingo functions as a phonetic banner proclaiming association with the peer group. When teenagers hear or use "their" words, they identify with and are strongly reminded of peer membership.

5) *Value statement.* Argot reflects what is important to members of the subculture. The index of argot is a sensitive indicator of peer values. Research finds that use of argot by itself is sufficient to determine the nature of delinquent or nondelinquent involvement (Lerman, 1967). Cultural linguists have discovered that the significance to a group or society of a given thing is indicated by the number of words they use to refer to it. The classic example is Whorf's oft-cited observation that Eskimos have seventeen various terms to refer to snow, while standard English has only one (Whorf, 1956). Similarly, North American teens have multiple words describing the sex act.

6) *Linguistic conditioner.* Once firmly established, value-laden lingo greatly influences the way members of a group perceive their social environment and pattern their behavior (Schwartz and Martin, 1967). There is a high correlation between argot, values, and behavior.

Teenage argot, as based on the above six functions, does not consist of a uniform body of linguistic expression. Innercity and black youths cultivate a version that is closely related to racial and ethnic lingos, the athletic jock illuminates another variation, while teenage surfers of the West Coast use a set of words and expressions all their own. These vocabularies, of course, overlap and are probably understood, although not spoken, by most teenagers. The frequency of argot use reaches its peak in the junior-high years. Researchers believe this is in part related to newly established linguistic competence among eleven- to thirteen-year-olds (Secord, Wiig, and Williams, 1989). Some topics prompt greater lingo increases for both sexes, such as alcohol drinking, drugs, and popularity. Among males however, athletics, cars, motorbikes, girls, and sex get special treatment, while girls tend to use more argot in reference to clothes, style, appearance, and being popular or unpopular (Nelsen and Rosenbaum, 1972). The normal lifespan for argot and slang expressions is short. Barzun (1975) illustrates this quite well, saying: "Only fifty years ago . . . young men and women said: isn't it the darb!, that's the bean!, pike along, pash, razz, bughouse, smack for him, and other mysterious remarks."

There is a notable lack of research on teenage argot. Those who seek to minister to youth will realize the functions teen lingo fulfills for young people. Although it changes, sometimes rapidly, its provides a unique window for understanding the ideas and values of adolescents from an insider's perspective.

Channels of Mass Communication

The role of mass communication in transmitting, and even creating, the youth culture cannot be understated. Mass communication solidifies a national adolescent culture via television, radio, magazines, home videos, MTV, and the record industry. It is beyond the scope of this chapter to go into a detailed review of the research related to the media and adolescents. A review of the significant functions of the media is delineated, followed by an overview of related issues and tensions.

The role of the visual media is most likely primary in disseminating ideas and styles. Equally tangible is the medium of the recording industry, which conveys the ideas of musicians, subculture values, and common joy and pain through lyrics. These two media are often combined in movies, videos, or on MTV. The amount of TV watching by adolescents has been increasingly documented (Liebert, 1982; Wilkins, 1982); the heaviest period of viewing occurs between the sixth and eighth grades. It is presumed the main reason for this increase is found in the new freedom that this age group experiences in staying up later in the evening. Several studies show a consistent correlation between some teenage obesity and the amount of TV viewing (Greenberg and Heeter, 1983; del Toro, and Greenberg, 1989). Prevalence of obesity among twelve- to-seventeen-year-olds increased by 2 percent with each hour of television viewed, in part because food is the most heavily advertised product shown on children's television. Significant research is now being done on adolescents' video usage. Roe (1987) studied the relationship between school achievement and video cassette recorder use in over 1,300 Swedish fifteen- and sixteen-year-olds. School achievement was significantly and negatively related to the distribution and duration of home access to VCRs and the amount of their use.

It is claimed that a number of prominent negative ingredients are consistently portrayed to adolescents via the television, music, movies, and MTV. Among them are: programing which implies that happiness comes from materialistic success, idealization of immaturity as desired behavior, stereotypical presentation of only the physical dimension of human sexuality, glorification of instant achievement and solutions to life's problems, supression of personal creativity, lessening of individual social interaction skills, desenstization toward the occult and Eastern religions, and excessive exposure to violence. Space will permit detailing of a brief history for the last category only. It serves as a representative sample.

Periodic upsurges in public concern over possible negative consequences of violence-filled TV and media have prompted a number of official inquiries. The first major inquiry was in 1972 by the Surgeon General's Scientific Advisory Committee on TV and Social Behavior, yielding five volumes of findings. Generally, the reports linked violence on TV with aggressive behavior in young people. Predictably the media reacted defensively and tried to capitalize on the technicality that though a correlation was established, there was no proof of a casual relationship. The matter was more or less laid to rest until 1982 when the National Institute for Mental Health published another notable report: *Television and behavior: Ten years of scientific progress and implications for the eighties*. The unambiguous conclusion: Television is a "violent form of entertainment" that clearly leads to aggressive behavior in children and teenagers. Network reaction was predictable. They rejected the report on the grounds that programs are giving the public exactly what they wanted. The networks, they believed, were justified because they only served what the public desired. In addition to these comprehensive reports on television and aggression, which integrate masses of research data, there are numerous specific studies that contribute valuable insights.

In spite of what appears to be overwhelming evidence for negative influence, some social scientists continue to remain aloof from the modeling theory. They are convinced that TV and the media are secondary causes of real-life violence and that other factors, such as the individual's family background and personality, are much more causative. A number of arguments are given to support this. Some researchers maintain that vicarious aggressive experience is therapeutic and calming (Feshbach and Singer, 1971). Another reason mentioned for nonimitation of violence is the viewer's ability to discern fiction from fact. Snow (1974) found that children were capable of interpreting acts of violence on TV as taking place in a "play" setting; they rarely attempted to reenact them. If seen in this light, Bandura's (1963) classic experiments with a Bobo doll in which children acted out aggressive behavior they had just viewed, lose some of their significance. Insofar as children knew the thing was play, the beating is not to be equated with a degree of violence against another human being. Others who study human behavior warn against overgeneralizing the influence of televised violence. They suggest such imitation occurs only under certain circumstances, as in cases where emotionally "disturbed" adolescents are exposed to violent fare. Most of this research concentrates on imitators and, indeed, finds many of them to be pathologically disturbed. While the assumption has a ring of plausibility, it raises unresolved questions regarding the specific definition of "disturbed" and "normal." A final argument used to negate the imitation theory is that, while some appear to copy what they have watched, they remain a relatively small number. It is claimed the more significant issues are an increasing tolerance for cruelty and its subconscious assimilation into one's values and morals. The last argument may be the most potent of all.

Recent research has focused on news stories about *teenage suicide* and the clustering of actual self-destructions following enactment of suicide on television. Phillips and Carstensen (1986) found that suicides significantly increased 0-7 days after stories were aired, even after factoring out the effects of the day of the week, month, holidays, and yearly trends. They conclude TV stories about suicide trigger additional suicides, perhaps because of imitation. Gould and Shaffer (1986) report similar results in their study of the variation in the numbers of suicides and attempted suicides by teenagers in the greater New York area following the showing of two fictional films on the subject. Others have taken issue with these findings. Marks (1987), for instance, criticizes the research design and suggests the apparent surge of suicides could be explained by coroners' misclassification of what were actually accidental deaths. A replicative study of Gould and Shaffer (1986) further clouded the research picture. No evidence of increased teenage suicide was found for California or Pennsylvania teens; this led to the suggestion that it is premature to be concerned about possible fatal effects of fictional televised films about suicide (Phillips and Paight, 1987). Still another study suggests that adolescents may not be influenced by news about suicide or that they may just deny such influence (Steede and Range, 1989). The debate regarding self-destructive imitation continues.

The tenet that media violence breeds imitation in real life is supported, to some degree, by multiple instances of reenactment (Belson, 1978; Sebald, 1984). There is little doubt that some individuals, both old and young, imitate what they see. While they remain a tiny minority of the viewing audience, their acts of mimicry destroy society and human lives.

Rock videos have become a relatively new force in communicating youth values, styles, and attitudes. They are usually short, just a few minutes in length, and often violent or sexual, or both. With the growth of MTV in the 1980s, teenagers can sit mesmerized by the constant playing of music videos. There is no plot just ever-changing action. To date, the long-term effects of watching hours of music videos every day are not well-documented, although many young adolescents have told the author that peers who watch these videos for any significant time become "hyper" and "cranky."

A medium of considerable importance is teen magazines. Reading a newspaper or magazine has been shown to have a greater effect on teen behavior than listening to the broadcast media (Garramone and Atkin, 1986). Processing printed media requires the brain to use higher level functions. Magazine publishers try to attract attention by "teen" connoting titles like *Teen World, Modern Teen,*

Seventeen, and simply, *Teen.* Others have taken their titles from slang vocabulary and assumed the terms would appeal to teenagers. The vast majority of these magazines have a limited circulation. They are aimed at a specific readership within the teenage population. The factor that remains constant throughout youth-oriented publications, and perhaps that of foremost importance, is the magazine's function of conveying a sense of collective identity. This unity function is illustrated by the large volume of "letters to the editor," and by fan clubs and pen pal departments, in which young people describe personal problems and give and ask advice.

Themes in books for the adolescent market have been studied longitudinally. Painter (1985) examined changes that occurred in the themes, characters, and settings of books for early adolescents over the past ten years. The conclusion: There was an upswing in readings about drugs, sex, alcohol, and violence.

Contemporary youth culture depends upon channels of mass communication for survival. It promotes unity and solidarity. In some instances the effects of the media on adolescents is not positive.

Fads and Styles

The major elements of a fad include temporality, novelty, triviality, creation of status criteria, identification with the in-group, compensation (for powerlessness, alienation, and sexual frustrations), and the security of "sameness" (Gold, 1964). These elements can be easily recognized in the fads and styles of modern youth. Almost all adolescent vogues are short lived, one displacing the other in rapid sequence. It is difficult to determine the average duration, it may range from a few months to several years. For a behavior style to qualify as a fad it must introduce a relatively new way of doing, speaking, grooming, or dressing. It should draw attention and be clearly distinguishable from preceding habits and customary behavior in the adult world.

The significance of a fad is usually trivial compared with the mores of society. Teen fads are meant for adolescents only. They spring up more or less spontaneously (in some cases being orchestrated by merchandizers and the media) and are imitated by teenagers without particular scrutiny toward purpose. Once established, these temporary quirks are jealously guarded and kept from outsiders. The fad is part of the identification function with the youth subculture, using the uniform appearance or habit as a boundary-maintaining device. Outlets for thwarted creativity and compensation for various frustrations are benefits of participating in the latest fad (Straton, 1985). An example would be rechanneling of sexual aggressiveness into harmless, "safe," and culturally tolerated behavior forms, such as teenage dancing. Many researchers claim that teenagers use stylish whims as status measurements (Roszak, 1969; Sebald, 1984; Lennon, 1986). They believe fads allow adolescents to achieve prestige in the eyes of their peers by conforming and excelling in the observance of that which is in vogue and reduce feelings of standing out and being vulnerable to the "imaginary audience" (Elkind, 1984, 33). Grunlan (1982), however, questions if fads do in fact designate increased status for an in-group.

Adolescents are noted for their fads and styles in four specific areas—clothing, music, dancing, and hair style. *Clothing* is a visual means of communication. Once clothing has given a teenager an idea of social identity, he or she is able to pattern his ideas accordingly. Clothing serves three additional functions, in addition to influencing the type of social interaction a person experiences (Brooks, 1981). It can be a medium of expressing rebellion from the adult world, allow for aesthetic expression, and afford in-group utilitarian control (Buckley and Roach, 1974; Lennon, 1986). If a certain period of time is exceeded, and certain clothes become customary for one or more generations, they can no longer be defined as faddish. Wearables such as blue jeans, for example, are not sufficiently novel or different from adult clothes to warrant the label of fad.

Vestiges of many, if not all, adolescent clothing fads are still around. Perhaps no fad ever dies completely; it only slumbers to be reawakened and go through a fascinating metamorphosis to reappear in a slightly altered form. While Grunlan and Reimer (1982) question the values behind fads, fads do leave us with a richer repertoire of choice for dress and appearance. For many young people they are colorful caprices that make existence in urban-industrial living more palatable.

Unlike clothing fads, *music* styles have proved of longer duration. Popular music, once primarily an adult-oriented entertainment, underwent radical changes in the mid-1950s and emerged at the end of that decade as the almost exclusive property of youth. It remained for the Beatles, however, to unify the actual rock revolution that subsequently defined an emerging segment of the American population, financed a counterculture, spawned the multibillion dollar music industry, and gave young people a common means of expression—a music, a language, and even a dramaturgy with roles of heros and martyrs (Martin, 1979; Conger, 1984).

Rock style has not remained uniform over the years. Perhaps this flexibility of styles (folk, sentimental, acid, punk, new wave, and heavy metal are only a few representations) has allowed it to remain a dominant medium for communicating to the adolescent subculture. Today rock is not the sole domain of teenagers. There is a massive adult following of those who listen to "the beat."

Like rock and roll, *dancing* has evolved. Modern dance is quite different from artistic, traditional dance with specific steps and gestures. Modern social dancing displays a degree of sexual suggestiveness that no other Western dance forms have dared before (Grafton, 1964; Conger, 1984). Some analysts have called contemporary dance "safe sex" for teenagers, noting inhibitions all but disappear under rhythmic anatomical gyrations which suggest highly sexual nuances and copulatory motions. Others, such as Harvard psychiatrist Philip Solomon, see these dances as healthy outlets for youthful restlessness and sublimated sexual desires. Studies have revealed that the predominant feelings experienced by young dancers are release and abandon, sensations that social scientists explain as the dancers' temporary retreat from the tensions and frustrations of being status-deprived adolescents (Blum, 1966; Scanzoni and Scanzoni, 1988). Explained on the basis of these functions, the longevity of dancing as an adolescent fad is not surprising.

Of all the fads and styles of the past decades, *hair* seemed to offend the mores and aesthetic sensibilities of the establishment most profoundly. The long hair controversy of the 1960s and '70s applied almost exclusively to boys. Each new hairstyle was not received as a fad but as a perversion. Some claimed that long hair had been a symbol of virility ever since biblical days and confessed they grew luxuriant tops because their girlfriends admired and liked it. Others wore their hair long simply because they wanted to and because they desired to look different from adults. Teenagers' insistence on long hair dissipated, possibly because adults gradually imitated it to some extent. Today's mousses, goos, and gels allow for light shadings or bold accentuations. This may be a recycling of the "tinting phase" that was popular in the 1950s while the "mohawk" style is identical to that of the same name from the 1960s.

In a fine treatment of the sociology of hair, Synnott (1987) describes developments in hair symbolism in the U. S. and Britain over the last forty years. Hair is seen as a symbol of the self, of group identity, and a mode of self-expression and communication. Three zones of social significance are identified: head, face, and body. Hair displays and concealment, according to Synnott, can be understood both as pattern and as process, and in terms of the three polar oppositions of gender, ideology, and physique. His conclusion is that hair enables in-group social distinctions and changes to be symbolized.

There have been many additional youth fads that were minor, regional, very short-lived, or subculture-specific. They range from wearing Neru jackets in the 1960s, to "streaking" in the '70s, to the wearing of "shades" or the violence of Skinheads in the '80s. A current practice for many teen subcultures is going to the shopping malls. Anthony's (1985) subjects considered themselves "regulars" in that they visited the shopping center at least twice a week, almost always with others. Only about half went to purchase an item. Other reasons included seeing and talking with friends, watching people, seeing members of the opposite sex, and playing video games.

It is important for the outsider to understand why adolescents participate in faddishness. Often adults have focused on the specific action—the "what"—without being sympathetic to the underlying messages. Following the latest style or fad provides novelty, security, exclusivity, and status for many youths.

Participation in adolescent faddishness defines the adolescent as someone who is different from children and adults, albeit at a highly superficial level. It amounts to a kind of growth by substitution, an attempt to give the impression of inner transformation by means of outer alterations. But true, constructive growth, growth by differentiation and integration, does not come about as easily as modifying language or wearing new clothing styles.

Sense of Solidarity

Esprit de corps is the organizing of collective feeling on behalf of a movement or group. It gives life, enthusiasm, and vigor to the participants and may well be related to what Griffin calls "cohesiveness" (1982; 16-19). There is actually no single dimension by which *esprit de corps* can be measured. The degree of youth's solidarity can be identified however, by examining several features such as teenage attitudes, values, lingo, fads and styles, status criteria, and hero worship.

A well-developed sense of solidarity helps fulfill many needs in a contemporary teenager's life. For example, a sense of belonging together is increased when teens join with one another in a common undertaking. Such an environment pervades with feelings of closeness and intimacy. Feelings of strangeness, difference, and alienation disappear. Under such conditions relations tend to be of cooperation instead of personal competition. Additionally, personal reserve breaks down as mutual sympathy and responsiveness are promoted. The individual teenager thus develops a new conception of himself, but it is in the direction of greater allegiance to the movement (Blumer, 1969).

Blumer (1969) notes the primary ways for developing a sense of solidarity. One of the surest indicators is the attempt to exclude adults from adolescent activities and styles. Habitual reference to the impersonal third-person "they" (parents, adults, or the establishment) as distinct from the first-person "we" and "us" is a constant reminder of modern youth's practice of setting themselves apart from the larger society (Eicher, 1974). The sense of solidarity is greatly enhanced if the in-group can identify a common adversary or "enemy," since it enables the followers to focus their dissatisfaction away from the in-group interaction and directs frustration and hostility to an out-group target (Cramer and Champion, 1975). Membership belief that the movement is being opposed (often unjustly and unfairly) by unscrupulous "others" serves to rally the members around their aims and values, and minimizes differences between leaders and followers, especially during periods of hardship (Hoult, 1979). A significant insight was made by Cramer and Champion when they determined that solidarity refers specifically to the affective content of in-group relations. It provides positive emotional elements which many teenagers do not otherwise receive. In certain instances church youth groups would be well served by using this *"In-Group-Out-Group" principle*.

The formation of *esprit de corps* also occurs through the use of *informal fellowship*. Both the adolescent subculture and the church use many kinds of informal and communal associations. Singing, recreation, picnics, joking around, having fun, and friendly informal conversation are important devices of this sort. Through them, the individual gets a sense of status and a sense of social acceptance and support in place of prior loneliness and personal alienation.

The final way to develop social solidarity is through the use of *formal ceremonial behavior and ritual*. The value of mass meetings, rallies, parades, huge demonstrations, and commemorative ceremonies is immense. A special sense of vast support is experienced by the teen who participates in a large assemblage. He or she gains an expanded view of being somebody distinctly important. The "paraphernalia of ritual" fosters feelings of common identity and sympathy. Slogans, cheers, poems, expressive gestures, and, in some cases, uniforms acquire symbolic and sentimental significance. They represent the common feelings about the movement; they serve as a constant reliving and reinforcement of the mutual bondedness.

A sense of solidarity may be regarded as group feelings of oneness and enthusiasm. These collectivities help many modern teenagers find temporary significance. The allegiance which *esprit de corps* fosters normally follows a "boom-and-crash" cycle. Based merely on heightened enthusiasm, it is likely to vanish with the collapse of such emotionalism. In order for feelings of oneness to last over time, persistency and determination must be given the group by instilling within participants a set of convictions (Blumer, 1969).

Hero Worship

Hero worship is observable in both adults and teenagers. Consequently, most identifiable cultures come equipped with leaders. Yet, when one looks at North American youth culture on the national level, leadership is conspicuously absent. This is because the peculiar hero-orientation of today's adolescents deals more with heroes from the entertainment world than world leaders in the real sense of the word.

The attractiveness that heroes have for the masses is composed of a number of complex elements. Some of them have been verified by research, and some have been assumed by theory. North American teenagers derive at least five major gratifications from hero worship.

1) *Romanticism.* Teenagers are particularly prone to adhere to romantic perceptions of the male-female relationship because they lack the experience of the older generation and are reluctant to accept adult standards. As a result, teen heroes can easily capitalize on the romance hunger of their followers, reinforce unrealistic perceptions, and become tangible foci of romantic identifications.Teenagers see in their heroes the incarnation of many of their fondest dreams and desires.

2) *Sex and fetishism.* Expressions of hero worship have frequently been interpreted as sublimation of sexual tension whereby some material aspect of the popular hero, such as his or her clothing or hair, becomes a fetish—a tangible substitute for the coveted person that can provide a certain degree of gratification. Hero fetishism has two forms. The most prominent is mild and socially acceptable, such as: collecting and/or pinning up pictures and posters of heroes, or being given a sweaty handkerchief from a hero-performer during a concert (Morgan, 1960). The second form of fetishism is less substitutional and more

direct. Groupies constitute a special institution of teen subculture and are mostly female hero worshipers who fulfill their erotic fantasies by engaging in sexual activities with rock stars and their immediate entourages. There is an internal status system that largely depends on which famous bands they have engaged. These "rock geishas" are a small minority. For the rest of the masses of teenagers, their heroes remain distant, romantic figures with whom they stay in touch by various fetishistic practices.

3) *Crowd ecstasy.* Youthful energy and excitement find an outlet when heroes perform in front of large teen audiences. Concert and festival settings give the young an opportunity to physically express exuberance by screaming, touching, and moving rhythmically. Being in a mass of peers is a visceral experience for the teenager and offers an outlet for frustration and tension. Such rallies are not intended exclusively for listening but as a testimony of belonging. A number of physical expressions of "worshiping," such as screaming, jumping, and even "fainting," have a mutually reinforcing effect in a crowd situation. The reinforcement is due to the rewards derived from the prestige assigned to such peer-approved and peer-encouraged actions.

4) *Fascination with the bizarre and the absurd.* Humans of any age category can be made into a captive audience by the bizarre and the absurd. Modern teenagers cultivate the fascination by a freak style that during previous epochs was confined to the semi-underground adult theaters. For those who do not desire to attend a Skinhead party, a safer and more comfortable seat is available in many movie houses. The Rocky Horror Picture Show has been offering its transvestic fare to youthful crowds for over a dozen years. Since the mid-1970s Alice Cooper, Mick Jagger, and Elton John devised gimmicks to win teen attention that included macabre appearance and sado-masochistic performances. Generally, however, the early 1980s initiated a more subdued entertainment style except for select elements of the heavy metal scene. Today's young adolescents have yet to find their own identity. There is both a resurgence in worshiping the milder heroes of the preceding teen generation and gravitation toward absurd Headbanger extremism.

5) *Heroes as "messengers."* Heroes are significant others who have influence on teenagers' thinking and value-orientation. One of the prominent means by which morale and convictions are built in a subculture is through the emergence of a "saint cult." There is usually a major saint (Lenin, Marx, and Mary Baker Eddy serve as examples) and a series of minor saints, chosen from the popular leaders of the movement (Blumer, 1969). However, of all the functions national teen heroes perform extending a unifying message is currently the least effective (Conger, 1984). On a local level, however, many youth pastors have built conviction into their teens by emerging as a cult-type leader.

One could classify some of the "folk rock" heroes of the 1960s as advocates of certain values for adolescents. Perhaps the best known was Bob Dylan, whose songs criticized social conditions and focused on civil rights, the threat of nuclear war, and Vietnam. Others like Joan Baez, Judy Collins, and Peter, Paul and Mary followed the lead of Dylan, expounding social commentary with their music. While the charisma achieved by these heroes made their message credible to many, the majority of young teen fans approached the message more from the visceral, musical, and hero worship angle. The folk rock following was never as broad as the rock enthusiasts in general. The political and philosophical messages of the protest heroes, however, made impressions on the older and more serious adolescent population. An example of which could be the hip Bohemians or the early Beatniks of the 1950s.

The 1980s found a teen scene devoid of almost any type of leader-hero. As young people have become more individualistic (Sebald, 1984), most rock bands are intent on appealing to only a select segment of the teen audience—a tacit admission that rock music is no longer the unifying force of a generation.

Activism, Radicalism, and Alternative Lifestyles

North American adolescents form a population that is hyper-receptive to countercultural ideas and radical suggestions. They look for an escape from the alienation that is caused specifically by adolescence and by an anomic society in general. A certain degree of alienation should not be judged as entirely negative. Teen ministries can profit from this provided the energy can be converted and channeled into meaningful, creative directions.

Only a minority of teenagers feel alienation keenly enough to express it in the form of *radicalism*. Most students go with the system and do not work to abolish or radically change it (Lipset and Schaflander, 1971). Still, hundreds of thousands of youth struggle intensely to overcome feelings of alienation and stress (Rowlison and Felner, 1988), to try to supplant anomie (Strommen and Strommen, 1985), to search for identity and acceptance as individuals (Stevenson, Roscoe, Brooks, and Kelsey, 1987), and to find meaning in life (Brake, 1980; Sebald, 1984).

The general pop culture is to goal-oriented youth movements as a cops-and-robbers game is to a military battle. In contrast to the faddishness and entertainment, radical movements focus on goals and action. They are dynamic and intent on proselytizing. In North America however, the general teen culture and the radical culture are not always diametrically different. There is no sharp boundary between the counterculture and the youth subculture; differences are best measured in degree. The teen subculture has, in reality, absorbed many countercultural characteristics, and vice versa (Yinger, 1982).

Three major streams seem to dominate contemporary adolescents' search for an alternative lifestyle: the pro-retreatist, pro-mystic, and pro-drug approaches.

Pro-retreatist. The retreatist youth tradition is firmly established in American life. During the 1950s through the 1970s, several groups of this nature stand out: the Bohemians, the Beatniks, the Hippies, the Communards, and the Street People. Each was a colorful splinter group from the previous and generally attracted younger audiences who were less sophisticated, less talented, and less literate (Lipset and Schaflander, 1971; Conway and Siegelman, 1978). The great upheaval of the counterculture, occurring 1965-72, "more or less swallowed up these splinter groups, temporarily unified them in a common cause, and later (during the calmer late 1970s) regurgitated a metamorphosis: the New Age movement" (Sebald, 1984, 286). During the 1980s the typical pro-retreatist had a predilection for communal living, vegetarianism, and a mixture of the occult and oriental religions; they lacked the militancy of their predecessors but preferred a more philosophical-religious retreat (Conger, 1984).

The pro-retreatist movement offers little for teenagers. There does not seem to be any consistent development or cultivation of a quality that could be judged as the germanic core of pro-retreatist youth philosophy. Instead, it appears that serials of unorganized and largely unremembered trial-and-error experiments go in circles and end up nowhere (Wuthnow, 1976).

Pro-drug. The escape routes from alienation, meaninglessness, and the search for identity jutted out into many different directions during the 1960s-80s. Those avenues have not remained constant but are continually shifting. One of the latest changes is a return to alcohol as the most common illegal drug used by youth (Solow and Solow, 1986). However, crack, the newest and perhaps most devastating form of cocaine, is making a serious claim to be the preferred drug of choice (Johnson, O'Malley, and Bachman, 1986).

There are many reasons why teens are drawn to drugs. What originally attracted the vast majority of adolescent followers was more the identity derived from submerging into an underground movement than a serious interest in finding "higher levels of consciousness" (Klapp, 1969). It may still be so today. It must also be argued that some participate in mind-altering drugs as a form of escapism from both personal problems and inhibitions (Solow and Solow, 1986). Other teenagers become members of the pro-drug movement through the force of social pressure. In an eight-year longitudinal study of the multiple influences on drug use, conformity was found to be the strongest variable (Stein, Newcomb, and Bentler, 1987). The pro-drug connection offers only temporary illusion to the searching teen; true insight and knowledge, alas, defy chemical instantness.

Pro-mystic. All radical youth movements have, in one sense, a religious core. It is the integrating, meaning-giving function at the heart of the definition of religion (from religare, "to bind together") that youth seek. Such movements typically possess creed, cult, and code. They proclaim a basic meaning, provide ritual and sensate implementation, and present guidelines for everyday life.

Many teens are finding fulfillment in "True Believer" cultic movements (Rome, 1985). The followers of the pro-mystic approach to life distinguish themselves from ordinary searchers by: 1) using their lives to serve the belief instead of the reverse; 2) making proselytizing their duty; 3) believing that their dogma is the only valid philosophy of life; 4) using "radical" means to accomplish the missions and visions; and 5) subordinating themselves to a totalitarian organization and leaders who demand absolute loyalty (Richardson, 1980; Bromley and Shupe, 1981; and Levi, 1982).

While writing from a social-psychological perspective, Sebald (1984, 298) testifies to the great religious longing found in many contemporary adolescents:

> No movement other than the religious-totalitarian provides so complete a gratification for youth's ideational search. It is in this perspective that a number of powerful religious youth movements must be understood. The revival of mystical religion, primitive lore, spiritualism, ritual occultism, astrology, and the preoccupation with meditation is beyond a mere fad—it is youth's attempt to expand awareness beyond the limits imposed by modern science and the objective approach to life.

Today's youth increasingly sympathize deeply with the mystic approach to life. They find credence in a mixing of oriental, occult, and Western beliefs; such is a testimony to the depth of their starvation for meaning, lack of personal identity, and spiritual vacuum.

Significant numbers of teenagers find fulfillment in choosing an alternative lifestyle from the pro-retreatist, pro-drug, and pro-mystic movements. Although the present era is subdued and nonmilitant, the potential for renewed youth upheaval remains immanent. The basic adolescent needs of identity, relationship, significance, and purpose remain unanswered for many teens. They await only a key idea around which to rally and bond together and perhaps a hero-messenger-leader to communicate the message.

Conclusion

Seven major dimensions of adolescent culture have been highlighted: in-group values and norms, teen argot, channels of mass communication, styles and fads, sense of solidarity, "hero" worship, and activism-radicalism. No claim is made for completeness in each dimension. They serve as representative samples of the contemporary teen scene. The nature of the age span is not rebellious, antisocial behavior. Teenagers are not necessarily getting worse (although more opportunities for mischief may be available now to all ages). Young people do not automatically throw out their parents' opinions nor reject their guidance at age thirteen.

Youth subculture is an invention (see chapter two) that accommodates a number of people whose needs and desires are not met within the main blueprint of society. In today's rapidly changing culture, teenagers have lost their once privileged position. Instead, they have had a pre-mature adulthood thrust upon them.

Elkind suggests they are "unplaced" in that there is no nook for a young person who needs a measured and controlled introduction to adulthood. This is compounded by the fact that society seems unable to accept the true reality of adolescence, that there are "young people in transition from childhood to adulthood who need adult guidance and direction" (Elkind, 1984; 4 and 5).

Benson, Johnson, Wood, Williams, and Mills' (1984) massive study of young adolescents and their parents clustered the need for guidance into seven goal areas:

Achievement—satisfaction of arriving at excellence in some area of endeavor;

Friends—broadening one's social base by having learned to make friends and maintain them;

Feelings—self-understanding gained through having learned to share one's feelings with another person;

Identity—the sense of knowing "who I am," of being recognized as a significant person;

Responsibility—confidence in knowing "I can stand alone and make responsible decisions";

Maturity—transformation from a child into an adult; and

Sexuality—acceptance of responsibility for one's new role as a sexual being.

The initial letters of each catchword form the acronym "AFFIRMS" (Strommen and Strommen, 1985). Like Betty in the beginning of this chapter, many teenagers are waiting for a willing adult to affirm them through the maze of options in the adolescent subculture.

REFERENCES

Anthony, K. H. (1985). The shopping mall: A teenage hangout. *Adolescence, 20,* 307-312.

Bachman, J., Johnson, L., and O'Malley, P. (1985). *Monitoring the future: Questionnaire responses from the nation's high school seniors (1975-1983).* Ann Arbor: The Institute for Social Research.

Ban, J. D. (1986). Adolescents in Canadian culture: Religious development. *Journal of Religious Education, 81,* 225-238.

Bandura, A. (1972). The stormy decade: Fact or fiction. In D. Rogers (Ed.) *Issues in adolescent psychology.* New York: Prentice Hall.

Bandura, A., Ross, D., and Ross, S. A. (1963). Imitation of film-mediated aggressive models. *Journal of Abnormal and Social Psychology, 66,* 3-11.

Barzum, J. (1975). *Simple and direct: A rhetoric for writers.* New York: Harper & Row.

Bauman, K.E., and Fisher, L. A. (1986). On the measurement of friend behavior in research on friend influence and selection: Findings from longitudinal studies of adolescent smoking and drinking. *Journal of Youth and Adolescence, 15,* 345-353.

Bellah, R., Madsen, R., Sullivan, W., Swidler, A., and Tipton, S. (1985). *Habits of the heart.* Berkeley, Calif.: University of California Press.

Belson, W. A. (1978). *Television, violence and the adolescent boy.* Lexington, Mass.: Heath.

Benson, P., et al. (1983). *Report on 1983 Minnesota survey on drug use and drug-related attitudes.* Minneapolis: Search Institute.

Benson, P. L. (1985). Teenage pregnancy. *Source,* Search Institute, *1*:1.

Benson, P. L., Donahue, M. J., and Erickson, J. A. (1989). Adolescence and religion: A review of the literature from 1970 to 1986. In M. Lynn and D. Moberg (Eds.), *Research in the social scientific study of religion,* Vol. 1, 153-181. Greenwich, Conn.: JAI Press.

Benson, P. L., Donahue, M. J., Guerra, M.J., (1989). The good news gets better. *Momentum,* November, pp. 40-44.

Benson, P., Johnson, A., Wood, P., Williams, D., and Mills, J. (1984). *Young adolescents and their parents.* Minneapolis: Search Institute.

Benson, P., Williams, D., and Johnson, A. (1987). *The quicksilver years: The hopes and fears of early adolescence.* San Francisco: Harper & Row.

Benson, P., Yeager, R., Wood, P., Guerra, M., and Manno, B. (1986). *The Catholic high school: Its impact on low-income students.* Washington, D.C.: American Psychiatric Association.

Bibby, R. W., and Posterski, D. C. (1985). *The emerging generation: An inside look at Canada's teenagers.* Toronto: Irvin.

Billy, J. O., and Udry, J. R. (1985). The influence of male and female best friends on adolescent sexual behavior. *Adolescence, 20,* 21-32.

Blum, L. H. (1966). The discotheque and the phenomenon of alone-togetherness. *Adolescence, 1,* 351-366.

Blumer, H. B. (1969). "Social movements" in A. M. Lee, (Ed.) *Principles of sociology.* New York: Barnes and Noble.

Brake, M. (1980). *The sociology of youth culture.* London: Routledge and Kegan Paul.

Bromley, D. G., and Shupe, A.D. (1981) *Strange gods: The great American cult scare.* Boston: Beacon.

Brooks, J. (1981). *Showing off in America.* New York: Little, Brown.

Brown, B. B., Lohr, M. J., and McClenahan, E. L. (1986). Early adolescents' perceptions of peer pressure. *Journal of Early Adolescence, 6,* 139-154.

Brownstone, J. E., and Willis, R. H. (1971). Conformity in early and late adolescence. *Developmental Psychology, 4,* 334-337.

Buckley, H. M., and Roach, M.E. (1974). Clothing as a nonverbal communication of social and political attitudes. *Home Economics Research Journal, 3,* 94-102.

Campolo, A. (1987). The youth culture in sociological perspective. In W. Benson and M. Sentor (Eds.), *The complete book of youth ministry.* Chicago: Moody.

Cauce, A. (1986). Social networks and social competence: Exploring the effects of early adolescent friendships. *American Journal of Community and Psychology, 14,* 607-628.

Chassin, L. A. (1986). Changes in peer and parent influence during adolescence: Longitudinal versus cross-sectional perspectives on smoking initiation. *Developmental Psychology, 22,* 327-334.

Clasen, D. R., and Brown, B. B. (1985). The multidimensionality of peer pressure in adolescence. *Journal of Youth and Adolescence, 14,* 451-168.

Coleman, J. C. (1980). Friendship and the peer group in adolescence. In J. Adelson (Ed.), *Handbook of adolescent psychology.* New York: John Wiley.

Coleman, J. S. (1963). *The adolescent society.* New York: Free Press.

Coleman, M., Ganong, L. H., and Ellis, P. (1985). Family structure and dating behavior of adolescents. *Adolescence, 20,* 537-543.

Coles, R., and Stokes, G. (1985). *Sex and the American teenager.* New York: Harper & Row.

Conger, J. J., and Petersen, A. C. (1984). *Adolescence and youth* (3rd ed.). New York: Harper & Row.

Conway, F., and Siegelman, J. (1978). *Snapping: America's epidemic of sudden personality change.* New York: Lippincott.

Cramer, J. A., and Champion, D. J. (1975). Toward the clarification of solidarity. *Pacific Sociological Review, 18*, 292-309.

Danesi, M. (1989). Adolescent language as affectively coded behavior: Findings of an observational research project. *Adolescence, 24*, 311-320.

del Toro, W., and Greenberg, B. S. (1989). Television commercials and food orientations among teenagers in Puerto Rico. *Hispanic Journal of Behavioral Sciences, 11*, 168-177.

Douvan, E., and Adelson, A. (1966). *The adolescent experience*. New York: John Wiley.

Dunphy, D. C. (1963). Adolescent love as a reflection of teenagers' search for identity. *Sociometry, 26*, 230-246.

Easterlin, R. A., and Crimmins, E. M. (1988). Recent social trends: Changes in personal aspirations of American youth. *Journal of Sociology and Social Research, 72*, 217-223.

Eicher, J. B. (1974). *A longitudinal study of high school girls' friendship patterns, social class, and clothing*. East Lansing, Mich.: Michigan State University Agricultural Experiment Station.

Elkin, F., and Westley, W. A. (1955). The myth of adolescent culture. *American Sociological Review, 20*, 680-84.

Elkind, D. (1981). *The hurried child: Growing up too fast, too soon*. Reading, Mass.: Addison-Wesley.

Elkind, D. (1984). *All grown up and no place to go: Teenagers in crisis*. Reading, Mass.: Addison-Wesley.

Erikson, E. (1968). *Identity, youth and crisis*. New York: W. W. Norton.

Eskilson, A., Wiley, M. G., Muehlbauer, G., and Dodder, L. (1986). Parental pressure, self-esteem and adolescent reported deviance: Bending the twig too far. *Adolescence, 21*, 505-515.

Feshbach, S., and Singer, R. D. (1971). *Television and aggression: An experimental field study*. San Francisco: Jossey-Bass.

Franzoi, S. L., and Davis, M. H. (1985). Adolescent self-disclosure and loneliness: Private self-consciousness and parental influence. *Journal of Personality and Social Psychology, 48*, 768-780.

Garramone, G. M., and Atkin, C. K. (1986). Mass communication and political socialization: Specifying the effects. *Public Opinion Quarterly, 50*, 76-86.

Gold, R. L. (1964). "Fad," in J. Gould, and W. L. Kolb, (Eds.), *Dictionary of the social sciences*. New York: Free Press.

Goldman, R., and Goldman, J. (1984). Perception of sexual experience in childhood: Relating normal development to incest. *Australian Journal of Sex, Marriage and Family, 5*, 159-166.

Gordon, M. M. (1974). The concept of the subculture and its application. *Social Forces, 25*, 38-46.

Gould, M. S., and Shaffer, D. (1986). The impact of suicide in television movies: Evidence imitation. *New England Journal of Medicine, 315*, 690-694.

Grafton, S. (1964). The twisted age. *Look* (Dec. 15), 37-38. Krau (1987).

Green, A. W. (1968). *Sociology*. New York: McGraw-Hill.

Greenman, B. S., and Heeter, C. (1983). Mass media orientations among Hispanic youth. *Hispanic Journal of Behavioral Sciences. 5*, 305-323.

Griffin, E. (1982). *Getting together*. Grand Rapids, Mich.: Baker.

Grunlan, S. A., and Reimer, M. (1982). *Christian perspectives on sociology*. Grand Rapids, Mich.: Zondervan.

Hajcak, F., and Garwood, P. (1988). Quick-fix sex. Pseudosexuality in adolescents. *Adolescence, 23*, 755-760.

Hare, B. R. (1988). *Black youth at risk: The state of black America.* New York, National Urban League.

Harman, L. D. (1985). Acceptable deviance and social control: The cases of fashion and slang. *Deviant Behavior, 6* (1), 1-15.

Harrison, D. F., and Pannell, R. C. (1989). Contemporary sex roles for adolescents: New options or confusion? *Journal of Social Work and Human Sexuality, 8,* 27-45.

Herzog, A. R., and Bachman, J. G. (1982). *Sex role attitudes among high school seniors.* Ann Arbor: Institute for Social Research, The University of Michigan.

Hill, R., and Aldous, J. Jr. (1969). Socialization for marriage and parenthood. In D. Goslin (Ed.) *Handbook of socialization theory and research.* Chicago: Rand McNally.

Hoult, T. F. (1979). *Sociology for a new day* (2nd ed.). New York: Random House.

Hunter, F. T. (1985). Individual adolescents' perceptions of interactions with friends and parents. *Journal of Early Adolescence, 5,* 295-305.

Hurlock, E. B. (1967). *Adolescent development* (3rd ed.). New York: McGraw-Hill.

Johnston, L., O'Malley, P., and Bachman, J. (1985). *The use of licit and illicit drugs by America's high school seniors 1975-1984.* Washington, D. C.: U. S. Government Printing Office.

Johnson, L., O'Malley, P., and Bachman, J. (1986). *Drug use among American high school students, college students, and other young adults.* Washington, D. C.: U.S. Government Printing Office.

Jones, E. F., et al. (1985). Teenage pregnancy in developed countries: Determinants and policy implications. *Family Planning Perspectives, 17,* 53-63.

Jorgenson, S. R. (1983). Beyond adolescent pregnancy research frontiers for early adolescent sexuality. *Journal of Early Adolescence, 3,* 141-155.

Keats, J. A., et al. (1983). Parents, friends, siblings, and adults: Unfolding referent other importance data for adolescents. *International Journal of Psychology, 18,* 239-262.

Kephart, W. M. (1981). *The family, society, and the individual* (5th ed.). Boston: Houghton Mifflin.

Kinsey, A., et al. (1963). *Sexual behavior in the human female.* Philadelphia: W. S. Saunders.

Klapp, O. E. (1969). *Collective search for identity.* New York: Holt, Rinehart and Winston.

Konopka, G. (1976). *Young girls: A portrait of adolescence.* Englewood Cliffs, N. J.: Prentice Hall.

Kovacs, G. T., Dunn, K., and Selwood, T. (1986). Teenage girls and sex: The Victorian Action Center survey. *Australian Journal of Sex, Marriage and Family, 7,* 217-224.

Krau, E. (1987). The crystalization of values in adolescence: A sociocultural approach. *Journal of Vocational Behavior, 30* (2), 103-123.

Lane, K., and Givartney-Gibbs. (1985). Violence in the dating relationship. *Journal of Family Issues, 23,* 136-147.

LeMasters, E. E. (1974). *Parents in modern America.* Homewood, Ill.: Dorsey Press.

Lennon, S. T. (1986). Adolescent attitudes toward designer jeans: Further evidence. *Adolescence, 21,* 475-482.

Lerman, P. (1967). Argot, symbolic deviance and subcultural delinquency. *American Sociological Review. 32,* 209-224.

Levi, K. (Ed.) (1981). *Violence and religious commitment.* University Park: Pennsylvania State University Press.

Levinson, D. (1978). *The seasons of a man's life.* New York: Knopf.

Levinson, R., Powell, B., and Stellman, L. C. (1986). Social location, significant others and body language among adolescents. *Social Psychology Quarterly, 49,* 330-337.

Liebert, R. M. (1982). *The early window: Effects of television on children and youth.* Elmsford, N.Y.: Pergamon.

Lipset, S. M., and Schaflander, G. M. (1971). *Passion and politics: Student activism in America*. Boston: Little, Brown and Company.

Marks, A. (1987). Television and suicide: Comment. *New England Journal of Medicine, 316*, 877.

Martin, B. (1979). The sacralization of disorder. *Sociological Analysis, 40*, 87-124.

McCoy, K. (1982). *Coping with teenage depression*. New York: New American Library.

Mehta, G. (1981). *Karma cola: Marketing the mystic east*. New York: Simon and Schuster.

Miller, B. C., and Olsen, T. D. (1986). Parental discipline and control attempts in relation to adolescent sexual attitudes and behavior. *Journal of Marriage and Family, 48*, 503-512.

Morgan, M., and Grube, J. W. (1989). Adolescent cigarette smoking: A developmental analysis of influences. *British Journal of Developmental Psychology, 7*, 179-189.

Morgan, T. B. (1960). Teen-age heroes: Mirror of a muddled youth. *Esquire*, March 1960, pp. 65-73.

Mussen, P. H., Conger, J. J., and Kagan, J. (1979). *Child development and personality*. New York: Harper & Row.

Nelsen, E. A., and Rosenbaum, E. (1972). Language patterns within the youth subculture: Development of slang vocabularies. *Merrill-Palmer Quarterly of Behavior and Development, 18*, 273-284.

Norman, J., and Harris, M. (1981). *The private life of the American teenager*. New York: Rawson Wade.

Offer, D., Ostrov, E., and Howard, K. I. (1981). *The adolescent: A psychological self-portrait*. New York: Basic Books.

O'Keeffe, N. K., Brockopp, K., and Chew, E. (1986). Teen dating violence. *Social Work, 31*, 465-468.

Opie, I., and Opie, P. (1959). *The lore and language of school children*. Oxford: The Clarendon Press.

Painter, H. W. (1985). Changing images in books for young people. *Child and Youth Services, 7*, 39-46.

Parsons, T. (1950). Psychoanalysis and the social structure. *Psychoanalytic Quarterly, 19*, 378-79.

Peters, J. F. (1985). Adolescents as socialization to parents. *Adolescence, 20*, 921-933.

Petersen, A. C., and Crockett, L. (1985). Pubertal timing and grade effects on adjustment. *Journal of Youth and Adolescence, 14*, 191-206.

Phillips, D. P., and Carstensen, L. L. (1986). Clustering of teenage suicides after television news stories about suicide. *New England Journal of Medicine, 315*, 685-689.

Phillips, D. P., and Paight, D. J. (1987). The impact of televised movies about suicide: A replicative study. *New England Journal of Medicine, 317*, 809-811.

Powell, L. H., and Jorgensen, S. R. (1985). Evaluation of a church-based sexuality education program for adolescents. *Family Relations Journal of Applied Family and Child Studies, 34*, 475-482.

Reiss, I. (1966). The sexual renaissance: A survey and analysis. *Journal of Social Issues, 22*, 123-137.

Remmers, H. H., and Radler, D. H. (1962). *I am teenager*. New York: Bobbs-Merrill.

Richardson, H., (Ed.) (1980). *New religious and mental health*. Lewiston, N. Y.: Edwin Mellen Press.

Rome, H. P. (1985). Perspectives on adolescence and society's values. *Psychiatric Annals, 15*, 11-14.

Roscoe, B., and Callahan, J. E. (1985). Adolescents' self-report of violence in families and dating relations. *Adolescence, 20*, 545-553.

Roscoe, B., Diana, M. S., and Brooks, R. H. (1987). Early, middle, and late adolescents' views on dating and factors influencing partner selection. *Adolescence, 22*, 59-68.

Roszak, T. (1969). *The making of a counter culture*. Garden City, N. Y.: Doubleday.

Row, K. (1987). Adolescents' video use: A structural-cultural approach. *American Journal of Behavioral Scientist, 30*, 522-532.

Rowlison, R. T., and Felner, R. D. (1988). Major life events, hassles, and adaptation in adolescence: Confounding in the conceptualization and measurement of life stress and adjustment revisited. *Journal of Personality and Social Psychology, 55*, 432-444.

Samet, N., and Kelly, E. W. (1987). The relationship of steady dating to self-esteem and sex role identity among adolescents. *Adolescence, 22*, 231-245.

Sapp, G. (Ed.) (1991). *Compassion in pastoral ministry*. Birmingham, Ala.: Religious Education Press.

Savin-Williams, R. C. (1980). Dominance hierarchies in groups of late adolescent males. *Journal of Youth and Adolescence, 9*, 75-83.

Scanzoni, L. D., and Scanzoni, J. (1988). *Men, women and change*. New York: McGraw-Hill.

Schwartz, G., and Merten, D. (1967). The language of adolescence: An anthropological approach to youth culture. *American Journal of Sociology, 72*, 453-468.

Sebald, H. (1972). The pursuit of 'instantness' in technocratic society and youth's psychedelic drug use. *Adolescence, 7*, 343-350.

Sebald, H. (1975). Subculture: Problems of definition and measurement. *International Review of Modern Sociology, 5*, 82-89.

Sebald, H. (1984). *Adolescence - A social psychological analysis* (3rd ed.). Englewood Cliffs, N. J.: Prentice Hall.

Sebald, H. (1985). New age romanticism: The quest for an alternative lifestyle as a force of social change. *Humboldt Journal of Social Relations, 23*, 234-248.

Sebald, H. (1986). Adolescents' shifting orientation toward parents and peers: A curvilinear trend over recent decades. *Journal of Marriage and the Family, 48*, 5-13.

Secord, W., Wiig, E. H., and Williams, G. H. (1988). Multiple perceptions of word relationships: Evidence of adolescent competence. *Folia-Phoniatrica, 40*, 197-204.

Selye, H. (1976). *The stress of life*. New York: McGraw-Hill.

Shapiro, T. (1985). Adolescent language: Its use for diagnosis, group identity, values and treatment. *Adolescent Psychiatry, 12*, 297-311.

Smith, E. A., Udry, J. R., Morris, N. M. (1985). Pubertal development and friends: A biosocial explanation of adolescent sexual behavior. *Journal of Health and Social Behavior, 26*, 183-192.

Snow, R. P. (1974). How children interpret TV violence in play context. *Journalism Quarterly, 51*, 13-21.

Solow, R. A., and Solow, B. K. (1986). Mind-altering drugs: Effects of adolescent sexual functioning. *Medical Aspects of Human Sexuality, 20*, 64-74.

Steed, K. K., and Range, L. M. (1989). Does television induce suicide contagion with adolescents? *Journal of Community and Psychology, 17*, 166-172.

Stein, J. A., Newcomb, M. D., and Bentler, P. M. (1987). An eight year study of multiple influences on drug use and drug use consequences. *Journal of Personality and Social Psychology, 53*, 1094-1105.

Steinberg, L. (1986). Latchkey children and susceptibility to peer pressure: An ecological analysis. *Developmental Psychology, 22*, 433-439.

Stevenson, B. W., Roscoe, B., Brooks, R. H., and Kelsey, T. (1987). Profiles of mod revivalists: A case study of a reemerging adolescent group. *Adolescence, 22*, 393-404.

Straton, J. (1985). Youth subcultures and their cultural contexts. *Australian and New Zealand Journal of Sociology, 21*, 194-218.

Street, S. (1985). Sex roles, feedback and self-concept. *High School Journal, 69.* 70-80.

Strommen, M. P. (1988). *Five cries of youth* (rev. ed.). New York: Harper & Row.

Strommen, M. P., and Strommen, I. A. (1985). *Five cries of parents.* San Francisco: Harper & Row.

Strouse, J., and Fabes, R. A. (1985). Formal versus informal sources of sex education: Competing forces in the sexual socialization of adolescents. *Adolescence, 20,* 251-263.

Swadi, H., and Zeitlin, H. (1988). Peer influence and adolescent substance abuse: A promising side? *British Journal of Addiction, 83,* 153-157.

Synnott, A. (1987). Shame and glory: A sociology of hair. *British Journal of Sociology, 38,* 381-413.

Thornburg, H. D., Thornburg, E., and Ellis, S. M. (1984). Assignment of personal value among adolescents. *Journal of Psychology, 118,* 65-70.

Verhoff, J., Douvan, E., and Kulka, R. (1981). *The inner American: A self-portrait from 1957-1976.* New York: Basic Books.

Walker, L. S., and Greene, J. W. (1986). The social context of adolescent self-esteem. *Journal of Youth and Adolescence 15,* 315-322.

Westney, Q. E., Cole, O. J., and Munford, T. L. (1986). Adolescent unwed prospective fathers: Readiness for fatherhood and behaviors toward the mother and the expected infant. *Adolescence, 21,* 901-911.

Wilkins, J. A. (1982). *Breaking the TV habit.* New York: Scribners.

Williams, R. M., Jr. (1960). *American society: A sociological interpretation.* New York: Knopf.

Whorf, B. L. (1956). *Language, thought, and reality.* Cambridge, Mass.: MIT Press.

Wuthnow, R. (1976). Recent patterns of secularization: A problem of generations? *American Sociological Review, 41,* 850-867.

Wynne, E. A., and Hess, M. (1986). Long-term trends in youth conduct and the revival of traditional value patterns. *Educational Evaluation and Policy Analysis, 8,* 294-308.

Yankelovich, D. (1981). *New rules: Searching for fulfillment in a world turned upside down.* New York: Random House.

Yinger, M. J. (1960). Contraculture and subculture. *American Sociological Review, 25,* 624-633.

Yinger, M. J. (1982). *Countercultures.* Riverside, N. J.: Free Press.

Youniss, J. (1980). *Parents and peers in social development.* Chicago: University of Chicago Press.

"Youth on the Move" (1981). *U. S. News and World Report,* January 5, p. 71-79.

Chapter Two

Adolescence as a Cultural Invention

RONALD L. KOTESKEY

"When I was a child, I talked like a child, I thought like a child, I reasoned like a child. When I became a man, I put childish ways behind me." (1 Cor 13:11 NIV)

The apostle Paul talks about when he was a child and when he was an adult, but not about when he was an adolescent. Why does he not tell us what he was like as an adolescent? Because, although he was a teenager, he never was an adolescent. Adolescence had not yet been invented in Paul's day, so he could not write about it. In fact, the modern concept of adolescence is so new that our language does not even have words for male and female adolescents. Adults are called "men" and "women." Children are called "girls" and "boys." Neither of these fit teenagers who are often called "guys" and "gals," slang for "boys" and "girls."

Adolescence Invented

The word *adolescens*, the Latin present participle of *adoelescere*, was used in Paul's day. It meant "growing one," referring to the sudden growth spurt shown by teenagers. Today adolescence is defined as the period between puberty and adulthood (*The Random House Dictionary of the English Language*, 1987; *The New Encyclopedia Brittanica*, 1986). Two hundred years ago people became adults at puberty, so there was no adolescence. However, both the meanings and the ages of puberty and adulthood have changed during the last century so that people pass through puberty several years before they are defined as adults.

Puberty

Like adolescence, the word "puberty" has changed in meaning. Puberty comes from the Latin *pubertas,* meaning "adulthood." In the apostle Paul's time puberty was the beginning of adulthood, not the beginning of adolescence. When we define adolescence as the time between puberty and adulthood, we are literally saying that it is the period between biological adulthood and social adulthood. Of course, today puberty means the age of sexual maturity, the age at which people can have children, not the age at which we treat them as adults.

Not only has the meaning of puberty changed, but so has its age. Systematic studies of the age of menarche (the first menstrual period, closely related to puberty) began at the end of the eighteenth century. Wyshak and Frisch (1982) reviewed 218 reports on age of menarche made between 1795 and 1981, covering 220,037 women. Of sixty-five studies done before 1880, *none* found an average age of menarche *below* 14.5. The age of menarche over that eighty-five-year period ranged from 14.5 to 17.5, with an average of about sixteen. Of twenty-four studies done after 1950, *only one* found an average age of menarche *above* 14.5. Since 1950 when the decline stopped in the United States, the average age of menarche has been about 12.5 years of age (Bullough, 1981; Tanner, 1981).

The age of puberty for males is not as obvious and not as well-documented. In the eighteenth century when Bach was choirmaster at St. Thomas' Church in Leipzig, choirboys sang soprano until they were seventeen or older (Lindzey, Hall, and Thompson, 1978). Today their voices break at a much earlier age, at about fourteen or fifteen years of age. Researchers argue over how much the age of puberty has declined, but all agree that it has. People reach puberty somewhere between two and four years earlier than they did in the early nineteenth century.

Adulthood

The word "adult" is from the Latin *adultus,* the past principle of *adolescere,* the same word from which adolescence comes. The only difference is that adult literally means "grown one," someone past their growth spurt. The dictionary defines an adult as one who has grown to full size and strength in one definition and as one who has reached the age of maturity as specified by law in another. The problem in our culture is that we have separated these two meanings so that people grow to full size and strength several years before they come of age. They are adults physically before they are adults legally.

Until the last century most people were considered adults at twelve to fourteen years of age, and society treated them as adults. At the age of thirteen plus one day for men and twelve plus one day for women the Hebrews went through bar mitzvah or bat mitzvah and attained religious and legal maturity. The father read from the Torah and recited the benediction, "Blessed is he who has now freed me from the responsibility of this one" (Kaplan, 1972, p. 244). Although many things are involved in being an adult, being able to marry and being responsible for yourself are the two major marks of adulthood.

Marriage

Hebrew Law. Among the ancient Hebrews not only could people marry at puberty, but they were also encouraged to do so. Although some well-known exceptions occurred in the Old Testament, many people married soon after puberty. Several passages from the *Talmud* encourage marriage at puberty. One passage praises the man who loves his wife as he loves himself, honors her more than himself, and "leads his children in the right path, and marries them just before they attain puberty" (Sanhedrin 76a).

Not only were parents encouraged to marry their daughters early, but they were seen as evil if they did not do so. Referring to Leviticus 19:29 which commands parents not to make their daughters prostitutes, Rabbi Akiba said, "This refers to the delay in marrying off a daughter who is already a *bogareth*" (Sanhedrin 76a). A footnote explains that since she has attained puberty (a *bogareth*) she may become unchaste if not married. It also notes that marriage then was at a far earlier age than it is now.

Rabbi Abaye asked, "Which poor man is subtly wicked?" He answered, "He who delays in marrying off his daughter, a *bogareth*" (Sanhedrin 76b). Again a footnote explains that his wickedness is that he keeps her unmarried to profit from her labor while endangering her chastity.

The Hebrews had ideal ages for many things. The best age to study scripture was five, to become subject to the commandments (bar mitzvah) was thirteen, to study the *Talmud* was fifteen, and "eighteen–for the bridal canopy" (Aboth 5). The school of Rabbi Ishmael taught, "When will he take a wife? As soon as one attains twenty and has not married. He exclaims, 'Blasted be his bones!'" (Kiddushin 29b). At that time puberty for men was probably about the age of eighteen as it was around the world 200 years ago.

What was the problem in not marrying soon after puberty? Rabbi Huna said, "He who is twenty years of age and is not married spends all his days in sin. 'In sin'–can you really think so?–But say, spends all his days in sinful thoughts." Rabbi Hisda continued, "The reason that I am superior to my colleagues is that I married at sixteen. And had I married at fourteen, I would have said to Satan, An arrow in your eye" (Kiddushin 29b-30a). A footnote explains that then he would have been able to defy Satan because he would have been free of impure thoughts. The problem with remaining unmarried was sexual fantasy.

Although the Rabbis wanted people to follow the social clock of the day, school before marriage, they granted exceptions. "If one has to study Torah and to marry a wife, he should first study and then marry. But if he cannot live without a wife, he should first marry and then study" (Sanhedrin 29b).

Roman Law. Under Roman law men could marry at fourteen and women at twelve. When a Roman girl reached her thirteenth year, her parents actively began to seek a husband for her. The law required that the girl's consent be given, but this was assumed unless she openly refused. The parents considered wealth and family convenience, and the children usually followed the parents' directions. An unmarried woman at nineteen was distinctly an old maid. Self-initiated courtship was virtually unknown as evidenced by the fact that the Latin language had no words corresponding to "court" or "woo" in our English language (Goodsell, 1934).

English Law. Under English law the legal minimum age for marriage remained at twelve for women and fourteen for men. In Saxon England during the Middle Ages, children could be betrothed as infants, but the agreement could be broken until the child was ten with no penalty. If the contract was broken when the child was between ten and twelve, the parent was fined. Both the parents and the "child" could be fined if the child was over twelve years old (Goodsell, 1934). At the age of twelve "children" were considered responsible enough to be fined for breach of contract.

Early marriages were common even into the eighteenth century. Any man of fourteen and woman of twelve could marry, without their parents' consent and at little expense. Hampstead Chapel advertised weddings for only five shillings if the couple brought a "Certificate according to the act of Parliament." In 1716 the chapel offered to marry the couple free if they "have their wedding dinner in the gardens" (Goodsell, 1934; p. 335).

In 1882 Parliament raised the age of consent from twelve to thirteen, but an attempt to raise it to sixteen failed. However, on August 14, 1885, Parliament, on a vote of 179 to 71, raised the age from thirteen to sixteen due to pressure from the London Salvation Army. General Booth wrote in *The War Cry* that he thanked God for the success he had given to "the first effort of the Salvation Army to improve the laws of the nation" (Collier, 1965; p. 125). Now young girls would not be forced into marriages they did not want.

When people could marry at twelve, that meant that those with earlier-than-average puberty could marry as soon as they matured. The law of 1885 meant that about half of the girls would have to wait a little while after they matured before they could marry. As the age of puberty went even lower and the legal minimum age of marriage went even higher, adolescence was created. A massive social experiment began, and teenagers of this century have been the guinea pigs. It is ironic that General Booth's Salvation Army was forced to open homes for unwed mothers, partly because of the cultural change he encouraged.

American Law. Early American law and practice was modeled after the English and other European precedents. In 1704 Madam Knight wrote that Connecticut youth usually married very young, that men were more likely to marry under the age of twenty than over, and that women often married at sixteen or under. Old maids were ridiculed, and they became "antient (ancient) maids" at twenty-five (Calhoun, 1917). Others noted that a woman single at twenty was a "stale maid" (Queen and Habenstein, 1974).

The Puritans in colonial America recognized the power of the human sexual drive and took precautions to prevent premarital sex. Getting suitable husbands and wives for their children was the best way to avoid premarital sex, pregnancy, and sexual perversion. Thomas Cobbett, a Puritan, wrote that such people "not being able to contain," would be guilty of "unnatural pollutions, and other filthy practices in secret; and too oft of horrid Murthers of the fruit of their bodies" (Morgan, 1978; pp. 369-370).

Many of the first people to move "west" married at fifteen or sixteen. In pioneer Kentucky a marriage between a man of sixteen and a woman of fourteen was "an occasion of merriment and brought out the whole fort" (Calhoun, 1918; p. 13). Calhoun went on to mention that according to another report, girls in North Carolina married so early that twenty-seven-year-old grandmothers were frequently found.

As in England, laws raising the minimum legal age for marriage were passed in various states. Early marriage became frowned upon as much as late marriage had been only a few years before. By 1926 Westermark wrote that marriage at the age of puberty was found among the "uncivilized races" (p. 31). In 1934 Goodsell wrote that laws permitting marriage at twelve and fourteen should long ago have disappeared from the law books of "enlightened states." He thought that laws permitting children to marry were a "social stupidity" (pp. 475-476). What was considered normal for 3000 years is, in the twentieth century, called uncivilized, unenlightened, and socially stupid.

Responsibility

Throughout history societies have expected people to take responsibility for themselves after passing through puberty. People were expected to work and held responsible for wrong acts. The *Talmud* says that, among other things regarding his son, the father was to "teach him Torah, take a wife for him, and teach him a craft." Rabbi Juda said that a man who did not teach his son a craft "teaches him brigandage. 'Brigandage!' can you really think so!–But it is as though he taught him brigandage" (Kiddushin 29a). That is, if the son had no occupation, he had to become a thief.

Occupational heredity and the guild movement were found in the Roman Empire. The naturalness of a father teaching his son his trade is evident enough, but the later Roman Empire gave such occupational heredity the force of law. With economic decay, some of the craftsmen wanted to escape into better paying, easier work. "Reforms" followed, forcing sons to follow their father's footsteps so that trades essential to the state would not die. Children and teenagers learned their trades from their fathers (Kranzberg and Gies, 1975).

Although the guilds nearly disappeared for some time, they reappeared even stronger toward the end of the Middle Ages. Sons usually learned the craft from their fathers. Masters could have only one or two apprentices, but as many sons, brothers, or nephews as they wished could work with them. After several years of hard work, an apprentice could become a master by fulfilling a set of obligations including the production of a "*master*piece," or example of his craft.

Among the Puritans a child started working at six years of age, but at fourteen his father chose a calling for him. Such a calling was more than a way of making a living because they believed that God called people to an occupation by giving talent and inclination. The father had to carry out God's plan in choosing an occupation for his son (Bremner, 1970).

In his autobiography, Benjamin Franklin wrote that he began grammar school at eight years of age. At ten he was taken home to help his father in the family business of a "Tallow Chandler and Sope-Boiler." At twelve he was indentured to serve as an apprentice until he was twenty-one. In his autobiography, Andrew Carnegie wrote that at fifteen years of age he got his "first real start in life . . . from the dark cellar running a steam engine . . . into paradise . . . with newspapers, pens, and sunshine about me . . . I felt that my foot was upon the ladder and that I was bound to climb" (Bremner 1970; pp. 112, 645).

Not only were teenagers expected to support themselves, but they were also held responsible for wrong actions. They could become criminals. Juvenile delinquency was officially invented with the passage of the Juvenile Court Act by the Illinois legislature in 1899. In that act a "delinquent child" was defined as "any child under the age of sixteen years who violates any law of this State or any City or Village ordinance" (Bremner, 1971; p. 507). Of course, at that time sixteen was about the age at which boys passed through puberty. The idea was to help teenagers by having informal, separate, confidential proceedings where lawyers were unnecessary, in a court which could not send people to prison. If teenagers could be helped early, the experts thought they would not enter a life of crime.

Today in the United States people are not allowed to marry, without parental consent, until they are eighteen in most states. Although states differ they usually cannot sign a contract, make a will, or serve on a jury until they are that age. Most adolescents must go to school and cannot work full-time until they are sixteen to eighteen. They cannot buy alcoholic beverages until they are twenty-one in all states (*Information Please Almanac*, 1989; *The Book of the States*, 1988).

Just as the age of puberty was decreasing so that people were maturing earlier, our culture increased the age at which they were considered adults. Twentieth-century Western culture has created another stage of development between these two, adolescence–the time between puberty and adulthood.

The contrast between cultures with and without adolescence is sharpest when refugees come into our Western culture. Le Gaiu, his wife, and three daughters moved from Vietnam to California. The parents expected their daughters to live at home until they married and hoped to arrange marriages for their daughters after they finished college. Daughter Trang (now called Jennifer) says, "If the decision is up to them, they'd chose a smart man in business. I want a nice, funny man who will not always worry about his work" (Toufexis, 1985; p. 85). Who knows more about picking a marriage partner, people who have lived in a marriage relationship for twenty years or someone who has never been married? Which makes a better husband, a smart businessman or a funny man who does not worry about work?

Why Create Adolescence?

Although the idea of adolescence does not seem logical, there had to be some reason to create it. Bakan (1971) dealt extensively with the development of adolescence into a social fact of life in the United States. From the initial settlement of the country until the end of the nineteenth century America had a chronic labor shortage which was rectified by slavery, immigration, and the working of children and teenagers. Farm work and simple factory work could be done by unskilled laborers.

However, by 1880 the frontier was gone and the railroad network was essentially completed. In the next decade the number of cities with more than 8,000 people nearly doubled. By 1900 more than a third of the population lived in cities. With increasing industrialization, the labor shortage disappeared and was replaced with a labor surplus (Bakan, 1971). Industrialization, urbanization, immigration, and mobility all played a role in the creation of adolescence. Although the concerns were always phrased in humanitarian rhetoric about "saving the children," many times the underlying motives were more economic and self-serving.

With the labor surplus, labor began to organize. The Knights of Labor (later called the AFL) had a membership of 100,000 in 1885 and a membership of 730,000 by 1886. From its beginning it campaigned to prohibit child labor, but effective child labor laws did not pass until after 1900 (Bakan, 1971). People interested in protecting children from the hazards of the workplace worked with the unions, which were also interested in creating a labor shortage to drive wages up.

Immigration also played a part in the creation of adolescence through the passage of labor laws and compulsory attendance laws in education. By 1890 more than a third of the population was of foreign parentage, which resulted in very restrictive immigration laws at about this time, laws supported by organized labor. Immigrants were also seen as having a lower level of morality expressed in sexual immorality, drinking, and vagrancy. Of course part of this behavior was because immigrants were more likely to be unemployed.

In 1875, Mary Carpenter (Bakan, 1971), in her address to the American Social Science Association, stated that society was suffering because of this unemployment and immorality and that it was the duty of the state to stand *in loco parentis* to see that the children were properly educated. The state must intercede in restraining and training its teenagers who were also becoming unemployed. If teens did not work, society had to do something with them, thus they were forced to go to school. Humanitarians pointed out that educated people would be better citizens and could get better jobs.

Seen in this light, the creation of adolescence made sense. "Children" were to be protected from forced labor, and wages for others were to increase. At the same time the "children" were to be educated well into their teens so that they would be socialized or Americanized.

Are They Adults?

When we observe adolescent behavior, we are tempted to ask, "Are they adults?" We may be tempted to think that they have just gone through an early puberty and are not really adults. But they *are* adults, as can be seen in various types of development.

Physical Maturity. Although his research was completed sixty years ago, Scammon (1930) is still cited in textbooks today. He found that the sexual system matures relatively late, compared to other physical aspects of maturation. The nervous system and the lymphatic system mature rapidly and relatively early in life. The adolescent growth spurt in body size comes at about the same time as sexual maturity. Physical maturity peaks at some time in the teens, and physical decline begins in the twenties. Although endurance may increase even through the thirties, other physical capacities begin to decline during the twenties.

A look at "Dosage and Administration" in the annual *Physicians Desk Reference* (1989) reveals dosages for children and adults, but rarely one for adolescents. Physiologically adolescents are much like adults. Pharmaceutical manufacturers grope for words to describe adolescents, and you will find phrases such as "adults and children over fourteen years of age" or "children (8-12) . . . and adults (over twelve) . . ." Even a look at the dosages on over-the-counter drugs like aspirin and decongestants reveals that children become adults physically at twelve to fourteen years of age.

Changes in the brain continue throughout life. The metabolic rate of the brain during late childhood is about twice that of an adult. However, between the ages of ten or eleven and thirteen or fourteen the metabolic rate declines to that of a typical adult. Then experience changes the brain by strengthening the circuits that are used and weakening those that are not, something like a sculptor building a framework, adding plaster to it, then chipping away the extra until the final form is achieved (Greenough, Black, and Wallace, 1987).

Cognitive Maturity. Swiss psychologist Jean Piaget (1972) has been the leading person to study the development of thinking. Although the apostle Paul wrote about this nearly 2000 years ago (the verse quoted at the beginning of this chapter), Piaget carefully documented that children think quite differently from adults. He found that cognitive development is virtually complete at about the age of puberty. People go through four stages in the development of their thinking, with the final stage of development for most (formal operations) coming at about eleven or twelve years of age. By then, many adolescents potentially can reason deductively, formulate and test hypotheses, and think in abstract terms. They can learn algebra, program computers, and use the scientific method (see chapter three).

Even if one disagrees with the concept of "stages," there is no denying the fact that the thinking of sixteen-year-old adolescents is quite like that of other adults, and remarkably different from that of six-year-old children. For the first time in their lives, adolescents can go beyond the concrete and actual world, and they can imagine the world as they would like to see it. Then they are likely to be distressed when they see how the real world falls far short of their utopia. They realize their parents are not perfect and complain about it to their youth ministers. Of course, they also realize their youth ministers are not perfect and complain to their parents. The idealism of adolescence is not just a result of the creation of adolescence. It occurs because these intellectual powers can be exercised for the first time (Piaget, 1967).

Moral Maturity. Lawrence Kohlberg has studied moral development and proposed at least six stages. The final two stages, which he calls "postconventional," begin to appear in adolescence (Kohlberg and Gilligan, 1971). Many people at this level of development can make moral decisions on the basis of moral principles rather than on the approval or authority of others. Rather than simply obeying rules, many adolescents can think of general rights of people and of universal ethical principles (see chapter seven).

Of course, any youth minister knows that adolescents do not make all their moral judgments on the basis of ethical and moral principles. However, they do have the capacity to do so if they have entered the stage of formal operations (see chapter three). Without question, the moral judgments of eighteen-year-old adolescents are quite similar to those of other adults and quite different from those of six-year-old children.

Why Don't They Act Like It?

If teenagers really are adults, "Why don't they act like it?" Before the invention of adolescence teenagers acted like adults, but most of them do not do so today. Why?

The Disease of Precocity. Although we view precocious children as gifted today, for nearly a century after 1830 such precocity was viewed as a disease. In 1834 Amariah Brigham declared that "precocious maturity of the mind is nearly always a disease." An article in the *Common School Journal* in 1843 advised that if children exhibited any symptoms of precocity, they should be taken immediately from books and encouraged to "ramble and play in the open air, or engage in manual labor." Precocity referred to more than intelligence. It included premature independence, assertiveness, sexuality, adult skills, mannerisms, emotional states, and attitudes. Children were not to develop any faster than the norm. Precocity was seen as becoming epidemic under such forces of modern society as urbanization, individualism, ambition, luxury, and wealth (Kett, 1978; pp. s184-s187). Rather than seeing their children as gifted, parents saw them as sick and in need of treatment, exactly the opposite of today.

Shortly after the turn of the century we invented organizations to turn teenagers into children instead of allowing them to be the adults they had been. The names of these organizations indicated what people thought of teens: Boy Scouts of

America (1910), Girl Guides, renamed Girl Scouts (1912), Boy's Clubs of America (1906), and many forerunners of 4-H, such as Boys' and Girls' Agricultural Clubs (Ohio, 1902), Farmers' Boys and Girls League (Texas, 1903), and Boys' and Girls' Demonstration Clubs (Mississippi, 1907).

Advice to slow down the development of teenagers continues into the end of this century. Writing to a secular audience, David Elkind (1981, 1984) advocates slowing the rate of development of children and adolescents. Writing to a Christian audience, Larry Richards (1984) said, "Unfortunately, our culture forces teenagers' development too rapidly.... I very consciously insulated my teens from the fast pace of growth that adolescent culture assumes" (p. 157).

Elkind (1981) was correct in cautioning people against hurrying the development of their children. However, he and Richards (1984) have extended that idea so far that now we try to keep adults (adolescents) from being adults. Elkind titled his 1984 book *All Grown Up and No Place to Go,* indicating they were adults but had no role in our culture. The real solution is not to keep them from growing up but to give back their role in adult society. Children should be allowed to be children, but adults should be expected to be adults.

A Self-Fulfilling Prophecy. Psychologist Robert Rosenthal has conducted several experiments showing that people (and even animals) behave as we expect them to, even when we do not intend to influence them. In one experiment he gave all students a test and *randomly* picked about 20 percent of the students, designating them "late bloomers." He told the teachers these children would show remarkable gains in intellectual competence during the next eight months. Eight months later he asked the teachers about these students and the teachers said that these students were more interesting, curious, happy, appealing, adjusted, and affectionate than other pupils in the class. Not only did their grades go up, but so did their scores on IQ tests eight months later (Rosenthal and Jacobson, 1968). Although psychologists do not always find this effect, they find it often enough to realize that expectations do have an effect on behavior.

The self-fulfilling prophecy ("Rosenthal effect") does not explain all of adolescence, but it helps explain some things about it. We expect adolescents to be immature, irresponsible, and prone to divorce when they marry. They are. Then we tell them they cannot be treated as adults because they are immature, irresponsible, and divorce-prone. When we say that adolescents are not socially or emotionally mature, what we are saying is that we (as a part of our culture) have not expected and demanded this maturity of them. Even though they are physically mature, cognitively mature, and morally mature, we have not allowed them to be socially mature. We have expected them to behave in some way less than adult.

What Can Youth Ministry Do?

Rather than conform to the culture the church must transform the culture. Rather than increasing adolescence, youth ministry must decrease it. In both Old and New Testament times people were babies, children, and adults. "Take

this baby and nurse him for me . . . When the child grew older . . . One day, after
Moses had grown up" (Ex 2:9-11, NIV). In verse 9 Moses was a baby, in verse
10 he was a child, and in verse 11 he had grown up. In Hebrews 11:23 Moses was
a child, in verse 24 he had grown up. He never was an adolescent.

A century or two ago our culture expected children to be as responsible as
adults and work in factories. Today our culture expects adolescents (who are really adults) to be as irresponsible as children. The church must correct the excess-
es of the culture, keep children children and make adults adults.

Although a Christian bar mitzvah ceremony may not be accepted in most
churches, there should be some ceremonies or activities in which adults participate but children do not. Although some churches baptize infants and allow
anyone to take communion, perhaps these two ceremonies could be made con-
tingent on children becoming adolescents and having a personal relationship
with God (the author did with his children).

Twenty years ago it became fashionable for teens to not trust anyone over thirty. Most cultures revere their elders, but we seem to worship our youth. Youth
need to realize that people who have lived through many different experiences
are in a better position to make many judgments about life. Youth must respect
the wisdom of those older than them in the church.

The invention of adolescence by the decrease in the age of puberty combined with the increase in the age of adulthood has resulted in three major problem areas. First, although we have created this stage of life, we have not yet
given people in it an identity in our culture. Second, we have forbidden marriage
for teenagers, but we have not told them what to do with their sexuality. Third,
we have made it illegal for them to work and forced them to spend their time in
school.

Identity Lost

"Why were you searching for me?" he asked. "Didn't you know I had to be
in my Father's house?" (Lk 2:49, NIV). As he was about to enter adulthood
(his teen years) Jesus knew who he was and his mission in life. This is in marked
contrast to the "Who am I?" question adolescents wrestle with so frequently in
our culture. In the more structured societies of the past, teenagers did not have
to deal with the question of identity—society told them. With our emphasis on freedom of choice and individuality, such societies sound restrictive. Identity came
from the culture, community, religion, and family. Of course, these were inter-
dependent and combined to give people their personal identities.

Cultural Identity
On the day after their thirteenth birthday Hebrew men went through their
bar mitzvah. The next time the Torah was read in the synagogue, the new man
was called up to read it. Likewise, on the day after their twelfth birthday the

women went through bat mitzvah. These new men and women were viewed as adults in their culture.

When a Roman boy reached his sixteenth year, he exchanged his *toga prae-texta* for a *toga virilis* as a symbol of his growth to manhood. On the morning of March 16, the day called *Liberalia,* the boy laid the symbols of his boyhood on the altar at home and went to an imposing ceremony at the forum (Goodsell, 1934).

Modern Western society has no uniform age or ceremony to mark the beginning of adulthood. At about age twelve people start paying adult prices in restaurants. At about age sixteen they can drop out of school and drive. At about age eighteen they can vote, marry, sign a contract, serve on a jury, and make a will. At age twenty-one they can buy liquor. Except for the age at which people can buy alcohol, the states have a great variety of ages (*The Book of the States,* 1988) at which people begin being treated as adults in various areas. One reason we have no rites of passage is because we have no agreement on when adulthood begins. The ambiguity of entering adulthood has fostered a fixation of some, a perpetual adolescence lasting into their twenties and thirties. Rather than assuming adult roles, they continue a culturally sanctioned irresponsibility.

Even within a single institution a teenager is treated as both child and adult in different areas. Checking into a motel a person is treated as a child at the front desk (allowed to stay free) if they are under eighteen. However, they are treated as an adult in the motel restaurant at twelve. Furthermore, they are considered a child in the bar until they are twenty-one. Is it any wonder that teenagers are confused about their identity in our culture? We have gone from the bar mitzvah to the bar as the final symbol of adulthood.

Community Identity

Throughout most of human history people have had not only a cultural identity but also a community identity. A person received an identity by simply growing up in the community. Every gospel writer refers to "Jesus of Nazareth." Even one of Jesus' own disciples, before he became a disciple, said, "Nazareth! Can anything good come from there?" (Jn 1:46 NIV). Several factors have combined to remove a sense of community identity from many people in our culture.

One factor is mobility. Rather than people remaining in one community for life or for extended periods of time, they move frequently. Between 1985 and 1986, 18 percent of the population over one year of age moved (U.S. Bureau of Census, 1987). Such movement makes it difficult for a person to develop much of a community identity. Furthermore, even people who do not move are affected because their friends move. If they do not move from their community, parts of their community move from them.

Another factor is schools. Schools used to be part of the community whether a one-room school in a village or a neighborhood school in a city. Then schools consolidated so people could pool their resources to provide a broader education.

This meant that adolescents had to be bussed from their community to a large school having hundreds or thousands of students. A by-product of this bussing is the reduction of community identity.

Yet another factor is urbanization. At the turn of the century two-thirds of all Americans lived either on farms or in small towns. Prior to World War II 52 percent of the U.S. population was still rural, and large cities still had neighborhoods. However by 1980, 75 percent of the population had moved to urban areas (U.S. Bureau of the Census, 1987). It is easy to feel like a part of the community in a village, but not in a metropolitan area.

Religious Identity

At one time belonging to a culture and a community meant that you received a religious identity too. In fact, the same word may be used to denote both a culture and a religion. A Jew is one who is a descendant of the ancient Hebrews or someone whose religion is Judaism. Of course, some countries have a state religion, and thus most in the society have a religious identity as a part of their cultural identity.

The Reformation brought a split in Christianity, the divergence of Protestants from Roman Catholics. Denominations within Protestantism held distinctly different theologies. Mainline churches became pluralistic, presenting a variety of beliefs and allowing people to pick those most satisfying to them. Even belonging to a church did not mean one received a religious identity. This is compounded by modern "Free Enterprise" religion where there is little or no loyalty to a specific congregation (Stellway, 1982).

From its beginning, the United States separated church and state. The first amendment to the Constitution said, "Congress shall make no law respecting an establishment of religion, or prohibiting the free exercise thereof." Although we prize this religious freedom, it results in less of a religious identity.

Family Identity

In the past, teenagers had family identities as well as cultural, community, and religious identities. God was not just an infinite, all-powerful Being. "I am the God of your fathers, the God of Abraham, Isaac, and Jacob" (Acts 7:32 NIV). Every Jew could tell you to which tribe he or she belonged. Genealogies like those in Matthew 1 and Luke 3 could be given by any good Jew. Today most teens cannot even give the first names of their great-great-grandparents. Several factors have resulted in the loss of family identity.

Some factors are related to the rising divorce rate. A century ago there was one divorce for every thirteen marriages. Today there is one divorce for every two marriages (*Information Please Almanac,* 1989). Closely related to that is the increasing number of remarriages. As recently as 1970 more than two-thirds of all marriages were first marriages for both the bride and the groom. Today only about one-half of all marriages are the first for both.

Other factors are related to not getting married at all. In 1970, 523,000 unmarried couples were living together. By 1986 this had increased to 2,200,000 couples (U.S. Bureau of the Census, 1987). More and more unmarried women are having children. In 1950, only 4 percent of the children born were to unmarried mothers. Today more than 20 percent are.

Identity Sought

The idea of adolescents having an identity crisis is closely related to the theories of Erik Erikson (1968). He called for the development of a more inclusive, industrial identity, but that has not occurred. Teenagers whose identities do not develop in their culture, community, church, or family try to find it in other ways. Let us now consider some of the ways they try to develop identities.

Negative identity. Erikson (1968) notes that some teens develop a negative identity by doing the opposite of what some authority says they should do. This behavior consists in rejecting the signs of identity that society offers, rather than designing a new identity, because no positive identity was offered.

Negative identity usually involves opposing the wishes of parents and school officials. Some adolescents wear certain clothes, cut their hair, listen to music, and so forth, to oppose what those in authority approve. If parents or schools have a dress code, teens want to wear something else. Brehm (1966) called this "psychological reactance." Whenever people are told that they cannot do something or have something, that is exactly what they want. Furthermore, they will take steps to get back the freedom they think they have lost.

The problem with a negative identity is that it is usually temporary; when the adolescent leaves home and school, no identity remains because it came only from parents and school officials. Furthermore, a negative identity does not work in adult life. If people keep trying the negative identity approach with their employers, they lose their jobs. Adolescents can get away with a negative identity only because our culture does not expect them to behave as adults.

Obedience. The opposite of negative identity is doing whatever an authority says to do. People trying to find their identity through obedience do whatever they are told. They want to please the authority and will do almost anything, good or bad.

Although we may not think of adolescents as obedient, the fact is that they, like the rest of us, are generally obedient to authority. Milgram (1974) did a long series of experiments during the 1960s and early 1970s. The question was how far people would go in hurting others when ordered to do so by an authority. The first experiments were done with Yale University students (adolescents), and about 60 percent of them were fully obedient, even when they thought they were causing intense pain. Remember that these experiments were conducted during the Vietnam War when college students were anything but docile.

The problem with much obedience, like that of negative identity, is that it is no identity at all. While this is a socially acceptable identity if they obey parents or school authorities, it is not socially desirable if the teen obeys a gang leader.

Conformity. Adolescents often seek an identity by conforming to other adolescents. Unfortunately, those adolescents also lack an identity, so peer pressure becomes a case of the blind leading the blind. In the past, adolescents could conform to their community or family to obtain an identity, but today they turn to their peers.

Asch (1952) found that adolescents tend to conform even to a group of total strangers. College students sat around a table judging which of three lines was equal to a fourth one. If all the people in the group gave the incorrect answer, the last one to judge felt pressured to give the same wrong answer. About one-third of the time they gave the answer the others gave, even with all of the lines immediately before them. Of course, many of the decisions adolescents have to make are much less clear than picking out a line of the same length, so they tend to conform a great deal.

Costanzo and Shaw (1966) found that conformity increases up to about twelve years of age, then begins to decrease. Other studies have generally confirmed these results. This is in agreement with the age of puberty as we saw earlier. Since adolescents are most unsure of themselves when they first become adolescents, they conform most at that point.

Conformity to a peer group is not an adequate answer to the search for identity. If the group breaks up or rejects the adolescent, he or she is again left without an adequate identity. This fact gives the group great power over each person in it. Adolescents find it difficult to act as individuals but easy to act as a part of the group.

Cults. Adolescents disappointed at not finding identity in the church become prime candidates for joining cults. Enroth (1977) said that more than anything else, young people joining cults are searching for identity and spiritual reality. In contrast to our culture, which offers uncertainty, fear of failure, discontent, isolation, and loneliness, cults offer a strong identity.

Unfortunately, cults do not offer a lasting identity either. In *Radical Departures: Desperate Detours to Growing Up,* Levine (1984) reports his study of more than 800 people in fifteen cult groups ranging in age from fourteen to thirty. He found that 90 percent of the teens who suddenly left to join a cult returned home within two years, and almost all returned ultimately. Shaving one's head and wearing a sheet may give a temporary feeling of identity, but it does not become a lasting identity for many.

What Can Youth Ministry Do?

Youth ministers cannot change the culture at large to have teens treated as adults. However, they can see that teens are treated as adults in the group itself to the degree possible. They can give teens real responsibilities and expect the teens to carry those responsibilities out. Teens can lead small groups, lead the entire group from time to time, be Bible school teachers, and do routine maintenance on church vehicles.

Youth ministers can help youth develop community identity, rather than taking an anti-establishment position. Youth groups can do community service projects to clean up or improve the community (see chapter nine). Programs should include discussion on what it means to be a Christian in the community where one lives, to relate faith to culture. The history of the community can be brought into the youth program in the form of telling what it was like to be a Christian in the early years of the community and how the church influenced the development of the community—or failed to influence it where it should have.

Community identity shades into religious identity because the church is a community within the larger community. Youth ministers should develop their own religious identity, then pass this pride in church and denomination along to their youth. This can be done in the form of historical skits and an emphasis on the Christian calendar to pass on the religious heritage. Teens can produce the church newsletter, serve on regular committees, and sing in the choir.

Religious identity can shade into family identity in the form of family suppers and featured families of the month. This is particularly difficult when teens are from broken homes, but those teens are the ones who need it the most. Mother-daughter and father-son (or father-daughter and mother-son) events can be effective in this respect. Encourage pride in the family name. Encourage youth to start or participate in family devotions at home. Have them share family traditions and funny stories of ancestors with the rest of the youth group.

Sex Forbidden

"But since there is so much immorality, each man should have his own wife, and each woman her own husband" (1 Cor 7:2 NIV). The invention of adolescence makes it illegal for people to carry out 1 Corinthians 7:2–people cannot marry before eighteen years of age without parental consent. Realizing that people are sexual beings, the apostle Paul knew that simply restricting marriage would not stop sexual activity.

Celibacy or Chastity?

Although celibacy during adolescence is required of nearly everyone in our culture, we must remember that celibacy does not necessarily equal chastity, in their original meanings. "Celibate" is from the Latin *celibatus,* which literally means "a single life." "Chaste" is from the Latin *castus,* which literally means "pure." In our culture most adolescents are celibate, (unmarried), but most are not chaste (pure).

Celibacy combined with chastity is a valid option. Two passages about celibacy in the New Testament are enlightening. First, in 1 Corinthians 7, Paul makes it clear that celibacy is as good as marriage. The chapter begins by saying that it is good not to marry (v. 1). When writing to the unmarried and the widows, he tells them that it is good to stay unmarried, as he is (v. 8). Second, after he taught some Pharisees about divorce, Jesus' disciples suggested that it might be better for a person not to marry. Jesus said that some refused to marry because of the kingdom of heaven–and that if you could accept celibacy, you should (Mt 19:10-12).

Notice that both Paul and Jesus make not marrying dependent on the decision of the individual. In fact, both made it clear that not everyone could live chastely in the unmarried state. In 1 Corinthians 7 where he spoke of not marrying, Paul also stated that since there was so much immorality, people should have their own spouses (v. 2). He said that if they could not control themselves, they should go ahead and marry because it is better to marry than to burn with passion (v. 9). Jesus also made it clear that not everyone could accept his teaching about not getting married. He said that being able to accept celibacy was a special gift, and it was to be accepted only if one had that gift (Mt 19:11-12).

Although our culture has been able to legislate adolescent celibacy, it has not produced chastity. Ideally the two concepts would coincide, but we must be realistic about the strength of the sexual drive. Living a chaste life is certainly a worthy goal, and one to be pursued. However, we are mistaken if we believe that we can force all adolescents to seek it, especially with the emphasis on sexuality by our culture. Both secular and Christian adults tell adolescents how wonderful sex is; then they tell adolescents they cannot have any.

Adolescents are clearly sexual beings. In their classic study, *Sexual Behavior in the Human Male,* Kinsey, Pomeroy, and Martin (1948) found that the age of maximum sexual activity was somewhere between sixteen and twenty years of age. The greatest number of sexual outlets occurs at about sixteen or seventeen years of age in both married and unmarried males. Not only was the total outlet greatest during adolescence, but so was the number of sources, such as intercourse, masturbation, nocturnal emissions, and homosexual contacts. The period of greatest sexual desire for women apparently occurs later in life, but nearly two-thirds of them had their first orgasm before marriage (Kinsey, Pomeroy, Martin, and Gebhard, 1953). This results from masturbation, petting, premarital sex, dreams, and homosexual contacts–and that was before the sexual revolution of the 1960s.

Solitary Sex

Since they are not allowed to marry, most adolescents try to satisfy their sexual desires by themselves. They experience sex in their sleep, in their fantasy, and masturbate.

Orgasms during sleep. Kinsey et al. (1948, 1953) found a great difference between men and women in terms of sexual orgasms during sleep. More than 80 percent of the men experienced nocturnal emissions and the highest incidence was during the late teens. Only 8 percent of the women had orgasms in their sleep by the age of twenty.

Nocturnal emissions occurred in Old Testament times and are dealt with briefly in Deuteronomy 23:10, where they are called things which "chanceth him by night" in the King James Version, and "nocturnal emissions" in more modern translations. During the nineteenth century, these were seen by some people as evil. They were called "vile personal pollutions," and were seen as sexual sin. The rationale was that you must be sinning unconsciously, even if you were not doing so consciously. Today people see them as a sign of biological maturity rather than of sin.

Sexual fantasy. Sexual fantasy is certainly nothing new, but fantasy by large numbers of single adults is a new development. When Jesus was elaborating on the commandment against adultery (Mt 5:27-28), he said that whoever looked at a woman to lust after her had committed adultery with her already in his heart. Notice that he was talking about adultery, not premarital sex. This is because many people married as soon as they became sexually mature, and most immature persons were not tempted to sexual fantasy.

Shaffer and Shoben (1956) found that 97 percent of college men and 96 percent of college women admitted having had sexual fantasies at some time. Furthermore 74 percent of the men and 73 percent of the women reported having such fantasies during the month before the survey. Why this high incidence of sexual fantasy? People fantasize about things they want but cannot have. Since adolescents cannot marry and have sex in marriage, they daydream about it.

Although the Bible does mention sexual fantasy by married adults, it does not discuss it among unmarried individuals. Contemporary Christians disagree about such fantasy. LaHaye and LaHaye (1976) point out that sexual fantasy about your own spouse is not evil. Of course, this is no help to adolescents, since they do not have spouses. The LaHayes tell singles to "force your mind" to have only pure (nonsexual?) thoughts about other people. Scanzoni (1973) maintains that some sexual fantasies can be good if they are a way of planning for the future, a way of thinking how one would act before the experience occurs. She says that if one concentrates on the beauty of sex in marriage and does not imagine intercourse with an acquaintance, fantasy is acceptable.

Masturbation. Probably no other sexual topic provides more disagreement among Christians at the present time than masturbation. A century ago it was blamed for almost every kind of physical and mental illness. Both secular society and Christians condemned it. However in this century rather than seeing it as harmful, people began advocating masturbation. For example, Haeberle (1978) says that it feels good, releases tension, stimulates fantasy, is legal, is always available, is not hazardous to health, and helps one to learn to control orgasm.

Most people masturbate during adolescence. Kinsey et al. (1948) found that by fifteen years of age 82 percent of the men had masturbated. In fact, that was the way 68 percent had their first ejaculation. Although Kinsey found masturbation much lower among women in the 1940s, reviewing all studies done over a sixty-year period, Chilman (1980) noted that among teenage women the rate of masturbation had doubled in a generation.

Although this is the most frequent sexual activity among adolescents, the Bible is completely silent on the subject. Of course, when the Bible says nothing, Christians disagree widely about a subject. At one extreme is Adams (1973) who has a section entitled "Masturbation Is Sin." He believes that the following four biblical principles can be extended to masturbation: We must not be mastered by anything; it is adultery of the heart; it is not presented as a biblical option; and it constitutes a perversion of the sexual act. At the other extreme is Shedd (1968) who has a chapter titled "Masturbation–Gift of God." He says that past generations may have just been blinded to the truth, that masturbation may simply be the "wise provision of a very wise Creator" who "gave it to us because he knew we'd need it" (p. 73). In the middle is Miles (1971) who has chapter sections entitled "When is masturbation sinful?" and "When is masturbation not sinful?"

Interpersonal Sex

While solitary sex may bring physical release, it is often not fully satisfying to a person because God designed sex to be shared. Thus adolescents are seldom content with sex by themselves.

Petting. With the advent of adolescence, marriage was forbidden and premarital intercourse was considered wrong. Since sexual desires were still present in teenagers, a new type of courtship came to be generally accepted. Social scientists do not agree on exactly when the custom of petting (physical contact intended to cause sexual arousal, but not followed by intercourse) developed as an accepted part of courtship. By the 1920s it was established as a part of the invention of adolescence.

Since petting has so many different definitions, accurate data on how frequently it occurs are sketchy. Kinsey et al (1953) found that 81 percent of the men and 84 percent of the women had engaged in some type of petting by the age of eighteen. In a series of surveys every five years between 1965 and 1980, Robinson and Jedlicka (1982) found that heavy petting among college students increased from 71 percent in 1965 to 85 percent in 1980 for men, and from 34 percent in 1965 to 73 percent in 1980 for women. Thus, the majority of adolescents engage in this type of sexual behavior.

As with other types of adolescent sexual behavior, the Bible is silent on petting. Since people could marry at sexual maturity, sexual contact before marriage was rare. Petting was not a part of courtship. When Abimalech looked out his window and saw Isaac caressing Rebekah, his first reaction was not that they were a courting couple but, "Surely she is your wife!" (Gen 26:9). Contemporary Christians disagree widely on the acceptability of petting. Smedes (1976) in "Part Two: Sex and Single People," has a chapter titled, "Responsible Petting." He says that petting can be a means of mutual discovery, communication, and sharing. Miles (1971) is much more critical of petting, maintaining that there is no such thing as unstimulating kissing and embracing and these usually lead to more sexual activity, often including intercourse.

Premarital sex. Adolescent premarital intercourse has increased dramatically in recent years. Summarizing an eight-page table of studies, Chilman (1980) notes that between 1925 and 1965 premarital intercourse remained rather stable with about 25 percent of high school senior men and 10 percent of high school senior women having premarital sex. By 1973 these percentages had risen to 39 percent for men and 35 percent for women. Of course, they are even higher today.*

Some people say that these are just surveys and people are talking about sex more, but not engaging in it more. However, several other more objective lines of evidence are available. The illegitimacy rates for teenagers tripled between 1940 and 1975. In fact, today more than 20 percent of all children born are to unwed mothers. In a randomly drawn national sample Zelnik and Kantner (1979) found that 21 percent of all unmarried women had conceived a child by age nineteen. Not all conceived children are born because for every two children born to a teenage mother, one is aborted. Another evidence for the increase in premarital sex is the increase in sexually transmitted diseases. Although figures of "specified reportable diseases" must be interpreted with caution because not all cases are reported, they are of value to indicate trends (U.S. Bureau of the Census, 1987). Gonorrhea cases nearly quadrupled between 1950 and 1975. In the late 1980s syphilis cases reached their highest levels since penicillin was discovered in the 1940s. Although it is not a specified reportable disease, an estimated 20,000,000 people have herpes.

Although it does have something to say about premarital sex, the Bible does not dwell on it as it does adultery. Since people could marry at sexual maturity, premarital sex was not much of a problem then. Passages in Exodus 22, Deuteronomy 22, and 1 Corinthians 7 make it clear that sex before marriage does not have God's approval. Although our culture generally says that sex requires only that two people care for each other, most Christians believe that sex requires the commitment of marriage.

Homosexual behavior. While premarital sexual activity is apparently practiced more often, homosexual behavior has remained constant or even decreased during the last century. Although Kinsey et al. (1948, 1953) reported an incidence of 37 percent for men and 20 percent for women having at least one homosexual experience to orgasm, most now agree that those percentages were exaggerated due to an error in his data analysis. Chilman (1980) concluded that although gays are very vocal, only about 10 percent of men and 5 percent of women have homosexual experience. If people are going to have a homosexual experience, chances are about two out of three that they will begin before

* As this went to press (January 1991) a CDC survey found that 51.5 percent of teenage girls reported having intercourse, ranging from 25.6 percent of fifteen-year-olds to 75.3 percent of nineteen-year-olds. -Ed.

they are fifteen years old. After adolescence very few are likely to initiate homosexual activity.

As with premarital sex, the Bible does not dwell at length on homosexual behavior. However both the Old and New Testaments prohibit it. Chapters 18-20 of Leviticus list homosexual behavior along with many other sexual activities as being sinful. Chapter 1 of Romans also discusses it in the same light.

What Can Youth Ministry Do?

The creation of adolescence is clearly related to, and even causative of, sexual difficulties. The only way to permanently solve these sexual difficulties would be to eliminate adolescence. However, youth ministry can help teens deal with some of these problems.

Most adolescents are not disturbed by nocturnal emissions. However, some who read Deuteronomy 23:10 may misinterpret the fact that these are called "unclean" as meaning they are sinful. Teens should realize that this means ceremonially unclean, and thus those affected were forbidden to participate in the Jewish religious exercises. One could become unclean by touching a dead body, a reptile, or a menstruating woman.

Masturbation is a controversial issue. Teens reading the King James Version may misinterpret three passages as relating to masturbation because of the particular wording used more than 300 years ago. First, in Genesis 38:9 Onan "spilled it on the ground" when having intercourse with his brother's widow. This displeased God who slew Onan. Although masturbation is sometimes called Onanism, this passage does not refer to masturbation, but to coitus interruptus, an ineffective form of birth control. Second, Micah 2:1 is sometimes interpreted as masturbation in bed in the morning. A modern translation will show that it refers to carrying out general evil planned during the night. Finally, 1 Corinthians 6:9 refers to "abusers of themselves with mankind." Again a modern translation will show that this was referring to homosexual behavior, not masturbation. Christian youth should realize that God did not deal directly with masturbation in the Bible and Christians disagree about it, so they will have to come to some decision about it themselves. Like other issues not dealt with in the Bible, we must respect the different opinions people reach on this topic.

Fantasy by unmarried adults is not dealt with in the Bible, but many Christians believe that it should be treated the same as fantasy by married people in Matthew 5:28. Adolescents should be warned about the dangers of becoming involved in pornography. It leads to misinformation about sex, incorrect expectations, and continual need for new (and often more intense) pornography. Howard, Reifler, and Liptzin (1970) found that being repeatedly exposed to the same erotic material resulted in less sexual arousal. Adolescents using pornography are setting themselves up for needing a new sexual stimulus every few weeks, not for a lifetime of marriage to one person.

Likewise, the Bible does not deal directly with petting. Some adolescents turn to petting to escape frustration, but find that it only increases frustration. Chilman (1980) notes that studies have shown that persons who pet, but do not go on to intercourse, are more restless and dissatisfied with their sex lives that those who do not pet at all, on the one hand, or those who have premarital intercourse, on the other. When "petting" takes place by married couples, it is called "foreplay" because it usually leads to intercourse. Stopping short of intercourse leaves a person frustrated, because each stage of petting calls for more until orgasm is reached. Some teens try to solve this by petting to orgasm. Although they maintain "technical virginity," they often feel guilty for going too far.

Finally, the Bible does speak to the idea of sex outside of marriage, either heterosexual or homosexual. It majors on adultery, sex outside the commitment of marriage by married people, because people could marry when mature. However, it also speaks to sex by unmarried people. The requirement for sex with someone is lifelong commitment, not that you simply "love" the other person.

Adolescents need to realize there is nothing wrong with them for having sexual desires. The problem is that our culture has prevented teens from expressing their God-given desires in a marriage relationship. However, this does not mean that they can have sexual relations outside marriage.

Work Restricted

"For even when we were with you, we gave you this rule: 'If a man will not work, he shall not eat.'" (2 Thes 3:10, NIV).

What do college students report daydreaming about more than sex? Work! Shaffer and Shoben (1956) found that while 97 percent of the men and 96 of the women reported daydreaming about sex, 100 percent of the men and 98 percent of the women reported daydreaming about vocational success. Why do they daydream about work? For the same reason they daydream about sex— because they are not allowed to pursue a full-time occupation. Another command found in scripture is now illegal to carry out.

Legal Restrictions

In 1823 Massachusetts state laws stated that welfare funds could not be used "for the support of any male person over the age of twelve, and under the age of sixty years, while of competent health to labor" (Bremner, 1970). People over twelve were expected to support themselves. What a difference between that and the laws a century later.

Child labor laws. Before the Civil War, a continual labor shortage resulted in children being employed everywhere. In fact, in 1834, 40 percent of the factory workers in New England were children. After the war people who cared about children, people who wanted to keep wages up, and people who wanted efficient labor persuaded legislators to pass child labor laws. However, rather than just making forced labor illegal, legislators made all labor illegal for children.

The ages set when the laws were passed made sense. People could begin to work at about the age of puberty. That is, children could not work and adults could. Since then the age of puberty has decreased by about three years, and the minimum legal age for work has increased. We now have a situation in which some adults (adolescents), not just children, are prevented from working full-time positions that pay enough to live on. Currently all but five states require people to be a particular age before working anything but the most menial part-time job. That age is eighteen in twenty-four states, sixteen in seventeen states, and various other ages in the remaining states (*The Book of the States 1988-1989*).

Minimum wage laws and hourly wages. For thousands of years people were paid for the quantity of work done. However, the invention of the assembly line made pay based on individual production impossible. In addition, under piece-work conditions some people worked too long and too hard, so unions successfully campaigned for hourly wages throughout industry. Inexperienced, low-producing adolescents must be paid the same rate as experienced, high-producing older workers. Employers want production, so adolescents are the last hired and first fired.

A federal minimum wage law was passed in 1938 as a part of the Fair Labor Standards Act. At that time it covered about half the workers in the private sector. Since then it has been expanded to cover more than 90 percent of all workers, including most adolescents. Although such laws were intended to protect workers, they had the effect of pricing adolescents out of the labor market. The National Commission on Youth (1980) recommended paying lower wages to youth gaining work training and experience in apprenticeship and internship programs.

Discrimination laws and work requirements. Although we hear much about age discrimination, that usually does not include adolescents. It is usually interpreted to mean discrimination against people forty to seventy years of age, not those twelve to twenty. Although statistics relating to teenage unemployment are not available before the 1940s, those available since then show that teenage unemployment runs consistently three to five *times* as large as that of other adults (*Handbook of Labor Statistics 1975–Reference Edition;* U.S. Bureau of the Census, 1987). Of course these statistics do not include adolescents who would be looking for work if they thought it was available. They also do not reveal the kinds of jobs adolescents get–often part-time temporary ones.

As if laws were not enough, employers have also set requirements for jobs, requirements which are often unnecessary. Many jobs unnecessarily require a high-school diploma. In addition, urbanization and industrialization have changed the nature of work and its requirements. In urban areas there are many adolescents, but little work for them.

School Required

Since adolescents were not allowed to work, our culture had to do something with them. Education seemed like a logical, even practical, thing.

Throughout history parents had been responsible for the education of their children. If they could not accomplish the task, they found someone to act *in loco parentis,* literally in the place of the parent. However, with the creation of adolescence, the state took responsibility for education.

Compulsory attendance. No country has attained universal education by just setting up schools and encouraging parents to send their children. The only way to get general literacy has been to enact compulsory attendance laws, and even compulsory attendance does not lead to 100 percent literacy. When such laws began to take effect in Germany, people thought that they would never be tolerated in a free society. However, the Massachusetts law of 1852 compelled everyone between eight and fourteen years of age to attend school twelve weeks a year and six of those weeks had to be consecutive (Good, 1960).

As more and more laws were passed, the general trend was toward lowering the age for starting attendance, raising the age for quitting, and increasing the length of the school year. Although parents objected, the courts consistently held that the state had ultimate authority for education. For example, the Supreme Court of Indiana upheld the constitutionality of the state's compulsory education law in 1901. Justice Dowling said, "The natural rights of a parent to the custody and control of his infant child are subordinate to the power of the State. . . The welfare of the child, and the best interests of society require that the State shall exert its sovereign authority to secure the child the opportunity to acquire an education" (Bremner, 1971; p. 1422).

Age grading. Compulsory attendance laws alone would not have created adolescence. Another factor that helped produce adolescence was age grading, the practice of placing people in a class (grade) in school, not on the basis of what they know, but on the basis of their chronological age. Exclusive age grading is a recent innovation in the United States and a part of our creation of adolescence.

Aries (1960/1962) gives a distribution of pupils in various classes in a school in seventeenth century France. In the 4th class, students ranged from eight-year-olds to twenty-one-year-olds. Nineteenth century France had a similar distribution and the range in the same class was from eleven-year-olds to sixteen-year-olds. Age-graded schools were introduced in the United States in 1844 and the transition to a graded system was accomplished in the large cities by 1860 and in all districts before 1900. Education became a twelve-year-long assembly line, and once a child starts on the line he or she finds it very difficult to move faster or slower in most schools.

High schools invented. In the early years of our country students went to grammar schools to master Latin and Greek well enough to meet the standards of their chosen college. During the eighteenth century another institution from Europe, the academy, became prominent. They were private schools, but the middle class could often afford to send their children. However, not everyone went to them so they did not create adolescence.

With ever-increasing compulsory attendance laws and age grading, the high school was the educational factor in the creation of adolescence. By 1860 there were about 300 high schools in the nation, but compared to more than 6000 academies, they were not much of a force in American higher education (Monroe, 1940). The issue of using tax money to support such schools was taken to court in several states. The Kalamazoo case in 1874 in Michigan became a legal precedent for other states when the state supreme court ruled that the high school was a proper part of the public school system.

Attendance at high school did not become the norm until adolescence was fully created in the first half of the twentieth century. In 1890 only seven out of every hundred people fourteen to seventeen years of age were enrolled in high school. By 1920 it was fifteen out of every hundred, and by 1930 it was fifty-one out of every hundred (Bremner, 1971). Today 95 percent of the people between fourteen and seventeen are enrolled in school, and below the age of sixteen 99 percent are in school (U.S. Bureau of the Census, 1987).

What Can Youth Ministry Do?

Like juvenile officers and high-school teachers, youth ministers are professionals who work with people in this newly created stage of development. Juvenile officers are employed by the legal system, teachers by the educational system, and youth ministers by the religious system. Youth ministers should work closely with these other professionals who deal with the same group.

Realizing that society does not hold teenagers responsible to support themselves, nor even be fully responsible for crimes they commit, youth ministers should emphasize responsibility. Since teenagers often cannot work, youth ministers can teach them job skills and positive attitudes toward work by requiring work in the youth program. Instead of just having them pay money for activities (money their parents supply) teenagers can learn about work and working with others if it is required in the youth program. Youth can learn about budgeting and saving money by being responsible for planning youth activities on a limited budget and actually carrying out the activity. When they want something more than the budget allows, they can work as a group by "renting" themselves out as yard workers, house cleaners, car washers, and so forth, to raise money for their activities.

Realizing that no one really likes being forced to do something, like going to school, youth ministers can help emphasize the importance of really learning, not just getting a diploma. The diploma is important for society, but learning is important for the development of the person. The youth minister can help by building up the school, not tearing it down.

Conclusion

Adolescence has been invented by our culture and handed to us. Although it has created problems of identity, sexuality, and work, these problems are not insurmountable. Youth ministers can help adolescents understand that the problems are not with teens but with their culture.

Youth ministers can also work toward reversing the trend in our society toward a longer and longer adolescence. Rather than keeping people unmarried and financially dependent, we need to work toward adult status for all people who are adults. But just as our society did not suddenly invent adolescence, so it cannot suddenly abandon it. However, we can gradually work toward its elimination.

REFERENCES

Adams, J. (1973). *The Christian counselor's manual*. Grand Rapids, Mich.: Baker.

Aries, P. (1962). *Centuries of childhood* (R. Baldick, Trans.). New York: Vintage. (Original work published, 1960.)

Asch, S. (1952). *Social psychology*. New York: Prentice Hall.

Bakan, D. (1971). Adolescence in America: From idea to social fact. *Daedalus, 100*, 979-995.

Brehm, J. W. (1966). *A theory of psychological reactance*. New York: Academic.

Bremner, R. H. (Ed.) (1970). *Children and youth in America: A documentary history. Vol. I: 1600-1865*. Cambridge, Mass.: Harvard University Press.

Bremner, R. H. (Ed.) (1971). *Children and youth in America: A documentary history. Vol II: 1866-1932*. Cambridge, Mass.: Harvard University Press.

Bullough, V. L. (1981). Age at menarche: A misunderstanding. *Science, 213*, 365-366.

Calhoun, A. W. (1917). *A social history of the American family from colonial times to the present. Vol. I: Colonial period*. Cleveland: Arthur H. Clark Company.

Calhoun, A. W. (1918). *A social history of the American family from colonial times to the present. Vol. II: From independence through the Civil War*. Cleveland: Arthur H. Clark Company.

Chilman, C. (1980). *Adolescent sexuality in a changing American society*. Bethesda, Md.: U. S. Department of Health, Education, and Welfare (Publication no. 80-1426).

Collier, R. (1965). *The general next to God*. New York: Dutton.

Costanzo, P. R., and Shaw, M. E. (1966). Conformity as a function of age level. *Child Development, 37*, 967-975.

Elkind, D. (1981). *The hurried child*. Reading, Mass.: Addison-Wesley.

Elkind, D. (1984). *All grown up and no place to go*. Reading, Mass.: Addison-Wesley.

Enroth, R. (1977). *Youth, brainwashing, and the extremist cults*. Grand Rapids, Mich.: Zondervan.

Erikson, E. H. (1968). *Identity: Youth and crisis*. New York: W. W. Norton.

Good, H. G. (1960). *A history of Western education* (2nd ed.). New York: Macmillan.

Goodsell, W. (1934). *A history of the family as a social and educational institution* (rev. ed.). New York: Macmillan.

Greenough, W. T., Black, J. E., and Wallace, C. S. (1987). Experience and brain development. *Child Development, 53*, 539-559.

Haeberle, E. J. (1978). *The sex atlas*. New York: Seabury.

Handbook of labor statistics 1975–Reference edition. (1975). Washington, D.C.: U. S. Department of Labor.

Howard, J. L., Reifler, C. B., and Liptzin, M. B. (1970). *Effects of exposure to pornography* (Technical Reports of the Commission on Pornography, Vol. 8) Washington, D.C.: U. S. Government Printing Office.

Information please almanac. (42nd ed.). (1989). Boston: Houghton Mifflin.

Kaplan, Z. (1972). Bar Mitzvah, Bat Mitzvah. *Encyclopaedia Judaica* (pp. 243-247). Jerusalem: Keter Publishing House.

Kett, J. F. (1978). Curing the disease of precocity. *American Journal of Sociology, 84,* s183-s211 (Supplement).

Kinsey, A. C., Pomeroy, W. B., and Martin, C. E. (1948). *Sexual behavior in the human male.* Philadelphia: Saunders.

Kinsey, A. C., Pomeroy, W. B., Martin, C. E., and Gebhard, P. H. (1953). *Sexual behavior in the human female.* Philadelphia: Saunders.

Kohlberg, L., and Gilligan, C. (1971). The adolescent as a philosopher: The discovery of the self in a postconventional world. *Daedalus, 100,* 1051-1086.

Kranzberg, M., and Gies, J. (1975). *By the sweat of thy brow.* New York: Putnam.

LaHaye, T., and LaHaye, B. (1976). *The act of marriage.* Grand Rapids, Mich.: Zondervan.

Levine, S. V. (1984). *Radical departures.* San Diego: Harcourt Brace Jovanovich.

Lindzey, G., Hall, C.S., and Thompson R. F. (1978). *Psychology* (2nd ed.). New York: Worth.

Miles, H. J. (1971). *Sexual understanding before marriage.* Grand Rapids, Mich.: Zondervan.

Milgram, S. (1974). *Obedience to authority.* New York: Harper & Row.

Monroe, P. (1940). *Founding of the American public school system,* Vol 1. New York: Macmillan.

Morgan, E. S. (1978). The Puritans and sex. In M. Gordon (Ed.) *The American family in social-historical perspective* (2nd ed.). New York: St. Martins.

National Commission on Youth. (1980). *The transition of youth to adulthood: A bridge too long.* Boulder, Col.: Westview.

Physician's desk reference (43rd ed.). (1989). Oradell, N.J.: Medical Economics Co.

Piaget, J. (1967). *Six psychological studies.* New York: Random House.

Piaget, J. (1972). Intellectual development from adolescence to adulthood. *Human Development, 15,* 1-12.

Queen, S. A., and Habenstein, R. W. (1974). *The family in various cultures* (4th ed.). Philadelphia: Lippincott.

Richards, L. (1984). The stages of adolescence. In J. Kesler (Ed.) *Parents and teenagers.* Wheaton, Ill.: Victor.

Robinson, I. E., and Jedlicka, I. E. (1982). Change in sexual attitudes and behavior of college students from 1965 to 1980: A research note. *Journal of Marriage and the Family, 44,* 237-240.

Rosenthal, R., and Jacobson, L. (1968). *Pygmalion in the classroom.* New York: Holt, Rinehart and Winston.

Scammon, R. E. (1930). The measurement of the body in childhood. In J. A. Harris, C. M. Jackson, D. G. Katterson, and R. E. Scammon (Eds.) *The measurement of man.* Minneapolis: University of Minnesota Press.

Scanzoni, L. (1973). *Sex is a parent affair.* Glendale, Calif.: G/L Pub.

Shaffer, L. F., and Shoben, E. J. Jr. (1956). *The psychology of adjustment* (2nd ed.). Boston: Houghton Mifflin.

Shedd, C. (1968). *The stork is dead.* Waco, Tex.: Word.

Smedes L. B. (1976). *Sex for Christians.* Grand Rapids, Mich.: Eerdmans.

Stellway, R. J. (1982). Religion. In S. A. Grunlan and M. Reimer (Eds.), *Christian perspectives in sociology.* Grand Rapids, Mich.: Zondervan.

Tanner, J. M. (1981). Menarcheal age. *Science, 214,* 604.

The book of the states 1988-1989 edition, (1988). Vol. 27. Lexington, Ky.: The Council of State Governments.

The new encyclopaedia Brittanica (15th ed.). (1986). Chicago: Encyclopaedia Brittanica, Inc.

The Random House dictionary of the English language (2nd ed. unabridged). 1987. New York: Random House.

Toufexis, A. (1985, July 8). Caught between two worlds. *Time,* pp. 84-85.

U. S. Bureau of the Census. (1987). *Statistical abstract of the United States, 1988.* (108th ed.). Washington, D.C.

Westermark, E. (1968). *A short history of marriage.* New York: Humanities. (Originally published, 1926).

Wyshak, G., and Frisch, R. E. (1982). Evidence for a secular trend in age of menarche. *New England Journal of Medicine, 306,* 1033-1035.

Zelnik, M., and Kantner, J. F. (1979). Reasons for nonuse of contraception by sexually active women aged 15-19. *Family Planning Perspectives, 11,* 289-296.

Chapter Three

Adolescent Thinking and Understanding

GARY L. SAPP

"They found him in the temple, sitting in the midst of the doctors, both hearing them, and asking them questions. And all that heard him were astonished at his understanding and answers. . . . And Jesus increased in wisdom and stature, and in favor with God and man" (Lk 2:46,47,52).

This poignant episode in the life of Jesus succinctly articulates the theme of this chapter. At twelve Jesus' powers of reasoning and understanding were highly developed. What is even more significant is that his intellectual development continued throughout his adolescence to such a degree that he not only impressed his peers and elders but pleased God as well.

This chapter examines adolescent thinking and understanding, conceptualizing them as developing phenomena that are transformed during the adolescent years. Achieving religious maturity is in part dependent upon a dynamic intellectual component that must develop throughout one's life. Other scriptural passages that reflect this developmental orientation include Paul's statement that "babes in Christ" are fed with milk because they cannot handle more substantive fare (1 Cor 3:1-2). Some individuals speak, think, and understand as children, but others mature and function as adults (1 Cor 13:11). We are instructed to not be as children, being deceived by every fanciful doctrinal claim. Instead we are to "grow up into him in all things" (Eph 4:15-16). Christ also emphasizes the importance of moving beyond a legalistic orientation toward a deeper concern for the principles underlying the law (Mt 5:17-48). The assumption is made that knowledge is hardwon: "If any man think that he knoweth any thing, he knoweth nothing yet as he ought to know" (1 Cor 8:2). And Paul's statements "For we know in part and we prophesy in part . . . but then shall I know even as also I am known (1 Cor 13:9,12), indicate a partial understanding of reality becoming more fully realized.

The chapter begins with a brief definition of thinking and then considers the development of thought processes from a Piagetian perspective. Piaget's notion of a stage of formal operations has dominated the field of adolescent development and his ideas have generated the bulk of research activity since the 1960s (Keating, 1980). The notion of formal operations is the central construct underlying development in a variety of areas of human personality. Of particular interest is the achievement of formal operations and its subsequent impact on adolescents' reasoning about social situations.

Recent literature has been critical of the Piagetian position and many cognitive researchers have shifted their attention toward applied research questions in which both the context and content of the cognitive activity is highly significant (Keating, 1990). These new approaches are important components of a contemporary cognitive psychology which has significant implications for our conception of the adolescent. Aspects of this approach will be delineated in the latter part of the chapter. Finally, the relationship of adolescent thinking to the development of personal religion will be considered.

A Definition of Thinking

Thinking is a symbolic activity culminating in understanding which requires the manipulation of symbols and the imposition of meaning (Neimark, 1987). The symbolic aspect of thinking is paramount because actions and objects are removed from their immediate physical contexts. These physical events are then transformed and represented verbally, graphically, or behaviorally. In children and adolescents, symbolization is often an inferred activity and is particularly significant as young people move from the childhood world of direct expression to the adult world of the *"double entendre."* To be interpersonally successful adolescents must become very adept at word games, nuances, and speaking euphemistically. To be accepted by peers one must be able to express hostility but not provoke retribution. In a world in which one's social status is paramount, adolescents must be acutely aware of subtle cues which are often conveyed in obscure ways.

The second aspect of thinking, the imposition of meaning, provides motivation and direction for thought processes (Neimark, 1987). Meaning is not necessarily intrinsic to a behavioral interaction but is usually ascribed to it after the fact. Paul illustrates this point when he indicates that what to the believer is precious and sacred may to the unbeliever be foolishness. Many religious persons have experienced a significant change in their understanding of and appreciation for a passage of scripture after undergoing a personal trauma. I can remember flying through a thunderstorm in a light plane that was thrashing around the sky. The words, "He that dwelleth in the secret place of the most high shall abide under the shadow of the Almighty" (Ps 91:1), suddenly became much more meaningful to me. Meaning is above all a personal construction that is imposed on events as they occur, and it is unique to the observer.

A third aspect of thinking is the increasing complexity of concepts and their rich interrelatedness. As the child matures cognitively, s/he develops increasingly complex and differentiated cognitive structures. These structures branch into infinitely diverse and specialized categories. In this context, concepts may be defined either as rules for grouping incoming information or categories that result from appropriate grouping.

When describing the process of understanding two components emerge: 1) the awareness of one's own thought processes and the "deliberate direction of them" and 2) "the application of procedures to achieve this direction and to bring order out of a constant stream of sense impressions" (Neimark, 1987). One might argue that one of the key markers of the development of adolescent thinking is the movement toward self-awareness and self-regulation of thought.

The Role of Thinking in Adolescent Development

If asked to identify the most significant transformation in adolescence, most adults would select physical changes. Changes in physique, accompanied by altered reproductive capacities, are obvious, important signs that adolescents are becoming adults. However, another important transformation is the adolescent's new way of thinking. These powerful, qualitative changes in cognitive capabilities result in an enhancement in scope and breadth of thinking, reasoning, and problem solving.

This fateful change has been characterized as "thinking in a new key" (Elkind, 1984). For not only is the advance profound, but it sets adolescents on a collision course with their previously immature understanding of reality. Also the adolescent's adjustment to the challenges posed by this change in worldview is one of the major developmental tasks that one will ever face. Elkind (1984) contends that the cognitive changes are even *more* significant and far-reaching than the physical ones. These new mental powers are the perceptual filter that bring about a transformation in the way adolescents react to their new physical appearance. The heightened sense of self-awareness and enhanced self-consciousness is not a product of the bodily changes themselves but is an adolescent response to the qualitative difference in thinking (Elkind 1984).

The central, dynamic role of thinking and perception related to problem solving has served as the underlying premise for much of the relevant research (Piaget, 1972; Elkind, 1984). While the development of new intellectual structures does not necessarily produce a different type of thinking, the new structures are a necessary precondition to advanced thinking. Understanding the changes in adolescent thinking abilities is integral to the broader understanding of adolescent functioning in the related areas of personality development, identity development, moral reasoning, and religious commitment.

Thought Processes in Childhood and Adolescence

Adolescents think in a qualitatively different way from children. Thought processes of children can be illustrated by the responses of two ten-year-old boys, one in Taiwan and one in the United States, who were presented with the well-known Heinz dilemma: "In Europe, a woman was near death from a cancer. There was one drug that the doctors thought might save her. It was a form of radium that a druggist in the same town had recently discovered. The drug was expensive to make, but the druggist was charging ten times what the drug cost him to make. The sick woman's husband, Heinz, tried to borrow the money, but he could only get together about $1,000.00, which is half of what it cost. He told the druggist that his wife was dying and asked him to sell it cheaper or let him pay later. But the druggist refused. So Heinz got desperate and broke into the man's store to steal the drug for his wife. Should the husband have done that?" (Kohlberg, 1958).

After considering the plight of the family, the children ventured their opinions about the "right" course of action. They said that the life of the mother should be saved, if possible; therefore, the drug should be stolen. The reason offered was that other family members, most particularly themselves, would be highly inconvenienced by the mother's death. The children's mode of reasoning was highly egocentric in that their thoughts were focused on their own needs. They were unable to relate to the needs of the mother in any real, deep human fashion.

Children's thinking, as illustrated by these responses to the Heinz dilemma, is oriented to self-gratification in the here and now. Children are often unable to defer satisfaction of their immediate needs to the future. In contrast, adolescents have a much better concept of the future and are fascinated by the possibilities inherent in a situation. They perceive so many ways to approach a problem that they are often unable to make up their minds. Further, life is so full of possibilities that the adolescent is often dazzled by the complexity of it all.

A second difference is adolescents' ability to test the hypotheses that they generate. Children possess a relatively limited memory capacity, being able to recall only four or five digits and even fewer discrete memory facts (Thorndike, Hagan, and Sattler, 1986), and a relatively rigid cognitive structure that limits their flexibility in achieving problem solutions. Adolescents not only generate hypotheses but can systematically test them. Problem solutions can be methodically evaluated and even improbable, or apparently impossible, solutions can be considered. Adolescents also apply the processes of inductive and deductive reasoning. Through inductive reasoning they systematically organize and criticize ideas in order to construct theories. Then by manipulating variables either singly or in combination they may test outcomes.

Adolescents also tend to think about their own thoughts and the thoughts of others (Keating, 1980). This may involve contemplation, introspection, and reflection. The willingness of adolescents to focus on the abstract and to speculate allows for the development of intellectual insight that was previously impossible. Much as young men develop muscles and then want to publicly flex them, when a new cognitive capacity is developed the adolescent revels in the joy of public display.

One outcome of the focus on "thinking about thinking" is the realization that other people may actually have different thoughts about the same situation. This "perspectivistic thinking" (Sprinthall and Collins, 1988) is facilitated by the intellectual games of give and take that occur among peers. It is closely related to one's social success, for empathy and an inordinate social sensitivity are required for effective social interaction.

An essential question that relates to the understanding of adolescent thinking concerns the dynamics of thought processes. How do children move from a concrete apprehension of reality to the intellectual wizardry and the soaring word play of the adolescent? Understanding these cognitive changes is most important, for it is the key to an appreciation of the spiritual struggle that confronts every adolescent. We may thereby come to understand why many adolescents will seriously question and often reject the religious values of their parents. Also, we may more effectively facilitate cognitive growth and thereby enhance the adolescent's readiness for religion (Goldman, 1965).

Formal Operational Thinking

The culminating stage of cognitive development, formal operational thought, begins during early adolescence, usually about eleven or twelve years of age. While the thought processes of formal operations become firmly established by the age of fifteen, some adolescents never achieve the stage, probably because of learning handicaps or a lack of relevant physical or social experiences. Formal operations, then, is a cognitive possibility but is by no means a certainty. Elkind (1967) indicates the dynamic nature of this construct when he describes formal operations as the "conquest of thought."

A major characteristic of formal operational thought is propositional thinking (Elkind, 1984). This higher mode of logic enables the adolescent to deal with possibilities, to go beyond the here and now and to extend reasoning across time and space. Adolescents are no longer restricted to short-term concrete experiences as a basis for thought. Rather, they may engage in fantasy, the hypothetical, and the abstract. This capability is illustrated by the adolescent's facility with handling contrary to fact propositions. If one says to a nine-year-old child, "Just suppose that dogs could talk. What would be the first thing they would say?" The child would look at you in disbelief and say, "But dogs can't talk." Adolescents, however, if in the mood, could reason about this anomaly as if it were logical.

The ability to use propositional logic allows adolescents to engage in hypothetical–deductive reasoning. This means that adolescents may develop hunches (hypotheses) about correct problem solutions, organize their ideas, test outcomes in some orderly fashion, and systematically reject outcomes that are ineffective. Hypothetical–deductive reasoning transcends the bounds of everyday experience and allows one to conjecture about premises which are hypotheses, not simple, concrete facts. Trautman (1984) suggests that these premises are testimony and/or pure conjecture. The former include statements which are true but momentarily unverifiable. The latter are those which are hypotheses not directly verifiable, fictitious statements, or statements contrary to fact. The term "formal" in formal operational thought refers to Piaget's conclusion that the mental operations in this stage may be performed wholly on a symbolic level. Since formal operational thought moves away from thinking about things to thinking about ideas, it may be said to transcend reality (Brainerd, 1978). Concrete referents from the external environment are unnecessary as "intelligence seems to have severed its ties with the real world" (Trautman, 1984).

The capacity to engage in scientific reasoning is a major aspect of formal operations. Brainerd (1978) suggests that as scientists attempt to answer questions they formulate "what if" questions. What would happen if one or more factors were changed in a situation and the others were held constant? An experiment is then conducted in which the factors (variables) are manipulated and outcomes are measured. The next step is to examine the results to determine if there is a significant relationship between the factors manipulated and the measured outcomes. If a functional relationship is determined and if the relationship is consistent with other supporting data, scientists may conclude that a general relationship (law) has been confirmed. An additional step is the collecting and processing of the results of many studies within a coherent framework to produce a theory. Piaget finds this theory-building process to be an appropriate model for adolescent intelligence.

A related characteristic of formal operational thought is the adolescent's ability to deal with abstractions in a reflective manner. For rather than reasoning directly from a set of concrete facts, they can understand and manipulate relationships between abstractions directly. They can be guided by the form of an argument and ignore its content.

Brainerd (1978) indicates that formal operations is "thought thinking about itself." This capability is better illuminated if one considers Piaget's distinction between the mental operations of concrete operational thought (first order) and those of formal thought (second order). Second order mental operations are capable of reflecting on themselves. Adolescents can arrive at generalizations and extrapolate rules that are not directly observable in the everyday world. Those who have achieved formal thought devise possible rules prior to the observation of events that may confirm or deny the rules. This process of formulating rules in advance is a unique characteristic of formal thought (Trautman, 1984).

Piaget suggests that adolescents' awareness of the possible, as contrasted with the real and literal, predisposes them to critically question their current understanding of religion. Also their propensity for theory building influences them to formulate and test theories about God, his origin, his role in creation, and his relevance to the contemporary world. This theory testing and the development of adolescents' personal, distinct faith and belief systems requires adult tolerance and support. For it is the questioning of a "borrowed faith" and the resulting doubt and ambiguity that paves the way toward a more personal and mature faith of one's own (Ratcliff, 1990). An unwillingness to accept adolescent questioning and religious exploration may produce a premature acceptance of a childhood faith. Maintaining a faith based upon prescientific conceptual views poses an extremely difficult challenge for the adolescent.

Adolescent Language

The implications of formal operational thinking for the adolescent's social world are extensive and profound. One of the most obvious social manifestations is the adolescent's advanced use of and understanding of language. Adolescents become very sophisticated in their ability to understand abstract words and concepts (Fischer and Lazerson, 1984). Terms like justice, truth, the brotherhood of man and the fatherhood of God are taken seriously because more adolescents become fully aware of connotations. For the first time they realize that the statements "man looks on the outward appearance but God looks on the heart" or "God is no respecter of persons" have direct implications for social conduct.

Other aspects of language which transform the quality of adolescent social interaction are the understanding of metaphor, simile, irony, and sarcasm (Elkind, 1980). One's faith may be compared to a mustard seed, a man's spiritual condition is illustrated by his feeding hogs. A son's personal arrogance and antipathy for his father is seen in his fancy dress and exaggerated personal appearance (Absalom), and one's faith may be compared to a piece of glass and may be easily shattered (Santrock, 1987).

Adolescents seem to especially enjoy satire (Fischer and Lazerson, 1984). The common practice of the class legacy in the high-school annual or caricatures in high-school newspapers seems to be a universal high-school phenomena. High-school students often make up satirical labels for teachers or peers, e.g., "stork," "blimp," "horse," "cabbage head." The labels are often based on some obvious (or not so obvious) physical characteristic or mannerism. Elkind (1984) suggests that word play is enjoyable to adolescents because it allows them to practice their new abilities and to express their reservations about the adult world. By using word play they may articulate their own beliefs, values, and preferences in a relatively safe fashion. They can be critical of adults yet can explore aspects of adults' roles that may be frightening or forbidding to them.

Formal Operational Religious Thinking

The impact of Piaget's writings has been so widespread that most studies in the development of religious thinking have been based on his approach (see chapter five). The primary advocate for applying Piagetian notions to the area of religion is Goldman (1964,1965). He used Piaget's clinical interview and the latter three stages of cognitive development (preoperational, concrete operational, and formal operational) as a conceptual framework to analyze levels of religious thinking of British children. Responding to three Bible stories and three religious pictures, the children, ages six to seventeen, fell in stages of religious thinking that closely paralleled Piaget's cognitive stages (Hoge and Petrillo, 1978).

After analyzing adolescent responses Goldman discerned that the major components of formal operational thinking were easily identified in adolescents' religious thinking. In point of fact, most adolescent responses to the Burning Bush story incorporated a statement that Moses was hesitant to look at God because he realized that he (as did all others) shared a sense of sin and unworthiness. Also, hypothesis testing may be seen in a statement given in response to why the ground was holy: "Can God have a greater degree of presence? I'm not sure. Wasn't it supposed to be the Lord's mountain? Wasn't it a volcano and what they couldn't understand they called holy, something dangerous to be left alone?" (Goldman, 1964, p. 60). Another similar hypothesis was that God would hallow the ground like a magnetic field.

The burning bush was perceived primarily as an internal phenomenon. "Instead of God appearing as a person he came in the bush. It seemed to be his eyes, but it wasn't really . . . he could have imagined it in his mind" (quoted in Goldman, 1964, p. 61). Hypotheses also may be developed from a naturalistic perspective as adolescents attempt to rationalize empirical accounts with biblical offerings. Some adolescents suggested that Moses was really hallucinating while some generated elaborate theories based on supernatural causes, "It was a continuous replacement of matter" (p.61).

The Red Sea story provoked both natural and supernatural explanations. One example of a natural explanation was, "It's been proved that at a special time the sea does part. It gets very shallow." (Question) "How do you mean?" "At a special time of the year, only once a year." (Question) "Did God do it?" "No, they just got there at the right time, God had nothing to do with the sea." The supernatural explanation related to God's simply making a path that rose up out of the water because "he can create things as he wants" (p.61). A fusion of the two explanations was evidenced by a wind theory developed by one adolescent. "It was God's force. . . . He'd just move it, remove the forces keeping the water there, such as gravity." The most sophisticated view was, "All things are possible with God. It quite literally happened. It's a comparatively simple thing for God to do" (p.61).

Propositional logic is manifested in the story of the temptation of Jesus. "He would not turn stone into bread because that would be using the power for his own good. If he didn't use it for some better purpose, he'd no right to go out and preach" (p. 62). Understanding that the story is a parable is reflected in the answer, "Jesus lives by the Word of God. . . . You have faith in him and he will provide all your needs." Another answer indicating the abstract nature of the encounter was, "He had gone to the desert to sort his own thoughts out and God gave him this test. It was his own conscience, to see if he would give in or go on" (p. 62).

Goldman also found a great deal of variability in levels and types of religious thinking at a given chronological age. He agreed with earlier research (Harms, 1944) that religious thinking lags behind development in other areas. Goldman suggested that the discrepancy between levels of religious thinking and thinking in other areas would lead to a rejection of religion as being childish and simple-minded. Further, he hypothesized that the greater the gap between the capacity for formal operations and level of religious thinking, the more adolescents would reject religious teachings (Hoge and Petrillo, 1978).

To test the hypothesis, Hoge and Petrillo (1978) conducted a study with adolescents from three denominations to compare measures of religious thinking and rejection of religious training. They found, contrary to Goldman's assumptions, that smaller gaps between religious thinking and overall cognitive capacity are usually associated with more rejection of religious doctrine and teaching of the church. The researchers also indicated that while the impact of overall cognitive capacity upon religious thinking was weak, the impact of religious education was strong.

The authors raise a dilemma pointing out that one of the goals of religious instruction in the American church is to raise the level of abstract religious thinking. Religious educators desire that our youth can apprehend God's handiwork in a variety of spheres: socially, emotionally, and intellectually. As one clergyman noted, "When I laid my burden down by the riverside, I didn't leave my brains there also." However this research suggests that the more one promotes cognitive growth, the more likely it is that the adolescent will become critical, rejecting, and negative toward church doctrine (Hoge and Petrillo, 1978).

Adolescent Egocentrism

The achievement of formal operations enables adolescents to not only conceptualize their thoughts but also to conceptualize the thoughts of others. This ability to more easily take the perspective of another, coupled with their preoccupation with self, results in a unique type of self-consciousness (Elkind, 1984). Piaget (1976) calls it a second egocentrism (the first taking place in early childhood). However, the overwhelming preoccupation with self becomes obsessive such that adolescents conclude that they are the center of attention to all others.

Since the adolescent can now view his own behavior from the perspective of others, he becomes the actor playing to what Elkind (1984) calls the "imaginary audience." All behaviors are now evaluated in terms of how the adolescent is faring in the judgment of the imagined audience. When one looks in the mirror first thing in the morning, judgments are rendered through the eyes of others. Boys are themselves imagining how they will look to the girls; whereas the girls are thinking about how attractive they will be to the boys and how envious other girls will be. However, when the young people meet they are more concerned with being seen than they are with observing others. As Elkind (1984) indicates, they are simultaneously actors to themselves and audiences to others. Given this perspective, confrontation with adults takes on a particular significance because the interaction may be a serious test of tenacity and willpower. The issue is no longer who is right or wrong, as the question for the adolescent is, "Am I winning?" "How am I being judged by my 'audience'?" This intellectual perspective heightens adolescents' sensitivity to public exposure. Thus it is important for adults to minimize public criticism and avoid ridicule when engaged in these tests of will.

The significant increase in self-preoccupation may have a profound effect on adolescents' spiritual lives (Strommen, 1988). They may experience powerful, overwhelming feelings of shame, guilt, and worthlessness and see themselves as "chief among sinners." Or there may be increases in destructive, rebellious, or criminal behavior. These experiences may provide an opportunity for spiritual growth and an enhanced religious understanding. It is illuminating to realize that both adolescent suicide and religious conversion experiences are highest around fifteen years of age (Goldman, 1964; Strommen, 1988).

One common theme during adolescence is a preoccupation with one's own death and the anticipation of others to it (Sprinthall and Collins, 1988). Elkind (1980) cites the scene from *Tom Sawyer* when Tom, having run away with Injun Joe and Huck, sneaks back home after he is presumed drowned. But this memory was too much for the old lady, and she broke entirely down. Tom was sniffling, now, himself–and more in pity of himself than anybody else. He could hear Mary crying and putting in a kindly word for him from time to time. He began to have a nobler opinion of himself than ever before. Still, he was sufficiently touched by his aunt's grief that he longed to rush out from under the bed and overwhelm her with joy. The theatrical gorgeousness of the thing appealed strongly to his nature too but he resisted and lay still (Twain, 1946).

Complementing the imaginary audience is a mental construction regarding the deep-seated belief in one's uniqueness. Elkind (1980) suggests that while adolescents may fail to differentiate personal concerns from concerns of others, they often overdifferentiate their feelings. They assume not only that they are important to many people but that their personal feelings are original and unique to them. Only they can suffer such agony or know unmitigated joy. Or in the sentiment of Tchaikovsky's song, "None but the lonely heart can know my sorrow." This assumption of specialness is labeled by Elkind as the "personal fable."

The belief in personal uniqueness may distort reality such that adolescents become convinced that they will never die. This belief may account for the propensity of adolescent males to attempt to set land speed records on public highways. Another example is the apparent mindless quality of adolescent thinking when they indiscriminately sample drugs at a party without knowing what chemicals the drugs contain. Or as a sixteen-year-old indicated, she needed *no* contraceptive because she would *never* get pregnant.

Evidence of the personal fable is also evident in the personal writings of adolescents (Elkind, 1984). They may keep a diary with the belief that their lives are of such significance that the world is waiting breathlessly for its publication. Another kind of evidence is that for the first time in their lives adolescents will begin to confide in a personal God. Adolescents value privacy highly and are often afraid that their personal secrets may become known. This desire for privacy, coupled with the belief in a personal uniqueness, can facilitate the opening of channels of spiritual communication. Adolescents may come to regard their relationship with God as an I-Thou relationship with a personal God as a trusted confidant. God may be turned to for loving guidance and support, not just for personal gifts or extricating one from potentially embarrassing situations (Long, Elkind, and Spilka, 1967). Elkind (1984) suggests that the personal fable persists throughout our lives, for if we faced the dangers of contemporary society without this shield of invulnerability we would be extremely threatened.

Adolescents may also internalize and generalize the assumption of personal uniqueness to such a degree that they more deeply understand the significance of each person in God's sight. They come to realize that God really does love all the children of the world. Everyone is precious in God's sight, and every believer is to be the salt of the earth, the bearer of the good news. The egocentric assumptions of adolescence, then, are not to be scornfully rejected, for they may serve as an underlying motivation for movement toward a more mature, productive faith.

Social Reasoning

The increasing complexity and abstractness of thought allows adolescents to grasp more effectively the nuances and complexities of social situations and relationships (Sprinthall and Collins, 1988). This developing cognitive capability, coupled with the qualitative change in adolescent egocentrism, and the emergence of the peer group as a powerful, motivating frame of reference produces a convoluted and complicated social mix. Compared to the way they functioned as children, adolescents no longer make decisions in relatively clearcut ways. Decision making now becomes complicated and stressful as any choice precludes the possibility of engaging in other desirable activities. For example, attending a church service may be perceived simultaneously as a choice to see one's girl friend, a place to be observed by one's peers, a way to get out of the house, a way to please parents, or a way to enhance one's spirituality.

A crucial factor in adolescents' decision-making process is their awareness of the discrepancies between the actual and the possible. The perceiving of reality as only one of a range of possibilities produces what Elkind (1984) describes as a strong degree of idealism and criticalness. Adolescents experiencing the "grass is greener" phenomenon may become intolerant, impatient, hypercritical, and angry about situations ranging from the nature of the family structure to the use of the family car (Elkind, 1976). Indeed, since most individuals have a heavy psychological investment in their families, the family becomes the first arena for the manifestation of adolescent critism. Some adolescents in an attempt to manipulate their perception of the family will go so far as to engage in a "foundling fantasy." The fantasy is that they have been adopted and that their real parents are wealthy or famous. So they really do not belong with their present family but perceive themselves as superior.

Adolescent idealism can also have profound effects on one's perception and acceptance of organized religion. The adolescent may become hypercritical of religious practices, scornful of the faithful, and rejecting of practices deemed to be mere charades. One young lady stopped attending a church that had relatively uninhibited worship services and went to one that was more restrained because she felt the former was undignified and unbecoming to her. A young man changed churches because he was embarrassed to take his girlfriend to his old church which he felt was shabby and decrepit. A third adolescent experienced a wholesale rejection of a denomination because he viewed its position on social issues as hypocritical.

Adolescent Self-Perceptions

Adolescents not only develop strong tendencies toward idealism and criticalness, they also develop rich, abstract, and complex conceptions of what they and others are like (Sprinthall and Collins, 1988). While children focus on overt, observable, more singular behavioral characteristics, adolescents attribute behavior to traits, predispositions, and motives. The background factors are then used to summarize, explain, and interpret observable behaviors. Consider the difference between the self-perceptions of the following individuals as reported by Santrock (1987):

Nine-year-old boy: "My name is Bruce C. I have brown eyes. I have brown hair. I have brown eyebrows. I am nine years old. I love! sports. I have seven people in my family. I have great! eye site. I have lots! of friends. I live on 1923 Pinecrest Drive. I'm going on ten in September. I'm a boy. I have an uncle who is almost seven feet tall. My school is Pinecrest. My teacher is Mrs. V. I play hockey! I'm the smartest boy in the class. I love food! I love fresh air. I love school."

Seventeen-year-old girl: "I am a human being. I am a girl. I am an individual. I don't know who I am. I am Pisces. I am a moody person. I am an indecisive person. I am an ambitious person. I am a big curious person. I am not an individual. I am lonely. I am an American (God help me). I am a Democrat. I am a liberal person. I am a radical. I am conservative. I am a pseudoliberal. I am not a classified person (e.g., I don't want to be) (Montemayor and Eisen, 1977; pp. 317-18).

Whereas the child's self-perception is rather concrete and specific, the adolescent's view of self demonstrates an increase in interpersonal disruptions, mood swings, and belief statements (Santrock, 1987). This expanding view of self and one's motives has a significant effect on adolescent's religious development, for it allows them to better comprehend the holiness of God and his relationship with persons. God may now be conceptualized as a beneficient being whose goodness is manifest in the blessings of nature, the goods of the material world, and through the caring of other people. Conversely, while God loves all humanity, divine justice must be meted out because God is also just. Punishment is related to one's guilt and is best understood when viewed in relation to the whole picture of who God is (Goldman, 1964). Further, the actions of God toward people are not whimsical because the adolescent's capacity for empathy allows him to understand the "mind" of God. Abraham's apparent bargaining with God regarding the lives of the people of Sodom and Gomorrah makes sense when the adolescent realizes that God's will is that none should perish.

Adolescent descriptions of both themselves and others are more reality-oriented and objective than judgments of children. While younger children often judge others based on shared activities, adolescents can assume the posture of a detached observer. Descriptions of self and others will contain more general and psychological characteristics and will be more evaluative than children's descriptions. Finally, adolescent descriptions tend to be more reflective about the self and the motives that determine one's behavior.

Another significant aspect of adolescent development relates to the changes in thinking and reasoning about their personal and social world. It is not until adolescence that formal theories about the self are formulated (Okun and Sasfy, 1977). Since early adolescents hold tenuous conceptions of their selves, these conceptions are easily disconfirmed. Thus they may engage in an ongoing search for feedback that will corroborate positive, fulfilling views of self. The development of physical characteristics such as broad shoulders, a deep voice, or facial hair are markers for boys that they are becoming men. As Barry White, a well-known singer, with a distinctive bass voice recently remarked, "When I was fourteen I got up one morning and what came out of my mouth scared both me and my mother to death."

Adolescent views of self are dynamic as Elkind (1971) indicates: "During adolescence the young person develops a true sense of self. While children are aware of themselves they are not able to put themselves in other people's shoes and to look at themselves from that perspective. Adolescents can do this and do engage in such self-watching to a considerable extent. Indeed, the characteristic self-consciousness of the adolescent period results from the fact that the young person is now very much concerned with how others react to them. This is a concern that is largely absent in childhood."

The Self, Identity, and Faith

Erik Erikson's work has profound implications for adolescent views of self. His conception of identity resolution and its implications for the understanding of adolescent personality are well known. Erikson has delineated eight developmental stages that cover the life cycle. Each of the stages focuses upon a crucial emotional and social crisis that stems from both biological and cultural factors. Resolution of these crises allows the individual to move productively into the next higher stage. For adolescents the crucial stage is identity versus role diffusion. Erikson (1968, p.87) describes identity as follows: "The wholeness to be achieved at this stage I have called a sense of inner identity. The young person, in order to experience wholeness, must feel a progressive continuity between that which he has come to be during the long years of childhood and that which he promises to become in the anticipated future; between that which he conceives himself to be and that which he perceives others to see in him and to expect of him. . . . Identity is a unique product, which now meets a crisis to be solved only in new identifications with age mates and with leader figures outside of the family."

To achieve a coherent identity the adolescent must face critical developmental issues such as choosing an occupation, developing a meaningful personal ideology, engaging in appropriate sex role behavior, and choosing a sexual orientation (Waterman, 1982). Dealing with these critical issues is facilitated by a period of role experimentation and open questioning. After the achievement of personal identity the older adolescent develops an enhanced, more focused self-concept. The more mature self-concept sets the stage for the assumption of personal responsibility to carry out commitments formulated during this time period (Newman and Newman, 1988). However, failure to resolve the identity crisis may result in a sense of confusion and uncertainty (role diffusion) and a disturbance in self-concept followed by lowered self-esteem.

The achievement of identity is closely tied to the notion of "moratorium, experimentation, personal choice, and the finding of one's self." Many writers (Erikson, 1968; Elkind, 1974) contend that articulating a strong sense of identity requires some minimum amount of time to carefully sort out one's beliefs. This suggests that dynamic periods in one's life must be followed by a time for reflection—a cessation of the struggle. Certainly the role of contemplation in religious development needs to be reevaluated.

The theme of identity resolution in adolescence is closely related to the study of self-concept. Possessing a poor self-concept and the concomitant low self-esteem is one of the major contemporary problems of adolescents. In a cross denominational study of 7,000 adolescents, low self-esteem was identified as a problem area by more than 20 percent of the respondents (Strommen, 1988). Poor self-esteem was manifested in a variety of ways: lack of self-confidence, poor academic achievement, impaired interpersonal relationships, hypercritical attitudes toward self, and excessive distress over personal faults (Strommen, 1988). Low self-esteem is particularly damaging to adolescents since it may distort the development of their relationship to God. It may also be generalized to anxiety about one's faith which may produce distancing and alienation from God. Anxiety may be experienced in many areas, whether it be spiritual lonesomeness, the inability to live congruently with one's religious convictions, or excessive concerns about eternal life. Further, the sense of alienation may be so profound that these self-hating youth cannot believe in a personal, caring God (Strommen, 1988).

Moore (1988) discusses strategies that might enhance adolescent self-esteem and thereby promote spiritual development. He refers to Fowler's (Fowler and Keen, 1978) stages of faith, particularly the synthetical-conventional stage that encompasses ages twelve to eighteen. At this stage adolescents are concerned with interpersonal relationships, and God can be viewed as a trustworthy, lifelong friend who can always be counted upon. The significance of Fowler's work in this context is that it emphasizes the centrality of self-esteem in establishing interpersonal relationships in the world. Thus it provides a starting point in dealing with adolescent needs for enhanced self-esteem. Moore's approach emphasizes Jesus as a friend and stresses his personal interest in each person. Moore suggests that passages of scripture such as John 15: 11-17 in which Christ enunciates the significance and power of friendship, "Greater love hath no man than this that a man lay down his life for a friend," can be extremely meaningful in helping adolescents deal with low levels of self-esteem.

Self-Understanding and Moral Reasoning

A developmental theory of the self has been delineated by Robert Selman (1980). Self-understanding and perspective taking are conceptualized as gradually emerging phenomena that move through a series of five stages. The stages commence with the three-year-old preoperational child and continue through the mutual perspective taking of the adolescent. Selman (1980) applies perspective taking to four dimensions of social development: Concepts of individuals, concepts of friendship, concepts of peers, and concepts of parent-child relationships. The following table is taken from Santrock (1987).

Selman's Levels of Interpersonal Understanding

Stage 0–Egocentric Viewpoint
(Age Range 3-6)

Child has a sense of differentiation of self and other but fails to distinguish between the social perspective (thoughts, feelings) of other and self. Child can label other's overt feelings but does not see the cause and effect relation of reasons to social actions.

Stage 1–Social-Information Role-Taking
(Age Range 6-8)
Child is aware that other has a social perspective based on other's own reasoning, which may or may not be similar to child's. However, child tends to focus on one perspective rather than coordinating viewpoints.

Stage 2–Self-Reflective Role-Taking
(Age Range 8-10)
Child is conscious that each individual is aware of the other's perspective and that this awareness influences self and other's view of each other. Putting self in other's place is a way of judging his intentions, purposes, and actions. Child can form a coordinated chain of perspectives but cannot yet abstract from this process to the level of simultaneous mutuality.

Stage 3–Mutual Role-Taking
(Age Range 10-12)
Child realizes that both self and other can view each other mutually and simultaneously as subjects. Child can step outside the two-person dyad and view the interaction from a third-person perspective.

Stage 4–Social and Conventional System Role-Taking
(Age Range 12-15+)
Person realizes mutual perspective-taking does not always lead to complete understanding. Social conventions are seen as necessary because they are understood by all members of the group (the generalized other), regardless of their position, role, or experience.

Following Kohlberg (1985), Selman outlines levels of perspective-taking beginning with relatively simple egocentric judgments and culminating in an understanding of the differing perspectives that unite individuals in a social system. Similar to other developmental areas, e.g., moral reasoning, adolescents are more likely to describe other individuals based upon internal, psychological characteristics. When judging the motives of another they are more likely to integrate both personal and situational factors (Keating, 1990). Similarly, when making moral judgments, adolescents, most of whom have moved into the conventional (social conformity) stage, recognize the relative significance of both individual and social factors in fulfilling moral obligations. Shifts from the conventional level to the postconventional level require an appreciation of the rights and responsibilities of citizenry (the social contract) and an adoption of a frame-work of universal principled ethics.

The achievement of the advanced levels of perspective taking and higher order moral reasoning does not come easily. As Keating (1990) states: "Their greatest difficulty occurs in trying to achieve an integrated understanding of this personal and social experience. Indeed, such coordination and integration seems to elude a substantial minority of individuals even into adulthood. This may be akin to the phenomenon of unsystematic or nonprincipled knowledge or "knowledge in pieces" found in adolescents' conceptions of the physical world (pp. 21, 22).

Challenges to Piaget's Theory of Intellectual Development

Piaget's emphasis on the central role of thinking and problem solving is seen by some critics as extreme (Cohen, 1983). The reality is that the near euphoria with which Piaget's theory was initially received has degenerated into a chorus of criticism (Sternberg, 1983). One major criticism rejects the primacy of formal operational reasoning as a core notion in the theory. For if Piaget's contentions are accepted, formal operations is the basic intellectual structure underlying the development of all other aspects of personality.

Wagner (1987) suggests that the attainment of formal operations logically appears to be a necessary precondition for the resolution of the identity crisis. This is true because resolving the identity crisis requires the adolescent to use cognitive abilities usually taken as evidence of formal operational thinking. These include the ability to select from "all possible and imaginable relations" and "make a series of ever-narrowing selections of personal, occupational, sexual, and ideological commitments" (Wagner, 1987; p. 245). In order to determine the relationship between formal operations and identity development, Wagner compared children and adolescents on formal operations tasks: combinatorial reasoning, a balance task, and degree of ego identity as measured by an incomplete sentence test, and a semistructured interview (Marcia, 1966).

The results did not indicate that formal operational thinking is a necessary con-dition for identity formation. There was, however, a complementary relationship between combinatorial ability and degree of identity as assessed in the inter-view. Wagner suggests that these positive findings have more to do with the requirements of the task, and thus they do not support a Piagetian notion of structural unity (a comprehensive stage of formal operations). These outcomes suggest that real-life problems are solved by a type of reasoning which is some-what different from formal logic.

Another important notion of Piaget's is the idea of stages as comprehensive structured units of thought. To make this claim one must assert that adolescents possess a cognitive structure which is universally shared. Further, they should pos-sess a logical system by which common tasks may be solved. If stages are meaningful explanatory constructs, there should be clear links between stages so that understanding foundational concepts predicts understanding of higher order concepts. Also, there should be some similarities in quality of thinking across tasks (Santrock, 1987). For example, if a child develops the capacity to conserve, s/he should concurrently develop the capacity to seriate and cross classify. The evidence suggests, however, that lack of predictibility and consistency is the rule (Fischer, 1980).

There also is the question of how universal structures relate to differing cultures and environments. Piagetians seem to ignore differences in levels of development between rich and poor and developed versus undeveloped societies. Cohen (1983) quotes Piaget writing in *Piaget and His School* (1976) on this point: "One finds among the children of a town individuals of a whole variety of social, family, and scholastic milieus, some of whom will show considerable advances or lags in development. This does not contradict the orderly succession of stages which remain constant. It shows that other variables are added to the mechanism of epigenesis. Despite differences due to culture or environment, the large Piagetian stages of growth follow each other like waves: *nothing* can modify a scenario so well-determined, though poverty and ignorance can retard them."

This statement implies that the sequence and characteristics of mental structure are unaltered no matter what the environmental conditions. Related research (Barrett, Radkey-Yarrow, and Cline, 1982), although not speaking directly to the question, indicates that inadequate early nutrition may have powerful detrimental effects on thinking. While most Piagetians have not paid a great deal of attention to a psychometric analysis of intelligence, there is substantial evidence that poor, disadvantaged children have lower IQs and fare more poorly in schools than do the advantaged. Further, IQ differences between racial and ethnic groups in the United States appear as early as age four (Lesser, 1965). What is normal intelligence in one country (Japan) may be quite different in other countries.

Another issue (Cohen, 1983) concerns the role of formal operations in the daily lives of adolescents. How often does informal human problem solving incorporate these highly sophisticated, orderly, rational procedures enunciated by Piaget? The answer appears to be very infrequently. (Czikszentmihalyi and Larson, 1984) reports that adolescents indicated that only 11 percent of their daily thoughts deal with logical thinking or problem solving.

Even in special situations such as the creativity of internationally renowned scientists there appears to be no reason to believe that they necessarily achieve their insights in any formal way. The classic example is the discovery of the double helix in DNA research from a dream of two intertwined snakes. Cohen (1983) criticizes Piaget for believing that the highest level of thinking consisted of an orderly sifting through a set of logical possibilities, even though much of Piaget's later work contained examples drawn from the history of science.

Cohen (1983) also identifies what he considers to be a paradox in Piaget's writing. It is now acknowledged that Piaget rather severely underestimated the intellectual capabilities of the preconceptual child in areas such as causal reasoning (Schultz and Kestenbaum, 1985), conservation (Hall, Lamb, and Perlmutter, 1986), and mental processes (Wellman, 1985). However, after the child achieves concrete operational thinking, Piaget perceives a shift to powers of rational thinking. Kohlberg (1974) echoes the point in his article, "The child as a moral philosopher." As Cohen (1983) euphemistically states, "By the age of fifteen most adolescents are dab hands at scientific methods, wizards of the syllogism, and all set to dazzle in the laboratory of life—a truly magical transformation" (p. 86).

The significant point is that Piaget considers these intellectual developments a matter of course and not particularly unusual. Further, the kind of thinking that characterizes a given stage, e.g., formal operations, characterizes the adolescent's total personality structure. This is a rather intense preoccupation with rationality or, as Cohen (1983) states, "a kind of delirium and delusion of logic."

In addition to the conceptual problems with Piaget's views, there are four theoretical and methodological challenges drawn from Brown and Desforges (1979) and Siegel and Brainerd (1978), enunciated by Sternberg and Powell (1983). The first challenge, replicability, relates to researchers' attempts to replicate Piaget's results on the conservation tasks. A major problem is the variability in outcome which is influenced by the lack of standardization in Piaget's clinical method. However, the arguments of Piaget's critics are directed more toward the validity of Piaget's methodology and the interpretation of his observations than to replicability per se (Brown and Desforges, 1979).

Determining successful task completion is another problem. This issue relates to the difficulty of identifying the ages at which Piagetian constructs appear. The challenges to the theory are twofold: What constitutes successful performance on a selected task, and how does one ensure that tasks are age—and culture—appropriate? Successful performance on conservation may be evidenced by an appropriate judgment; or the subject might also be expected to justify his responses, often in the face of conflicting evidence (Kaye, Hall, and Baron, 1979).

Cross-cultural attempts at task validation find that non-Western children often fail a conservation task if it is presented in a traditional form. Familiarity with a task (and with the language of the task) does affect the outcome. Identifying age-appropriate tasks has proven to be difficult because of the extensive reliance on language in Piagetian tasks. When more appropriate nonverbal tasks are generated they produce evidence for Piagetian constructs at earlier ages than predicted by Piaget's research (Braine, 1964).

A third set of issues relates to the specificity of task measurement. For example, does a Piagetian task measure conservation of area and nothing else?

Speaking to this point Riley and Trabasso (1974) analyzed Piagetian tasks and suggested that little attention had been devoted to analyzing the information-processing demands of the tasks. They trained preoperational children to solve a transitive inference task involving a series of sticks of different lengths. The outcome contradicted Piaget's theory, but upon closer examination they found that the children were employing a successful strategy different from that which was predicted. This finding suggests that a more precise analysis of task information-processing requirements is necessary if the validity question is to be answered.

A second point concerns whether the appearance of a given cognitive operation indicates that the child is necessarily in a particular stage of development, possessing the full complement of cognitive capabilities described by Piaget.

Support for stages as characterized by underlying cognitive structures requires a consistency in performance across tasks. However, while cognitive structures are conceptualized apart from content, the content of a task produces significant variability in individual performance (Martorano, 1977). Considering this evidence, Sternberg and Powell (1983) suggest that the challenges to Piaget's stage theory are so telling that it might be better if this part of the theory were abandoned. Further, other alternatives fit Piaget's data quite well such that the theory is losing credibility.

Sternberg and Powell (1983) also contend that Piaget's theory is not particularly useful because it labels children generally without telling much about how they function in daily life. They suggest that a more constructive approach would be to look first at the child's ordinary and usual performance—including the cognitive processes and strategies that the child uses—and at the nature of the interaction between external and internal determinants of performance.

The Development of a Personal Religion

Following Piaget (1923), Elkind (1979) suggests that adolescents' enhanced cognitive capabilities set the stage for a profound change in their personal religious development. These capabilities are manifested in the adolescents' capacities to generate theories, to grasp abstract relationships, and to comprehend the underlying reasons for them. This desire to understand principles and the need to engage in theory construction is characterized by Elkind (1979) "as the search for comprehension."

Given denominational differences in theology, the clash of empirical science versus revealed truth, and the excruciating social pressures exerted upon contemporary youth, it is no wonder that their attempts to comprehend reality often end in failure and despair. Religion provides a particularly appropriate solution to this dilemma since it contains a body of beliefs, legend, and history which provides the adolescent with a vehicle for understanding God (Elkind, 1979).

A crucial factor in this search for comprehension is the degree of approximation between the personal religion of the adolescent and the requirements of the institutional religion. A lack of agreement between the two will lead to doubts and rejection of institutional religion. Ideally the preconceptual, magical, fantasy orientation of the child's spontaneous religion will be cognitively transformed in an orderly manner to better conform to the belief system of the organized religion (see Tamminen et al., 1988). However, recent research (Adams, 1976) suggests that greater numbers of contemporary youth are not making this transition either happily or successfully. More young people appear to be retaining a personal religion while rejecting institutional religion (Conger 1977), and fewer young people today, as compared with twenty years ago, view themselves as religious. Fuller (1988) believes that a crucial factor in this transition is the adolescent's rejection of religious values of parents and society and an articulation of his/her own faith by selecting self-chosen values.

A personal religion may also enhance the sense of self and positive self-esteem and provide the adolescent with a sense of direction. "Because religion roots the meaning and purpose of life in the transcendental reality of God, it makes it possible for individuals to locate themselves and their actions within a larger frame of reference. Religious doctrines enable individuals to make confident choices about who they are, what they stand for, and what they stand against. Religious faith also frees individuals from being at the total mercy of events in the world. Instead of being subjected to every new external influence, they are prepared to bring their own set of values and goals to bear upon the interpretation of everyday life. This makes possible conduct motivated by self-chosen values rather than by environmental or instinctual forces. And, too, religious faith reinforces a positive sense of self-worth by aligning our personal identity and moral outlook with an understanding of God's creativity in the world" (Fuller, 1988; p. 39).

Another aspect of the evolving personal religion is the religious paradox (Paloutzian, 1983), which is the questioning of one's religious values and beliefs while appearing to be religious. This period of questioning is often accompanied by a decline in religiousness (Potvin, Hoge, and Nelson, 1976), an increase in the influences of competing reference groups (Stark, 1984), and on overt or covert "teenage rebellion" (Hill, 1986). Those within the church have often interpreted these behaviors as responses to the influence of a sinful, pleasure-seeking world (Hill, 1986), the inadequacies of the church in responding to developmental needs of youth (Dean, 1982), or the adolescents' perception of a lack of care or concern by the adults in the church (Strommen, 1988). However, Hill (1986) contends that even if adolescents enjoyed a perfect church they would still express disillusionment and dissatisfaction. She perceives questioning and doubt as a normal part of the adolescent's developmental process. Without this questioning and soul searching the development of a mature, personal, internalized, and steadfast faith would not be possible (Hill, 1986).

Fuller (1988) classifies adolescent religious doubts into three areas: personal, scientific, and rational doubts. Personal doubts come into play when we believe that our religion no longer serves our personal needs. Adolescents may experience doubts due to being rejected in love, failing to be accepted by peers, or failing to gain admittance to a valued college. Scientific doubts arise when unavoidable tensions arise between knowledge as produced by empirical methods of science versus knowledge as the mystical, personal, revealed truths of religious experiences. There is also the ongoing, raging debate in America's public schools regarding the controversy between evolution and creationism. Living in a technological age driven by scientific research places a great burden upon individuals who, in order to be perceived as religious, may be required by their peer group to accept prescientific descriptions of the origins of man and the development of the species. Rational doubt relates to criticisms of religion in regard to perceived hypocrisy of adults in the church, adults' support of bigotry and intolerance, and adolescents' awareness of the role of culture in shaping one's religious beliefs.

Fuller (1988) believes that doubt can be a very positive force in the movement toward spiritual maturity. As evidence he offers Tillich's (1957) comment that a dynamic religious faith necessarily contains an element of intellectual doubt. Tillich also contended that one's faith is flawed if it requires the acceptance of ideas for which there is insufficient evidence. This posture makes religious faith appear irrational when it is rational or better yet, suprarational. Fuller perceives faith as "the condition in which individuals are 'grasped' by something that confronts them as unconditional, ultimate, and in some way intrinsic to the life process itself" (p. 44). Longitudinal studies of religious development suggest that most adolescents return to the religion of their parents (Elkind, 1984; Waterman, 1982). Yet the key issue is when adolescents reach maturity, will they incorporate the religious element into their identity and claim ownership of a dynamic personal faith? As Allport (1966) pointed out, many religious individuals are external in their orientation, going through the motions and following some institutional religion without any sincere commitment or internalization of religious values. Elkind (1984) believes that a religious orientation is most effectively fostered in childhood so that young people should experience a time when they are free from any particular institutional religion. Religious experiences for adolescents should provide opportunities for young people to socialize, to discover their true selves, to enhance their identities, and to explore other religious traditions. This "sabbatical" from institutional religion will pave the way for a "later integration of personal and formal religious beliefs and values" (p. 43).

Metacognition, Context, and Memory

One important feature of cognitive activity is *metacognition*. This process refers to knowledge adolescents have about their own thought processes. It is also the ability to effectively monitor one's cognitive activity for accuracy, consistency, and veracity. In adolescence there is a developmental enhancement of metacognitive activity which is produced by the increase in self-awareness and reflectivity. However, empirical attempts to increase the level of metacognitive activity have encountered difficulty in producing transfer of self-regulation strategies from one content area to another (Cavanaugh and Perlmutter, 1982). Keating (1990) suggests that an overemphasis on metacognitive activities early in the learning process might be deleterious to performance since attention may be drawn to activities that should process toward a greater degree of automaticity. An illustration of the phenomenon is disrupting someone's golf game by asking him to explain how he made a certain putt. Keating (1990) suggests that once a difficult skill or domain has been mastered, attention can be directed to determining if the system is operating smoothly.

Glover et al (1990) points out the importance of context in influencing the acquisition of knowledge. One of the major difficulties in religious instruction is the decontextualization of knowledge. If religious instruction is neglected in the home, then children and adolescents may obtain the majority of their religious knowledge in informal or institutional settings. Unfortunately their use of that knowledge might well be confined to that setting. The Good Samaritan might be an exemplary person on a Sunday morning, but does the story have any real applicability to social relationships or charitable endeavors outside of the church? For many people there is no transfer (see Sapp, 1991).

Knowledge in human memory is not stored semantically (like a dictionary), rather some elements are stored schematically or structurally (Glover et al., 1990). The key to achieving expert knowledge in any area is to acquire information that can be used in many contexts and then to link this knowledge in some meaningful way to knowledge already stored in memory. If one is teaching in a church school it is not sufficient to assume that students will automatically draw appropriate conclusions from the beatitudes and parables. The key element is for the student to experience the information in a variety of contexts before the learning will be contextually broad-based. This, of course, is a major problem for any organization, school, or church that refuses to "get their hands dirty" with real world problems.

Synthesis and Reformulation

Earlier in the chapter I pointed out that Piaget's pioneering work has come under a great deal of criticism. At this writing some researchers (Glover, Ronning, and Bruning, 1990; Keating, 1990) are explicating applications of cognitive psychology for children and adolescents and finding a negligible role for Piaget's theory. Others (Brynes, 1988) continue to find Piaget's constructs to be theoretically fruitful. Brynes proposes a systematic reformulation of formal operations, finding four aspects to be crucial: operations on operations, the construction of all possible combinations, propositional reasoning, and hypothetical reasoning.

A more radical departure from Piaget's theory combines a neo-Piagetian approach with an information-processing perspective (Case, 1985). This synthesis focuses on adolescent conceptual gains in many content areas. Broad conceptual reorganizations do occur but they are influenced by the adolescent's capability to generate and consider different representations of information. The dynamics of conceptual change are that adolescents overlearn and automatize basic cognitive processes; they have an increased memory capacity, and they know more content. These factors, in combination, provide for a more efficient cognitive apparatus such that adolescents can retain and manipulate several different dimensions of a problem. Keating (1990) suggests that Case's approach may muddle somewhat the relationship between shifts in the structure of knowledge, changes in basic processing, content knowledge, and other developments (p. 16).

The approaches described above are only a subsample of the discipline of contemporary cognitive psychology. The area is quite dynamic, and there has been a considerable loss of consensus such that researchers may disagree regarding the core questions of research on adolescent thinking (Keating, 1990). This theoretical divergence has provided an impetus for consideration of more applied issues such as the teaching of thinking skills and procedures for successfully implementing cognitively oriented intervention programs.

Final Thoughts

When we consider the pivotal role of thinking and understanding in the lives of adolescents, we should not lose sight of the fact that thinking is a product of a complex personality structure. For every thought there must be a thinker, and that person has many dimensions. Adolescent thinking is also powerfully influenced by social structures, the family constellation, and the larger society. Facing a myriad of conflicting forces it seems impossible for adolescents to avoid doubts, fears, and confusion. Is it any wonder that some will say with Cain, "My burden is greater than I can bear"? Those who effectively channel their developing cognitive capabilities will most successfully deal with a confusing, convoluted world.

Cognitive processes are integrated, working holistically. The employment of a relatively discrete analysis should not distort that fact. It is also a truism that persons often do not behave as they should. Behavior is assumed to be controlled by rational thinking, yet there are numerous cognitive socialization factors, e.g., television and peer culture, which have a deleterious effect on the attitudes and lifestyles of adolescents. These social forces appear to be oriented toward undermining reflection, overwhelming thoughtful analysis, and substituting transitory emotional states for significant human relationships (Keating, 1990).

Adolescents deserve all the understanding, love, and support that their families, churches, and culture can muster. Hopefully our appreciation of the dynamic changes in their cognitive processes will enhance our commitment to better assist teens in their search for personal and religious maturity.

REFERENCES

Adams, J.F. (1976). *Understanding adolescents*. Boston: Allyn & Bacon.
Allport, G. (1966). The religious context of prejudice. *Journal for the Scientific Study of Religion, 5*, 447-457.

Allport, G. W., and Ross, J. M. (1967). Personal religious orientation and prejudice. *Journal of Personality and Social Psychology, 5,* 432-443.

Anderson, J.R., and Reder, L.M. (1979). An elaborative processing explanation of depth of processing. In L.S. Cermak and F.I.M. Craik (Eds.), *Levels of processing in human memory.* Hillsdale, N.J.: Erlbaum.

Barrett, D., Radkey–Yarrow, M., and Cline, R. L. (1982). The effects of malnutrition on cognitive growth. *Developmental Psychology, 18,* 541-61.

Braine, M.D. (1964). Development of a group of transitivity of length: A reply to Smedslund. *Child Development, 35(3),* 799-810.

Brainerd, C. (1978). *Piaget's theory of intelligence.* Englewood Cliffs, N.J.: Prentice Hall.

Brown, G., and Desforges, C. (1979). *Piaget's theory: A psychological critique.* New York: Methuen.

Byrnes, J.P. (1988). Formal operations: A systematic reformulation. *Developmental Review, 8,* 66-87.

Case, R. (1985). *Intellectual development: Birth to adulthood.* New York: Academic Press.

Cavanaugh, J. C., and Perlmutter, M. (1982). Metamemory: A critical reexamination. *Child Development, 53,* 11-28.

Cohen, D. (1983). *Piaget: Critique and reassessment.* New York: St. Martin's Press.

Conger, J.J. (1977). *Adolescence and youth* (3rd ed.). New York: Harper & Row.

Cowen, P.A. (1978). *Piaget with feeling.* New York: Holt, Rinehart and Winston.

Craik, F.I.M., and Lockhart, R.S. (1972). Levels of processing: A framework for memory research. *Journal of Verbal Learning and Verbal Behavior, 11,* 671-684.

Csikszentmihalyi, M., and Larson, R. (1984). *Being adolescent.* New York: Basic Books.

Dean, R.A., (1982). Youth: Moonie's target population. *Adolescence, 17,* 567-574.

Desforges, C., and Brown G. (1979). The educational utility of Piaget: A reply to Shayer. *British Journal of Educational Psychology, 49 (3),* 277-281.

Elkind, D. (1974). *A sympathetic understanding of the child.* Needham Heights, Mass.: Allyn & Bacon.

Elkind, D. (1979). *The child and society.* New York: Oxford University Press.

Elkind, D. (1984). *All grown up and no place to go.* New York: Addison-Wesley.

Erikson, E.H. (1968). *Identity: Youth and crisis.* New York: W.W. Norton.

Fischer, K.W. (1980). A theory of cognitive development: The control and construction of hierarchies of skills. *Psychological Review, 8C,* 477-531.

Fischer, K.W., and Lazerson, A. (1984). *Human development.* San Francisco: W.H. Freeman.

Fowler, J. and Keen, S. (1978). *Life Maps: Conversations on the journey of faith.* J. Berryman (Ed.). Waco, Tex.: Word Books.

Fuller, R.C. (1988). *Religion and the life-cycle.* Philadelphia: Fortress Press.

Glover, J.A., Ronning, R.R., and Bruning, R.H. (1990). *Cognitive psychology for teachers.* New York: Macmillan.

Goldman, R. (1964). *Religious thinking from childhood to adolescence.* New York: Seabury Press.

Goldman, R. (1965). *Readiness for religion.* New York: Seabury Press.

Harms, E. (1944). The development of religious experience in children. *American Journal of Sociology, 50,* 112-122.

Hill, C.I. (1986). A developmental perspective on adolescent "rebellion" in the church. *Journal of Psychology and Theology, 14(4),* 306-318.

Hoge, D.R. and Petrillo, D. H. (1978). Development of religious thinking in adolescence: A test of Goldman's theories, *Journal for the Scientific Study of Religion, 17 (2),* 139-154.

Jacoby, L., and Craik, F.I.M. (1979). Effects of elaboration of processing at encoding and

ADOLESCENT THINKING AND UNDERSTANDING   95

retrieval: Trace distinctiveness and recovery of initial context. In L.S Cermak and F.I.M. Craik (Eds.), *Levels of processing in human memory* (pp 1-22). Hillsdale, N.J.: Erlbaum.

Kaye, D.B., Hale, V.C., and Baron, M.B. (1979). Factors influencing rule discovery in children. *Journal of Educational Psychology, 71 (5),* 654-668.

Keating, D.P. (1980). Thinking processes in adolescence. In J. Adelson (Ed.), *Handbook of adolescent psychology.* New York: John Wiley & Sons.

Keating, D.P. (1990). Adolescent thinking. In S. Feldman and G. Elliot (Eds.), *At the threshold: The developing adolescent.*

Kohlberg, L. (1958). *The development of modes of moral thinking and chance in the years 10 to 16.* Unpublished doctoral dissertation, University of Chicago.

Lesser, G., Fifer, G., and Clark, D.H. (1965). Mental abilities of children from different social-class and cultural groups. *Monographs of the Society for Research in Child Development, 30,* (4, Whole No. 102).

Long, D., Elkind, D., and Spilka, B., (1967). The child's conception of prayer. *Journal for the Scientific Study of Religion, 6,* 101-109.

Marcia, J.E., (1966). Development and validation of ego-identity status. *Journal of Personality and Social Psychology, 3,* 551-558.

Martorano, S.C., (1977). A developmental analysis of performance on Piaget's formal operations tasks. *Developmental Psychology, 13 (6),* 666-672.

Montemayor, R., and Eisen, M. (1977). The development of self-conceptions from childhood to adolescence. *Developmental Psychology, 13,* 314-319.

Moore, J. (1988). Adolescent spiritual development: Stages and strategies. *Religious Education, 83(1),* 83-100.

Newman, P. R., and Newman, B. M. (1988). Differences between childhood and adulthood: The identity watershed. *Adolescence, 23* (Fall), 551-557.

Neimark, E.D. (1987). *Adventures in thinking.* New York: Harcourt Brace Jovanovich.

Neves, D.M., and Anderson, J.R. (1981). Knowledge compilation: Mechanisms for the automization of cognitive skills. In J.R. Anderson (Ed.), *Cognitve skills and their organization.* Hillsdale, N.J.: Erlbaum.

Okun, M.A., and Sasfy, J.H. (1977). Adolescence, the self concept and formal operations. *Adolescence, 12,* 373-379.

O'Malley, P., and Bachman, J. (1983). Self-esteem: Change and stability between ages 13 and 23. *Developmental Psychology, 19,* 257-268.

Palincsar, A.S., and Bown, A.C. (1984). Reciprocal teaching of comprehensive-fostering and monitoring activities. *Cognition and Instruction, 1,* 117-175.

Paloutzian, R. (1983). *Invitation to the psychology of religion.* Glenview, Ill.: Scott, Foresman.

Piaget, J. (1923). *La psychologie et les foi religieuses.* Geneva: Labor.

Piaget, J. (1967). *Six psychological studies.* New York: Random House.

Piaget, J. (1972). Intellectual evaluation from adolescence to adulthood. *Human Development, 15,* 1-2.

Piaget, J. (1976). *Piaget and his school.* B. Inhelder, H. Chipman, and C. Zwingmann (Eds.). New York: Springer-Verlag.

Potvin, R.H., Hoge, D., and Nelson, H. (1976). *Religion and American youth.* Washington, D.C.: United States Catholic Conference.

Ratcliff, D. E. (1990). Personal correspondence.

Riley, C.A., and Trabasso T. (1974). Comparatives, logical structures, and encoding in a transitive inference task. *Journal of Experimental Child Psychology, 17(2),* 187-203.

Santrock, J.W. (1987). *Adolescence: An introduction* (3rd ed.). Dubuque: William C. Brown.

Sapp, G.L. (1991). Psychological foundations of religious compassion. In G. Sapp (Ed.), *Compassion in pastoral ministry*. Birmingham, Ala: Religious Education Press.

Schultz, T.R., and Kestenbaum, N.R. (1985). Casual reasoning in children. *Annals of Child Development, 2,* 195-233.

Selman, R.L. (1980). *The growth of interpersonal understanding.* New York: Academic Press.

Siegel, L.S., and Brainerd, C.J. (Eds.) (1978). *Alternatives to Piaget: Critical essays on the theory.* New York: Academic Press.

Spada, H., and Kluwe, R.H. (1980). Two models of intellectual development and their reference to the theory of Piaget. In R.H. Kluve and H. Spada (Eds.), *Developmental models of thinking.* New York: Academic Press.

Sprinthall, D.A., and Collins, W.A. (1988). *Adolescent psychology: A developmental view* (2nd ed). New York: Random House.

Stark, R. (1984). Religion and conformity: Reaffirming a sociology for religion. *Sociological Analysis, 45,* 273-82.

Sternberg, R. J., and Powell, J.S. (1983). The Development of intelligence. In Paul H. Mussen (Ed.), *Handbook of child psychology:* Volume III. New York: John Wiley & Sons.

Strommen, M. (1988). *The five cries of youth,* (rev. ed.). New York: Harper & Row.

Tamminen, K., Viannello, R., Jaspard, J., and Ratcliff, D. (1988). The religious concepts of preschoolers. In D. Ratcliff (Ed.), *Handbook of preschool religion education.* Birmingham, Ala: Religious Education Press.

Thorndike, R.L., Hagen, E.P., and Sattler, J.M. (1986). *The Stanford-Binet intelligence scale.* (4th ed.). Chicago: Riverside Publishing Company.

Tillich, P. (1957). *Dynamics of faith.* New York: Harper & Row.

Trautman, M.C. (1984). *Theoretical analysis of the cognitive demands of the concept "church."* Pittsburgh: University of Pittsburgh.

Wagner, J.A. (1987). Formal operations and ego identity in adolescence. *Adolescence, 22,* 23-35.

Waterman, A.S. (1982). Identity development from adolescence to adulthood: An extension of theory and a review of the research. *Developmental Psychology, 18 (3),* 341-358.

Wellman, H.M. (1985). The child's theory of mind: The development of conceptions of cognition. In S. Yussen (Ed.), *The growth of reflection in children,* Orlando: Academic Press.

Wiklegren, W. (1974). *How to solve problems.* San Francisco: Freeman.

Chapter Four

Preadolescence

JERRY ALDRIDGE

Preadolescence is the critical period between childhood and adolescence which occurs between the ages of nine and thirteen (Kohen-Raz, 1971). Preadolescents hold fast to childhood one day and want to be treated like adults the next. The issues and problems of this age are developmentally distinct from either childhood or adolescence. To better address this period, journals such as *Childhood Education* include a column or section devoted specifically to preadolescent development. From the preadolescent column in *Childhood Education,* O'Brien (1990) reports, "Perhaps the most crucial years for children are between ages one and two and eleven and twelve. More developmental experiences occur during those two periods than at any other time in their lives. Decisions about independence and trust and their own self-worth are based on personal experiences with people in their near environment" (p. 163).

Churches often separate the preadolescent from the adolescent while the media continually treats the preadolescent (as well as the teenager) as a young adult (Elkind, 1981). The markers of childhood are disappearing and with them go the lines between the preadolescent and the adolescent, but there are differences between these two groups. These differences can be seen in personality, physical, cognitive, moral, faith, and self-esteem development.

Personality Development

Preadolescent development is dependent on both internal and external influences. The social world of the child interacts with the individual's psychosocial development in a specific and unique manner. Comer (1989) indicates, "Some preadolescents and early adolescents are poised and articulate in social situations—at parties, with relatives, in school, and at weddings and other special occasions. Others—even when carefully taught—are much less graceful" (p. 132). While developmental norms are somewhat helpful in understanding preadolescent personality development, this information should be balanced with the fact that each preadolescent expresses his own emotional uniqueness within the context of the social world.

Preadolescents are influenced by three groups—the family, the school, and informal and formal peer groups which include everything from cliques and gangs to church youth groups. As a child moves into preadolescence, parents, teachers, and other significant adults may have less influence and control over the preadolescent. The peer group becomes a major focus of social development (Minuchin, 1977). There is a renewed developmental need for autonomy and separateness from adults. Just as a two-year-old begins to assert his individuality, the preadolescent asserts himself, but this time he is significantly influenced by his peers. This peer influence peaks between the ages of eleven and twelve and then begins to decline (Hetherington and Parke, 1986).

Even though the peer group has a predominant influence over the preadolescent, the family still has the major impact on values and beliefs (Jung, 1954; Strommen, 1988). Preadolescents ranked having a happy family as their highest value listed in the "Listening to Early Adolescents and their Parents" (LEAP) survey conducted by the Search Institute (The myth of the generation gap, 1984). The majority of preadolescents are close to their parents, and it is within the family context that most preadolescents want to discuss their problems.

Function of the Peer Group

The consequences of peer group participation are strongly related to self-concept, self-esteem, and typology which will be discussed later in this chapter. The peer group is generally the indicator of social acceptance or rejection (Bukowski and Newcomb, 1985). Two important factors in peer group participation are physical attractiveness and shared values.

Concern about physical attractiveness increases during this period. During the childhood years, the "ugly duckling" stage emerges in which physical appearance is less important in socialization (Minuchin, 1977). During the early elementary years, the child is less concerned with grooming or neatness than he is during the preadolescent years. He does not pay close attention to the way he looks (hence the "ugly duckling" stage), but this changes. The preadolescent is thrown into a vulnerable position since his increased interest in physical attractiveness comes when biological changes often result in awkward movements and less than flattering appearance. Several studies have shown a relationship between peer group acceptance and physical attractiveness (Lerner and Lerner, 1977; Stephan and Langlois, 1984). Preadolescents are quick to stereotype body types and personality traits. Muscular and athletic children are seen as strong, brave, smart, and helpful while stout individuals are often viewed as sloppy and lazy. Skinny children are often thought of as weak, anxious, quiet, or worrisome (Staffieri, 1972). These stereotyping tendencies are important for religious educators to note for numerous reasons such as helping the outcast preadolescent cope as well as encouraging spiritual values in youth groups to help counter the superficial interest in good looks.

Shared values also "play a critical part in influencing people's social interactions" (Vander Zanden, 1989; p. 336). This is particularly important for youth ministers to ponder since the values of the church will hopefully be the values of the youth group. Because preadolescents are so influenced by their peer group, it stands to reason that the values of the peers will impact on the values of the individual.

Activities planned by the youth minister can influence the values of the peer group and support individual social and emotional development. Positive peer interactions can be enhanced by planning activities which avoid inappropriate competition, comparison, and conformity (Aldridge, 1989). When children are placed in individual competitions within the church, such as memorizing scripture, participating in Bible drills, or reading a text out loud, their social acceptance and self-esteem can be at risk. This especially applies when team leaders have to choose who will be on their team. Competition is more appropriate when it is tied to cooperation. Games and activities which have groups of children competing together against another group, allow preadolescents to work cooperatively to achieve a common goal. Competition can be minimized in group situations if members of the groups exchange team members during the competition. Later, if someone asks, "Who won the game?" it is difficult to ascertain since many have been members of more than one team during the activity.

Comparisons among preadolescents are also developmentally inappropriate and should be avoided by youth ministers (Aldridge, 1988). Teachers and parents sometimes compare children with siblings or others children and this serves to inflate the feelings of some preadolescents at the expense of others. There are some occasions in which peer modeling is acceptable, but this is best accomplished through a volunteer process. A preadolescent who volunteers to share a talent or explain a skill can serve as a role model without emphasizing comparisons. Comparison using biblical references is also questionable. To say to a preadolescent, "You ought to be more like Paul" could imply that the child's own God-given talents are not as good as Paul's, when indeed they might just be different. Comparing children can have negative consequences on both their socialization and self-esteem (Clark, Clemes, and Bean, 1980).

Conformity is also a concern this age. The preadolescent is at a time when skepticism about adult authority increases and the peer world is becoming more important. This increases preadolescent vulnerability to peer pressure. The individual who is insecure will often do anything to achieve group approval. This is partially why alcohol and drug dependency occurs within cliques that support such habits. The youth minister can sometimes serve as a role model and help preadolescents develop skills to stand firm against negative conformity (Bandura, 1986).

Industry and Identity Issues

Industry and identity are important to psychosocial development during preadolescence (Erikson, 1968). Erikson's theory of psychosocial development involves "eight major stages of intrapsychic conflict that are dealt with sequentially in identity formation" (Richter, 1982; p. 14). Stages leading to preadolescence include 1) basic trust versus mistrust (birth to two); 2) autonomy versus shame and doubt (two to three years); and 3) initiative versus guilt (four to six years). During preadolescence, subjects are usually in the stage of 4) industry versus inferiority while moving toward a new psychological dilemma known as 5) identity versus role confusion. Some preadolescents attempt to integrate previous stages to develop basic trust, autonomy, initiative, and industry, and thus in a sense must work through these earlier stages once again in the process of identity formation. The issues of trust, autonomy, initiative, and industry are necessary for the preadolescent to eventually develop a strong sense of identity (Erikson, 1980).

The development of industry occurs as the child finds out what he can do academically and how he relates socially. Industry issues involve acquiring a sense of competence and mastery in school. If the individual is not achieving a sense of competence at school, the religious setting may provide some opportunity for competence. The church setting is most often smaller than the school setting and hopefully more nurturing. Opportunities for music, sports, and participation in small group social activities are often provided by the church. This setting may allow the preadolescent to develop a sense of competence and participation. Mastery of tasks within social and learning situations are necessary to develop a foundation for coping with the adolescent task of achieving an identity.

Once industry issues have been dealt with the developmental task of forming an identity can occur. How does one go about achieving an identity? How can adults help preadolescents in this search for identity? According to Ganiere and Enright (1989) "there are three key concepts for intervention that consistently emerge in the literature. One of them is that identity consists of self-perceptions and images derived from others' perceptions of oneself" (p. 284). This point is similar to Mead's "looking glass self" in which an important aspect of identity and self-concept is the ability to take the role of others and see ourselves as objectively as possible through other people's perceptions (Mead, 1934). The second concept is that early identifications strongly influence perceptions of the social-self and identity. Finally, values influence social-self perceptions. So, preadolescents are influenced by others, their early life experiences, and the value system within which they live. The youth minister cannot change earlier life experiences, but he may be able to change the perception of those events. He also has limited control over the perceptions of others concerning the preadolescent, although he can model acceptance and value the individuality of each preadolescent. The value system is one area in which the youth minister can have a profound influence since the church is part of the value system in which the child operates.

Physical Development

Preadolescence is an important period with regard to three significant changes related to physical development. First, there is a growth spurt about the time of puberty, sometimes occurring during the preadolescent years (Baldwin, 1986). Second, the differentiation in ectomorphic, mesomorphic, and endomorphic body types becomes more pronounced during this period (Santrock and Yussen, 1984). Finally, the self-esteem and social development are profoundly affected by the physical changes happening during this period (Vander Zanden, 1989).

Girls in preadolescence begin their growth spurt before boys, which is very apparent in the physical changes and size of girls when compared to boys in the fifth and sixth grades (Shaffer, 1985). During this time, children experience the lengthening of the limbs and trunk (Santrock and Yussen, 1984).

The average age of menarche, defined as the first menstrual period, has fallen approximately a year and a half since 1905 (Vander Zanden, 1989). This trend has appeared to stabilize and is now at an average of 12.8 years. The onset of menarche varies considerably among girls. One study of middle-class girls in the Boston area found that among 781 girls, menarche ranged from 9.1 years to 17.7 years (Zacharias et al., 1976). Early puberty among both males and females is associated with a tendency toward a stout physique while late menarche often is characteristic of a thin body type (Faust, 1977).

Differentiation in body types becomes more noticeable during the preadolescent period. Endomorphs are those with noticeably chubby body types. Mesomorphs have more of an athletic build which is more desirable in Western society, while ectomorphs exhibit the skinny body build (Hurlock, 1980). Each body type is also associated with certain personality types and thus, physical development interacts with personality and social development (Sheldon, 1940). This belief, however, has been questioned and the relationship between body type and personality type is still not clear (Stager and Burke, 1982).

Self-esteem and social acceptance are strongly connected to the preadolescent's physical development (Faust, 1960). Early maturation is often seen as a plus for males. "For example, the value placed on manly appearance and athletic excellence means that early maturing boys often enjoy the admiration of their peers" (Vander Zanden, 1989; p. 366). Early maturation and social acceptance appear to be more complicated for girls. Early maturation among girls is often seen as a handicap (Faust, 1960). Late-maturing girls seem to be at a disadvantage in middle or junior high school.

Physical changes are also associated with initiation rites in many cultures (Campbell, 1989). The Christian tradition also involves certain religious experiences which are associated with the preadolescent period. During this age period, confirmation or receiving of salvation are often emphasized, while the bar mitzvah or bat mitzvah is found in the Jewish tradition. Some social scientists believe that this initiation into "adulthood" has been lost in Western spirituality. A greater preparation and emphasis on religious initiation into adulthood is found in other cultures and religions. This lack of emphasis on initiation may result in the individual's loss of significance in religious participation (Campbell, 1989).

Cognitive Development

During the 1960s and 1970s, new insights into cognitive development were a major contribution of developmental psychology (Gardner, 1983). Piaget's theory of cognitive development was translated into education practice (Wadsworth, 1990). Piaget's stage theory traces cognitive development from a sensorimotor orientation of infants to the abstract reasoning of adolescents and adults. The preadolescent period of cognitive development is a critical time of transition between the concrete style of thinking and the abstract level of reasoning.

During the concrete operational stage, characteristic of children from seven to eleven, there is an increased ability in classifying concrete objects and performing many of the school-oriented operations such as adding, subtracting, multiplying, and dividing. There is also an increased awareness and understanding of geographic space and historical time (Sund, 1976).

Some preadolescents are in transition to the next stage of formal operations, often characteristic of individuals from eleven to fourteen, in which they are better able to perform more abstract conceptual thinking. Characteristics of the formal operational period include hypothetical-deductive thinking, reflective thinking, propositional logic, and syllogistic reasoning (Ginsburg and Opper, 1979). The abstract reasoner is capable of creating theories, understanding time and space more completely, and questioning ethics (Sund, 1976). This period is also a time in which idealistic egocentrism occurs; they often believe that what they think should be that way in reality (Ginsburg and Opper, 1979).

An important distinction in Piaget's theory of cognitive development is that it treats children's thinking as qualitatively different from adult thinking. Applying Piaget's theory to youth ministry would involve taking into account that children think in ways unlike adults. According to Miller (1976), eight- to-eleven-years-olds are often very literal in their understanding of biblical concepts. They may fragment and illogically sequence events (Ratcliff, 1987). Further, this age group often focuses on the physical properties rather than the spiritual significance of events. According to the Miller (1976) study, early adolescents in the twelve-to-fourteen range were equally distributed between the concrete, transition, and abstract stages, "while the abstract stage was clearly dominant in the fifteen to eighteen year range" (Ratcliff, 1987; p. 23). Teaching the Bible to preadolescents often requires a different approach and content. Ratcliff (1987) recommends that Bible concepts which require formal operational thinking should be avoided until the preadolescent is cognitively ready for them.

Six suggestions can be made for developing instruction based on Piaget's theory (Sund, 1976). These are appropriate for youth ministers in planning learning activities for preadolescents. Suggestions include:

1) emphasize active involvement;
2) focus on helping children reflect upon ideas, not just memorizing facts;
3) develop activities which move from concrete to abstract;
4) sequence activities according to the stages of cognitive development represented in the group while simultaneously attempting to individualize activities as much as possible so as to meet the needs of those preadolescents who are functioning cognitively at different levels;
5) adjust the curriculum to the preadolescent and not the preadolescent to the curriculum;
6) focus on the process of learning rather than on the product. For example, focus on how the preadolescent arrives at biblical concepts as opposed to just encouraging him to give the right answers.

Cognitively, the preadolescent is moving to a better understanding of historical time and geographic space. It is during this period that the individual begins to grasp the nature and importance of historical events in the Judeo-Christian tradition and the place in which these events occurred. He is also better able to extract and apply abstract principles.

While some preadolescents are moving into the formal operational period, others have not yet reached this stage. Several studies indicate that a large percentage of high-school students have difficulty with certain abstractions and have not reached a formal operational level (Elkind, 1961; Sund, 1976). Other studies report that abstract thinking is clearly predominant during the adolescent years (Goldman, 1964; Miller, 1976).

Recently, Piaget's theory of cognitive development and traditional views of intelligence and psychometry have been questioned by developmental psychologists, particularly Howard Gardner (1983). Gardner says that traditional views of intelligence are general and somewhat analogous to a container of water. Some people have full amounts and others lesser amounts of intelligence. Gardner suggests that this analogy is insufficient; intelligence is more specific and individual. He has proposed a theory of multiple intelligences and has identified at least seven types of intelligence which include linguistic, musical, mathematical-logical, visual-spatial, bodily kinesthetic, social-interpersonal, and intrapersonal (Kitano and Kirby, 1986).

Gardner points out that if the backgrounds and education of Einstein and Mozart were interchanged, the results would have been a mediocre musician and an average scientist. From Gardner's perspective of multiple intelligences, youth ministers are encouraged to ask the question, "How is this child smart?" not "How smart is this child?" Church workers are encouraged to apply Gardner's theory by searching for each child's individuality as a means of helping that individual develop spiritual values and work out his own contribution and ministry to others. The youth minister can also help the preadolescent discover and develop his spiritual gifts.

Other recent developments in cognitive psychology include an emphasis on learning styles (Carbo, 1987). Some preadolescents show a preference for visual learning while others are more auditory oriented. Still others learn better through kinesthetic and tactile modalities. Children also show preferences for learning during different times of the day. Specific learning styles and time preferences are challenging variables to consider when designing a quality youth ministry. The task involves paying close attention to individual needs and time preferences in order to reach the preadolescent.

Moral Development

Moral development refers to the process of forming values, learning right from wrong, and the ability to guide one's own actions in terms of these values (Vander Zanden, 1989). There are several approaches to moral development, including the psychoanalytic view, cognitive learning theory, and the cognitive-developmental approach. The psychoanalytic view describes the child as an individual possessing aggressive and sexual drives which need to be channeled to meet both parental and societal standards (Shaffer, 1985). Internalization of external standards helps children develop moral behavior.

Cognitive learning theory postulates that children learn moral values primarily through observational or "see-and-do" learning from significant others (Bandura, Ross, and Ross, 1963). Cognitive-developmental theory views moral development as a succession of stages with different kinds of thinking and behavior occurring at each level of moral development (Wadsworth, 1990). The cognitive-developmental theory of moral development has been researched thoroughly and has specific implications for preadolescents. This theory has its roots in the research of Piaget and Kohlberg (Ginsburg and Opper, 1979).

Piaget believed moral development progressed through two broad stages. The first stage was that of *heteronomous morality* in which the child depends on adults for moral rules and judgments. In this stage, the child is very rigid and inflexible in his understanding of morality. During the preadolescent period children begin to develop the second stage of moral development known as *autonomous morality*. Simply put, heteronomy is being governed by others, while autonomy is being governed by one's self. Kamii (1985) focused much of her research on how parents, teachers, and significant adults in the lives of young children continually reinforce heteronomy. Heteronomy in preschool and early elementary aged children is one thing, but as children enter the preadolescent stage, peers become the significant others instead of adults. Adults who do not help children construct appropriate autonomy may find preadolescents caught in a moral dependence upon an undesirable peer group. Piaget believed that the limitations of heteronomous morality were correlated to the child's cognitive development. However, if cognitive learning theory is also considered, it is easy to see how peers also influence the preadolescent.

Lawrence Kohlberg refined Piaget's theory of moral development and continued to research and change his own theory of moral development (Kohlberg, 1984). His research has recently received wide criticism, especially for his exclusion of females in some of his studies. Gilligan (1982) reports that Kohlberg has developed a theory of male moral development which is a morality of justice. She suggests that women have more of a morality of nurturance and care which is not captured by Kohlberg's research.

Kohlberg's stage theory of moral development is divided into three levels, with two stages at each level (see chapter seven). The overwhelming majority of preadolescents fall into the first two levels (four stages). The lowest stage of moral development is one in which the individual makes a choice out of fear of punishment. The next stage involves making decisions with the thought, "What's in this for me?" A still higher stage is that of good girl/nice boy orientation in which the individual makes a moral decision based on the idea of what an exemplary child would do. The interest in reciprocity is still present. Many preadolescents are in the "law and order" stage in which fixed laws prevail and moral decisions should be made based on the laws.

Moral development in preadolescence is also associated with prosocial behavior and altruism. Shaffer (1985) defines prosocial responses as "behaviors such as cooperation, helping, sharing, or comfort giving that benefit other people" (p. 23). He further defines altruism as "a concern for the welfare of others that is expressed through prosocial acts such as sharing, cooperating, and helping" (p. 487). As children approach adolescence, they may help others and become more cooperative, but the dynamics of the situation, which include many variables such as context and family background, often dictate whether a preadolescent will come to the rescue of a peer. Social factors are extremely important in the moral development of the preadolescent. These would include upbringing, peer group acceptance, and societal expectations just to mention a few.

One reason why preadolescents are more prosocial and altruistic is due to new advancement in role-taking. Selman (1976) has proposed a developmental stage theory in which most preadolescents fall into Stage 3, *mutual* role-taking. This roughly corresponds to children ages ten to twelve. According to Damon (1983), "This stage is characterized by the fact that the child realizes that both self and other can view each other mutually and simultaneously as subjects. Child can step outside the two-person dyad and view the interactions from a third-person perspective" (p. 125). This corresponds to Mead's looking glass self (Mead, 1934).

Cognitive development, observational learning, prosocial and altruistic development, and new abilities in role-taking result in many changes in moral development for the preadolescent. These new developments are experienced in a new social context in which peer relations are dominant. Relating authentically to the preadolescent requires effort in accepting both the cognitive and social changes involved.

Faith Development

The development of faith is also changing for the preadolescent (Fowler, 1986). Fowler has developed a theory of structural stages of faith development. He recognizes the complexity of operationally defining faith but sees it as a human universal in which we shape our lives through convictions and assumptions about reality. For Fowler, it is a way of leaning into or meeting life.

Fowler's stage of faith development for the early adolescent period is what he calls "synthetic-conventional" faith. This stage is filled with conflict and dissonance in which there is a "mutual interpersonal perspective-taking" (p. 29). There are several activities of this stage which typically characterize the preadolescent. These include:

1. Identity and interiority (what we find inside ourselves), one's own and others', become absorbing concerns.
2. Style and substance of personality become a conscious concern.
3. Values, commitments, and relationships are seen as central to identity and worth at a time when worth is heavily keyed to the approval and affirmation of significant others.
4. A seeking for values and beliefs to call forth our trust and to direct our loyalties.
5. Selfhood derives from important relations and roles (pp. 29-30).

This stage of faith development involves a holistic characteristic of the preadolescent; all areas of development are interrelated and critical to one another. Notice Fowler's emphasis on identity and personality, as well as values and commitments. Physical changes also feed into the faith development, since physical development as well as personality development is now a conscious concern. Fowler reports that this period roughly corresponds to Piaget's early formal operational period because the preadolescent is better able to use his mind. It is at this time that he or she is better able to take the role of others and new relationships are possible.

What are some of the major religious concerns of preadolescents? Benson, Williams, and Johnson (1987) studied approximately 8000 fifth through ninth graders to answer this question. Their study involved thirteen agencies, most of which were major denominations. Their sample for this study is generally considered representative of American preteens. The findings are particularly helpful to youth ministers seeking to understand the concerns of preadolescents.

Most preteens report that religion is an important influence in their lives. Religion to them is multidimensional as they see spiritual development as both vertical (relating to God) and horizontal (relating to others). Religion is more often seen by preteens as being liberating rather than restrictive.

During preadolescence, males and females are somewhat different in their view of religion. Boys generally attach less significance to religion while girls consistently hold more positive attitudes toward church. Further, boys are more likely than girls to see religion as restricting. Both sexes, however, experience a decline in interest toward religion, but this trend is more noticeable among boys.

The importance of appropriate religious education cannot be overstressed during this developmental period. The more important religion is to preadolescents, the more likely they are to have high self-esteem, good attitudes toward church, engage in helpful behaviors, and refrain from drug abuse (Benson, Williams, and Johnson, 1987).

Self-esteem Development

Social, physical, cognitive, moral and faith development are all strongly tied to self-esteem development in preadolescence. Aldridge (1989) defines the self-concept as what one thinks about the self. For example, the preadolescent may think of himself as a sixth grader, a member of the soccer team or youth group at church. This makes up his self-concept. Self-esteem, in contrast, is how one feels about the self-concept. How does the child feel about herself as a sixth grader, a member of the soccer team, or a participant in the youth group?

There are basically four requirements for the development of positive self-esteem (Clark, Clemes, and Bean, 1980; Coopersmith, 1967). These include a sense of belonging, a feeling of individuality, the opportunity to choose, and the presence of good models. The preadolescent is at-risk in each of these areas.

Clark, Clemes, and Bean (1980) have listed eight characteristics of children and adolescents which indicate high self-esteem and eight which imply low self-esteem. The preadolescent with high self-esteem will "act independently, assume responsibility, be proud of accomplishments, approach new challenges with enthusiasm, exhibit a broad range of emotions and feelings, tolerate frustration well, and feel capable of influencing others" (pp. 7-8). However, individuals with low self-esteem will "demean their own talents, feel others do not value them, feel powerless and easily influenced by others; will express a narrow range of emotions and feelings, and avoid situations that provoke anxiety. They become defensive and easily frustrated and blame others for their own weaknesses" (p. 8). A sense of belonging, individuality, the opportunity to choose, and the presence of good models are variables which interact with the preadolescent's individual typology and biology to determine or contribute to the preadolescent's high or low self-esteem.

Developing a Sense of Belonging

Where does the preadolescent belong in the youth ministry? The unique nature of preadolescent development has been considered earlier in this chapter. The preadolescent is not the typical elementary child, and yet he is not fully into the adolescent period. Providing a sense of belonging within the church requires careful consideration of the preadolescent, the extended peer group in the church, and the current structure for serving children and youth in this setting. This decision is critical since Strommen (1988) reveals that this age is an important one with regard to spiritual values.

Some preadolescents are ready to participate in church youth activities, others are not. Individual differences increase during this period and the placement of children into one peer group or another demands much thought. The current structure of youth programs adds to the confusion of where to place preadolescents—especially in church programs which are small in number. For example, if there are only two active preadolescents and one is immature and prefers to remain with children but the other is ready to participate as an adolescent, what can be done to provide the best appropriate placement for each? Rigid age requirements and structures based on age add to this problem of placement. As noted earlier, the curriculum should fit the child instead of the child being made to adapt to the curriculum (Sund, 1976).

A lack of connectiveness and belonging can be observed in preadolescents who exhibit many of the following traits. Children who do not communicate well and have few or no friends may have trouble with this sense of belonging. Those who talk negatively about the church, family, or peer group and are disliked by their peers have special problems with connectiveness. Sometimes the preadolescent who does not belong tries to be the center of attention or constantly tries to get others to notice him (Clark, Clemes, and Bean, 1980).

Providing a strong sense of community for the preadolescent can help change feelings of isolation. Avoiding unnecessary competition, comparison, and conformity while looking for ways to encourage cooperation can help the child who has difficulty with connectiveness (Aldridge, 1989).

Developing a Feeling of Individuality or Uniqueness

Just as the preadolescent has the need to belong, he or she also has the need to be distinct. A sign of individuality is expressed in individuals who feel they know information that no one else knows and who feel that their differences are appreciated and enjoyed by others. Hobbies, talents, interests, or cultural background can be opportunities for children to express their uniqueness. There exists a paradox of wanting distinctiveness while at the same time gravitating toward conformity.

Children who have difficulty with individuality take little pride in their appearance or accomplishments. They often speak negatively about themselves and conform to peers' wishes without considering their own desires. They may show off when it is not appropriate and interact with people in a way that is not authentic, spontaneous, or creative.

A sense of uniqueness can be enhanced in church settings by encouraging youth to express their own ideas and share their own talents. Since preadolescents are concerned with autonomy, it is important to take the time to listen to their ideas and opinions and respect their visions. The opportunity to share opinions, concerns, and talents is especially important during these years.

Encouraging the Ability to Make Choices

A sense of power is important to the development of self-esteem (Coopersmith, 1967). The preadolescent has a need to make decisions and solve problems. The ability to maintain and develop a certain amount of control over the environment is important to the development of healthy self-esteem. Assumption of responsibility increases during preadolescence when individuals take on more roles which include everything from baby-sitting to choosing social groups and friends.

Preadolescents who have difficulty with power and choices may act helpless or be excessively stubborn or demanding. Learning emotional control is especially important during this period. Youth ministers can help through modeling, listening, and setting realistic expectations in which the individual is given the opportunity to make choices. This is often accomplished through child-centered activities rather than adult-directed processes (Clark, Clemes, and Bean, 1980).

The ability to make appropriate choices increases over time. Young children lack the ability to make difficult, responsible choices. The preadolescent can begin to accept more power over his actions if youth ministers will encourage personal responsibility and help children by making them more aware of their decision making abilities. Church programs can increase personal responsibility in youth if there is an increased opportunity to share talents and participate in decision-making processes of the youth group. A sense of power will be influenced by the nature and dynamics of the church peer group in which the preadolescent is functioning. If the preadolescent is with younger children, there may be more opportunities for a leadership role. If the pre-teen is with the youth group, there may be less chance for choices due to the age and social nature of the group. There is no doubt, though, that active involvement of the preadolescent will enhance his or her power and decision-making abilities.

Providing Good Models

The fourth requirement of self-esteem is the presence of good models. There are three types of models which influence the preadolescent. These include human models, philosophical models, and operational models. Human models include parents, teachers, church workers, and peers who make an impact. The peer group is now serving as the primary role model for the child since the shift at ten to twelve years is from adults to the peer group. Philosophical models include religion and family philosophy which tend to solidify in adolescence. Operational models are processes of decision making. The preadolescent is faced with the question, "How do I go about solving this problem?" since he now has more power and opportunities to choose. Operational models are influenced by the preadolescent's human models.

Preadolescents who have poor role models often have trouble with moral decisions. They are often confused as to how to work with others and may be easily influenced and uncertain in social situations. They may also avoid traditional social settings.

The youth minister's role is partly one of modeling. Because of this role, inadequate philosophical and operational models of the preadolescent may be counteracted by the youth worker. The preadolescent may be open for experiences in religion and decision making and is often affected by the moral development of a significant adult within the church. The adult can help the preadolescent understand what the adult believes. The importance of open communication and modeling acceptance and caring cannot be overstated.

Becoming an exemplary model for preadolescents requires an awareness of the major concerns which face preadolescents and adolescents (see Benson, Williams, and Johnson, 1987). Strommen (1988) found self-esteem, family well-being, welfare of people, personal advantage, and personal faith to be areas of great concern to young people. From his research he describes five cries of youth which include 1) the cry of self-hatred, 2) the cry of psychological orphans, 3) the cry of social concern, 4) the cry of the prejudiced, and 5) the cry of the joyous. The last three cries are especially characteristic of adolescence. However, the first two cries, that of self-hatred and psychological orphans, are deeply part of the preadolescent's experience and deserve detailed consideration.

The cry of self-hatred. Strommen contends that there are few sufferings as difficult as feelings of inadequacy and worthlessness. He lists three self-relational characteristics associated with low self-esteem. These are personal faults, lack of self-confidence, and low estimate of worth. What causes self-hatred in the preadolescent? There are both internal and external variables which interact to produce this self-hatred.

The typology of the preadolescent as well as environmental factors work together to place the preadolescent at risk for self-hatred and low self-esteem. The introverted child is at risk because North American culture values gregarious, extroverted youth. Robert Johnson (1988) has reported that the United States is an "extroverted-thinking" culture. The introverted preadolescent may have difficulty with adults, but more importantly, he or she may have problems with peers.

External sources which influence self-hatred include the family, the school, and the peer group. Elkind (1981) has documented the effects of the family on the middle school child. Several factors he cites include the adultification of children and the eroding of family values. The preadolescent is treated more and more like a little adult, noticeable in the clothing children wear and in the information children acquire. Elkind states that preadolescents and younger children have no distinction in their dress from adults. More importantly, adults in disjointed families are confiding more and more in their preadolescents about issues that are beyond their level of maturity. For example, a divorced mother may make the preadolescent son the "man of the house" and then confide in him about her personal problems such as finances and dating. Salary information and family disgraces are no longer protected from children and this overwhelming responsibility of dealing with adult information is often more than the child can handle. The result is often a feeling of responsibility over variables beyond their control. Such information is difficult for the preadolescent to process when they already must deal with their own personal issues such as puberty, school, and peer pressures.

Self-hatred, though, is not always the result of hurrying children into adulthood. It is sometimes the product of not allowing them to grow up. In some cases, overprotection contributes to self-hatred. Just as giving the preadolescent too much responsibility before he is ready can do damage, so can not giving him enough. Parents who are overprotective often try to live their lives through their children. The preadolescent is unconsciously (or consciously) required to remain a helpless child so that the parent will feel needed and useful. The preadolescent's task is to become gradually more and more independent from the parents and other adults and attempts to keep him from this are also associated with self-hatred.

The school is another external source of self-hatred. Manning and Manning (1981) have documented what they refer to as the school's six assaults on children. These include a "heavy emphasis on testing, homogeneous grouping, the use of a large number of worksheets, heavy drill, and long periods of sitting and listening" (Aldridge, 1989; p. 4). Children usually begin to change classes in middle school or junior high school and feelings of loneliness and helplessness can creep in at this time due to a loss of a stable reference point or location. School systems are in a quandry as to how to serve preadolescents. Whether the concept of the middle school (grades six-eight) or the junior high school (grades seven-nine) is best suited for preadolescents is still an unanswered question (Hetherington and Parke, 1986). It seems that no one knows the best structure for teaching preadolescents but it is certain that most schools create a tremendous amount of stress on this age group.

Peer competition is now the rule instead of the exception in middle and junior high schools. The preadolescent self-esteem is highly influenced by competition. What used to be reserved for senior high schools is now very much a part of the middle school. All types of competitive sports, beauty pageants, and proms push the preadolescent into the adolescent world, often before he or she is developmentally ready. The physical changes and differences of preadolescent development are enough with which to cope, without magnifying these differences in academic, athletic, and social settings. The preadolescent who exhibits the cry of self-hatred is especially concerned about how he is accepted by his peers. The overemphasis on competition can undermine acceptance by the peer group and a feeling of connectedness between them.

The cry of psychological orphans. The second cry of youth rises from the need to have a stable home life which is supportive, accepting, and loving in which people care for one another (Strommen, 1988). This need is often undermined by significant changes in the family structure.

The family system has changed so drastically in the past thirty years that there has been a sharp increase in the number of psychological orphans. Before 1969, most women with children at the preadolescent age spent their time at home. As late as 1940, only one-tenth of mothers worked outside the home. Today, well over one-half of mothers with preadolescents are in the work force. Working mothers do not necessarily create psychological orphans, but the stress placed on the family contributes to the preadolescent's sense of being alone. Many other factors such as divorce and parental job mobility are issues which can contribute to a preadolescent's feeling of abandonment.

Institutions such as the school and church are left with responsibilities for preadolescents which were previously the territory of the family. Psychological abandonment in the family places more and more responsibility on other social institutions to facilitate spiritual and moral development. The youth minister may find the large majority of the preadolescents in a state of psychological abandonment. The role of providing psychological, moral, and emotional support for preadolescents is the challenge of the church workers whether they want it or not.

What can be done to help the preadolescent achieve healthy self-esteem at a time when sociological factors are creating preadolescents with the cry of self-hatred and the cry of psychological orphans? O'Brien (1989) suggests that preadolescents can be taught to build their own self-esteem which is not dependent on someone else saying "You are an OKAY person. You can achieve on your own. You can be successful" (p. 36). She further cites a recent survey reporting that 93 percent of preadolescents know when they feel good about themselves. Since preadolescents are aware of their self-esteem, they can be taught to manage positive self-esteem by identifying what they have done, what skills it took and how they felt when achieving success.

Conclusions and Suggestions

What conclusions can be made about preadolescence and how church workers and youth ministers can help the preadolescent? From the research reported, fifteen conclusions can be made about the pre-teen years from ten to twelve. Suggestions for working with preadolescents are made for each of the fifteen conclusions provided.

1. *The preadolescent is neither a child nor an adolescent. Unique developmental issues and problems exist during this period* (Kohen-Raz, 1971).
Suggestions:
   a. Understand that the preadolescent may want to be a child one day and adult the next. Accept the fact that they are in a developmental transition.
   b. Help parents understand that this is a difficult age. Virtually every area of development is in turmoil. Changes are happening rapidly in the social, physical, cognitive, moral, and spiritual domains.
   c. Listen to the preadolescent as he expresses his frustration over all of these changes.

2. *The peer group is becoming more and more important* (Damon, 1983).
Suggestions:
   a. Understand the importance the preadolescent places on looking good in front of the peer group.
   b. Avoid unnecessary comparisons and competitions.
   c. Facilitate peer discussions and keep the highest standards by modeling respect for each pre-teen group member.

3. *The peer group preference is same-sex grouping in early preadolescence but by the end of preadolescence most individuals prefer cross-sex grouping* (Vander Zanden, 1989).
Suggestions:
   a. Make adjustments in group activities as the interests of preadolescents shift.
   b. Adjust activities when the social situation becomes awkward.
   c. Keep in mind that the girls go through puberty earlier than boys. Girls may be physically more mature at this age. Avoid situations that accentuate such differences.

4. *Industry and identity are both issues for the preadolescent* (Ritcher, 1982).
Suggestions:
   a. Help preadolescents develop a sense of accomplishment by helping them achieve reasonable and appropriate goals.
   b. Design activities in which the preadolescent is challenged to learn more about himself and his abilities.

5. *Physical changes influence self-esteem and socialization* (Santrock and Yussen, 1984).
Suggestions:
   a. Try to find individual gifts and talents for the pre-teen to share. If a preadolescent is given the opportunity to demonstrate his strengths, this may off-set some of the negative feedback experienced from peers during this ugly duckling period.

b. Provide experiences in which physical development is played down and spiritual growth is emphasized, such as helping each individual discover his or her spiritual gifts.

6. *The preadolescent's thinking is qualitatively different from adults* (Wadsworth, 1990).

Suggestions:

a. Recognize that the preadolescent is just beginning to understand historical time and geographic space in the adult sense. Plan activities which begin to address these two issues with regard to biblical concepts.

b. Understand that the preadolescent may not be able to think in abstractions like adolescents. Provide concrete examples and situations for them.

c. Search for experiences which will be developmentally appropriate.

7. *Individual talents and types of intelligence exist during this period* (Gardner, 1983).

Suggestions:

a. Provide varied experiences which may actualize an individual's specific type of intelligence.

b. Actively seek specific talents in preadolescents.

c. Find ways to help the preadolescent express individual talent.

8. *Preadolescent moral development is influenced by observational learning* (Bandura, 1986).

Suggestions:

a. Be aware of what types of observations the preadolescent is making.

b. Provide a good role model of moral development.

c. Remember that the preadolescent is being influenced more and more by his peers.

9. *Prosocial and altruistic behaviors are situational* (Vander Zanden, 1989).

Suggestions:

a. Plan social activities in which cooperation and caring are part of the process.

b. Plan group projects that can only be completed through cooperation.

c. Develop multi-age group activities for the preadolescent. Design these projects in such a way that the pre-teen will have to help and be helped.

10. *The preadolescent is capable of seeing another person's perspective and taking the other person's role* (Selman, 1976).

Suggestions:

a. Develop problem-solving activities in which the preadolescent has to take the role of another person.

b. Plan a series of role-playing activities so that the individual can consider what others might think or do in specific situations.

11. *Synthetic-conventional faith is characteristic of the preadolescent period* (Fowler, 1986).

Suggestions:

a. Provide opportunities to explore commitments, relationships, and values.

b. Help the preadolescent explore identity and interiority by making opportunities for cooperative learning and discussion.

c. Develop programs in which the preadolescent participates in and explores various roles.

12. *Self-esteem develops out of a sense of both belonging and individuality* (Aldridge, 1989).

Suggestions:

a. Use caution in placing the preadolescent in group activities. Acceptance into the group is a key issue in self-esteem and the pre-teen might not fit into either the children's or the adolescent's group.

b. Find outlets for the pre-teen to both explore and share interests and ideas.

13. *Self-esteem in the preadolescent is dependent on human, philosophical, and operational models* (Clark, Clemes, and Bean, 1980).

Suggestions:

a. Provide authentic adult role models for preadolescents while remembering that the peer group also serves as human models.

b. Present religious information at a level at which more preadolescents can grasp, yet do not oversimplify or become condescending.

c. Model problem-solving through real life experiences as well as hypothetical dilemmas.

14. *Preadolescents are not only aware of their self-esteem, but they are able to monitor it* (Glenn and Nelson, 1989; O'Brien, 1990).

Suggestions:

a. Help preadolescents identify when they feel good about themselves.

b. Explore with pre-teens what makes them feel good about themselves.

c. Discuss the process and skills involved in doing things which provide a feeling of self-worth.

15. *The cries of self-hatred and psychological orphans relate to pre-teens as well as adolescents* (Strommen, 1988).

Suggestions:

a. Identify with pre-teens the variables within the family, school, church and peer group which contribute to feelings of self-hatred.

b. Explore with preadolescents the intrapsychic conflicts which influence self-hatred individually.

c. Discuss the changing roles of families and institutions (such as school and church).

d. Help preadolescents identify times and situations when they feel abandoned.

e. Present possible alternatives to coping with feelings of abandonment.

Summary

The preadolescent period is characterized by storm and stress which is experienced by both the pre-teen and those who work with him. Virtually every area of development is in transition. Further, the various areas of development interact and influence each other. Physical changes affect social and self-esteem development while cognitive changes impact moral development. Where the preadolescent fits in is a major concern for adults. Schools, churches, and social organizations have not found the "ideal place" for the pre-teen. Wherever the preadolescent is placed, a major consideration is enhancing self-esteem.

REFERENCES

Aldridge, J. (1988). How to build self-esteem in children. *Exploring 2 for Leaders, 18*, 4-5.

Aldridge, J. (1989). Helping children build self-esteem. *Day Care and Early Education, 17*, 4-7.

Baldwin, B. (1986). Puberty and parents: Understanding your early adolescent. *Pace, 13*, 15-19.

Bandura, A. (1986). *Social foundations of thought and action: A social cognitive theory.* Englewood Cliffs, N.J.: Prentice Hall.

Bandura, A., Ross, D., and Ross, S. (1963). Imitation of film-mediated aggressive models. *Journal of Abnormal and Social Psychology, 66*, 3-11.

Benson, P., Williams, D., and Johnson, A. (1987). *The quicksilver years.* San Francisco: Harper & Row.

Bukowski, W., and Newcomb, A. (1985). Variability in peer groups perceptions: Support for the "controversial" sociometric classification group. *Developmental Psychology, 21*, 1032-1038.

Campbell, J. (1989). *This business of the gods . . . In conversation with Fraser Boa.* Caledon East, Ontario, Canada: Windrose Films.

Carbo, M. (1987). Reading styles research: 'What works' isn't always phonics. *Phi Delta Kappan, 68*, 431-435.

Clark, A., Clemes, H., and Bean, R. (1980). *How to raise teenagers' self-esteem.* San Jose, Calif.: Enrich.

Comer, J. (1989). What's normal? *Parents, 64*, 132.

Coopersmith, S. (1967). *The antecedents of self-esteem.* San Francisco: Freeman.

Damon, W. (1983). *Social and personality development.* New York: W. W. Norton.

Elkind, D. (1961). Children's discovery of the conservation of mass, weight, and volume: Piaget replication study II. *Journal of Genetic Psychology, 98*, 219-227.

Elkind, D. (1981). *The hurried child.* Reading, Mass.: Addison-Wesley.

Erikson, E. (1968). *Identity: Youth and crisis.* New York: W. W. Norton.

Erikson, E. (1980). *Identity and the life cycle.* New York: W. W. Norton.

Faust, M. (1960). Developmental maturity as a determinant in prestige of adolescent girls. *Child Development, 31*, 173-186.

Faust, M. (1977). Somatic development of adolescent girls. *Monographs of the Society for Research in Child Development, 42* (1, Serial No. 169).

Fowler, J. (1986). Faith and the structuring of meaning. In C. Dykstra and S. Parks (Eds.), *Faith development and Fowler* (pp. 15-42). Birmingham, Ala.: Religious Education Press.

Ganiere, D., and Enright, R. (1989). Exploring three approaches to identity development. *Journal of Youth and Adolescence, 18*, 283-295.

Gardner, H. (1983). *Frames of mind: The theory of multiple intelligences.* New York: Basic Books.

Gilligan, C. (1982). Why should a woman be more like a man? *Psychology Today, 16*, 68-77.

Ginsburg, H., and Opper, S. (1979). *Piaget's theory of intellectual development* (2nd ed.). Englewood Cliffs, N.J.: Prentice Hall.

Glenn, H., and Nelson, J. (1989). *Raising self-reliant children in a self-indulgent world.* New York: St. Martin's Press.

Goldman, R. (1964). *Religious thinking from childhood to adolescence.* New York: Seabury.

Hetherington, E., and Parke, R. (1986). *Child psychology: A contemporary viewpoint* (3rd ed.). New York: McGraw-Hill.

Hurlock, E. (1980). *Developmental psychology* (5th ed.). New York: McGraw-Hill.

Johnson, R. (1988, May). *Healing the wounded feeling function.* Paper presented at the meeting of the Atlanta Jung Society, Atlanta, Ga.

Jung, C. (1954). *The development of personality: Papers on child psychology, education, and related subjects.* Princeton, N.J.: Princeton University Press.

Kamii, C. (1985). *Young children reinvent arithmetic: Implications of Piaget's theory.* New York: Teachers College Press.

Kitano, M., and Kirby, D. (1986). *Gifted education: A comprehensive view.* Boston: Little, Brown.

Kohen-Raz, R. (1971). *The child from 9 to 13: Psychology and psychopathology.* Chicago: Aldine-Atherton.

Kohlberg, L. (1984). *Essays on moral development. Vol. 2, The psychology of moral development.* San Francisco: Harper & Row.

Lerner, R., and Lerner, J. (1977). Effects of age, sex, and physical attractiveness on child-peer relations, academic performance, and elementary school adjustment. *Developmental Psychology, 13*, 585-590.

Manning, M., & Manning, G. (1981). The school's assault on childhood. *Childhood Education, 57*, 84-87.

Mead, G. (1934). *Mind, self, and society.* Chicago: University of Chicago Press.

Miller, K. (1976). *The relationship of stages of development in children's moral and religious development.* Unpublished doctoral dissertation, Arizona State University.

Minuchin, P. (1977). *The middle years of childhood.* Monterey, California: Brooks/Cole.

O'Brien, S. (1989). How can I help my preadolescent? *Childhood Education, 66*, 35-36.

O'Brien, S. (1990). The critical years: Ages 10-12. *Childhood Education, 66*, 163-164.

Ratcliff, D. (1987). Teaching the Bible developmentally. *Christian Education Journal, 7* (2), 21-32.

Richter, D. (1982). A bibliographical survey of youth and youth ministry. In D. Wyckoff and D. Richter (Eds.), *Religious education ministry with youth* (pp. 1-53). Birmingham, Ala.: Religious Education Press.

Santrock, J., and Yussen, S. (1984). *Children and adolescents: A developmental perspective.* Dubuque, Iowa: Wm. C. Brown.

Selman, R. (1976). Social-cognitive understanding. In T. Lickona (Ed.), *Moral development and behavior: Theory, research, and social issues.* New York: Holt, Rinehart and Winston.

Shaffer, D. (1985). *Developmental psychology: Theory, research, and applications.* Monterey, California: Brooks/Cole.

Sheldon, W. (1940). The varieties of human physique. New York: Harper.

Staffieri, J. (1972). Body build and behavioral expectancies in young females. *Developmental Psychology, 6*, 125-127.

Stager, S., and Burke, P. (1982). A reexamination of body build stereotypes. *Journal of Research in Personality, 16*, 435-446.

Stephan, C., and Langlois, J. (1984). Baby beautiful: Adult attributions of infant competence as a function of infant attractiveness. *Child Development, 55,* 576-585.

Strommen, M. (1988). *Five cries of youth* (2nd. ed.). San Francisco: Harper & Row.

Sund, R. (1976). *Piaget for educators: A multimedia program.*Columbus, Ohio: Charles E. Merrill.

Vander Zanden, J. (1989). *Human development* (4th ed.). New York: Random House.

Wadsworth, B. (1990). *Piaget's theory of cognitive and affective development* (4th ed.). New York: Longman.

Zacharias, L., Rand, W., and Wurtman, R. (1976). A prospective study of sexual development and growth in American girls: The statistics of menarche. *Obstetrical and Gynecological Survey, 31,* 325-337.

Chapter Five

Adolescents and Religion

KENNETH E. HYDE

Adolescence is a time of making personal choices. The constraints of childhood are relinquished now that they are more responsible for their behavior, and adult life draws near with its freedom of choice. This is evident in terms of religion; for some adolescents, belief develops into a committed faith, for others it fades and dies, while for some it may remain dormant (Williams, 1989) as a seed waiting for the right conditions to stimulate germination. In this process of growing into or out of belief there are many factors. The beliefs acquired in childhood are not adequate for the critical examination to which they must now be subjected; will prior beliefs be reaffirmed or will doubts give rise to guilt or to the rejection of belief? Those to whom adolescents may turn for help need to understand the manner in which religious beliefs develop. Throughout the years of childhood adolescents have been subject to parental influence; now the effects of that influence become clear. Many may for a time reject some of their parents' wishes but tend to retain what they perceive to be the fundamental values of their homes. The example of parents and their agreement, or lack of it, on religious issues now bears fruit. Consistency in talking about beliefs and living them out is a strong influence when the atmosphere of the home is one of acceptance and of warmth. Adolescents need to find the same acceptance and support in their congregations, and belief is reinforced when the same attitudes are found in parochial schools.

Bealer and Willets (1967) commented that even though there was much research about the religious interests of college students, there was relatively little about adolescents. The existing studies were unsystematic and often lacked an adequate definition of the religiousness they set out to study; many had failed to distinguish between the different dimensions of religion.They took Glock and Stark's (1965) five dimensions of religion as a model and summarized the findings of more than forty studies. On the ritualistic dimension, a number of studies indicated a high level of church attendance and daily prayer. For the experiential dimension, most adolescents were concerned about religion but were unsure about faith. Many professed belief in God, but few felt close to God. On the ideological dimension, almost all accepted doctrine in general terms, or at the most expressed some doubts about it. The intellectual dimension—knowledge about dogma, doctrine, and history—had few studies, but factual knowledge of the Bible among adolescents was low. The consequential dimension—the effect of religion on behavior—was poorly researched. Most American adolescents embraced a traditional belief system with a reasonable degree of participation; the level of religious knowledge was low, but interest was quite high, even though the development of this into faith was not typical. Adolescents were reluctant to deny the supernatural, yet unwilling to commit themselves firmly, so that their religious position was one of hedging. Adolescents would not risk social rejection by making their doubts public. However, some held strong religious commitments and acted on them.

More than twenty years later the situation is similar, although information about adolescent religion has been filled out by other studies. When those from outside America are considered, cultural differences must be kept in mind; some continental studies are of adolescents within particular Catholic cultures, and European research is about more secular societies than the United States. There can be substantial variations among Protestant, Catholic, and Jewish believers, and different people believe in very different kinds of God (Piazza and Glock, 1979). Adolescents show a similar variety.

First, we will consider the findings which more recent research has added to this profile and then attempt to explore the roots of religion in adolescence. The consequential dimension—the effect of religion on moral thinking and behavior—is dealt with in chapter seven.

Religious Behavior

Religious behavior is one of the most important indicators of an individual's religion. Regular attendance at a church or synagogue is a mark of commitment, the more so when it is accompanied by a habit of private personal prayer. Yet attendance may arise from quite different motivations; one person attends because of deep religious needs which are only satisfied in corporate worship, while another attends because it is the pleasant meeting-place of a group of friends lacking deep religious conviction. Religious orientations have been described in a number of ways—committed or consensual, intrinsic or extrinsic, means, end, or quest (Hyde, 1990). This is a reminder that behavior is not the sole indicator of religion, since it does not disclose its motivation.

Adolescent lifestyles are related to their religious commitment. They can be seen as complex symbols which have to do with an individual's identity. In many of the new religious movements there are striking stylistic affinities, from clothing to living arrangements, which distinguish the groups from the rest of society; the weakest groups lack such identifying lifestyles. The authority of tradition, of law, or of a charismatic personality is being overtaken by taste as the hallmark of personal choice. Religiousness can be just one choice of personal taste, but, alternatively, it can give direction to all choices (Miller, 1981). In Canada most adolescents value highly friendship, love, freedom, and honesty, and relationships and music are very important. Most claim to believe in God, but only a quarter attend church with any regularity, even though they hold positive views about organized religion (Ban, 1986).

Studies of adolescent church attendance need to be related to the pattern of adult attendance, which has many variations. A comparison of church attendance over a period of thirty years showed that each of five groups defined by the decade in which they were born had its own characteristic pattern, which changed with age (Wingrove and Alston, 1974). Since each generation establishes its own pattern, children's church attendance follows at first the pattern of their parents; in adolescence fresh habits are formed, possibly starting a new trend. At any one time there are also persistent regional differences. Even so, adult church attendance in the United States has shown a steady increase over a long period. In their examination of statistics and estimates for American church membership, Finker and Stark (1986) gave the percentage of population regularly attending church as follows:

Year	1850	1860	1870	1890	1906	1916	1926	1952	1980
Rate of attendance	34%	37	35	45	51	53	58	59	62

Church attendance is erratic among adolescents, with no consistent age change. Williams' (1989) review showed from extensive surveys that the church attendance of more than ten thousand pupils had markedly declined between twelve and sixteen. The attendance and interest of high-school seniors had increased a little from 1978 to 1980 but then declined, so that 35 percent reported weekly attendance. A Gallup poll indicated that two-thirds claimed membership of a church or synagogue, and of them 40 percent attended church the previous week—52 percent Protestant and 30 percent Catholic; there was only a small sex difference, but many more blacks (68 percent) than whites (49 percent) attended. Attendance was greater in the South than elsewhere, and lowest in central cities (Gallup and Jones, 1989).

The churches with a formal youth program gain increased support; girls attend slightly more than boys at every age. Adolescent boys with older brothers exhibit lower church-attendance rates, and those with older sisters the highest rate (De Bord, 1969). There is not a great difference in religious behavior between Lutheran adolescents and adults, but adolescents are the most heterogeneous in beliefs, attitudes, and lifestyle (Johnson, Brekke, Strommen, and Underwager, 1974). Affluent young adults show low levels of church involvement, and white-collar adolescents give low scores on religiousness, with a growing loss of interest among Protestants (Nelsen and Potvin, 1980). Yet those from white-collar backgrounds are a little more likely to attend church than the others (Gallup and Jones, 1989). Religious practices and orthodoxy are both affected by age and denominational allegiance. The decline in religiousness in adolescence is a complex process (Sloane and Potvin, 1983). Attending church at least once a month is associated with regular private prayer and the satisfactory development of religious concepts; in turn these are strongly associated with positive religious attitudes and behavior. Year by year, religious learning only occurs among church-attending adolescents (Hyde, 1963, 1965).

Between 1964 and 1974 the religious involvement of black and white high-school adolescents declined, particularly among boys (Dickinson, 1976). By 1979, some reversal was seen, especially among boys. The smaller decline recorded for girls still continued to some extent, so that the difference between the sexes had narrowed (Dickinson, 1982). The frequency of private prayer—an index of religiousness outside the church—showed a general decrease; this was true also of parents, who had a strong influence on their children's prayer habits (Morgan, 1981).

Attitudes to Religion

It is necessary to distinguish between the popular phrase "religious attitude" and the psychometric term attitude to religion, which measures the extent of an individual's feelings about religion. The technique of constructing reliable attitude scales has for a long time been a favorite activity of many social psychologists. Their popularity is due to the ease with which they are used—respondents have only to mark a number of statements, indicating the extent to which they agree or disagree with them. They have been used over a broad field of interests, although there is still no firm consensus about what they measure, nor how a professed attitude is related to actual behavior. An attitude to religion scale measures an emotional reaction to particular religious concepts. Hepburn (1971) complained that there was a dearth of information about the development of religious attitudes in adolescence, which he regarded as one of the least researched areas of religious life. He found there is a high level of interest in religion among American adolescents, but some studies have shown that those who are more intelligent begin to question religious belief.

While such scales have been widely used with college students, their use with adolescents has been almost entirely British. There is convergence from many of these results, spread over almost fifty years, but care is needed in applying them to the American situation, where a much larger proportion of adolescents are likely to show positive attitudes. The description of attitude development and change appears to be a universal one, but the extent to which positive attitudes are found varies considerably in different societies, even in the same country. Nearly all the English studies show that younger children display more positive attitudes to religion than older children, and girls score more highly than boys. Age brings doubt and a more critical attitude. There is no peak age for conversion. Several studies report a significant relationship between intelligence and attitude to religion scores. Church attendance has a significant relationship with these scores, and there is a strong relationship between the attitude scores of children and the religious behavior of their parents. Church attendance, the maintenance of favorable religious attitudes, and the growth of religious understanding go hand in hand. Apathy rather than hostility is frequently reported, yet with a latent interest in religious issues but not in religious institutions. Stricter moral codes are related to conventional religiousness but not a compassionate attitude. Regional differences persist in England but are much more marked between England and Ireland. There are wide differences in pupils' attitudes in apparently similar schools, in single sex schools and coeducational schools, and between state schools and some church schools (Hyde, 1990).

There is no difference between attitude scores of English youth club members still at school and those who have left. Church youth club scores are similar to others. Prayer, which is favored by most members, is practiced by few and is strongly associated with belief in God, but not in the divinity of Jesus. The Bible is highly regarded, but for most it holds no personal significance. Only a minority read it because it gives them strength; most find no dynamic quality in it—girls no more than boys. Most believe in a future life, and many have an orthodox belief in Jesus Christ; this is significantly associated with regular church attendance and other areas of religious belief. Doubt is more prevalent among boys than girls (Kesteven, 1967). Pupils in religion classes in West German schools appear hostile to the church, but really they are indifferent to it. Despite this, it is possible to interest them in religion (Miller, 1977).

A substantial English study of attitude to Christianity has been undertaken by Francis (1976), who has given a number of accounts of this extensive project (e.g., Francis, 1977, 1978a,b, 1980a,b,c, 1984a; Francis, Wesley, and Rust, 1978; Kay and Francis, 1983). His objective was to secure accurate information about the Christian development of children, and variations of this development between different groups of children. His results indicate a steady decline in attitude to religion scores between the ages of eight and fifteen. No age is of special significance in this change, but there seems to be a growing disenchantment with Christianity, and a more hostile attitude is found among fifteen-year-olds. On attitude, involvement, and behavior, girls score higher than boys; involvement declines in the same way as attitude, but religious behavior shows some increase up to eleven, when it starts to decline. Religious behavior is the most powerful predictor of attitude to religion scores. Parents and Catholic schools exert a significant influence. Improvement in attitude to religion requires religious behavior to be fostered, since maintenance of favorable attitudes is associated with the influence of the church.

In an eight-year study of pupils' attitudes to Christianity (Francis, 1978b) these trends were confirmed but with a marked increase of alienation from Christianity at about fourteen rather than fifteen. A still further decline in these attitude scores was found in further replications in 1982 (Francis 1984a, b) and in 1986 (Francis, 1989).

While much of this research records a decline in attitude to religion with increasing age, a decline which becomes greater with the passing of time, very little attention has been given to enhancing attitudes. A very experienced teacher once told the author that when groups of older adolescents were able to discuss religious issues at length with recognized exponents of Christianity, they adopted critical stances, whereas when confronted with critics of Christianity, they adopted believing stances. The critics were better evangelists than fervent believers, who inoculated their audience against belief. Such an insight is supported by Batson's (1975) study; having persuaded a church group of students to affirm their belief in the divinity of Jesus, he produced evidence which denied the resurrection and which identified leading churchmen who had discarded their faith. Some students dismissed the evidence, but the belief of those who accepted it was intensified.

Religious Experience

There is a great deal of confusion regarding what is variously described as religious experience, intense religious experience, mystical experience, ecstasy, peak experience, nature experience, and transcendental experience. Some people regard such experiences as profoundly religious, but others see them as having no religious significance. For some, they are a one time experience, but for others they may continue over a long period of time, as in the earlier life of the poet Wordsworth. They are usually distinct from a conversion experience, which still is the subject of psychological study, though to a less extent than formerly. Charismatics would certainly regard glossolalia—speaking in tongues—as an important religious experience. Research has been mainly of two styles; either accounts of such experiences from many individuals are studied, or experiments are made to investigate what psychological states are associated with them. Lukoff and Lu (1988) discussed the problems of research into mystical experience in their review of its methods and results and the relationship between the findings of such qualitative and quantitative studies. The growing literature about this does not often distinguish particular characteristics of adolescence.

Young American adolescents feel close to God most frequently in church or synagogue, in times of solitude, anxiety, worry, prayer, and of moral action. Such experiences include an appreciation of divine intervention, or meditation bringing a heightened awareness, grief over bereavement, religious initiation, and experiences of direct communication. Girls have more of these religious experiences than boys, although boys report more church experience. The most intelligent are most likely to feel close to God in solitude. Religious experience is a significant part of their lives (Elkind and Elkind, 1963). Between seventeen to twenty-nine a third are likely to feel close to a powerful spiritual force (Thomas and Cooper, 1978), a finding confirmed by a recent Gallup poll (Gallup and Jones, 1989). Half the adolescents questioned said they had never experienced the feeling that they were in close contact with something holy or sacred, although half of these said they would like to have such an experience. Many who reported such an experience said it had made a lasting impression on their lives. A large proportion reported having experienced the beauty of nature in a deeply moving way, but only a third reported having had the feeling that they were in harmony with the universe (Glock and Wuthnow, 1979). Of those seventeen and older a third reported an intense spiritual experience and a quarter had undergone a "near-death" experience. There is a significant association between these two types of experience (Thomas, Cooper, and Suscovich, 1982).

A distinction can be made between normative religious experiences, such as conversion or an awakening to religious commitment, and nonnormative experiences, due to personal psychological factors. More than half the adolescents from some Baptist, Catholic, and Methodist churches reported many types of experience although few spoke of ecstatic or revelatory experiences. A salvation or inspiration experience was normative for those from Protestant churches, consistent with the expectations and encouragement of such groups. It was more frequent among girls and often occurred at eleven or twelve. Nonnormative experiences were diverse and could not be associated with particular styles of church involvement or personal relationships. They were more frequent among Catholics and were idiosyncratic and unpatterned. Cognitive ability was never associated with religious experience, nor was family influence predictive of it (Hoge and Smith, 1982).

In England, more than half of a group of older adolescents and students reported some kind of religious experience, girls more than boys. About three-quarters of them were religious. Nearly all those reporting transcendental experiences had attempted some creative art and were interested in poetry. A great variety of experiences was recorded. Most occurred after childhood; they were often associated with solitude, with evening or night, and with being outdoors in the country. Among the arts, music had considerable predominance in inducing such experiences. A great deal of what was described had to do with feelings of awe, joy, fear, enhancement, calm, trance, pleasure, melancholy, longing, and pain. They called their experiences religious or aesthetic or described them in some other way consistent with their basic beliefs (Paffard, 1970, 1973). In another group, more than half reported transcendental experiences; they were more likely to be creative, to spend time alone, to be religious, and to read poetry for pleasure. There was no difference between the sexes, but mental ability was significantly related to an increased likelihood of such experiences. Only 20 percent had an experience before eleven; more than half reported up to ten such experiences; many were alone when such experiences occurred; rather more reported they took place in the evening or night, and for most they occurred out of doors. They were best described as mysterious, lonely, serene, awesome, exciting, or frightening. While they could simply be a monumental event, for many they had been a means of either personal enrichment or personal transformation and conversion (Miles, 1983).

A similar diversity was found among the recollections of distant childhood experiences from English respondents of a wide age range. Parental influences had been prominent for many but for others entirely lacking. Some recalled words used in church and its rituals as a stimulus; for others, rituals were dull, to be endured as a duty, and ultimately to be rejected. A sense of identity was the hallmark of religious experience in some cases, or a sense of timelessness. An awareness of death proved to be momentous for some; with others a sense of morality and rightness was associated with the experience. For some these experiences were obviously intense; peak experiences seemed to be extreme instances of a capacity that was normally much more ordinary (Robinson, 1977). Children need to be taught to recognize such experiences in themselves and others and, even more, to cope with them (Robinson, 1971). The myths, legends, and sagas learned in childhood can be used for this purpose (Robinson, 1975). When Farmer (1988) interviewed adults about the religious experiences of their early childhood, many of them complained that the validity of their experiences had been destructively denied by their education. Involvement in imaginative activities was the primary means by which they can be interpreted. Early spiritual awareness is the beginning of a lifelong development.

Learning to understand life spiritually starts with nourishing the imaginative life, more particularly guiding the imagination into creative forms of activity. While this is not religious, it can be used to stimulate questions which are basically religious. Scholarship and theology are needed to keep Christian tradition alive, but they do not necessarily make any demands on the imagination (Robinson, 1982). The experiential element in religion is related to those arts which stimulate the imagination. Active involvement in social responsibility programs can lead to growth in religious awareness. Those who participate in religious activities tend to have greater religious awareness and theistic religious experiences. They tend to be satisfied with the language and beliefs of their church, to be less cynical about morality and less concerned with the materialistic values of the good life. Many adolescents who are unresponsive to established forms of religion show a positive interest in what are essentially religious questions, and nearly four-fifths of them say they have had an experience which could be described as mystical (Robinson and Jackson, 1987).

A third of the adolescent boys and half the girls in a Northern Ireland Protestant sample reported an experience of God. They described experiences of guidance and help, couched in terms of assurance, and spoke of a constant awareness of God's presence, rather than of moments of special illumination. Prayers about matters of great practical concern could be an occasion of experiencing God.

Others referred to a conversion experience. A minority gave examples of transcendental experiences—when climbing a mountain, at a scenic view, in a church building, or at a service of holy communion. The experience and its interpretation are so closely interwoven as to be virtually inseparable, and the claims to have direct experience of God suggest that religious experience is relatively common. Although more than half were regular church attenders, few had a sense of the church as a building or community mediating the presence of God; rather it was the place where the gospel was proclaimed. This theological framework provides the means of interpreting their experiences, and sheds light on a strong evangelical tradition (Greer, 1981a,b). When Catholics and Protestants were compared, marked differences between sexes and denominations were found (more girls than boys, more Catholics than Protestants). The high proportion of Catholic girls (64 percent) was striking. The most frequent experiences were again of guidance and help, followed by experiences of answered prayer, and then death, depression, and illness. Others described situations when this sense of presence became very real to them, as in solitude or in the celebration of the sacraments. Some experiences came from dreams, deliverances, or the papal visit. Catholic pupils were more inclined to report religious experiences although conversion experiences were not found among them (Greer, 1982).

Among Swedish children from nine to thirteen the most common factors producing a religious experience were distress at illness—their own or of someone close to them (more for girls than boys), misfortune, and loneliness, especially in the dark or in isolation. Few referred to worship, to nature, or to feelings of guilt. Their experiences were similar to those of adults. Their writing indicated a rich inner life with a strong sense of serenity, security and trust, longing for purity, receiving forgiveness and answers to prayer, a sense of thankfulness, joy and certainty and of the presence of God. A few had experienced a mystical sense of the presence of God. Conversion experiences were described by children belonging to churches emphasizing such experiences; they appeared to be serious, despite the children's limited ability to deal with the emotions that might arise (Klinberg, 1959). In a large Finnish group aged seven to twenty, 90 percent of those between nine and ten gave positive responses to questions about religious experiences, but only 55 percent of those aged fifteen or sixteen. A sense of God's nearness was associated with prayer, loneliness, fear, and emergencies (Tamminen, 1981).

There is much agreement between the various descriptions of the experiences in these accounts. They are associated with feelings of mystery, awe, joy, fear, peace, sadness, longing, pain, and ecstasy, and may be auditory or visionary. They are recognized to be sacred, pleasurable, exciting, or sensual. They bring enhancement, heightened perception and enlightenment, and tend to occur in solitude, in the evening or at night, outdoors in the country or in a church or synagogue. They tend to arise with particular states of mind—in times of anxiety, worry, prayer, and of moral action. Their subjects tend to be creative, to respond to poetry, to natural beauty, and to religion. They also may have negative elements associated with evil.

Religious Conversion

The religious experience designated conversion is not restricted to adolescence, but adolescence is frequently the time when some form of religious commitment takes place. Earlier studies were summarized by Argyle and Beit-Hallahmi (1975), and recently by Silverstein (1988). Once prolific, reports of conversion experience have more recently decreased. The debate about the age of conversion has been resolved by the recognition that better religious education brings an earlier commitment, and it is affected by adult expectations of children being converted. Inevitably a great range of conversion experiences have been recorded, both sudden and gradual. In consequence, it is not surprising that it has proved difficult to make satisfactory psychological theories about it. Gradual conversion is twice as frequent for American evangelicals and other Protestants, and even more frequent for Catholics (Gallup and Jones, 1989).

There is a distinction between sudden, gradual, and unconscious conversion. Sudden converts are religiously more conservative, are more authoritarian and show less personality control and intellectual efficiency. Sudden conversion has a strong emotional element; it is unexpected, without prior consideration of religious belief. Gradual conversion is a slower process in which particular aspects of religious belief are slowly adopted as the subjects change from rejecting religion to accepting it. Gradual converts are more conservative than the unconscious converts who have never rejected belief, but acquire it in the same way as other attitudes, from parents and peers, throughout the process of childhood development. Most of them hold similar beliefs to their mother or father (Scobie, 1973, 1975). Among five hundred adolescents, eleven had been converted during a period of several months without being subjected to intensive tactics. When compared with the unbelievers and former converts they showed that conversion remains unpredictable. No personality characteristics give a predisposition to conversion, nor is any radical personality change involved, although subsequently converts increase in self-sufficiency, introversion, optimism, dogmatism, and mental health. Rural adolescent converts show greater social distance and are more tough-minded and practical than their urban counterparts (Wilson, 1976).

Religious Beliefs

There is a sense in which everyone has a religious belief—even extreme atheists have religious beliefs and ideas of God which they reject, and they may be angered when informed that some religious people do not hold such beliefs either. No matter what the belief, or the strength with which it is held, it developed in the first place from more primitive, childish ideas, however they were originally acquired.

There is no lack of research into the religious beliefs of American adolescents. In a time of an apparent decline of belief, it is necessary to distinguish between a loss of belief and a gain in disbelief. Gallup poll data about belief in the after-life still shows little change over four decades (Gallup and Jones, 1989), although more recently fewer express doubts and more express disbelief (Hertel and Nelsen, 1974). Religious defection among youth is part of a larger syndrome of reaction against institutions and disaffiliation from society. Since the values and cultural styles which originate with youth spread throughout society, an increased defection from institutional religion can be expected in the future (Roof, 1978). What then are the religious beliefs of adolescents, and how do they vary?

They see religious belief as less important to themselves than to their parents, yet only one in five regard belief as unimportant. Its importance is stressed most in the South, more by young women and by above average ability students. Almost nine out of ten regard honesty, responsibility, and self-respect as very important. Three-quarters of the Protestants value hard work, as do two-thirds of the Catholics. Belief in the after-life still shows little change over four decades (Gallup and Jones, 1989), although fewer express doubts and more express disbelief (Hertel and Nelsen, 1974). However, the more that adolescents practice their faith, the higher their scores tend to be on a forgiveness scale, although forgiveness also develops with age (Enright, Santon, and Al-Mabuk, 1989).

Catholic adolescents have many misconceptions and erroneous ideas about the vocabulary of their catechism—words such as divinity, providence, or omnipotence. These are not replaced by more mature ideas with increasing age but rather the learning process ceases in the upper grades. Before learning is complete and at a time when increasing maturity might be expected to bring an improved rate of learning, it seems to stop for boys about thirteen and for girls after fifteen (McDowell, 1952). These findings were subsequently confirmed, although some improvement in learning continues for longer than previously recorded. Those attending public schools but receiving religious instruction in classes organized by the Confraternity of Christian Doctrine (CCD) do less well than those in parochial schools. There is a significant drop in scores at fourteen, suggesting a "crisis of faith" or a consequence of the style or content of teaching. Unlike boys, younger girls in CCD classes compare favorably with those in parochial schools in some aspects of learning, but their better performance grows less in the high-school years and little subsequent difference is found. It is still being taken for granted that many technical terms are comprehended (Cerney, 1965).

The strong religiousness of Catholics is well established, but variations have been recorded. Older American Catholic high-school students tend to be more liberal in their beliefs than the younger, and at every age girls are more liberal than boys. There is also some association between academic ability and liberal thinking, which continues through adult life (Coursey, 1971). Denominational labels

are not predictive of beliefs (Toch and Anderson, 1960). However, English adolescents who are Catholics differ in the prominence they give to Mary and to
sacramentalism; the Protestants are unsympathetic to the concept of Mary and
sacramentalism but give greater support to the concept of God as judge. The
Indwelling Spirit has the greatest prominence among the Quakers (Rees, 1967).

Over a three-year period an increase in orthodoxy was found in an American
group aged thirteen to seventeen, and although girls scored higher the boys
showed the greater increase, although it did not extend to a belief in God as a
heavenly father watching over and protecting people. A general belief in God is
apparently relatively stable over a long period of time (Zaenglein, Vener, and
Stewart, 1975). Many adolescents profess a religious faith and believe in the
necessity of religion in life, with a high level of church attendance (Jersild,
Brook, and Brook, 1978). There are inconsistencies of belief among Catholic
high-school girls; whether or not they believe in astrology or reincarnation their
religious beliefs do not differ, although believers in astrology are significantly
more likely to believe in reincarnation (Brink, 1978). Over the past decade there
has been an increase in the beliefs of the eighteen to twenty-one age group in the
supernatural. Three-quarters believe in angels, more of those who regularly
attend church than others. More than a half believe in astrology, and a half
believe in ESP; a third believe in reincarnation, more than a quarter in witchcraft,
and almost a quarter in ghosts and clairvoyance (Gallup and Jones, 1989). An
eleven-year longitudinal study showed that high-school students' religious attitudes had become more secular (Funk and Willits, 1987).

Hauser's (1981) review of relevant research indicates that many adolescents
suffer doubt. Despite the decline in church attendance with age, lapsed attenders
usually profess belief. The better educated tend to reject traditional beliefs, but
those in the churches are more involved. Cults tend to appeal to those who cling
to a childhood morality, seeking the security of complete, definitive answers. For
many adolescents, belief has to be literal and simplistic.

The beliefs criticized in adolescence are often those acquired early in life. The
traditional place given to religion is learned early in life and is associated with
attitudes of acquiescence to civil laws and political leaders, as well as with attitudes of support for the American political system. In adolescence these come
under review (Smidt, 1980). The theory that adolescent cognitive development
brings pressure upon religious belief was investigated by Ozorak (1987); existential questioning is often associated with change away from orthodox belief,
but it is not the cause of it. Beliefs of the strongly committed are strengthened by
questioning; those whose beliefs change have been affected by bereavement or
disappointment with religious rites or leaders.

Concepts of God

Christian groups of English adolescents regard God primarily in terms of
Jesus, favoring immanent rather than transcendent descriptions. Jewish adoles-

cents reject concepts of Jesus and Mary and regard God as father and judge in transcendent terms (Rees, 1967). French Catholic children under eleven think of God mainly as creator, or speak of his greatness, goodness, justice, strength, and beauty in an anthropomorphic manner. From eleven to fourteen God is seen in personal terms, such as father or sovereign; an emphasis on virtues indicates a refinement of what is still anthropomorphic thinking. As they grow older they think more of God in parental terms; at nine fewer than one in ten of the children think of God as father, but a quarter or more of boys aged thirteen and girls aged fifteen do so. This is followed by an interiorization when God is conceived subjectively as love or trust; anthropomorphic ideas disappear and the image of God becomes abstract and vague. The decline in thinking of God as creator continues through adolescence, but girls, unlike boys, continue to hold personalized ideas, linking Christ as Savior with attributes of greatness and goodness and an attitude of trust (Deconchy, 1964, 1967). English results are similar; little anthropomorphism is found at fourteen, but more abstract concepts do not develop very much either. Confusion between God and Jesus is still found. Few refer to an all-loving, all-knowing God, although more than half, greater with girls, regard God as beneficient, despite increasing skeptical comment from older boys. Those with greater religiousness tend to secure higher scores with age, but the scores of the less religious fall with age. Girls always tend to score more than boys (Shuttleworth, 1959).

Among young French Catholics the question "What does God mean to you?" yielded much relevant information. Ideas which become dominant in late adolescence are of God as great and powerful, as guide, and as an ideal, and fewer regard him as a confidant, as mysterious, and as source of life and light. Ideas of God as creator, as spirit, as merciful, and the seldom mentioned trinitarian ideas weaken in significance. Ideas of God as a loving father, eternal, just, and perfect weaken temporarily during adolescence but subsequently recover (Babin, 1963, 1965, 1967).

Babin also notes the tendency to see God in moral terms, and this brings a marked difference between the sexes. Girls, sensitive to personal relationships, report strong relationships with God, whom they regard as a protector, friend, and a consoling presence. Boys are more concerned with the nature and order of things and envisage God in terms of being and action, the great explanation of the world. Girls see God as one who watches over them, a view more static than that of the boys who regard God as a support in the warfare they have to wage, helping them reach their goals and strengthening them against temptation, a view which is more utilitarian and egocentric than that of the girls. One consequence of adolescent development is in the understanding of God as father; for many, father meant creator representing power or ruler; such an image contrasts with father representing love. It is noticeable that the love of God is perceived less among older adolescent boys but increasingly among older adolescent girls.

Some earlier English studies of adolescent ideas of God showed that material conceptions of God tend to disappear about the age of fourteen, except with those of lower intelligence. Even though references to a spiritual form can be found as early as eleven, it is not certain that using the word "spirit" indicates an abstract form even by fifteen. The idea of God as someone who is loving, caring, and possessing the attributes of an ideal parent is widespread (Bradbury 1947). After fifteen or sixteen few boys speak of God as a father; the idea of God as creator decreases with age, and similarly the idea that God is good. The belief that God hears prayer seems to be consistent, but older adolescents are less willing to believe that he speaks to them in prayer or answers prayer. Disbelief in the divinity of Christ arises about fifteen or sixteen. At eleven most believe in God; the movement away from belief with growing age is toward agnosticism and not to atheism (Bradshaw, 1949). At the start of adolescence, the dominant concepts of God are his power, his concern for the individual and his role as creator. Many boys of eleven or twelve are still at a realistic stage, but an individualistic stage is beginning with some of them, and its proportion increases with age. The disbelief encountered is usually of an intellectual origin. God's power, even if only conceived as that of a super-man, is the most prominent idea in boys, followed by the idea of God as concerned for individuals as their helper, guide or friend, and God as creator. The dominant concepts—of God as power, father, and creator give a sense of security, an object of authority, and meaning to the world. Many boys do not distinguish between God and the historical Jesus. In adolescence, as boys grow away from their parents, the sentiment for Jesus rather than God may become dominant (Dawes, 1954). Some associate a sense of awe with God, who then seems to be mysterious and fearful (Walker, 1950). When statements of beliefs about God are categorized, the cosmological is the least preferred by religious adolescents, and the most preferred by the nonreligious. All of them place the other categories in the same order—personal, epistemological, and social (Stevens, 1975).

Another English study showed a developing concept of God among secondary school children in regular contact with a church, girls securing higher scores than boys, but those no longer in touch with a church make no such progress. This learning is strongly associated with positive attitudes to religion and to the church. The decline of anthropomorphism with age is steady and not concentrated on any particular year. The acceptance of ideas of God as creator and as father show a marked reduction with age, except for church-going girls, nearly all of whom accept these ideas at every age tested. Similarly, age brings a reduced acceptance of orthodox ideas of Christology, except among the church-going girls (Hyde, 1965). When teaching biblical material with fifteen-year-olds, the method used makes no significant difference; the dominant factor in learning is church attendance, not school attended, denomination, or parental social status (Poole, 1986).

Mentally retarded adolescents' and adults' concepts of God are significantly affected by their mental age. Those who are older and more intelligent regard God as involved in human life to a greater extent than those who are more retarded, who, with a mental age from five to seven, think of God in universal rather than omnipotent terms, and as very much available to them. They attribute human characteristics to him more than the less retarded group (Stubblefield and Richard, 1965). Art work proves to be a more reliable means of expressing religious concepts for less able English adolescents; it shows a lower level of development than written work and provides a better indicator of real understanding (Hindley, 1965). Emotionally disturbed children, like normal children, dissociate God from punitive concepts; however, disturbed children associate God with authority figures and relate the meaning of God to their negative self-concepts (Price, 1970). Smith (1976) explored the God concepts of forty moderately retarded children and adolescents aged eleven to eighteen to assess the extent of their concepts of love and fear for mother, father, and God. God concepts were found to be similar to those of their mothers and fathers, with the maternal influence the stronger. Age had no effect since their mental development had been arrested at a preoperational stage. There was no evidence to indicate a relationship with religious affiliation or church attendance. In an institutionalized retarded teenage group, Peterson (1960) found the educable could remember Bible stories and repeat them and remember the moral of a story after it had been explained. The severely retarded gave immediate responses to joy, stories, and class activities but retained little, and the retention of religious concepts for many of them was not possible.

Much attention has been given to the extent that the image of God is modeled on that of parents. Different religious groups hold varying God concepts, and in an apparently homogeneous group a variety of views are to be found. A very religious group of Catholic girls had a concept of a wrathful, avenging, and punishing God, whereas their peers' concepts contained many attributes such as comforting, patient, faithful, or kind (Spilka, Armatas, and Nussbaum, 1964). The image of God is closely related to that of the preferred parent—usually the mother—but it also has some relation to the image of the parent of the opposite sex (Nelson, 1971). In primitive cultures a punitive image of God is found when the father is punitive, but a benevolent father is associated with a benevolent image of God (Spiro and D'Andrade, 1958).

A notable series of studies about parental figures and the representation of God has emanated from the Centre of Religious Psychology at the University of Louvain, with more than a dozen contributors (Vergote and Tamayo, 1981). They distinguish between the idealized figures of the father and the mother and the images of the subject's own actual parents. The real parents are significantly different from the symbolic parental figures; to some extent everyone shares in the recognizably different perceptions of an individual who says "I never had a real father" or "a real mother." It is claimed that these symbolic figures rather than the images of the actual parents influence the psychological development of children and in turn their representation of God (Vannesse and de Neuter, 1981). Some aspects of the adolescent image of God show stability and permanence; in particular, God is conceived as the absolute. While at every age in adolescence God is viewed as father, friend, helper, or benefactor; this idea is primarily held by those in mid-adolescence seeking some degree of help or support. The view of God as creator or as providence is also found in all age-groups, but its significance tends to decrease with age, and older groups think rather in such terms as "the meaning of life" or "the finality of life." Doubts and difficulties about religious faith are quite regular in later adolescence (Hutsebaut, 1972).

The characteristics of the parental figures themselves, on which the image of God is formed, vary from one culture to another, particularly those of the mother; this is due to cultural differences in the affective mother-child relationship (Tamayo, 1981). It is the culture, and not individual psychology, that determines which components of the parental figures are attributed to God (Vergote, 1981). The image of God of American adolescents is more paternal than that of the Belgian adolescents, but in the Americans it becomes more maternal with increasing age. All perceived parental qualities tend to correspond to the respondents' own sex (Vergote et al., 1969). Delinquents demonstrate marked deviations in their perception of parental roles and in particular, the absence of the law or authority factor, which affects their image of God (Tamayo and St-Arnaud, 1981). The three figures of father, mother, and God which have fully developed by adolescence do not change in any fundamental way in adult life (Tamayo and Cooke, 1981). Some support for these insights, and an indication of variations between individuals, is provided by Godin (1975), who found that responses of French-Canadian Catholic adolescents to his question, "To what are you referring when you say 'Word of God'"? could be classified into three groups. In the first, the dominant thought was of authority and competence, of giving direction, of being expert or father. The second group responded in terms of help, friendship, need, warmth, gentleness, brotherhood, intimacy, proximity, encounter and feeling, while the third group used such terms as abstraction, conscience, doctrine, idea, question, and thought.

An independent investigation of boys and girls aged seven to fifteen in Scotland showed the image of God is like the image of both the mother and the father. The image of God of the youngest children is very dependent on their parental images. This similarity of the images decreases with age, consistent with children first modeling God from their parents and later modifying their ideas. At all ages the images of boys and girls are significantly different, boys having a more primitive and judgmental image of God. The image of God is closer to that of the father than of the mother, in accord with the findings of Vergote and Tamayo (1981). There are wide individual variations; some children even show a negative relationship between parental and divine imagery (at least for one parent), which confirms that the quality of family life affects the image of God (Bulkeley, 1981). Since the image of the mother is so important in influencing children's images of God, Bulkeley considers it would be helpful to broaden religious language to express more adequately maternal aspects of God, setting psychological and theological perspectives side by side. Another study shows that the God concept is similar to that of the preferred parent; it is more complex than has been usually acknowledged, and it has a more cognitive surface structure and a more emotional underlying structure (McKenzie, 1987). Studies in this area continue; results remain inconclusive as to whether the God concept is better predicted from the symbolic father, the symbolic mother, the actual mother, or the actual father. There could be variations between individuals due to extraneous factors as yet undetermined.

The ideas of God as loving and protecting and an idea of God as a mother are found in those Catholic adolescents with the most advanced religious ideas, and they are associated with an understanding of Jesus and Mary as warm and loving. The emergence of these "positive optimistic beliefs" is primarily related to the perceived quality of Catholic education and religious experience but also to the influence of friends and parents, church attendance, and spiritual readings (Greeley, 1981).

Belief systems are not created by individuals but are transmitted from generation to generation; they are accepted because the fantasies and images of individuals correspond to their cultural traditions. Similarities between the image of God and the father are to be expected since they are openly expressed by many religions, and religious traditions themselves are learned in the first place through parents (Beit-Hallahmi and Argyle, 1975). Some eminent psychologists are critical of these studies. A basic difficulty is that there is a fundamental similarity between any concepts of goodness as applied to God or to parents. Any two elements that both meet a criterion of goodness will show some positive association. Further, the correlations recorded in these studies, while significant, are nevertheless weak (Gorsuch, 1988).

Knowledge about the Bible

It must not be assumed that because formal operational thinking is achieved in adolescence there is no longer any problem in understanding biblical material. In an English study of the effects of a year's academic biblical teaching on groups of sixteen- and eighteen-year-old students, formal operational thinking about it was not fully secured until eighteen (Miles, 1971). Ignorance of this late development underlies many misconceptions. It is often assumed that although children may have difficulty in understanding the Bible, adults do not. This is far from the truth. The Good Samaritan parable is scarcely understood by a fifth of adults with the lowest mental ability, and more than a third of those of average intelligence have little more insight. There is only a minimal understanding of the Bible by almost all church members, and neither preachers nor Sunday school teachers effectively communicate cognitive material, so that Christian tradition, the nature of God, or the meaning of Easter is much less understood than is generally supposed (Schroeder and Obenhaus, 1964). These limitations apply equally to adolescents.

Most studies about understanding parables have been with younger children. By the age of ten most are able to deal with the metaphors on which parables are based. Much research into the comprehension of metaphors has shown that part of the difficulty of understanding them relates to the degree that their context is familiar. Fagerlind (1974) has described some Swedish studies of the religious thinking of children aged ten to twelve which shed light on those a little older. They think in such a way as to make it impossible for them to interpret and explain the meaning of a parable directly. Yet when it is taught with a concrete illustration they can extract something meaningful from it. This is especially so if the teaching relates to their own experiences, when they can understand the ethical content of some parables. They cannot generalize about unfamiliar situations, but given something familiar to their experience they can discover a general meaning which is applicable to themselves. They are able to understand and use symbolic expressions about problems they have already met, even though they are not yet able to analyze them in logical terms. Teaching about parables at this age is viable providing the problems that emerge are familiar and important to the children. This does not imply that a full understanding is possible. The style of teaching encouraged by these results was subsequently found to produce much more positive attitudes than was formerly the case.

English boys of thirteen and seventeen often think "prodigal" means "pleasure seeking" and so misunderstand the parable of the Prodigal Son. The improved understanding of the older boys arises from their greater experience of life rather than from their better religious comprehension. This maturity can inhibit religious understanding; being more down-to-earth than younger boys they show less insight into the significance of the parable of the Workmen in the Vineyard. Many boys do not fully appreciate the meaning of the Good Samaritan story because of their limited knowledge of its background. The majority accept that the Bible contains a true message, even if it is hard for them to grasp, and they do not think every word of it is true (Gregory, 1966).

English school children aged eleven to fourteen who were well below average intelligence were tested about short sayings of Jesus, such as that about the broad road and the narrow gate, with the saying linked to a related event within their experience. Their responses were compared with groups of normal children aged seven to ten. The younger children show a consistent increase of scores with age, but the older, less able group show a much smaller increase in scores. Only at fourteen do these pupils achieve scores equal to those of normal ten-year-old children. This demonstrates the great difficulty that less able adolescents have in understanding even simple parables and metaphoric material (Hyde, 1969). Such students can deal with background and narrative material in the gospels, but a proper study of the historical Jesus cannot succeed before they are thirteen, although the passion story was found to have a profound effect on a boy with a long history of being rejected (Hebron, 1959).

The question of understanding parables raises other issues of biblical understanding. Various translations vary in the difficulty of their comprehension. Modern versions are more comprehensible than the King James version, and the Living Bible and Today's English Version are judged more comprehensible than the Revised Standard Version of the New English Bible. Liberal or conservative theological stances make no difference to comprehension (Yeatts and Linden, 1984). Despite popular opinion, the resonant language of the King James Version does not make its recall simpler. Narrative passages are less well recalled from the New English Bible than from the other versions used. Expository passages, which are more theological, are the most difficult of all; however, meaningfulness is not related to their recall, which is better from the New English Bible and Today's English Version (Yeatts, 1988).

If parables present problems of understanding, how much more difficult is the comprehension of myth? There is only one major study of the topic, that of Doran (1978), whose consideration of myth includes some empirical research. English children and adolescents were interviewed about five creation stories and their responses categorized into five groups. Younger children give inadequate responses. A girl of thirteen sees parallels between the infant Hercules and the infant Jesus, remarking doubtfully, "If one's true, the other must be as well—they're both about the same sort of thing." The largest group is characterized by disbelief which increases with age. These children reject nonbiblical stories out of hand. After eleven a scientific attitude comes to the fore; there is skepticism about creation stories; the account of the sun god Ra is thought to be just a good story, but stories about Jesus are "a load of rubbish." After thirteen skepticism is accompanied by a more mature attitude, e.g., rejecting the Greek idea of Zeus but not declaring another person's belief was wrong; dismissing nonbiblical stories; regarding Jesus as son of Mary and Joseph, or taking a science fiction approach to Ra.

The next largest group accept stories as literally true. Few believe all of them; literalism reaches a peak at nine, but some believe all Bible stories literally. After fifteen, most in this group believe the Genesis story but deny the others, and after seventeen some still take one or more of the stories literally. A smaller group give rationalistic responses, so that a girl of eleven mentions the possibility of symbolism, and a boy of seventeen says that details do not matter, the mind "needs something to hang on to." The final group is characterized by affective responses. Creation and resurrection themes are regarded as both true and comforting; a girl of fifteen comments, "It looks after everything; it puts all the power man hasn't got into categories; its a warm kind of feeling and is poetry as well. . . . It doesn't make us want to believe it, there are so many things to question." Another speaks of a supreme power but not of God as a person; she is a thoughtful, intelligent, and essentially religious person who over a decade has not been convinced by her teachers and church of the credibility of the Christian faith.

Many rely on the authority of the Bible, but none have been taught how biblical stories can be true. Biblical authority is for many children a pivotal point; for some, if the Bible story is true, the others cannot be; for others, because the biblical story is true, the others also could be. Many feel that science has made religion untenable, yet the children are still capable of wonder and awe. Intellectually they need help to recognize that science also uses myth-making ideas, such as, for example, the concept of the "running down universe" that must come to an end, which is stated, like religious eschatology, in the form of factual knowledge. One group, with their parents, will not tolerate the slightest critical consideration of the Bible or investigate the beliefs of other religions; such literalism seems to them to be an essential part of Christian belief.

Difficulties in understanding the creation story show a developmental progression. Scientific understanding begins about ten, when children regard the scientific and theological ways of looking at creation as conflicting. Subsequently, a few achieve a simple understanding of the creation story symbolically, but they do not necessarily believe it holds any relevance for them. Most, even older children, struggle with the problems raised by a literal interpretation of symbols (Greer, 1972).

From a theological perspective, Heimbrock (1986) argued that mythical thinking is a half-way house; it is not consistent with developed formal operational thinking since it is not a purely rational and objective kind of thought about reality. His contention that we lack an adequate psychological account of the development of symbolic and mythical thinking is a point to be taken. It would seem that religious symbolism requires a social interaction for its understanding. It is affective as well as cognitive, but its rationale, even if not formally logical, still needs mature thought forms for its full comprehension and expression.

One aspect of understanding biblical material is the need to have an adequate historical perspective, and a few English studies on this are relevant. Concrete thinking in history begins in the twelfth year and formal thinking begins soon after sixteen. At times a few younger pupils are capable of formal operational thinking in this area, yet even preoperational thinking occurs among the oldest pupils. At sixteen most historical reasoning is at the concrete operational level. Before this age it is difficult to teach history other than at the level of factual description since it is generally concerned with the inner motives of adults living in another century with a culture very different from that of contemporary society (Hallam, 1966, 1975). There are evident changes in styles of thinking at about fourteen and at fifteen. With more intelligent students logically restricted thinking declines with age, so that a high proportion of deductive conceptualizations are found, whereas in the less intelligent, not nearly so much advanced thinking is found (De Silva, 1969). The comprehension of historical narratives among girls below average intelligence is the same as that of normal students a year younger, but they never adequately achieve the abstract explanatory thinking which begins to appear at fourteen (Stones, 1965). Mature explanatory thinking is observed earliest when it is about material most closely related to students' experiences; in this respect, history and religious education are the most difficult subjects (Best, 1967).

In geography, students of twelve or over give descriptive replies which attempt an analysis of problems based on a single piece of evidence. Beyond thirteen a realistic stage is reached, when they offer more than one piece of evidence and begin to relate cause and effect, but not until after fourteen is full hypothetico-deductive reasoning attained (Rhys, 1966). Students' reactions to literature about violence show the expected improvement in understanding between the ages of thirteen and fifteen, but it also depends on how near a particular passage comes to their personal experience. In teaching such material, particular help is needed to understand metaphorical language (Ellis, 1970). The development of an affective response in judgments about poetry is similar to that of general cognitive development; after fifteen the number of mature explanatory judgments is about equal to the number of partial responses, and not until seventeen is mature judgment finally reached (Mason, 1974).

Parental Influence on Adolescent Religion

Parental religious values have a strong bearing on adolescent church attitudes. They are far more important than socio-economic factors, the type of school attended, the years of formal religious training, either in Sunday school or parochial school, or religious education programs. The level of activity in clubs or organizations in the school or community is irrelevant to adolescent religious attitudes. More important are the types of relationships with other people. The very strong influence of parents is mostly through their behavior, not through a conscious effort to socialize their children into the church (Hoge and Petrillo, 1978). Parental religious practice is a major determinant of adolescent religiousness among Catholics, even more with girls than with boys, and parental church attendance is related to many aspects of their children's religiousness. (Suziedelis and Potvin, 1981). Parental influence is stronger when both parents hold the same beliefs (Middleton and Putney, 1962). Adolescents have a great similarity with their parents' understanding of religious symbols, and there is some similarity in religious belief but not in their attitudes to the church (Wieting, 1975). The religiousness of Catholic adolescents is primarily influenced by the quality of the parents' relationship with them (McCready, 1979). The continuing church participation of recently confirmed Lutheran adolescents is associated with a high level of parental religious activity, consistency, education, and good family relationships. It is also associated with worship and religious teaching being related to daily life, a sense of belonging to a congregation which provides meaningful social experiences, an approachable minister, a view of religion as being practical, and a feeling of personal relationship with Christ (Jarvis, 1967). Adolescent dogmatism and beliefs are associated with that of their parents

(Thompson, 1973). The educational level of the family is another a factor. A liberal, open-minded climate in a family, whatever its social background, exposes children to information that is conducive to the development of friendly attitudes toward various outgroups (Schönbach et al., 1981).

Parental influence may vary between different denominations. Family attitudes to the church are most influential among Jews, then Catholics, and least among Protestants. Protestant children tend to diverge more from parental conservatism regarding change than do Catholic children (Newcome and Sevehla, 1937). The religiousness of high-school students in Evangelical Free Churches is significantly less than that of their parents, although they share the same beliefs, behaviors, and outlooks. Among Presbyterians, parental influence is the major factor in religious development, whereas in Evangelical Free churches, church and parents are both influential. Christian schools have no extra influence, despite popular expectation (Inskeep, 1986). The spiritual growth of evangelical high-school students is more strongly associated with parental church attendance than any other factor such as attendance at a Christian school or by the form of biblical teaching (White, 1985). Differences in religious outlook are strongly associated with parental orthodoxy, and denominational influence retains no significant effect (Nelsen, 1982). However, the complexity of the interactions is shown by another study which showed that church membership predicts adolescent values better than those of the parents, so that that socialization in religious values appears to take place in cultural subgroups more than in nuclear families (Hoge and Petrillo, 1982).

At the postconventional stage of moral development, parents and teachers no longer influence the moral judgments of boys but are replaced by adolescents' peers. Girls at the same stage are still influenced by their mothers to some extent. The ambivalence and hostility of a conservative, authoritarian family structure is associated with conventional morality. Postconventional morality altogether rejects such values, and this represents a legitimate expression of resentment against the authority of a parent who is perceived as unjust (Henry, 1987). Adolescent alienation is associated with the poor quality of their relationships with parents and other authority figures, with peer groups, with their own self-concepts, the influence of the media, and with negative influences from the church such as uninteresting sermons, restrictions on lifestyle and deficient devotional life (Laurent, 1986). Parental religiousness and adolescent religious belief are strongly related to religious practice but neither affect the decline in practice with age, although the decline varies with different categories of religious experience and parental control (Potvin and Sloane, 1985).

Parental control often has a religious outcome. The image of God, as has been shown, is closely related to the image of the parents; ideas of God, sin, guilt, and forgiveness grow out of experiences of parental love and authority and their parents' reactions to their successes and failures, and their joys and sorrows (Hirschberg, 1955). Harsh parental discipline with a rigorous religious training motivates children to present themselves in a favorable light, even if it means reporting things of doubtful truthfulness (Crandall and Gozali, 1969). An unhappy childhood is associated with the rejection of religious belief (Vetter and Green, 1932). Parental discord adversely affects the religiousness of children, especially with boys from troubled homes where they are also subjected to corporal punishment (Nelsen, 1981).

Adolescent religiousness relates positively to parental acceptance and negatively to rejection and power control. An intrinsic orientation is associated with parental empathy and acceptance and psychological control, and an extrinsic orientation is associated with an uncontrolled environment in which parents are perceived as distant (Lindquist, 1980). Authoritarian parents tend to have extrinsically oriented children with impaired spiritual growth, a closed cognitive style and a degree of over-dependency (Ernest, 1982). Parental indifference gives rise to feelings of insecurity and a craving for recognition, as does an over-strict or inconsistent discipline. Parental control that makes use of fear is associated with high religiousness and low scores on self-esteem (Batres, 1984). Nurturing family practices with democratic control encourage children from eight to thirteen toward commitment to a church and involvement in youth organizations. Restrictive parental regimes encourage antisocial behavior, alcohol use, racism, and sexism (Forliti and Benson, 1986).

Differing conclusions have been reached regarding the relative religious influence of mothers and fathers. A number of studies conclude that fathers are more influential than mothers on adolescent religiousness (Hoge and Petrillo, 1978, 1979). Chesto (1987) found that a crucial aspect of passing on Christian faith is the amount of God-talk in the home, and the involvement of the father in this is of particular importance. In a study of a broad range of adolescent religious activities, Kieren and Munro (1987) found that girls are influenced by their fathers and not their mothers, whereas boys are influenced by both parents.

However, stronger maternal influence has also been recorded. In the substantial parental influence on adolescents, that of the mother is the stronger, and there is no evidence for any sex-linked effects (Acock and Bengtson, 1978). Both parents have similar effects on their children, but maternal religion is an especially strong influence on daughters. When mothers have low levels of religiousness, their sons are adversely affected to a marked degree (Nelsen, 1980). The mother's influence in the home is the dominant one (Schmidt, 1981; Hunsburger and Brown, 1984; Dudley and Dudley, 1986). The religiousness of young adults is associated with that of the mother and that of the sons with the father as well (Philben, 1988). Girls perceive the parental power structure as more equalitarian than do boys, since they see the mother as being more powerful than boys do (McDonald, 1980).

These different conclusions are not necessarily in conflict if their areas of influence are carefully defined. The relationships of adolescent sons with their fathers and mothers are different from those of adolescent daughters, and relationships with friends of the same sex are also quite different (Youniss and Smoller, 1985). In the transmission of religious beliefs and practices by parents to their first-born adolescent sons, mothers and fathers have different roles. Adolescent church attendance is associated with that of the father, but their religious experience and practical application of religion is associated with the mother (Clark, Worthington, and Danser, 1988).

Social Constraints on Adolescent Religion

Peer group influence is a strong social constraint. Membership of a group brings pressure from the group, whether the influence is religious or secular (Davies, 1971). Adolescents with practicing parents and from more conservative denominations are strongly influenced by their own religious involvement. Between thirteen and fourteen their religious practice is strongly related to parental religiousness, and they are generally submissive to religious authority and to their parents. Between fifteen and sixteen their beliefs exert a greater influence, and peers influence religion and beliefs directly. Adolescents begin to construct with their peers a specific worldview. This affects their personal religiousness, and it becomes their dominant religious influence. Religious beliefs and practices are affected when they are in conflict with this newly formulated philosophy. Between seventeen and eighteen parents again become influential, but now adolescents tend to reconcile their early religiousness with the modifications they have made to it by their interactions with their peers. Religious practice becomes autonomous and an individual religious lifestyle has been formed, so that the influence of religious practice is reestablished, and either traditional beliefs are confirmed or new beliefs and experiences generated. Age itself does not cause the development; nor do all adolescents develop to the point of constructing religious meanings, or do so at the same age, although at fifteen or sixteen the process appears more salient (Potvin and Lee, 1981, 1982). The influence of peers is important for adolescents' self-concept, but there is no evidence that adolescent religion is a product of a distinctive youth sub-culture. A youth sub-culture is a matter of ritualistic conformity, but it is not important in the maintenance of ideals, values, and religion. These owe much more to the home. Parental support appears to be more important for religious belief than for religious activity (De Vaus, 1983).

Parochial schools are expected to nurture adolescent religion, but much of the research about this is inconclusive, and at times, contradictory. The problem in comparing the religiousness of former parochial school students with nonattenders is that often it is assumed that differences must arise from school influence. This overlooks parental influence, which is always found to be more strongly related to adolescent religiousness when it is taken into account. When it has been overlooked exaggerated claims have been made about school influence, as will be seen. Schools differ in many ways. Their admissions policy can affect the religiousness of their students, and socio-economic differences in their catchment area will affect the level of ability of the pupils and their religiousness on admission. Some pupils will be at a parochial school because, like their family, they are committed to their church and want to attend it; some will be there under duress—the school was chosen for them by their parents for reasons of convenience or family tradition but against their own desire to go to another school, perhaps with their friends.

So, there appeared to be little difference in religiousness between Catholics who had attended parochial schools and those who had not (Rossi and Rossi, 1957). A definitive study showed a significant association between Catholic education and subsequent adult religious behavior, which is strongest for those with a religious family background. There are significant differences which distinguished those who have all their education in parochial schools from those who do not. Catholic schooling and the religiousness of parents operates with a multiplier effect. There is a direct relationship between social class and sending one's children to Catholic schools. The differences between Catholics who have attended Catholic schools and those who have not are impressive, contrary to the earlier finding (Greeley and Rossi, 1966). A replication at a time when religious observance was decreasing suggests that the decline in religiousness for those who attend Catholic schools is much less (Greeley, McCready, and McCourt, 1976). Catholics in the most positive category of religiousness—the hopefuls—were much more likely to have been to a Catholic school (McCready and Greeley, 1976). In a comparison of adolescents attending Catholic parochial schools and public schools, all showed a decrease of religiousness with age. Protestant children in the sample read the Bible slightly more than parochial school Catholics, and were more literal in their approach to it, but on all other items the Catholics attending a church school scored highest, followed by Catholics at a public school (Nelsen, Potvin, and Shields, 1977). Although Catholic schools provided more religious education, on many issues those who had attended them did not differ from those who had not, although they showed greater Mass attendance and private prayer (Ridder, 1985). Answers to the question, "Do you believe in life after death?" were strongly associated with Catholic school attendance, an apparent proof that Catholic schools had a lasting effect on their pupils (Greeley, 1979). Catholic education was positively associated with religiousness when other variables such as parental influence were controlled (Fee, Greeley, McCready, and Sullivan, 1981). Among students at Catholic high schools there was greater church attendance and higher self-ratings of religiousness (Convey, 1984; Benson, Donahue, and Guerra, 1989), but parental influence was not considered.

Attendance at a Catholic school is most rewarding academically for students disadvantaged by their racial background, by the educational background of their family, or by their own prior lack of educational achievement. For these, academic rather than religious attainment is most evident. Many Catholic schools were established for the poor children of immigrants, and they are still doing successfully what they have always done. Religiousness is less associated with academic performance for Hispanics, and not at all for the blacks, half of whom are not Catholics (Greeley, 1982).

A few studies in other church schools have produced similar results. There is no difference between the religiousness of secondary school pupils in fundamentalist schools and fundamentalist pupils in public schools; their religiousness is related to that of their parents, their relationships with their parents, and to their church training (Erickson, 1964). There is no difference in academic achievement or doctrinal commitment between students in Adventist or in state schools (Meltz, 1980). Students who have attended all grades of an Adventist school are much more likely to join and stay in the Adventist church (Minder, 1985). Attendance at a private school makes no difference to the religious values held by the Mennonite students (Wiebe and Vraa, 1976).

Lutheran schools produce no significant differences in attitudes toward social and political issues among their students, whose greater involvement in church activities arises from family influence, disregarding those from homes only marginally associated with the church (Johnstone, 1966). When religiousness is held constant, school attendance at a Lutheran school makes no significant difference (Mueller, 1967). Students in Lutheran schools generally have a deep commitment to their faith, with high scores for religious belief but not for religious knowledge. Their religiousness is related to a number of factors including race, sex, home, environment, parental church membership, their own church attendance, the length of their Lutheran education, the religious curriculum studied, and their general mental ability (Kaiser, 1978).

The time given to Jewish schooling only begins to have an effect after 2,000 hours, but 4,000 hours are needed for a significant effect, and still greater time has no effect until 10,000 hours. Only with sufficient time can curriculum revision and better teaching methods make a greater contribution. The main agents of religious socialization include the religiousness of parents, the time spent on Jewish studies in Jewish schools, and participation in Jewish organizations (Himmelfarb, 1974, 1977). These results are supported by Fuchs (1978) and Bock (1976).

In Australia, after a similar history of inconclusive studies, it was Leavey's study (1972a, b) of senior girls in Catholic high schools that broke new ground. She not only confirmed that the major religious influence on these students is parental but also demonstrated that a Catholic school can have an independent influence, depending on the school climate. Comparisons were made between religiously high- and low-achieving students, on parental religiousness, socio-economic status of the home, socio-economic status of the school, school religious achievement, and students' examination successes—variables frequently overlooked. The most successful girls were the type of students which the schools hoped to produce, holding highly internalized beliefs, Catholic values, and morality. They tended to come from professional and managerial homes, not only from religiously high-achieving homes, but also from the religiously high-achieving schools. Some schools tended to be high-achieving and others low-achieving on all religious outcomes. The school climate which produced this difference arose from a complex interaction of relationships and goals, in which the role of the principal was crucial. The procedures of the successful schools reinforced their religious content, so that their students experienced the school as a religious environment. These high-achieving schools tended to include the high-achieving examination groups. Students from similar religious and social backgrounds responded differently in both religious and academic outcomes to schools with different climates. All schools tended to have a stronger effect than parents on the cognitive areas of religious knowledge. The differences between the two types of Catholic schools are marked. Students from high-religious homes did less well in a low-achieving school, and students from low-religious homes in a high-achieving school performed well above the average of the total sample. The schools had an impact on the students independent of their homes. Unless students experience the school as a Christian environment, they are not open to the Christian message; the procedures of the school must in some way reinforce its Christian content, or else it is not mediated, and religious education is not successful.

Confirmation of these results came from a similar study of students in Australian Catholic boys' schools. A religious school has its best effect when it reinforces and supports a good religious atmosphere at home, and a good religious school has a better influence on students from homes with low-religious influence than poor-religious schools. Once more, the school is shown to have an influence independent of students' homes. The climate of the school is the key factor in its religious influence; students' morale, their attitude to the principal, and the degree of freedom allowed have an important role in producing this climate, as do the school procedures in its day to day administration, the style of life it values, and what it celebrates or rewards (Flynn, 1974, 1985). A subsequent study in Catholic boys' high schools again indicated that students' religiousness is most strongly related to parental religiousness, but other outcomes—Christian faith and sensitivity to issues of social justice and a sense of Christian community in the staff—are related to the boys' perception of the social environment of the school. School-related factors are positively and uniquely associated with students' religious faith and awareness of social justice, an effect that is independent of home, peer group, or personality (Fahy, 1980). Rossiter (1983) regarded these studies as the most comprehensive and sophisticated sociological work in this area in English-speaking countries.

The cumulative effect of these studies in the United States, the United Kingdom, and Australia shows that while parents have the strongest influence on their children's religiousness, the school also may have an independent influence arising from its climate. This influence is not the result of formal religious education, but arises from the attitudes that are fostered and the effectiveness of pastoral care. That influence can be negative, even in a church school.

Churches also exert a strong influence on adolescent religion. An extensive research program was undertaken into the priorities and outcomes of the religious education programs of several denominations (Hoge and Petrillo, 1978, 1979; Hoge et al., 1982). From this a clear picture of adolescent involvement in religious activity emerged as well as the intentions of their leaders to help them handle the moral problems of sex, drugs, and the popular culture. The principal determinant to church attendance is parental attendance and parental religious values. Peer pressures and types of leadership determine youth group participation; attitudes toward the church depend on past religious education, types of leaders, and beliefs. In fostering church commitment among the young, personal relationships with parents, peers, and church leaders are foremost. Baptists have stronger church commitment and involvement because their system emphasizes these issues to a greater extent, so that adolescents liked their past religious training more than the others, described their leaders as more sincerely religious, and were more orthodox. Liberal influences, which often induce attitudes of individualism, relativism, and doubt about some types of religious training, have some impact. Cognitive and intellectual factors are not strong determinants of church participation and attitudes, and a large range of factors have little effect. Bible knowledge has little relation to other variables, and factual knowledge has little relation to church commitments. Support for some of these findings came from the study Dudley and Laurent (1984) undertook of high-school students at a church-related youth conference. Religious alienation is strongly related to the quality of relationships with pastors and parents as well as to opportunities for involvement in the church. It is also less strongly related to their self-concept, to peer group influence, and to the influence of the media.

Personality Traits, Identity Development, and Religiousness

In his extensive survey, Strommen (1974) identified the effects of Christian faith in over 7,000 American adolescents. Some are marked by low self-regard, self-criticism, lack of self-confidence, and anxiety about academic problems, religion, their families, and the opposite sex. Others participate regularly in church activities, pray for others, seek divine guidance, and respond to help made available by the church; these adolescents are marked by their optimism, high self-regard, and hope of greater church involvement in the future. Such observations raise questions about the relationship between personality traits and religion.

Studies investigating the association between religiousness and personality are inconclusive and sometimes contradictory. Most of them have been with college students or church members, but a few involve adolescents. Religious adolescents tend to be more sensitive, less dominant, and more conservative than others; they are less prone to guilt and anxiety as they grew older (Barton and Vaughan,

1976). When the categories of Jung's psychology are employed, personality differences are associated with more or less orthodox systems of belief (Lee, 1985). The religious have less worry and are more secure (Hauser, 1981). The anxiety caused in childhood by a stern father who does not understand them and a rigid rather than a loving mother leads to the development of a dogmatic system as a defensive reaction (Raschke, 1973). Such authoritarian adolescents are attracted to orthodox doctrine (Weller et al., 1975), and are more resistant to change, while upward social-class mobility is related to liberal religiousness (Baggot, 1978).

In one high school self-esteem is associated with religiousness among the younger boys but not the girls (Moore and Stoner, 1977), a finding confirmed for adolescents by Potvin (1977) but inexplicably contradicted—it is greater among girls than boys—by Smith, Weigert, and Thomas (1979). In many countries Catholic adolescents with marked religiousness have a positive sense of self-esteem. The girls show an association between self-esteem and an image of a loving God, and negative self-esteem is associated with an image of a rejecting, punitive God (Benson and Spilka, 1973). Religiousness relates to self-esteem for all boys and intrinsically oriented girls among Catholic adolescents. Since some aspects of the stereotyped male role are incompatible with aspects of religiousness, religious training influences boys' sex-role identity and tends to affect their social development (Suziedelis and Potvin, 1981). Religious maturity is associated with self-esteem and intrinsic religiousness and negatively with anxiety and extrinsic religiousness (Marthai, 1980). In a group of cancer patients aged ten to twenty-three, half claimed that their religion gave them security in the face of death and helped them to understand and accept their illness, although they were not more religious than the others; their condition had accelerated the development of an internalized faith among the younger patients (Tebbi et al., 1987).

Adolescents discover themselves as unique individuals, still uncertain and questioning. Their moral judgment moves from the preconventional to the conventional levels (see chapter seven). Ego-development proceeds from a conformist to a conscientious stage through a transitional stage. Individual acceptance of the rules of the group moves to a stage characterized by a conscious preoccupation with obligations, ideals, traits, and achievements measured by inner standards. This development comes about through social interaction, and not all adolescents advance in this manner, for many adults remain in the conformist stage. Adolescents need to examine their personal conflicts and experience using their judgment. They are most powerfully affected by their peers, and the interactions of any peer group are related to changes in self-development. The integration of every new generation of adolescents into society requires some change on the part of the adolescents but also some change on the part of society (Hayes, 1982).

Marcia (1966) extended Erikson's concept of adolescent identity achievement to four categories—(i) achievement, where one is relatively free from authoritarian values; (ii) moratorium, in which achievement is delayed; (iii) foreclosure, in which authoritarian values are endorsed, and (iv) identity confusion, illustrated in the continuum from the playboy to the schizoid personality. Identity achievement increases with cognitive ability (Skinner, 1983).

In one group of girls identity achievement was marked by their facing doubts and considering alternatives and then making a commitment to a definite position. Others who also question goals and values but remain doubtful are at moratorium. Both of these tend academically to be high achievers. Foreclosure represents those who doubt values without appraising alternatives, and their choices frequently reflect parental preferences. Identity diffusion subjects might or might not experience such doubts, but they have no serious intention of examining alternatives and express no commitment to an ideology. They are low-achieving academically and also lack the flexibility and purposefullness of those with stronger self-esteem (Hummel and Roselli, 1983). Adolescent girls with the lowest identity status also have the lowest religious values (St. Clair and Day, 1979). Although individuals with low identity status are associated with lower levels of moral reasoning, the converse is not established (Mischley, 1976). Adolescents tend to be diffuse, but this is largely owing to inexperience, uncertainty, and hesitation (McCready and Greeley, 1976). Almost all children from ten to sixteen are in more than one identity status, depending on the context, and identity status develops with age. Better educated parents give their children greater freedom of choice and as a result of this they make firm choices later. There are great variations between individuals in coming to firm religious conclusions (Archer, 1982). Intrinsic, committed religiousness is significantly associated with ego-development and tolerance. Each ego stage is associated with qualitatively different forms of religiousness (Terrance, 1987).

Hill (1986) considered Fowler's stage of conventional faith to be parallel to Kohlberg's conventional moral reasoning. Conventional faith is inflexible and stereotyped in contrast to an internalized committed postconventional faith, which in turn is related to identity resolution. Conservative churches tend to encourage the maintenance of conventional morality and conventional faith, and Meissner (1984) regarded this as the result of a critical superego, which produces unhealthy feelings of guilt resulting in an immature and unbiblical legalism. Before adolescence, conventional faith is normal, and this usually develops without difficulty into a concrete faith which relates to other people, although this development could be inhibited by a lack of formal operational thinking. The achievement of formal operations does not necessarily result in further progress to postconventional faith. Most adults remain at the conventional levels in both faith and morality, which shows that in adolescence their transition to postconventional faith did not take place.

The postconventional stage is primarily an inner acceptance of community values which does not come about without initial dissonance. Hill indicated five ways by which this dissonance could be resolved. Four of them are defensive: (i) individuals can refuse to recognize the dissonance, (ii) they can repress it, (iii) they can discount its source and render it invalid, or (iv) they can castigate themselves, regarding the dissonance as resulting from their own failure, and reaffirm their existing system of values. Such reaffirmation produces a legalistic stance. The other way is to challenge the validity of one's own values. Adolescents who do this, rejecting for the time being parental and religious values, are often thought of as rebellious. They become alienated, angry, confused, moody, and in conflict with authority—the classical description of identity confusion. Most of those who reach this stage pass through it to reestablish their values, values appropriate for postconventional faith and morality, retaining many of those that had been temporarily rejected (Young, 1981).

The plausibility of this suggestion depends on whether religious and moral development are associated, about which research is inconclusive, although Getz (1984) concluded that the relationship is established within narrow boundaries. Recently, Oser and Reich (1990) reviewed the conflicting findings about this, and compared them with their own findings about the relationship between Kohlberg's moral judgment and Oser's religious judgment. A dynamic model was necessary which varied according to stage and was also affected by socialization and individual experiences.

In some families and churches, adolescent questioning may be discouraged, leading to a forced compliance, so that adolescents adopt a defensive mechanism to quell their doubts. Then they remain entrenched in a highly structured society that consistently reinforces its values. Alternatively, their rebellion may become a permanent attitude, with their doubts never resolved unless subsequently they come to see it as experimentation and recognize that it holds the potential for growth. This model explains why some adolescents face a period of storm and stress. It warns that compliance may not indicate development but should rather be seen to show a foreclosed identity status associated with a less mature, conventional level of faith. However, Martin (1985) thought that the self-concept of adolescents is a continuous, stable growth which provides no evidence for such storm and stress.

In strict terms, identity achievement is not a personality trait. No personality trait, however described, is related to religiousness, although in a number of instances some traits may affect the expression of an individual's religiousness. The important distinction lies between the religious orientations. Authoritarian people are not necessarily religious, but when they are they adopt an authoritarian form of religion. Anxiety appears to be enhanced by some forms of religion, notably the authoritarian, but it is reduced by others. It is apparent that as personality develops in childhood and adolescence it affects the style of religiousness adopted, but it does not predispose to either acceptance or rejection of a religious outlook. However, because adolescence is the period when identity is resolved, Hill (1986) contends that it is the ideal time to make a transition from a consensual, extrinsic, conventional faith to an intrinsic, committed, postconventional faith.

Psychological Theories of Adolescent Religion

The application of attribution theory to religion is gaining in importance. People need to explain what happens. They attribute events to causes and interpret them in terms of their accepted meanings and values. New experiences, frustrations or failures, the loss of personal control or freedom, or the threat of fear and pain all require an explanation. When a meaning system is strongly held, people behave in terms of it. Often inferences have to be made about the causes of behavior and events as being due to oneself, to other people, to chance, or to God. The study of such perceived causation has come to be known as attribution theory. Spilka, Hood, and Gorsuch (1985) use it to provide insights into a wide range of topics, including religious experience, mysticism, conversion, moral behavior, and religious development, although Proudfoot and Shaver (1975) appear to be the first to relate it to the psychology of religion. It offers a means of explaining how experiences are interpreted on the basis of religious beliefs, and an attribution system provides a single conceptual framework which embraces a broad range of attitudes, beliefs, and behavior (Spilka, Shaver, and Kirkpatrick, 1985).

Elkind (1970) has shown how religion has an individual as well as a social origin, as it meets cognitive needs. Children develop an understanding of permanence; when they discover death, they feel the need for the conservation of their own life, an issue which arises fully in adolescence, and a religious solution for this need is possible. When the ability to make logical deductions is achieved, children try to relate things to one another with respect to time, space, causality, and origin; this search for relations, if the idea of God has been accepted, requires a religious means of establishing a relationship with the transcendent. Finally, adolescents develop the introspective ability to examine objectively their own thoughts and feelings and to make overriding theories as to the underlying reasons for things. This search for comprehension never meets with complete success, but religion provides a solution to the problem of comprehension.

Brown (1965) regarded belief as a relatively independent and predominately cognitive activity, acquired and sustained by social influences within a supportive and believing context. It arises from social learning rather than from emotional factors, even though metaphysical questions are asked and religious answers to them may show an emotional dependence and willingness to accept nonrational interpretations. The affective concomitants are probably not specific to religion, although they influence the way individuals express their beliefs. He noted that there is a single factor to which a variety of religious variables are related, and this factor is independent of a general response set, opinion strength, and certainty about matters of fact and opinion. When he repeated tests of political, religious, and social attitudes after thirty years (Brown, 1981) religiousness remained a stable factor almost identically structured in both tests. It is an underlying ideology rather than a deep psychological structure which indicates that religion should be seen as a relatively isolated cognitive system.

To conclude, this review of research findings confirms what has long been understood. Religion is learned first of all in the home, and it is the quality of the religious life of parents, and their active involvement in their own religious group, which in the long run is the greatest single influence on adolescents. Children adopt the attitudes and opinions of their parents; adolescence brings greater intellectual and emotional maturity and with it a more critical outlook, in which childish ideas are rejected. The influence of peers becomes of greater importance—but their choice of friends will have been affected by the attitudes they have already formed in their homes. Now the fundamental reality of their belief becomes evident; it may develop into a faith which controls their response to all of life's issues, it may remain in a secondary place, or it may fade into insignificance. The schools they have attended may have played a part in such decisions, but it is not the case that a school with a religious foundation must have a positive influence. They will judge the church in the first instance by the degree of its acceptance and the warmth of its friendship and only then by the message it transmits to them. Parents, church members, and church leaders with understanding and insight will recognize the many facets of this development from childhood into adult life, and the individual difficulties adolescents must overcome in the process. This takes place against a background of an increasingly secularized society, where people have as their first priority increased material possessions and comfort. In contrast, the innate idealism of young people is today focused on questions of the environment, freedom from pollution and the preservation of natural resources, and concern about the impoverished peoples of the third world. In a biblical tradition, these are religious issues, and to searching but critical adolescents the response made to them may be a key question in determining the integrity of adult religion.

REFERENCES

Acock, A. C., and Bengtson, V. L. (1978). On the relative influence of mothers and fathers: A covariance analysis of political and religious socialization. *Journal of Marriage and the Family, 40,* 519-530.

Archer, S. L. (1982). The lower age boundaries of identity development. *Child Development, 53,* 1551-1556.

Argyle, M., and Beit-Hallahmi, B. (1975). *The social psychology of religion.* London: Routledge and Kegan Paul.

Babin, P. (1963). *Crisis of faith.* New York: Herder and Herder (trans. *Les jeunes et la foi,* Lyons, 1960).

Babin, P. (1965). The idea of God: Its evolution between the ages of 11 and 19. In A. Godin (Ed.) *From religious experience to religious attitude.* Chicago: Loyola University Press.

Babin, P. (1967). *Faith and the adolescent*, London: Burns, Oates (trans. *Dieu et adolescent*, Lyons, 1963).

Baggot, A. L. (1978). *Religious attitudes, authoritarianism, selected personal values, and probabilistic upward social-class mobility in working-class adolescents*. PhD thesis, New York University.

Ban, J. D. (1986). Adolescents in Canadian culture: Religious development. *Religious Education, 81*, 225-238.

Barton, K., and Vaughan, G. M. (1976). Church membership and personality: A longitudinal study. *Social Behaviour and Personality, 4*, 11-16.

Batres, A. L. (1984). *Parental methods of control/influence as antecedents to belief systems*. PhD thesis, University of Colorado at Boulder.

Batson, C. D. (1975). Rational processing or rationalization? The effects of disconfirming information on stated religious beliefs. *Journal of Personality and Social Psychology, 32*, 178-184.

Bealer, R. C., and Willets, F. K. (1967). The religious interests of American high school youth. *Religious Education, 62*, 435-444.

Beit-Hallahmi, B., and Argyle, M. (1975). God as a father projection. *British Journal of Medical Psychology, 48*, 71-75.

Benson, P. L., Donahue, M. J., and Guerra, M. J. (1989). The good news gets better. *Momentum, 20*, 40-44.

Benson, P., and Spilka, B. (1973). God image as a function of self-esteem and locus of control. *Journal for the Scientific Study of Religion, 12*, 297-310.

Best, O. G. (1967). *The development of explanatory thought in the adolescent in out-of-school social situations*. DPC dissertation, University of Birmingham.

Bock, G. E. (1976). *The Jewish schooling of American Jews: A study of non-cognitive educational effects*. EdD thesis, Harvard University.

Bradbury, J. B. (1947). *The religious development of the adolescent*. MEd thesis, University of Manchester.

Bradshaw, J. (1949). *A psychological study of the development of religious beliefs among children and young people*. MSc thesis, University of London.

Brink, T. L. (1978). Inconsistency of belief among Roman Catholic girls concerning religion, astrology, and reincarnation. *Review of Religious Research, 20*, 82-85.

Brown, L. B. (1965). Aggression and denominational membership. *British Journal of Social and Clinical Psychology, 4*, 175-178.

Brown, L. B. (1981). The religionism factor after 25 years. *The Journal of Psychology, 107*, 7-10.

Bulkeley, S. G. (1981). *The image of God and parental images: A dialogue between theology and psychology*. PhD thesis, University of Glasgow.

Cerney, M.S. (1966). *The development of the concept of God in Catholic school children*. PhD thesis, The Catholic University of America.

Chesto, K. O'C. (1987). *F.I.R.E. (Family-centered Integenerational Religious Education): An alternative model of religious education*. DMin thesis, Hartford Seminary.

Clark, C. A., Worthington, E. L., and Danser, D. B. (1988). The transmission of religious beliefs and practices to firstborn early adolescent sons. *Journal of Marriage and the Family, 50*, 463-472.

Convey, J. J. (1984). Encouraging findings about students' religious values. *Momentum, 15*, 47-49.

Coursey, R. D. (1971). Liberal and conservative Roman Catholics. *Proceedings of the Annual Conference of the American Psychological Association, 6*, 133-134.

Crandall, V. C., and Gozali, J. (1969). The social desirability responses of children of four religious cultural groups. *Child Development, 40,* 751-762.

Davies, J. (1971). Shaken with the wind: The effects of group pressure on the expression of moral belief. *Journal of Moral Education, 1,* 49-52.

Dawes, R. S. (1954). *The concepts of God among secondary school children.* MA thesis, University of London.

De Bord, L. W. (1969). Adolescent religious participation: An examination of sib-structure and church attendance. *Adolescence, 4,* 557-570.

De Silva, W. A. (1969). *Concept formation in adolescence through contextual clues, with special reference to history material.* PhD thesis, University of Birmingham.

DeVaus, D. A. (1983). The relative importance of parents and peers for adolescent religious orientation. *Adolescence, 18,* 147-158.

Deconchy, J-P. (1964). The idea of God: Its emergence between 7 and 16 years. *Lumen Vitae, 19,* 285-296.

Deconchy, J-P. (1967). *Structure genetique de l'idee de Dieu chez des catholique francois.* Brussels: Lumen Vitae.

Dickinson, G. E. (1976). Religious practices of adolescents in a Southern college, 1964-1974. *Journal for the Scientific Study of Religion, 15,* 361-363.

Dickinson, G. E. (1982). Changing religious behaviour of adolescents 1964-1979. *Youth and Society, 13,* 283-288.

Doran, F. D. (1978). *Myth, Bible, and religious education.* PhD thesis, University of Exeter.

Dudley, R. L., and Dudley, M. G. (1986). Transmission of religious values from parents to adolescents. *Review of Religious Research, 28,* 3-15.

Dudley, R. L., and Laurent, C. R. (1984). Alienation from religion in church-related adolescents. *Sociological Analysis, 49,* 408-420.

Elkind, D. (1970). The origins of religion in the child. *Review of Religious Research 12,* 1, 35-42.

Elkind, D., and Elkind, S. (1963). Varieties of religious experience in young adolescents. *Journal for the Scientific Study of Religion, 2,* 102-112.

Ellis, J. I. (1970). *Response to literature: A study of the responses of thirteen and fifteen year-olds to five passages on a theme of violence.* MEd dissertation, University of Birmingham.

Erickson, D. A. (1964). Religious consequences of public and sectarian schooling. *School Review, 72,* 21-33.

Ernest, J. R. (1982). *Personal religious orientation and God-concepts as a function of remembered family authoritarianism.* PhD thesis, Rosemead Graduate School of Professional Psychology.

Fagerlind, I. (1974). Research on religious education in the Swedish school system. *Character Potential, 7,* 38-47.

Fahy, P. S. (1980). The religious effectiveness of some Australian Catholic high schools. *Word in Life, 28,* 86-98.

Farmer, L. J. (1988). *Religious experience in childhood: A study of adult perspectives on early spiritual awareness.* EdD thesis, University of Massachusetts.

Fee, J. L., Greeley, A. M., McCready, W. C., and Sullivan, T. A. (1981). *Young Catholics in the United States and Canada.* Los Angeles: Sadlier.

Finker, R., and Stark, R. (1986). Turning pews into people: Estimating 19th century church membership. *Journal for the Scientific Study of Religion, 25,* 180-192.

Flynn, P. F. (1974). *Some Catholic schools in action: A survey of sixth form students at 21 Catholic boys' high schools in New South Wales and A.C.T.* MA thesis, Macquarie University, Sydney, Australia.

Flynn, P.F. (1985). *The effectiveness of Catholic schools*. Sydney: A Saint Paul Publication.

Forliti, J. E., and Benson, P. L. (1986). Young adolescents: A national study. *Religious Education, 81*, 199-224.

Francis, L.J. (1976). *An enquiry into the concept 'readiness for religion'*. PhD thesis, University of Cambridge.

Francis, L.J. (1977). Readiness for research in religion. *Learning for Living, 16*, 109-114.

Francis, L.J. (1978a). Attitude and longitude: A study in measurement. *Character Potential, 8*, 119-130.

Francis, L.J. (1978 b). Measurement reapplied: Research into the child's attitude towards religion. *British Journal of Religious Education, 1*, 45-51.

Francis, L.J. (1980a). Paths of holiness: Attitudes towards religion among 9-11 year old children. *Character Potential, 9*, 129-138.

Francis, L.J. (1980b). The young person's religion: A crisis of attitude. *Scottish Journal of Theology, 33*, 159-169.

Francis, L.J. (1980c). Christianity and the child today. *Occasional Papers: Farmington Institute for Christian Studies*, No. 6.

Francis, L.J. (1984a). *Monitoring the Christian development of the child*. Abingdon: Cullham College Institute, reprinted in *Family, School and Church in Religious Education*, Edinburgh: University of Edinburgh, Department of Christian Ethics and Practical Theology.

Francis, L.J. (1984b). Roman Catholic schools and pupil attitudes in England. *Lumen Vitae, 39*, 99-108.

Francis, L.J. (1989). Monitoring changing attitudes towards Christianity among secondary school pupils between 1974 and 1986. *British Journal of Educational Psychology, 59*, 86-91.

Francis, L. J., Wesley, C. B., and Rust, J. N. (1978). Research in progress: An account of the religious attitude research project at the London Institute of Education. *Bulletin of the Association for Religious Education, 11*, 10-15.

Fuchs, J. L. (1978). *Relationship of Jewish day school education to student self-concepts and Jewish identity*. EdD thesis, University of California.

Funk, R. B., and Willits, F. K. (1987). College attendance and attitude change: A panel study 1970-81. *Sociology of Education, 60*, 224-231.

Gallup, G. and Jones, S. (1989). *Religion in America*. Princeton, N.J.: The Princeton Religion Research Center.

Getz, I. R. (1984). Moral judgement and religion: A review of the literature, *Counselling and Values, 28*, 84-116.

Glock, C. Y., and Stark, R. (1965). *Religion and society in tension*. Chicago: Rand McNally.

Glock, C. Y., and Wuthnow, R. (1979). Departures from conventional religion: The nominally religious, the non-religious, and the alternatively religious. In R. Wuthnow (Ed.) *The religious dimension*. New York: Academic Press.

Godin, A. (1975). Words of man—Word of God. *Lumen Vitae, 30*, 55-60.

Gorsuch, R. L. (1988). Psychology of religion. *Annual Review of Psychology, 39*, 201-221.

Greeley, A.M. (1979). Ethnic variations in religious commitment. In R. Wuthnow (Ed.) *The religious dimension*. New York: Academic Press.

Greeley, A.M. (1981). *The religious imagination*. New York: Sadlier.

Greeley, A.M. (1982). *Catholic high schools and minority students*. New Brunswick: Transaction Books.

Greeley, A. M., McCready, W. C., and McCourt, K. (1976). *Catholic schools in a declin-*

ing church. Kansas City: Sheed and Ward.

Greeley, A. M., and Rossi, P. H. (1966). *The education of Catholic Americans.* Chicago: Adline.

Greer, J. E. (1972). The child's understanding of creation. *Educational Review, 24,* 99-110.

Greer, J. E. (1981a). Religious attitudes and thinking in Belfast pupils. *Educational Research, 23,* 177-189.

Greer, J. E. (1981b). Religious experience and religious education. *Search, 4,* 23-34.

Greer, J. E. (1982). The religious experience of Northern Irish pupils. *The Irish Catechist, 6,* 49-58.

Gregory, H. M. (1966). *Parables in the secondary school.* DipRE dissertation, University of Nottingham.

Hallam, R. N. (1966). *An investigation into some aspects of the historical thinking of children and adolescents.* MEd thesis, University of Leeds.

Hallam, R. N. (1975). *A study of the effect of teaching method on the growth of logical thought.* PhD thesis, University of Leeds.

Hauser, J. (1981). Adolescents and religion. *Adolescence, 16,* 309-320.

Hayes, R. L. (1982). A re-review of adolescent identity formation: Implications for education. *Adolescence, 17,* 153-165.

Hebron, M. E. (1959). Religious instruction for the less able pupil in a secondary modern school. *Religion in Education, 26,* 101-105.

Heimbrock, H.-G. (1986). The development of symbols as a key to the developmental psychology of religion. *British Journal of Religious Education. 8,* 150-154.

Henry, R. M. (1987). Moral belief structure and context, self-identity and parental favouriteness as determinants of moral judgment stage. *Journal of Moral Education, 16,* 3-17.

Hepburn, L. R. (1971). Religion in the social studies: The question of religious attitudes. *Religious Education, 66,* 172-179.

Hertel, B.R., and Nelsen, H.M. (1974). Are we entering a post-Christian era? Religious belief and attendance in America, 1957-1968. *Journal for the Scientific Study of Religion, 13,* 409-419.

Hill, C. I. (1986). A developmental perspective on adolescent 'rebellion' in the church. *Journal of Psychology and Theology, 14,* 306-318.

Himmelfarb, H. S. (1974). *The impact of religious schooling: The effects of Jewish education upon adult religious involvement.* PhD thesis, University of Chicago.

Himmelfarb, H. S. (1977). The interaction effect of parents, spouse and schooling: Comparing the impact of Jewish and Catholic schools. *Sociological Quarterly, 18,* 464-477.

Hindley, A.H. (1965). *The religious concepts of secondary modern children tested by their art work.* AdCertEd dissertation, University of Sheffield.

Hirschberg, J. C. (1955). Some comments on religion and childhood. *Bulletin of the Menninger Clinic, 19,* 227-228.

Hoge, D. R., et al. (1982). Desired outcomes of religious education. In D. C. Wyckoff and D. Richter (Eds.) *Religious education ministry with youth.* Birmingham, Ala: Religious Education Press.

Hoge, D. R., and Petrillo, G. H. (1978). Determinants of church participation and attitudes among high school youth. *Journal for the Scientific Study of Religion, 17,* 359-379.

Hoge, D. R., and Petrillo, G. H. (1979). Youth and the church. *Religious Education, 74,* 305-313.

Hoge, D. R., and Petrillo, G. H. (1982). Transmission of religious and social values from parents to teenage children. *Journal of Marriage and the Family, 44,* 569-580.

Hoge, D. R., and Smith, E. I. (1982). Normative and non-normative religious experience among high school youth. *Sociological Analysis, 43*, 69-82.

Hummel, R., and Roselli, L. (1983). Identity status and academic achievement in female adolescents. *Adolescence, 18*, 17-27.

Hunsburger, B., and Brown, L. B. (1984). Religious socialization, apostacy and the impact of family background. *Journal for the Scientific Study of Religion, 23*, 239-251.

Hutsebaut, D. (1972). The representation of God: Two complementary approaches. *Social Compass, 19*, 389-406.

Hyde, K. E. (1963). Religious concepts and religious attitudes. *Educational Review, 15*, 132-141, 217-227.

Hyde, K. E. (1965). *Religious learning in adolescence.* Edinburgh: Oliver and Boyd for the University of Birmingham Institute of Education.

Hyde, K. E. (1969). *Religion and slow learners: A research study.* London: SCM Press.

Hyde, K. E. (1990). *Religion in childhood and adolescence.* Birmingham, Ala.: Religious Education Press.

Inskeep, K. W. (1986). *Religious organizational socialization in the Evangelical Free Church of America.* PhD thesis, Loyola University of Chicago.

Jarvis, W. L. (1967). *A limited study of the continued participation of recent confirmands of the American Lutheran Church.* STM thesis, Wartburg Theological Seminary.

Jersild, A. T., Brook, J.S., and Brook, D.W. (1978). *The psychology of adolescence.* New York: Macmillan.

Johnson, A. C., Brekke, M. L., Strommen, M. P., and Underwager, R.C. (1974). Age differences and dimensions of religious behaviour. *Journal of Social Issues, 30*, 43-67.

Johnstone, R. L. (1966). *The effectiveness of Lutheran elementary and secondary schools as agencies of Christian education.* St. Louis: Concordia Seminary.

Kaiser, R. G. (1978). *A study of selected religious practices, beliefs and knowledge of eighth grade students in the Lutheran schools of Michigan.* EdD thesis, Wayne State University.

Kay, W. K. and Francis, L. J. (1983). Progress in the psychology of religious development. *Lumen Vitae, 38*, 342-346.

Kesteven, S. W. (1967). *An enquiry into attitudes to religion of youth club members in Stafford and district.* MEd thesis, University of Birmingham.

Kieren, D. K. and Munro, B. (1987). Following the leader: Parents' influence and adolescent religious activity. *Review of Religious Research, 26*, 249-255.

Klinberg, G. (1959). A study of religious experience in children from 9 to 13 years of age. *Religious Education, 54*, 211-216.

Laurent, C. R. (1986). *Selected variables related to alienation from religion among church-related high school students.* PhD thesis, Andrews University.

Leavey, M. C. (1972a). *Religious education, school climate and achievement: A study of nine Catholic sixth form girls' schools.* PhD thesis, Australian National University, Canberra, Australia.

Leavey, M. C. (1972b). The transmission of religious and moral values in nine Catholic girls' schools. *Twentieth Century, 27*, 3, 167-184.

Lee, S. W. (1985). *The orthodoxy of Christian beliefs and Jungian personality type.* EdD thesis, University of South Dakota.

Lindquist, B. E. (1980). *Relationships among personal religion, dimensions of moral character, and parent-child interactions.* PhD thesis, California School of Professional Psychology.

Lukoff, D. and Lu, F. (1988). Transpersonal psychology research review topic: Mystical experience. *Journal of Transpersonal Psychology, 20*, 161-184.

Marcia, J. E. (1966). Development and validation of ego-identity status. *Journal of Personality and Social Psychology, 3*, 551-558.

Marthai, R. (1980). *Construction and validation of a measure of phenomenal process religious maturity.* PhD thesis, University of Southern Mississippi.

Martin, J. (1985). *A longitudinal study of self-concept and school related attitude during the adolescent years.* MEd dissertation, University of Birmingham.

Mason, J. S. (1974). Adolescent judgment as evidenced in response to poetry. *Educational Review, 36*, 124-139.

McCready, W. (1979). The family and socialization. In A. Greeley (Ed.) *The family in crisis or in transition.* New York: Seabury Press.

McCready, W. C. and Greeley, A. M. (1976). *The ultimate values of the American population.* Beverly Hills: Sage Publications.

McDonald, G. W. (1980). *Adolescent characteristics affecting parental power perception in the family.* Paper presented to the Southern Sociological Society.

McDowell, J. B. (1952). The development of the idea of God in the Catholic child. *Educational Research Monthly.* Washington: The Catholic University of America.

McKenzie, D. W. (1987). *The symbolic parent versus actual parent approaches in examination of similarities between parent and God concept.* PhD thesis, United States International University.

Meissner, W.W. (1984). Developmental aspects of religious experience. In W.W. Meissner (Ed.) *Psychoanalysis and religious experience.* New Haven and London: Yale University Press.

Meltz, H. E. (1980). *A study of the academic achievement and religious effectiveness of Seventh-Day Adventist education.* EdD thesis, Oklahoma State University.

Middleton R. and Putney, S. (1962). Religion, normative standards, and behaviour. *Sociometry, 25*, 141-152.

Miles, G. B. (1971). *A study of logical thinking and moral judgement in G.C.E. Bible knowledge candidates.* MEd thesis, University of Leeds.

Miles, G. B. (1983). *A critical and experimental study of adolescents' attitudes and understanding of transcendental experience.* PhD thesis, University of Leeds.

Miller, D. E. (1981). Life style and religious commitment. *Religious Education, 76*, 49-63.

Miller, G. (1977). Attitudes of schoolchildren to the church. *Lumen Vitae, 32*, 71-93.

Minder, W. E. (1985). *A study of the relationship between church sponsored K-12 education and church membership in the Seventh-Day Adventist Church.* EdD thesis, Western Michigan University.

Mischey, E. J. (1976). *Faith development and its relationship to moral reasoning and identity status in young adults.* PhD thesis, University of Toronto.

Moore, K., and Stoner, S. (1977). Adolescent self-respect and religiosity. *Psychological Reports, 4*, 55-56.

Morgan, S. P. (1981). *The intergenerational transmission of religious behaviour: The effect of parents on their children's frequency of prayer.* Paper presented at the annual meeting of the American Sociological Association, Toronto.

Mueller, D. J. (1967). Effects and effectiveness of parochial elementary schools: An empirical study. *Review of Religious Research, 9*, 48-51.

Nelsen, H. M. (1980). Religious transmission versus religious formation: Preadolescent-parent interaction. *Sociological Quarterly, 21*, 207-218.

Nelsen, H. M. (1981). Gender differences in the effects of parental discord on pre-adolescent religiousness. *Journal for the Scientific Study of Religion, 20*, 351-360.

Nelsen, H. M. (1982). The influence of social and theological factors upon the goals of religious education. *Review of Religious Research, 23*, 255-263.

Nelsen, H. M., and Potvin, R. H. (1980). Toward disestablishment: New patterns of social class, denomination and religiosity among youth? *Review of Religious Research, 22,* 137-154.

Nelsen, H. M., Potvin, R. H., and Shields, J. (1977). *The religion of children.* Washington, D.C.: United States Catholic Conference.

Nelson, M. O. (1971). The concept of God and feelings towards parents. *Journal of Individual Psychology, 27,* 46-49.

Newcome, T., and Sevehla, G. (1937). Intra-family relationships in attitude. *Sociometry, 1,* 180-205.

Oser, F. and Reich H. (1990). Moral judgment, religious judgment, world view and logical thought: A review of their relationship, I. *British Journal of Religious Education, 12,* 94-101.

Ozorak, E. W. (1987). *The development of religious beliefs and commitment in adolescence.* PhD thesis, Harvard University.

Paffard, M. (1970). Creative activities and 'peak' experiences. *British Journal of Educational Psychology, 40,* 283-290.

Paffard, M. (1973). *Inglorious Wordsworths: A study of some transcendental experiences in childhood and adolescence.* London: Hodder and Staughton.

Peterson, S. (1960). *Retarded children: God's children.* Philadelphia: Westminster Press.

Philben, K. M. (1988). *The transmission of religiosity from parents to their young adult children.* PhD thesis, Illinois Institute of Technology.

Piazza, T., and Glock, C.Y. (1979). Images of God and their social meanings. In R. Wuthnow (Ed.) *The religious dimension.* New York: Academic Press.

Poole, J. W. (1986). *An investigation into the effect of the method of teaching a Bible story on the cognitive domain of fourth year pupils in secondary schools.* MEd thesis, University of Birmingham.

Potvin, R. H. (1977). Adolescent God images. *Review of Religious Research, 19,* 43-53.

Potvin, R. H., and Lee, C. F. (1981). Religious development among adolescents. *Social Thought, 7,* 47-61.

Potvin, R. H., and Lee, C. F. (1982). Adolescent religion: A developmental approach. *Sociological Analysis, 43,* 131-144.

Potvin, R. H., and Sloane, D. M. (1985). Parental control, age and religious practice. *Review of Religious Research, 27,* 3-14.

Price, J. H. (1970). *A study of the God concepts of emotionally disturbed children at a child care center and the God concepts of the children in three Methodist church schools.* EdD thesis, Syracuse University.

Proudfoot, W., and Shaver, P. (1975). Attribution theory and the psychology of religion. *Journal for the Scientific Study of Religion, 14,* 317-330.

Raschke, V. (1973). Dogmatism and committed and consensual religiosity. *Journal for the Scientific Study of Religion, 12,* 339-344.

Rees, D. G. (1967). *A psychological investigation into denominational concepts of God.* MA thesis, University of Liverpool.

Rhys, W.T. (1966). *The development of logical thought in the adolescent with reference to the teaching of geography in the secondary school.* MEd thesis, University of Birmingham.

Ridder, N. F. (1985). *The religious beliefs and practices of Catholic graduates of Catholic and public high schools in the state of Nebraska from 1972-1981.* DEd thesis, University of Nebraska-Lincoln.

Robinson, E. A. (1971). Religious education: A shocking business. *Learning for Life, 11,* 5-8.

Robinson, E. A. (1975). The necessity for dream: Religious education and the imagination. *Learning for Living, 14*, 194-197.

Robinson, E. A. (1977). *The original vision*. Oxford: Religious Experience Research Unit, Manchester College.

Robinson, E. A. (1982). Professionalism and the religious imagination. *Religious Education, 77*, 628-641.

Robinson, E. A., and Jackson, M. (1987). *Religion and values at sixteen plus*. Oxford: Alister Hardy Research Centre, and London: Christian Education Movement.

Roof, W.C. (1978). Alienation and apostacy. *Society, 15*, 41-45.

Rossi, P. H., and Rossi, A. S. (1957). Some effects of parochial school education in America. *Harvard Educational Review, 27*, 168-199.

Rossiter, G. M. (1983). *An interpretation of normative theory for religious education in Australian schools*. PhD thesis, Macquarie University, Australia.

St. Clair, S., and Day, H. D. (1979). Ego identity status and values among high school females. *Journal of Youth and Adolescence, 8*, 317-326.

Schmidt, C. E. (1981). *The relationship of parents' belief systems to their parenting practices and to the belief systems of their children*. PhD thesis, University of Colorado at Boulder.

Schönbach, P., Gollwitzer, P., Stiepel, G., and Wagner, U. (1981). *Education and intergroup attitudes*. London: Academic Press.

Schroeder, W. W., and Obenhaus, V. (1964). *Religion in American culture*.Glencoe, Ill.: The Free Press.

Scobie, G. E. (1973). Types of Christian conversion. *Journal of Behavioural Science, 1*, 265-271.

Scobie, G. E. (1975). *Psychology of religion*. London: Batsford.

Shuttleworth, A. (1959). *Children's concepts of God*. DCP dissertation, University of Birmingham.

Silverstein, S. M. (1988). A study of religious conversion in North America. *Genetic, Social and General Psychology Monographs, 114*, 261-305.

Skinner, P. J. (1983). *The interaction between formal operational thought and ego identity development in late adolescence and early adulthood*. PhD thesis, Texas Technical University.

Sloane, D. M., and Potvin, R. H. (1983). Age differences in adolescent religiousness. *Review of Religious Research, 25*, 142-154.

Smidt, C. (1980). Civil religious orientations among elementary school children. *Sociological Analysis, 41*, 25-40.

Smith, C. B., Weigert, A. J., and Thomas, D. L. (1979). Self-esteem and religiosity: An analysis of Catholic adolescents from five cultures. *Journal for the Scientific Study of Religion, 18*, 51-56.

Smith, D. T. (1976). *The relationship between the moderately retardeds' God concept and their parental concepts*. MA thesis, Ohio State University.

Spilka, B., Armatas, P., and Nussbaum, J. (1964). The concept of God: A factor analytic approach. *Review of Religious Research, 6*, 28-36.

Spilka, B., Hood, R. W., and Gorsuch R. L. (1985). *The psychology of religion: An empirical approach*. Englewood Cliffs, N.J.: Prentice Hall.

Spilka, B., Shaver, P., and Kirkpatrick, L. A. (1985). A general attribution theory for the psychology of religion. *Journal for the Scientific Study of Religion, 24*, 1-20.

Spiro, M. E., and D'Andrade, R. G. (1958). A cross-cultural study of some supernatural beliefs. *American Anthropologist, 60*, 456-466.

Stevens, V. (1975). *An application of attitude testing to the identification of religious sentiment in adolescents*. MPhil thesis, University of Nottingham.

Stones, S. K. (1965). *An analysis of the growth of adolescent thinking in relation to the comprehension of school history material*. DPC dissertation, University of Birmingham.

Strommen, M. (Ed.) (1974). *Five cries of youth*. New York: Harper & Row.

Stubblefield, H. W. and Richard, W. C. (1965). The concept of God in the mentally retarded. *Religious Education, 60*, 184-188.

Suziedelis, A. and Potvin, R. H. (1981). Sex differences in factors affecting religiousness among Catholic adolescents. *Journal for the Scientific Study of Religion, 20*, 38-51.

Tamayo, A. (1981). Cultural differences in the structure and significance of the paternal figures. In A. Vergote and A. Tamayo, *The parental figures and the representation of God*. The Hague: Mouton.

Tamayo, A., and Cooke, S. (1981). The influence of age on the parental figures and the representation of God. In A. Vergote and A. Tamayo, *The parental figures and the representation of God*. The Hague: Mouton.

Tamayo, A., and St. Arnaud, P. (1981). The parental figures and the representation of God of schizophrenics and delinquents. In A. Vergote and A. Tamayo, *The parental figures and the representation of God*. The Hague: Mouton.

Tamminen, K. (1981). *Religious experience among children and youth: Project on the religious development of children and youth, Report II*. University of Helsinki, Department of Practical Theology.

Tebbi, C. K., Mallon, J. C., Richards, M. E., and Bigler, L. R. (1987). Religiosity and locus of control of adolescent cancer patients. *Psychological Reports, 62*, 683-696.

Terrance, F. (1987). *Religiousness, ego development, and adjustment*. PhD thesis, Miami University.

Thomas, L. E., and Cooper, P. E. (1978). Measurement and incidence of mystical experiences: An exploratory study. *Journal for the Scientific Study of Religion, 17*, 433-437.

Thomas, L. E., Cooper, P. E., and Suscovich, D. J. (1982). Incidence of near-death and intense spiritual experiences in an intergenerational sample. *Omega, Journal of Death and Dying, 13*, 35-41.

Thompson, D. D. (1973). *A study of the relationship of Rokeach's dogmatism with the religious orientation and religious orthodoxy of Catholic high school students and their parents*. PhD thesis, The Catholic University of America.

Toch, H., and Anderson, R. (1960). Religious beliefs and denominational affiliation. *Religious Education, 55*, 193-200.

Vannesse, A., and de Neuter, P. (1981). The semantic differential parental scale, in A. Vergote and A. Tamayo, *The parental figures and the representation of God*. The Hague: Mouton.

Vergote, A. (1981). Overview and theoretical perspectives. In A. Vergote and A. Tamayo, *The parental figures and the representation of God*. The Hague: Mouton.

Vergote, A., and Tamayo, A. (1981). *The parental figures and the representation of God*. The Hague: Mouton.

Vergote, A., Tamayo, A., Pasquali, L., Bonami, M. Pattyn, M-R., and Casters, A. (1969). Concept of God and parental images. *Journal for the Scientific Study of Religion, 8*, 79-87.

Vetter, G. B., and Green. M. (1932). Personality and group factors in the making of atheists. *Journal of Abnormal and Social Psychology, 27*, 179-194.

Walker, D. J. (1950). *A study of children's conceptions of God*. EdB thesis, University of Glasgow.

Weller, L., Levinbok, S., Maimon, R., and Shaham, A. (1975). Religiosity and authoritarianism. *Journal of Social Psychology, 95*, 11-18.

White, R. E. (1985). *Christian schooling and spiritual growth and development*. EdD thesis, Northern Arizona University.

Wiebe, B., and Vraa, C. W. (1976). Religious values of students in religious and in public high schools. *Psychological Reports, 38,* 709-710.

Wieting, S. G. (1975). An examination of intergenerational patterns of religious belief and practice. *Sociological Analysis, 30,* 137-149.

Williams, D. L. (1989). Religion in adolescence: Dying, dormant or developing? *Source, 5,* 4, 1-3.

Wilson, R. W. (1976). *A social-psychological study of religious experience with special emphasis on conversion.* PhD thesis, University of Florida.

Wingrove, E. R. and Alston, J. P. (1974). Cohort analysis of church attendance 1939-1969. *Social Studies, 53,* 324-331.

Wuthnow, R. (Ed.) (1979). *The religious dimension.* New York: Academic Press.

Yeatts, J. R. (1988). Variables related to the recall of the English Bible. *Journal for the Scientific Study of Religion, 27,* 593-608.

Yeatts, J. R., and Linden, K. W. (1984). Text comprehension of various versions of the Bible. *Journal for the Scientific Study of Religion, 23,* 1-18.

Young, R. C. (1981). Values differentiation as stage transition: An extension of Kohlberg's moral stages. *Journal of Psychology and Theology, 9,* 164-174.

Youniss, J., and Smoller, J. (1985). *Adolescent relations with mother, father, and friends.* Chicago: University of Chicago Press.

Zaenglein, M. M., Vener, A. M., and Stewart, C. S. (1975). The adolescent and his religion: Beliefs in transition. *Review of Religious Research, 17,* 51-60.

As this goes to press a major study on adolescent religion was released [January, 1991] titled "Today's teenagers: A generation in transition." The report is available from Barna Research Group, P.O. Box 4152, Glendale, Calif. 91222-0152. Also, Nick Stinnett at the University of Alabama—Tuscaloosa and well-known for his healthy family research, is currently conducting research on adolescent wellness. An early pilot study found teenagers reporting religious faith to be integral to coping at all grade levels [see *The Christian Journal of Psychology and Counseling,* Vol. 4 #1]. As of February, 1991, the ongoing results are generally consistent with the pilot study. In addition, the Search Institute, founded by Merton Strommen, regularly conducts research on adolescence that includes religious variables. Their newsletter *Source* is available by writing 122 W. Franklin, Suite 525, Minneapolis, Minn. 55404.

-Ed.

Chapter Six

Communication and Relationships

BLAKE J. NEFF

In a fascinating study of three thousand teenagers and their families, conducted by Gordon Sebine (1984) at the University of Michigan, 79 percent of the parents involved reported that they communicated well with their teens. However, in a near-complete reversal, 81 percent of the teens from those same families said their parents were not communicating with them. It seems apparent that:

1. There is little common understanding between parents and teens as to the meaning of communication. (This observation may undoubtedly be expanded to a much larger population). And,
2. At the very least 21 percent of parents and 81 percent of their teens say that whatever it is, it needs to be improved.

In response to these, the purpose of this chapter shall be first to postulate a usable definition of communication, and second, to suggest ways that the Christian education ministry to teens can assist the family in improving communication.

Communication Defined

There have been a great number of attempts to define communication (Dance, 1970). No author seems willing to accept the definition of another. B. Aubrey Fisher, in an attempt to make sense of the matter suggests, "I can only respond to the request for a definition of communication with the most pervasive of all qualifications—it depends on your perspective" (Fisher, 1978; p. 10).

Attempting to discover the elusive definition led others to conclude, "We feel that it is naive to suppose that only one definition of interpersonal communication exists or that only one conceptualization is possible" (Goss and O'Hair, 1988; p. 8).

At the risk of naivete it is necessary to posit a working definition of communication which can be effectively used by the Christian educator. As Infante and his colleagues suggest, "If at any time in the study of a phenomenon we stop and define it, the definition would simply represent our present thinking. As we learn more we would surely change our definition" (Infante, Rancer, Womack, 1990; p. 7).

Hence current thinking leads to the suggestion that communication be defined as all of the behavioral and verbal processes by which individuals share meanings.

Notice that the ultimate purpose of communication is shared understanding or shared meaning. However, failure to accomplish this quality of communication does not necessarily interrupt the ongoing process of attempting.

Since communication is a process, indicating a dynamic, ever-changing activity, it is difficult to demonstrate pictorially. The diagram below illustrates a point in the communication process, and thus serves to clarify the definition. Circles A and B represent two persons. The overlapped and shaded area demonstrates the degree to which meaning is shared on a particular subject at a particular point in time. Those portions of the circles which do not intersect the other represent the part of the understanding which is unique to one participant and not shared.

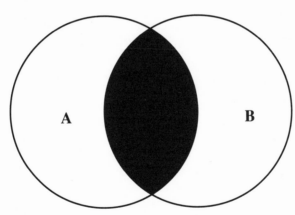

Of course communicators may share a great deal of meaning on one subject, but in another area the communication has been much less effective. For example, in one family parents and their teens have a great deal of shared meaning on the subject of teenage premarital sex. On the subject of teen alcohol abuse however, there is less understanding.

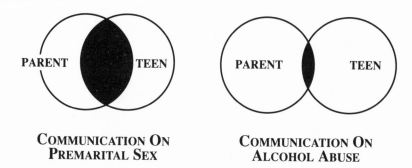

COMMUNICATION ON   COMMUNICATION ON
PREMARITAL SEX   ALCOHOL ABUSE

Misconceptions

This working definition points to several common misconceptions about what communication is and how it works. Examining each of these improves understanding of the communication process.

The Impossibility of Not Communicating

"My teenagers don't communicate anymore." "There is simply no communication between my kids and me." "I can't communicate with this younger generation." Actual comments like these from parents of teens indicate the prevalent misconception that it is possible to not communicate. Pioneer researchers in the pragmatic view of communication, Watzlawick, Beavin, and Jackson (1967), postulated in their *Pragmatics of Human Communication* that human beings cannot not communicate since communication and behavior are in their view synonymous terms.

Similarly, the definition posited above suggests the impossibility of not communicating. Of course there may be little shared meaning between two persons on a particular subject, but the process of exchanging toward the goal of mutual understanding continues.

A pair of illustrations serve to explain. Let us imagine that the father of a particular teen is deeply engrossed in the evening paper when his son walks into the room and attempts to strike up a conversation. For a time the boy converses in spite of the paper, but ultimately gives up and leaves the room. Later the younger participant is likely to declare that his father does not communicate with him. That is not accurate according to our definition. The father has indeed communicated. His behavior message, at least for this particular moment, is that what he is seeing on the printed page has priority over what he is hearing from the boy.

Similarly, consider the teen who falls asleep during what the youth director at the church considered a most interesting Sunday evening lesson. Sleeping during the discussion does not necessarily constitute lack of communication, nor even lack of interest. It may mean the youth needed sleep.

Accepting either of these events as evidence that parents or teens do not communicate fails to recognize the nature of the communication process. Both of these illustrations describe an activity for which there is very little shared meaning. Communication, as we have seen, is a process which includes interpreting the other's behaviors and meanings toward a goal of shared meaning.

Ironically, it is the teen in the first example who, while saying Dad does not communicate, accepts a snap conclusion rather than exploring the meaning of the behavior.

Similarly, the youth director who simply alerts parents to their teen's lack of attentiveness in the second example may have missed a great opportunity to discover a shared meaning with a young person. That shared meaning could include the nature of a fatiguing social schedule or appropriate Sunday evening meeting behavior.

At any rate, it is impossible to not communicate. There may be little mutual understanding, but the behavior/behavior-interpretation process continues. Communication improves (there is an increase in shared meaning) when participants recognize that fact and seek to discover the underlying meaning of evasive actions.

All Communication Is Not Verbal

Tangentially related to the first misconception is the notion that in order to be true communication there must be an exchange of words, that all communication is verbal.

In contrast, researchers in the area of nonverbal communication (defined as "attributes or actions of humans other than the use of words themselves which has socially shared meaning" [Burgoon and Saine, 1978; p. 9]) place a relatively high degree of importance in this type of communication. Albert Mehrabian (1981) reports that when a verbal and nonverbal message do not correspond, we rely on nonverbal cues 93 percent of the time and on the actual words that are spoken only 7 percent of the time in determining what to believe.

Other researchers offer different percentages; but all agree that nonverbal cues take precedence over verbal ones (see for example Birdwhistell, 1979, or Thompson, 1972). Regardless of the precise figure, it seems clear that much of the impact of communication comes from other than verbal cues.

Eye contact constitutes one type of nonverbal cue. Mark Knapp (1978) reports that eye contact serves four primary functions. These include establishing or defining relationships, controlling communication patterns, displaying emotion, and reducing distractions.

The importance of eye contact in dealing with children was highlighted by Marilyn Anderes (1989). While the emphasis in this brief piece is on the importance of eye contact with preschoolers, anyone who has felt the frustration of not being able to gain the undivided attention of another will recognize the importance of the concept for all ages.

In addition to eye contact, touching constitutes an important nonverbal cue. Jesus utilized touch extensively in his earthly ministry. On one occasion, recorded in the book of Mark, chapter five, the issue of touch comes to the fore when Jesus raises the question of who touched him in the crowd. The disciples, unclear on the importance of touch, scoff at the question, but Jesus persists. Finally, he identifies the woman who has relied on the healing properties of his touch.

Blondis and Jackson (1977) suggest a twentieth-century counterpart to the healing ministry of Jesus. They believe that in nursing touch may be the most important of all the nonverbal behaviors. They further point out that other nursing procedures depend upon touch.

Other functions of touch include communicating empathy and caring, friendship, or love and the desire to intimacy. The very common handshake ritual used extensively in the West is of course a common touching behavior.

This often overlooked means of communication may be extremely significant for those working with teens. Willis and Hoffman (1975) discovered that junior-high-age students experience only about half as much touch as their counterparts in the primary grades. In fact, there is a steady decline from infancy in the amount of tactile communication until that point when young people begin to experiment with touching members of the opposite sex.

Another area of nonverbal study with enormous implications for those who work with teens is territoriality and personal space. One teen reported that his father was always crowding him, trying to be his buddy. Observation revealed that while the father saw closeness as availability, the son saw the same distance as invasion of his personal space. As a result the younger participant was constantly backing away or turning his body.

Edward Hall (1966) in a pioneer work on the subject of territoriality and personal space observed four distances among middle-class adults. While the limits associated with these zones will vary from culture to culture (Wallace and Wallace, 1989), and even within cultures, general estimates of personal space are nonetheless helpful for understanding the concept, at least for the United States context.

Hall observed that *intimate distance,* which ranges from actual contact to eighteen inches, is reserved for those with whom people are emotionally close. A high degree of trust is associated with allowing someone to enter this zone.

The second territory surrounding the individual Hall labeled *personal distance.* This zone ranges from one-and-one-half to four feet. Persons allowed inside this zone enjoy candid closeness, but not intimacy.

Social distance, four to twelve feet, is usually used to conduct business, or at a social gathering. Salespeople intuitively use this zone to communicate availability but not overbearingness.

Public distance which occurs at twelve to twenty-five feet is usually used for public gatherings such as a speech or lecture. The diagram below illustrates

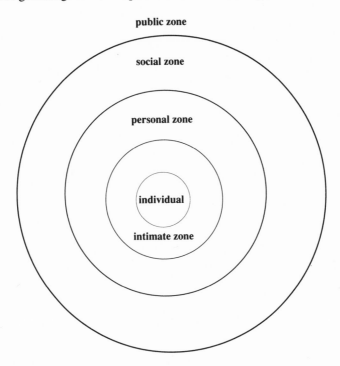

how these zones emanate from an individual like invisible bubbles which keep others at the proper distance.

While the appropriate interpersonal space or territory is clearly a function of relationship and culture, what may be less obvious is that age also plays a part (Malandro and Barker, 1983). Studies indicate that adult spacing is usually learned by the age of twelve years. Prior to that time, adults tend to dismiss inappropriate invasion of personal space on the basis of childishness. However, the emotional impact of suddenly imposing adult territorial standards on teens has yet to be discovered.

These brief discussions of eye contact, touch, and territory serve to refute the notion that communication must be verbal. In fact the sharing of understanding, more often than not, occurs without the benefit of words.

All Communication Is Not Oral

Closely aligned to the argument that all communication is verbal is the notion that all communication is oral. The difference in these two positions can be better understood when it is recognized that the world "verbal" comes from the Latin term for "word." On the other hand, oral means "mouth" (Stewart and

D'Angelo, 1988). Hence a verbal communication is communication with words, while an oral communication is by mouth. A note on the refrigerator door is therefore verbal but not oral, while the tone of voice used to get a message across is oral without verbal communication.

One aspect of verbal communication is listening. Listening is a vital, yet often neglected part of the process of mutual understanding of meaning.

The act of listening is the most time-consuming aspect of interpersonal communication. In a pioneer study cited by Wolvin and Coakley (1988), Rankin discovered that adults spend more than 42 percent of their communication time, and nearly 30 percent of their total waking time, in listening. The study has been replicated repeatedly since its original publication.

Yet, conversation with teens and their parents reveals that a large portion of what has been labeled "the generation gap" is really a gap in effective listening. Accusations from both generations abound that the other fails to listen carefully.

One teen revealed that a drug-dependent despair caused her to write a poem announcing her intention to commit suicide. In a last attempt to seek help from her pastor-father and his active in the church wife, she read the poem at dinner one evening. The measured response was only that the whole topic seemed rather "weird." The young person goes on to relate that only a miraculous intervention spared her life and brought her to the place of sharing the story on the campus of a church-related college. Of course, not all listening problems reach such extremes, but a listening crisis certainly exists.

One of the reasons for the crisis of listening in America today is that so few people have actually taken the time to consider the nature of listening. Many believe that listening is synonymous with hearing. Therefore they reason, "If my audio acuity is good, then I am a good listener." Nothing could be further from the truth.

In fact, hearing is only the first step in a three step process of good listening. The second step is "tuning in." Try this experiment. Stop reading for a moment, and just listen to what is going on around you.

What did you hear? Chances are you tuned in to some sounds that were there before but that you had effectively filtered out through your attention process.

Since society bombards continually with messages, most people have learned to effectively filter out that in which they have no immediate interest. Advertisers, recognizing this fact, use the repeat message over the airways in order to increase the likelihood of gaining attention. Often small children will use the same approach with Mom and Dad. Sadly however, by the teen years, most young people have stopped repeating their messages.

The third step in the listening process is attempting to understand. Herein lies the most difficult part of listening across the generation gap. Many times the family counselor will respond to the accusation of youth that, "Mom and Dad just don't listen to me," by demonstrating that parents do indeed know every word that has been said. Youth, however intuitively sense that real listening involves more than parroting words. It also includes an attempt to understand.

For example, the parent who replaces, "Because I said so," with some solid reasons for a particular prohibition gains increased respect from young people. That parent demonstrates listening skill in having seen the teen's point of view prior to making a decision. Ironically, instead of losing control and parental authority, many times this family leader gains status in the eyes of teens. Perhaps that is because those teens actually are looking for some firm boundaries that make sense, and which are established by persons who are secure enough to consider opposing sides of an issue.

Hence, we see that far from being all oral, communication is to a large degree non-oral. Further, when this aspect of communication is improved, especially in the area of listening, great benefits result.

Communication Is Not Just Information Exchange

While the exchange of information is an important aspect of communication, it is not the sum and substance of the process. In fact, taking their cue from Watzlawick, Beavin, and Jackson (1967), many researchers agree that every communication act has two elements. One is information, but equally important is the relational aspect of the act.

For example the sentence, "Finish reading this chapter," carries with it both informational and relational aspects. On the informational side there is the message that the author wants the reader to complete the chapter. On the relational side of the cue, however, is the implication that the author has the authority to tell the reader how to spend his or her time.

Similarly, the parent who fails to recognize that every communication event has both an informational and a relational aspect will fail to see the difference between, "Because I said so," and "Because I feel responsible for you and am concerned about your welfare." Both messages may insist on the same compliant behavior. The first, however, rationally says, "I am in charge. You have no voice in the matter. I make all the rules." The second approach conversely proclaims, "Authority brings with it responsibility. I care for you and about you."

Students of the relational aspect of communication suggest that relationships are best understood as either complementary or symmetrical. In *complementary relationships* each person's behavior complements the other. Typical complementary relationships include the boss-employee, teacher-student, or doctor-patient. These are based on the differences of the participants.

On the other hand *symmetrical relationships* are based upon the sameness of the participants. The participants behave on the basis of equal status. Close friendships, the relationship of many identical twins, and healthy, close husband and wife relationships serve as examples.

This understanding of the relational nature of communication becomes particularly interesting in the relationship between parents and teens. Obviously, when children are born, their relationship with their parents is strictly complementary. Children cry, adults respond; children wet, parents change; children sleep, parents sigh with relief. So goes the pattern of complementary roles in the earliest years.

As a child becomes older, however, he or she increasingly develops the ability to care for and think for himself. This process is accepted as natural by children, but it is not nearly so natural for their parents. One parent lamented that the big yellow monster had gobbled up his youngster when the child boarded the school bus for the first time and entered a world outside the rigid complementarity of the parent-child relationship. Helpful friends of teenagers, however, comforted, "Wait until it's not a school bus but an old jalopy driven by one of her friends."

Without realizing it, these advisors were explaining that as children mature the relationship with Mom and Dad becomes less and less complementary, and more and more symmetrical. That is, increasingly the child develops opinions, attitudes, values, and beliefs apart from parental influence.

For example, one marvels at the father in Jesus' story of the prodigal son. How the man avoided the urge to argue or retaliate when his son asked for his share of the inheritance, defies understanding. Instead, in Jesus' parable the father resists the temptation to retain a complementary pattern and allows symmetry to occur. Through his actions the father says, "I respect you as a fellow human being who has the right to make his own decisions" (and by implication, his own mistakes).

In order for a truly symmetrical relationship to develop, both persons must have freedom to choose other alternatives. Hence, we can trace the progression from childhood's complementarity to an adult relationship. In infancy, the relationship is necessarily complementary. As time passes the child develops other alternatives based on experiences beyond the home. Finally, the young adult has the ability to be totally independent of parental values and authority. At this point he/she establishes a great deal of shared understandings with parents on some topics but in other areas does not share understanding with Mom or Dad.

Obviously then, the teen years are critical in the relationship between young people and their parents. Parents who believe that appropriate information exchange is all there is to communication will settle for notes on the refrigerator, while their young people are making crucial life and death decisions.

Goals of Religious Education for Teenagers

This understanding of communication not only addresses the relationship between parents and teens but also suggests some important goals for the church's ministry to youth. Three such goals particularly emerge.

Maximize Communication Between Teens and God

While Christians express it in a variety of ways, the purpose of Christian education programs includes helping people develop an appropriate relationship with the divine. In other words the ministry serves to increase the shared understanding or shared meaning between participants and God.

Of course, developing a relationship with divinity takes on a different dimension than any other relationship, since scriptures clearly teach that God is unchanging. Therefore, to increase the overlap of shared meaning necessitates a change in the human participant.

Maximize Communication Between Teens and Parents

In the case of teenagers, the goal of Christian education is expanded to include assisting in the development of shared meanings between young people and their parents. That is, to assist in the improvement of communication between these two generational groups.

Someone will surely offer as an exception the young person who has aligned with the church and its mission but whose parents are not in harmony with that same mission. To maximize shared understandings in this case may actually draw the teen away from the church and its gospel message, or so the argument goes.

While it is true that these circumstances require special care, it does not seem to follow that the two goals suggested thus far are mutually exclusive. Enabling a young person to better understand his or her parents may in fact better equip the teen to one day win Mom and Dad to religious faith. In other words, understanding and communication do not necessarily imply agreement.

Provide a Christian Environment for Maturation

A third goal of effective Christian education, given an understanding of communication and relationships, is to provide an appropriate environment for the maturation process to take place. The teen years are the time when young people move out of complementary relationships with most adults and seek their own points of view and positions on issues. The church, believing that it has a point of view with which people of all ages may align and find fulfillment and meaning, offers a distinct perspective for decision-making teens.

Potential Problems

Accepting these three goals does not automatically guarantee success in the church's ministry to teens. One potential pitfall stems from the fact that in the real world of the Christian education professional there are at least three participants, or triadic communication. The discussion above considered the first two.

Triads intensify the difficulty of communication in the best of circumstances. A simple experiment will serve to explain. Sit between two friends and ask each of them to pretend for a few moments that they share the setting alone with you.

Ask them to carry on a conversation as if the third person were not there.

You will soon discover that while you attempt to carry on each conservation separately you fall far short of quality communication in each case. Your colleagues, on the other hand, will become increasingly frustrated with your lack of attentiveness.

Something similar occurs any time triads are involved in an attempt at shared meaning. Pictorially the small shaded area demonstrates the difficulty in finding shared meaning with more than one person at a time.

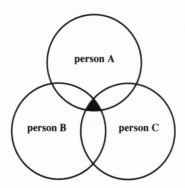

The tendency is for the problems of triads to be reconciled by the development of a dyad plus one (Wilmot, 1987). That is, there develops a primary relationship between two of the participants while the third is included only to a small degree.

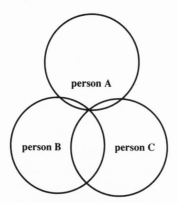

This does not imply that three people can never get along. However, the depth of shared meaning that is the hallmark of quality communication is at best difficult to attain in the triadic circumstance, since "when three people are in a face to face transaction, the transaction at any point in time is composed of a primary dyad plus one" (Wilmot, 1987; p. 22).

The implications of this problem for the youth minister are enormous. One youth pastor expressed genuine surprise when the governing board of the church dismissed him after several months of what he deemed successful ministry. Closer observation revealed that while the ministry was successful in terms of building relationships with teens, the parents of those teens had largely been left out of the dyadic coalitions.

In another situation, the minister to youth did an effective job of building a program which met the expectations of the adults in the congregations. The teens, however, found the same program less than exciting and drifted away.

In each of these situations, the problem was the same. The Christian educator to youth failed to recognize triadic involvement and adjust appropriately.

While much remains to be learned about the nature of triads, and what can be done to minimize their impact, research does give some clues. For example Mills (1953) discovered that the least active participant in a threesome is most likely to be left out of the coalition. In other words, the church youth program which includes activities with parents as well as teens will minimize the coalition formation of youth pastor and teens.

One church responded to this idea by scheduling a series of youth activities in which the teens did the planning and organizing and then invited parents to participate as their guests. Whatever approach is used, it must be remembered that the ultimate goal is not just for the youth educator to build shared meaning with the teens but to facilitate the building of teen relationships with God and with parents. Sometimes the wise Christian educator will sacrifice his relationship with the teen to accomplish the broader task.

A second potential problem in the accomplishment of these three goals involves the question of confidentiality. Jim and Sally Conway (1984) describe a personal example. When Sally told a friend over the telephone what a daughter had shared in confidence about her feelings for a certain boy, the youngster determined never to tell her mom anything again. Similarly, nothing will destroy the relationship between a Christian educator and the teens of a church quicker than the discovery that openness with that professional may mean revelations to someone else. While parents will from time to time need to know that kids are talking to some Christian adult, it should be a well-publicized, and never-violated rule that the nature of those conversations are not revealed.

Similarly, the wise parent encourages open conversation with sons and daughters when the atmosphere indicates that the conversations do not leave the confines of the family. In short, no matter what the relationship, enhancement will come when participants recall the ancient maxim that God provided two ears and only one mouth for a reason.

Accomplishing the Goals

The busy professional educator seeks a practical series of strategies for the accomplishment of these goals. Four general categories encapsulate these strategies.

Model Effective Communication

Having gained an understanding of the nature of the communication process, the Christian educator to teens will want to consciously model the best ways of developing shared meanings. This modeling process is most effective when it is consistently exemplified before both the teens of the church and their parents.

Understanding that communication does not necessarily imply verbal exchange, the professional Christian educator will accept silence and other nonverbals as appropriate at certain times. This is especially important when teens pass through a stage where the use of verbals seems to decline significantly (see Campbell, 1984).

Of course appropriate modeling will always include a generous amount of listening. The most skilled communicators in the Christian education profession remember that it is not sufficient to listen only to verbal and oral communication, but one must also strain to hear the nonverbals from both teens and parents.

Another aspect of effective modeling of communication for the Christian education professional involves appropriate use of touch. While societal standards of appropriateness must be strictly adhered to, and even surpassed, there are indeed proper and necessary times and places to communicate through touch. The slap on the back in jest, or the understanding hand on the shoulder in time of crisis says more than scores of words.

Good questioning techniques also are a part of the effective Christian educator's role. Open-ended questions, to which respondents cannot answer with a simple "yes" or "no," go a long way in getting at the heart of what another is feeling.

The consistent use of these and similar communication techniques aids greatly in the accomplishment of the goals of a quality Christian education program to teens.

Develop a Ministry of Presence

Realizing that communication and relationship go hand in hand, the effective Christian education communicator concentrates on a ministry of presence. Simply being available to do what teens choose to do says, "I care about you and want to be a part of your world."

One professional in ministry to teens discovered that she was most effective in a lunch-time program during the school year. She simply made it a point to visit high schools during teens' lunch periods. There was no agenda, or formal gathering, just an attempt to be involved where her young congregates spent time.

Another minister to youth with responsibility for Christian education to teens found that one of his most effective avenues of ministry came on the golf course. While only a handful of the teens from the youth fellowship played golf, they were quick to invite other nonchurch friends who later became a part of the fellowship.

Similarly, the effective professional performs the ministry of presence with parents. A most effective method for reaching unchurched households includes developing an interest in their activities.

The wise professional recalls that parents, like teens, have interests outside the church and family. Recognizing these interests, and developing ways to participate in them, earns the right to assume the more traditional aspects of ministry. Special care should be given to search out and utilize the interests of parents who are not a part of the regular church family.

Educate in Communication

As indicated in the Sebine study mentioned earlier in this chapter, many parents and teens are unsure as to the real meaning of communication. Still others have never taken the time to develop the necessary skills for effective communication. One responsive aspect of the church's ministry to families with teens includes programs which teach these important skills.

Seminars on listening or on nonverbal communication can be conducted on the local church level as ongoing programs, or as a special weekend ministry. Also, making available appropriate literature from the abundance of material on the subject of family communication will enable the Christian family to gain important communication skills.

Facilitate Communication

Ironically, many times the program of the church minimizes communication in the families of teens. For instance, those ministries which demand a great deal of parental time for church administration may need to be evaluated as to their real mission.

Further, the regular or special services of the church are often geared toward adults exclusively. While teens may be welcome, they seldom feel welcome unless the program applies directly to their interests and needs. Typical age-oriented programing does little to enhance family communication, since it inadvertently suggests that the church has nothing for the common life of parents and teens.

Instead, the effective church planner recalls that shared meaning often comes from shared experiences and thus designs activities to encourage the participation of the entire family. Opportunities are also given for meaningful evaluation of those programs across generations (see chapter ten).

One local church Christian educator became serious about this aspect of ministry and suggested an intergenerational Sunday school for one quarter. At first the reactions were negative, but once the elective program got under way adults discovered there was much to learn from the younger generation. Similarly, the teens involved responded favorably to being included as an equal in the discussion periods of the lesson.

Conclusion

Visitors to another culture will often try to communicate by speaking slower and louder in hopes of being understood. As children move into the alien culture of adolescence, a similar phenomenon occurs. Their exchanges with the adult world become much less frequent and may be punctuated with loud, even angry, outbursts.

In the midst of this confusion, the effective Christian educator recognizes the inseparability of communication and relationships. As a result, that educator seeks to strengthen families and the individuals within those families by acting as translator and guide across the cultural gap.

REFERENCES

Anderes, M. (1989). Point your face at me. *Decision* (May), 39.

Birdwhistell, R. (1979). *Kinesics and context.* Philadelphia: University of Pennsylvania Press.

Blondis, M. N., and Jackson, B. E. (1977). *Nonverbal communication with patients.* New York: John Wiley.

Burgoon, J., and Saine T. (1978). *The unspoken dialogue.* Dallas: Houghton Mifflin.

Campbell, R. (1984). The "grunt" stage. In J. Kessler with R. A. Beers (Ed.) *Parents and teenagers.* Wheaton, Ill.: Victor Books.

Conway, J., and Conway S., (1984). The silent treatment. In J. Kessler with R. A. Beers (Ed.) *Parents and teenagers.* Wheaton, Ill.: Victor Books.

Dance, F.E.X. (1970). The concept of communication. *Journal of Communication, 20,* 201-210.

Dausey, G. (1984). Communication killers. In J. Kessler with R. A. Beers (Ed.) *Parents and teenagers.* Wheaton, Ill.: Victor Books.

Fisher, B. A. (1978). *Perspectives on human communication.* New York: Macmillan.

Goss, B., and O'Hair, D. (1988). *Communicating in interpersonal relationships.* New York: Macmillan.

Hall, E. T. (1966). *The hidden dimension.* Garden City, N.Y.: Doubleday.

Infante, D. A., Rancer, A. S., and Womack, D. F. (1990). *Building communication theory.* Prospect Heights, Ill.: Waveland.

Knapp, M.L. (1978). *Nonverbal communication in human interaction* (2nd ed.). New York: Holt, Rinehart and Winston.

Malandro, L. A., and Barker L. L. (1983). *Nonverbal communication.* New York: Random House.

Mehrabian, A. (1981). *Silent messages.* Belmont, Calif.: Wadsworth.

Mills, T. M. (1953). Power relations in three person groups. *American Sociological Review, 18,* 351-357.

Sebine, G., cited in Dausey, G. (1984). Communication killers. In J. Kessler and R.A. Beers (Eds.) *Parents and teenagers.* Wheaton, Ill.: Victor Books.

Stewart, J., and D'Angelo, G. (1988). *Together.* New York: Random House.

Thompson, J. J. (1972). *Beyond words: Nonverbal communication in the classroom.* New York: Citation Press.

Wallace, R.C., and Wallace, W.D. (1989). *Sociology* (2nd ed.). Boston: Allyn and Bacon.

Watzlawick, P., Beavin, J.H., and Jackson, D.D. (1967). *Pragmatics of human communication.* New York: W.W. Norton.

Willis, F.N., and Hoffman, G.E. (1975). Development of tactile patterns in reaction to age, sex, and race. *Developmental Psychology, 11,* 866.

Wilmot, W.W. (1987). *Dyadic communication* (3rd ed.). New York: Random House.

Wolvin, A., and Coakley, C.G. (1988). *Listening.* Dubuque: Wm. C. Brown.

Chapter Seven

Adolescent Moral Development and Sexuality

BONNIDELL CLOUSE

Morality to a teenager is not the same as morality to a child nor is it what it will be when the teenager becomes a mature adult. There is a progression from early childhood to adulthood in an understanding of what is right, what is wrong, and what it means to be a good person. Moral development is concerned with changes that occur over time in behaviors, emotions, and cognitions relative to the realm of the moral.

Theories of Moral Development

Psychologists approach the study of moral development from various perspectives (Clouse, 1985a). Learning psychology has its roots in the philosophy of British associationist John Locke, who held that the child is born as a *tabula rasa,* or blank slate. It is the experiences children have that make them what they become. Learning psychologists such as John B. Watson (1931) and B.F. Skinner (1978) focused on observable behaviors that are shaped by environmental events. Albert Bandura (1965), a social learning theorist, emphasized the importance of appropriate models. Moral development occurs when the child imitates the actions of responsible adults and is reinforced for socially acceptable behavior and punished for socially unacceptable behavior.

Humanistic psychology stems from the philosophy of Jean-Jacques Rousseau who saw the child as a noble savage. Children are "noble" in that they are born with the potential for self-development including the propensity to develop morally; they are "savage" in that they seek to go their own ways and make their own decisions. Humanistic psychologists such as Carl Rogers (1978) and Abraham Maslow (1970) favor the encouragement of children's natural desire to be moral by letting them choose their own values and act upon their own decisions. Moral development comes from within the individual rather than being imposed by an outside source.

Psychoanalytic psychology, as proposed by its founder Sigmund Freud (1913/1949), views the person in still another way. The child is born as an *id* or an "it" with irrational passions and instincts, and thus is oriented to gratification and pleasure. In time, the *ego* or "I" emerges which is oriented to a real world, and later a *superego* or "conscience" develops which is oriented to matters of right and wrong. Development from infancy to adulthood is seen as bringing about a more goodly or moral individual, goodly in the sense of the person being able to live in a society with others and also in the sense of a developing conscience that monitors attitudes and behavior.

The bulk of the literature on moral development relates to cognitive psychology with its emphasis on stages of moral reasoning as given by Jean Piaget (1932) and Lawrence Kohlberg (1984). Piaget, a Swiss-born, French-speaking biologist and philosopher, watched children at play and told them stories involving a moral dilemma to see what their responses would be. He found that prior to the time children start to school they look at the *consequences* of behavior to determine if the behavior is good or bad. If they are rewarded, they perceive what was done as the right thing; if they are punished, they perceive it as wrong. Parents and other adults make the rules and these rules must be followed. The small child brings no further understanding to bear on the matter; one does what one is told. This morality of heteronomy, to use Piaget's term, is unilateral and imposed by those in authority. Children accept that they must obey because the rules are given by those who have the power to punish or reward. The first morality of the child, then, is one of constraint. It demands unquestioning adherence to the will of another.

The second morality of the child, more apt to be seen in children at the elementary school level, involves an understanding of right and wrong not so much in terms of the objective consequences of the act as in terms of the *circumstances* surrounding the event. The wrongdoer's intentions should be taken into consideration, not just the amount of damage done. In the context of peers or equals, getting along with age-mates becomes as important as obeying those in authority. Furthermore, rules are flexible and subject to change. The reason for obeying rules is because these rules have been agreed upon by those involved and must be followed out of consideration for all concerned. This morality of autonomy, again using Piaget's term, is bilateral and based on mutual agreement with others. It is a morality not of constraint but of cooperation. Children are beginning to do their own thinking as to what is good and what is bad.

Kohlberg's Theory

Lawrence Kohlberg expanded Piaget's two-process morality system to a six-stage sequence that extends from early childhood through mature adulthood. This was accomplished by focusing on the adolescent and young adult. Like Piaget, Kohlberg (1973a) emphasized the reasoning or intellectual functions that occur in moral development and measured the stage of moral thinking by what a person said in response to stories involving a moral dilemma. Stages are invariant, hierarchical, and universal. Kohlberg found that most people make statements at more than one stage depending on the circumstances at the time.

A key term used by Kohlberg is *conventional* which means that right and wrong are determined on the basis of convention or what society expects of its members. The conventional level is at the midpoint of moral development and includes the two middle stages (Stages 3 and 4) in the hierarchy of moral reasoning. A person whose reasoning is at Stage 3 equates good behavior with whatever pleases or helps others and believes one should live up to the expectations of family, friends, and neighbors. Good people are considerate and kind to the significant people in their lives. A person whose reasoning is at Stage 4 has a genuine understanding and respect for the law and willingly submits to rules and regulations. The law assures fairness or justice not only to us, our friends, and the people we know but also to those with whom we may never have contact. The law treats everyone equally, and an appreciation of this makes for law-abiding citizens who can live together in peace and harmony. Without rules, regulations, and laws, society as we know it could not exist. Most adult Americans reason at the conventional level.

At the earlier *preconventional* level (Stages 1 and 2) a person interprets goodness and badness on the basis of the physical consequences of the act. Kohlberg's first stage clearly parallels Piaget's morality of constraint or heteronomy. Avoidance of punishment and unquestioning deference to power are valued in their own right. Moving on to Stage 2, some elements of Piaget's second morality of cooperation or autonomy can be seen. Fairness, reciprocity, and equal sharing are present. Social interaction becomes possible and is a step higher than the first stage in which the person is not involved in the decision-making process. However, right and wrong are still based on the consequences of behavior to the self. The Stage 2 person believes the good is that which satisfies one's own needs, and human relations are viewed in terms like those of the marketplace where reciprocity is emphasized ("you scratch my back and I'll scratch yours").

Adults who advance to the *postconventional* level (Stages 5 and 6), having progressed through the previous four stages, are able to see beyond their own personal interests (preconventional) and beyond the norms and regulations of the family and social groups to which they belong (conventional) and are in a position to make decisions based on universal principles that apply to all people everywhere. Stage 5 provides a rationale for choosing among alternative social systems and supplies guidelines for the creation of new laws and arrangements.

It is an understanding that the law was made for man not man for the law. Stage 6 reasoning is exemplified by an obligation to self-chosen ethical principles that include the worth and dignity of every human being regardless of race, nationality, socio-economic status, or contribution to society. The postconventional level, then, allows for judging right and wrong, not in terms of one's own interests (preconventional level) or in terms of what is best for one's group (conventional level) but rather by what is basic to the dignity of people everywhere. The individual at this highest level has progressed in moral reasoning from one who is directed by the consequences of behavior to the self (Stages 1 and 2) to what society says is right (Stages 3 and 4) and finally to a self-directed socially responsive and responsible person who has an integrated set of values that apply to the whole human race (Stages 5 and 6). Approximately 20 percent of adult Americans make statements at Stage 5 and less than 2 percent make statements at Stage 6.

Adolescents at Different Stages

Adolescents, like adults, may be found at all stages of moral understanding, although some stages are more prominent than others during the teen years. A teenager whose reasoning is at Stage 1 may say it is all right to copy test answers as long as the teacher is not looking or to drive fast as long as parents do not find out or to cheat on one's boyfriend or girlfriend as long as he or she does not know you are doing it. It is only wrong if one is caught and the consequences are not to one's liking.

The adolescent at Stage 2 goes a step further in that reward and punishment come as the consequences of behavior rather than being the determiners of whether the behavior is good or bad. Copying test answers may result in a failing grade, driving fast may mean driving privileges are suspended, cheating on a friend may give rise to a broken relationship. One does not want these things to occur. However, a person is obligated only to those who are in a position to return the favor. The teacher must reward the student for being honest, the parents must hand over car keys if driving is acceptable, and one's boyfriend or girlfriend must remain true. If others do not do their part, you are no longer responsible to do your part. Turnabout is fair play.

Stage 3 thinking is a big step up from Stages 1 and 2 for now the adolescent equates good behavior with loyalty to the groups to which he or she belongs. What others *think* of you takes precedence over what they may *do* to you. Being moral implies concern for the approval of others. "Let's have an understanding" becomes more important than Stage 2's "let's make a deal." Most adolescents view themselves as members of several groups or subgroups and this may cause confusion if allegiance is given to those with differing definitions of how a person should act. If the teenager wants to get along with teachers and also with classmates, and if teachers frown on copying answers while classmates say it is all right, then a decision must be made as to the direction one will go. Parents and peers may not agree as to what constitutes "good" driving, and although both parents and peers would applaud relationships that would involve mutual commitments, they may not agree on who those friends should be. Stage 3 usually begins in preadolescence and is a dominant stage during the adolescent period (Hersch, Paolitto, and Reimer, 1979).

The inadequacy of Stage 3 becomes apparent when the adolescent must deal with problems on a societal level. Now the larger society takes precedence over the particular groups to which one belongs. The adolescent comes to understand that there are rules that are binding on everyone and that respect for delegated authority is essential to keep the society all in one piece. The law should be followed not only when it benefits the self and one's friends but also when it benefits people we do not know and have never met. Reasoning at Stage 4 means we will obey the speed limit not only for our protection and the protection of the occupants of the car we are driving but for the safety of everyone on the road. Others have the same right to a safe environment that we have. Everyone is obligated to the law and protected by the law.

Adolescents on occasion may make statements at the postconventional level, Stages 5 and 6, although this is not common (Kohlberg, 1984; Keasey, 1975). Adopting self-chosen ethical principles that are at variance with the attitudes of others or seeking alternative social arrangements that meet the needs of a larger portion of the citizenry usually comes later than the teen years if it comes at all. Adolescents may say that certain laws or rules are unfair and may demonstrate against institutions such as a nuclear plant or an abortion clinic even though these institutions are operating within the law, but one must look at the reasoning behind the statements or behind the demonstrations to determine the stage of moral development. If a young man refuses to register for the draft, is he doing it to preserve his own life and health (preconventional), because the church says it is wrong to engage in combat (conventional), or because he feels within himself that war is a moral evil and does an injustice to people everywhere (postconventional)? Only when right is determined by conscience, in accordance with the dignity and worth of human beings as ends in themselves rather than as means for some other good, can it be said that one is reasoning at the postconventional or principled level.

Kohlberg (1973b, 1981) also postulated a seventh stage having psychological and religious significance. Stage 7 involves a sense of oneness with the universe, a feeling of being an integral part of all creation. Rather than seeing oneself as a finite being, alienated and alone, one comes to view himself or herself as a part of all that exists, a portion of the totality of life. Many people have experienced this rush of mystic awareness, perhaps while watching the ocean or listening to beautiful music, but moments like this are fleeting. Adolescents also may feel a sense of unity with God, life, or nature that engulfs their whole being, although such feelings are more apt to occur during life's later years. Stage 7 is not a true moral stage for it has no definable structure nor is it logically or cognitively more adequate than the previous stage. The sense of euphoria and well-being that accompanies Stage 7 could occur to someone at any stage of moral development.

Research on Adolescents and Kohlberg's Stages

Kohlberg (1984) presented data for stage responses of middle-class urban boys in the United States, ages ten, thirteen, and sixteen. Approximately 40 percent of ten-year-olds were at Stage 1, 30 percent at Stage 2, 20 percent at Stage 3, and 10 percent at Stage 4. By contrast, the dominant stage for thirteen-year-olds was Stage 3 (approximately 30 percent) with about equal numbers responding at Stages 2 and 4 (approximately 20 percent each). Not until one tests sixteen-year-olds are statements seen at the postconventional level. Stage 5 accounted for about a fourth of the responses of sixteen-year-olds with Stages 4 and 3 following close behind. Stages 1 and 2 were less frequent and Stage 6 was the least frequent of all. Charles Keasey (1975) compared thirty twelve-year-old and twenty-four nineteen-year-old girls as to their level of moral understanding. Twenty-six of the twelve-year-olds scored at the preconventional level and four scored at the conventional level; nineteen of the nineteen-year-olds scored at the conventional level and five scored at the postconventional level.

James Rest (1986) of the University of Minnesota reports scores of junior high and senior high students on the Defining Issues Test (DIT), a standardized, objective style measure of moral judgment. The DIT has been used in over 500 studies to assess the stage or level of moral reasoning of over 10,000 teenagers and adults. Scores may be obtained for Stages 2, 3, and 4, and for the postconventional level (Stages 5 and 6), although Rest recommends using the percent of responses at the postconventional level (P level) as being more valid than responses at earlier stages. Combining studies, Rest found the average P level of 1,322 junior high students to be 21.90. For 481 senior high students the P level was 31.80. The slightly higher scores at the postconventional level in comparison with scores obtained in other studies may be accounted for by the fact that on the DIT students choose from a list of statements accompanying each of six moral dilemma stories. Because a person is naturally drawn to reasoning a little higher than one's own, having a higher stage presented as an option may inflate the scores somewhat. Adults, in general, plateau at the stage accounted for by their level of education, their scores being comparable to those of students currently enrolled at that level. The P level for college students is in the 40s, for graduate students in the 50s, and for moral philosophy and political science doctoral students in the 60s (Rest, 1980).

Adolescents and Stage Four and One-Half

Kohlberg's research indicated that the Stage 5 thinking seen in some high-school students is probably not a true Stage 5; rather it is symbolic of a transition period between the conventional and the postconventional levels. Sometimes referred to as Stage 4 1/2, the reasoning takes on a subjectivism and relativism not seen in Stage 5 adults (Kohlberg, 1984). The Stage 4 1/2 teenager does not believe that right and wrong should be prescribed for anyone including himself or herself. One should not have to do what others say but rather decide on one's own what is moral. At the beginning of Stage 4 1/2 the adolescent may confuse relativism with an egocentric perspective, but as he or she advances in moral understanding a self-centered view of individual natural rights gives way to a recognition that social demands are sometimes necessary to preserve the rights of all persons.

Thomas Lickona (1983) writes that Stage 4 1/2 is more apt to come in the late teens as the result of "diversity shock." When young people go to college, for example, they meet all sorts of people who believe all sorts of things about sex, God, politics, and morality.

> For kids who have been exposed to only one "system" of morality or truth, that's a bucket of cold water in the face. They go from thinking, "There's only one right system—mine," to thinking, "If so many people believe so many different things, it must be just a matter of opinion. There's no right or wrong" (pp. 242-243).

Such an attitude is understandably disconcerting to parents and youth leaders, especially when accompanied by a change in behavior. If the young person stops going to church, argues from a political position quite different from that of the family, or has a live-in boyfriend or girlfriend, the thinking may be Stage 4 1/2 but the behavior cannot be differentiated from Stage 2 egocentrism.

Richard Young (1981) calls this a period of hedonistic experimentation in which the introjected values of childhood are rejected. It is a confusing time for many adolescents who feel fear, anger, and alienation while at the same time experiencing the emotions of freedom, anticipation, and excitement. The adolescent is sorting out which values to retain and which values to reject. Both affective and cognitive conflict are present. Young maintains that after the period of experimentation "the individual will be faced with the need to reestablish order and coherence in his or her system of values in order to provide for stability and predictability" (p. 169). A return to the church and to the values taught earlier is not atypical in adulthood.

But this is less apt to occur if leaders within the church, many of whom reason at the conventional level, take the attitude that the rebelliousness of youth is the result of satanic influence rather than a normal process of growing up. Youthworkers, pastors, and other adults cannot condone attitudes and behaviors that are contrary to their religious faith, but they should understand the importance of each individual adopting self-chosen ethical principles rather than merely obeying rules laid down by those in authority. Morality by definition must come from within. Not deciding for oneself is what DiGiacomo (1979), an educator in a Catholic high school, calls "a Stage 4 cop-out." Rather than trying to understand the principles behind the moral life, such as *why* premarital sex, stealing, and lying are wrong, students just say that their religion is against it. "For this mentality, religion becomes the arbiter of morals, and church membership is a short-cut to enlightenment by way of the unexamined life. Dogmatism in any form is unacceptable to the postconventional mind, and should be" (p. 69).

In an article entitled "A Developmental Perspective on Adolescent 'Rebellion' in the Church," Cathryn Hill (1986) elaborates further on the importance of a period of doubt on the part of the adolescent. Hill believes that a time of questioning is necessary in order to achieve steadfastness in one's faith. Even as youth from unchurched homes may rebel against their parents' godlessness and join a church, youth from religious homes may react against their parents' lives and values and reject for a time what they have been taught. To accept the former as right and the latter as wrong may be in accordance with one's theology but does not reckon with a basic principle of adolescent development. Hill writes that "if adolescents do not return to their original values, perhaps this may be a result of the church's inability to grow beyond a conventional level of development and meet the developmental challenge of adolescent faith" (Hill, 1986; pp. 316-317).

Kohlberg's Stages and Religious Belief

Is religious belief a prerequisite for moral development? Do adolescents who are firm in their religious faith score higher on Kohlberg's stages than their counterparts who are agnostic or uncommitted? In a summary of the research on this topic, Kohlberg (1981) did not find a relationship between religion and moral reasoning. Nor did he believe that one religion is more advantageous than another.

> Our evidence of culturally universal moral stages, then, is also direct evidence against the view that the development of moral ideologies depends on the teachings of particular religious belief systems. No differences in moral development due to religious belief have yet been found. Protestant, Catholic, Moslem, and Buddist children go through the same stages at much the same rate when social class and village-urban differences are held constant (p. 303).

Harris (1981), using a sample of 438 subjects from nine Catholic high schools, would support this statement as he did not find religious belief or religious practice to be significantly correlated with moral judgment scores. Religious knowledge, however, was related. In two other doctoral dissertations in which high-school students were the subjects, religious knowledge (O'Gorman, 1979) and religious education (Stoop, 1980) were seen to be positively correlated with moral judgment. Rather extensive reviews of the research have been published by Getz (1984) and by Rest (1986), both concluding that religious affiliation appears to be less important than religious ideology (conservative-liberal). Adolescents and young adults who are conservative in their religious beliefs tend to have lower postconventional scores than their peers. Some differences between Protestant denominations have been found (Blizard, 1980/1982; Ernsberger and Manaster, 1981) but again, these reflect whether the denomination espouses a more conservative or a more liberal position. Most of the studies, both published (e.g., Clouse, 1985b; Haan, Smith, and Block, 1968; McGeorge, 1976) and unpublished (e.g., Cistone, 1980; Lawrence, 1978/1979; Moore, 1979/1980; Sanderson, 1973/1974) support this inverse relationship between religious conservatism and principled moral reasoning. Sapp and Jones (1986) conclude that "while religion may stimulate earlier movement toward conventional moral reasoning, adoption of a restrictive set of religious beliefs may preclude the possibility of moving to postconventional levels" (p. 209).

A rationale given (Clouse, 1985b) is that the conservative nature is to conventionalize or to conserve. The conservation or preservation of the society is based on getting along with others (Stage 3) and obeying the law of the land (Stage 4). Without large numbers of citizens at Stages 3 and 4, the society as we know it could not survive. Those who are conservative are more apt to accept without question the teachings of their religion whereas those who are liberal place more value on change and look for ways to modify the existing system (Stage 5). Blizard (1980/1982) found that the major differences between adults in nine Protestant denominations could be attributed to the doctrines of the church. Members of churches that teach a personal God, an external source of authority, and an evangelical social perspective did not score as high as members of churches that teach an abstract God, an internal source of authority, and a humanitarian social perspective. Rest (1986) writes that: "A liberal religious ideology would place more responsibility on the problem-solving capacities of the individual and less reliance on external authority, thus encouraging more self-struggle with moral dilemmas and fostering more practice in working out just solutions" (p. 126).

Criticisms of Kohlberg's Theory

Research on religious ideology and moral stages has caused some consternation among religious academics, especially those whose persuasion lies at the conservative end of the theological continuum. For example, Wolterstorff (1980) and Vitz (1983) claim the stages lack empirical confirmation especially at the postconventional level, and they criticize Kohlberg for adopting the humanistic assumption that morality develops from within the self rather than being learned by an external authority. To their way of thinking, Kohlbergian morality and Christian morality are diametrically opposed. Supporters, however, see a striking similarity between Kohlberg's concept of justice and the justice of God's righteousness as revealed in scripture (Joy, 1983). They have applied the stages of moral judgment to God's progressive dealings with his people (Motet, 1978), and to solving problems that arise within the religious community (Clouse, 1986; Duska and Whelan, 1975; Pressau, 1977).

Critics also are quick to point out that some people regress as well as progress in moral reasoning, that the more verbally fluent achieve higher scores than those less capable of expression, and that Westerners appear to be at an advantage when compared to peoples in Third World countries who believe meeting the needs of relatives takes priority over adopting universal principles that apply to everyone alike. Still others say that giving teenagers an opportunity to choose for themselves what is right and what is wrong and to decide which rules to follow and which rules not to follow encourages civil disobedience, thereby working against the best interests of the society.

In contrast to religious conservatives who hold that divine revelation provides the basis for an understanding of morality (Blizard, 1982), secular humanists agree with Kohlberg that morality must come from within (Humanist Manifesto II, 1980). However, some humanists take exception to Kohlberg's assertion that higher stages are better than lower stages. The avoidance of relativism, although compatable with Judeo-Christian theology, leaves the secular humanist decidedly uncomfortable. Secular humanists wish to respect the choices of all individuals, preferring not to place people's choices on an evaluative dimension (Kohlberg and Simon, 1972).

Another concern often cited in the literature has to do with the relationship between moral judgment and moral behavior. What a person does affects others more directly than what a person thinks or says. So the charge is made that unless higher stages of moral judgment are accompanied by moral acts not seen at lower stages, an understanding of the reasoning processes has little value. Cognitive theorists are aware that to know the good is not necessarily to do the good and that thinking about moral issues is not a substitute for moral living. They agree that moral reasoning is only one part of a much larger picture and that a connection needs to be established between judgmental processes and moral behavior. "The sheer capacity to make genuinely moral judgments is only one portion of moral character. . . . One must also apply this judgmental capacity to the actual guidance and criticism of action" (Kohlberg, 1967; p. 179).

Numerous studies have been conducted on the relationship between judgment and behavior. Some of these are reviewed by Golda Rothman (1980) and by Rest (1986). Although specific acts do not relate exclusively to specific stages, there are positive correlations between moral thought and moral behavior. Sprinthall and Sprinthall (1981) reported that 75 percent of thirteen-year-olds at the preconventional and conventional levels cheated, whereas only 11 percent of the postconventional students cheated. They concluded that there is an obvious direct relationship between levels of moral judgment and behavior on tests of cheating. Ziv (1976) found a significant correlation between resistance to temptation and level of moral judgment, supporting Kohlberg's (1964) statement that the same variables that favor advance in moral judgment also favor resistance to temptation. Most of the studies in which adolescents are the subjects compare delinquents and nondelinquents. Moran (1988) and Fodor (1972) found delinquents to be lower in moral reasoning than nondelinquents. Rest (1986) also cites studies using the DIT in which the same conclusions are drawn.

Kohlberg also has been criticized for not giving sufficient consideration to the place of emotions in moral development. Opponents say that the affective cannot be ignored. One cannot be certain that a moral concept is grasped unless it is accompanied by an appropriate emotion. For example, showing glee over someone's misfortune would indicate a lack of moral maturity regardless of what the person might say. In *The Philosophy of Moral Development,* Kohlberg (1981) acknowledges that moral judgment often involves strong emotional components and that sentiment and cognition cannot be separated. He writes that each stage has its own motive. Stage 1 action is motivated by a fear of punishment, Stage 2 by a desire for reward or benefit, Stage 3 by an anticipation of disapproval of others, and Stage 4 by anticipation of dishonor. The emotion of fear is more prevalent at the preconventional level, whereas the emotion of guilt is more apt to be experienced at the conventional level. Anxiety may be included in both fear and guilt. Kohlberg's observation has been supported by a number of researchers, including Ruma and Mosher (1967) and Ziv (1976) who found significant correlations between guilt and moral reasoning.

Regardless of the relationship between thinking and feeling, Kohlberg (1981) maintains that the cognitive takes precedence over the affective.

Two adolescents, thinking of stealing, may have the same feeling in the pit of their stomachs. One adolescent (Stage 2) interprets the feeling as "being chicken" and ignores it. The other (Stage 4) interprets the feeling as "the warning of my conscience" and decides accordingly. The differences in reaction is one in cognitive-structural aspects of moral judgment, not in emotional "dynamics" as such (p. 141).

According to Carol Gilligan (1982), the moral development of girls and women differs from that of boys and men. In her book *In a Different Voice,* she says that females are more responsive to social relationships, the feelings of others, and real-life moral problems. Concern for the needs of others takes precedence over the rights of others, and harmony and compassion come before reciprocity and respect. Females are more inductive; males are more deductive. Females are attached; males are separated or detached. Females accept caring as the basis for morality; males believe justice to be the foundation of the moral quest.

Gilligan faults Kohlberg for using only males in his studies, thereby relegating the moral characteristics of females to a lower position (Stage 3) than those of males of the same age (Stage 4). She believes that individual rights and justice should not take priority over human relationships and caring. This is not to say the men are not capable of caring or that women do not believe in justice but rather that there are gender differences in moral progression that must be recognized in order to adequately understand the human condition. Ideally, both the ethic of responsibility and the ethic of justice should combine in moral decision making.

Kohlberg's response to Gilligan's charge of sex-bias is that the psychological study of the moral domain may be enlarged to include the affective ideas of caring, love, loyalty, and responsibility, but these should not be construed as a separate morality quite apart from the rational reconstruction of justice reasoning. Rather, these special relationships and obligations complement and are included within a basic understanding of moral development as a growing differentiation of the prescriptive and the universal. For example, personal decisions as to the way aging parents will be cared for supplement and deepen the generalized or universal obligation of justice for the well-being of the elderly. The moral issue is adequate care not the method employed. By including affective responses to real-life moral dilemmas the scope of the psychological assessment of the moral domain is broadened, but this in no way changes the fundamental position that the basis of moral development is an understanding of justice for all people (Kohlberg, Levine, and Hewer, 1983).

Research that supports or refutes Gilligan's claim of gender differences has, for the most part, been done with adults rather than with teenagers. Gilligan interviewed twenty-nine women who were considering abortion, a real-life moral dilemma involving care and responsibility both for the self and for the unborn child. It would be difficult to find a comparable group of men. Reflections of the ego or self do not lend themselves to "hard" research. However, in response to Gilligan's "different voice," a literature review on sex differences has been conducted by Bebeau and Brabeck (1987), Rest (1986), Thoma (1984), and Walker (1984). In each survey, gender differences were negligible. Whatever differences were found could be accounted for by age, education, type of moral dilemma story, or the situation in which the moral dilemma was framed. Studies need to be done with adolescents. Adolescence is a critical time for young girls who have to struggle with the powerful cultural messages to think, feel, and act in stereotypic feminine ways. The transition from childhood morality to adult morality may indeed be different for females than for males. Research should include all ages to verify or deny Gilligan's thesis.

Havinghurst's theory

At every stage of life there are challenges one must face in order to move to the next stage with confidence. Robert Havinghurst (1953) referred to these challenges as *developmental tasks*. During adolescence developmental tasks include achieving new and more mature relations with age mates, achieving a masculine or feminine social role, accepting one's physique and using the body effectively, achieving emotional independence from parents, selecting and preparing for an occupation, preparing for marriage and family life, desiring and achieving socially responsible behavior, and acquiring a set of values and an ethical system as a guide to behavior. These tasks are met when the adolescent is biologically and psychologically ready and when the society exerts pressure on the adolescent to perform. Successful achievement of a task leads to happiness, success with later tasks, and social approval; failure to achieve leads to unhappiness, difficulty with tasks that lie ahead, and social disapproval. The adolescent must take into consideration the very real world of the here-and-now while at the same time preparing for adulthood.

Two of the developmental tasks deal specifically with moral development; namely, desiring and achieving socially responsible behavior and acquiring a set of values and an ethical system as a guide to behavior. These tasks are critical during the teen years when young people begin to consider their place within the community and their accountability to the society in which they live. Early adolescence is especially critical in the decisions made concerning self-worth, the worth of others, and the value of education, health, work, and citizenship (Jackson and Hornbeck, 1989).

Peck and Havinghurst (1960) conducted a six-year study of fifteen boys and fifteen girls in a small American town, following them from their eleventh to their seventeenth years. Peck and Havinghurst wanted to see if success in one task correlated with success in other tasks, if success at one age correlated with success at a later age, and if poor performance on one task might be compensated for by good performance on another. There was evidence of positive correlations between tasks at the same age and between tasks at different ages. There was less support for the concept of compensation. Peck and Havinghurst also studied the character types of these young people and found that adolescents who came closest to reaching the highest type of morality which they called "rational-altruistic" were those adolescents whose parents were neither permissive nor highly controlling but rather they encouraged in their children an optimal balance between independent thinking and social conformity.

Havinghurst's theory has not generated as much research as would have been expected considering the popularity of his concept of developmental tasks. However, the theory is found in textbooks on child and adolescent development and has been applied to curricular and extracurricular activities (Tryon and Lilienthal, 1950). It has also sparked an interest in developmental tasks in Christian education (Godin, 1971) and in developmental tasks within the family (Duvall, 1971). Godin views the young adolescent as seeing Jesus as a historical figure, the middle adolescent as having faith in God, and the late adolescent as wanting to be moral, not to earn favor with God, but to please God. Duvall presents what she believes to be predictable stages of developmental tasks within the family unit.

Erikson's Theory

Erik Erikson (1968) views adolescence as a transition period between childhood and adulthood in which the adolescent is searching for identity. The teenager asks himself or herself such questions as: "Who am I?" "Where did I come from?" "Am I leading toward some kind of understandable future?" "What is life all about?" The goal is to harmonize one's past and future, to achieve self-certainty, to come to terms with sexual identity, and to develop an ideology or set of beliefs. One's ideology is confirmed by fidelity or commitment to others, by ritualization or everyday habits that make for balanced stable living, and by taking an anti-authoritarian stance. Erikson would agree with Piaget and Kohlberg that morality comes from within the person rather than being mandated by an outside source.

Some adolescents are not successful in achieving a sense of identity. They are uncomfortable with their uniqueness as persons and with their lack of connectedness to others. Erikson would say they are experiencing role confusion. They do not know who they are, where they came from, or where they are headed. They may be isolated, directionless, or, in some cases, they accept without question the roles others impose upon them.

James Marcia (1980) has extended Erikson's ego psychoanalytic theory to describe four identity types: identity diffusion, moratorium, identity achievement, and foreclosure. *Identity diffusion* types tend to be aimless, disorganized, and opportunistic. They give little thought to past or future, play different roles depending on who they are with, and generally have poor self-concepts. In school they take the easiest classes and do not care what others do as long as they are allowed to do whatever they please. Family relations are often poor, with a father who takes an authoritarian approach to child rearing. Identity diffused adolescents seemingly have no desire to join the adult world with its responsibilities and values. This type appears to be more numerous today than in past generations.

Moratorium types are aware that they must come to terms with occupation, sex role, and values but they are not prepared to make these decisions while in their teens or early twenties. They need a period of experimentation in which they change majors, try different jobs, go from one intense relationship to another, and convert to a succession of ideologies or religions. They tend to be anxious, extreme in their views, independent, competitive, and quite unpredictable. Because a period of moratorium is a luxury working youths cannot afford, moratorium types are more visible among college students who have been raised in financially comfortable circumstances.

Identity achievement types tend to be stable and mature, consistent in behavior and attitudes, and effective in interpersonal relationships. They often have a firm commitment to occupational choice and are comfortable with their religious values. They know who they are and where they are going. If all goes well, there is little identity crisis. If, however, doors are closed to their chosen profession, or they are jilted by their boyfriend or girlfriend whom they intended to marry, or their religion does not meet their scrutiny, identity achievement types are thrown into a time of searching for what went wrong. Given their desirable personality characteristics and a supportive family, they usually come to terms with alternatives and make a satisfactory adjustment. Compared with the other types, these young people have a distinct advantage.

Foreclosure types also know what occupation they wish to pursue, the kind of person they will marry, and the religious ideology they espouse. However, these aspirations come directly from the parents and are accepted without question. The young woman who becomes a beauty operator like her mother and gets her training at the same beauty school is probably an example of foreclosure, that is, if she has always understood that this is what she will do. Foreclosure types are often working youths who marry early and raise a family. They seem not to go through the identity crisis seen in their peers. Studies show, though, that they are more vulnerable to criticism, more accepting of traditional values, and more inclined to do what they are told by authority figures (Marcia, 1967). They usually come from families in which the father is controlling but not harsh. Of the four groups, they are lowest in autonomy and highest in need for social approval (Orlofsky, Marcia, and Lesser, 1973). If their place of work closes or their spouse leaves or the minister of their church is involved in a scandal, it is more difficult for foreclosure types to pick up the pieces and get on with their lives.

Given the characteristics of each identity type, it is not surprising that a review of the research (Marcia, 1980) reveals that identity diffusion and foreclosure types are more apt to reason at Kohlberg's preconventional and conventional levels whereas identity achievement types and moratorium types are more apt to reason at the postconventional level. Identity diffusion and foreclosure both represent an external locus of control in which the young person looks outside the self for an understanding of right and wrong. Identity achievement and moratorium are both indicative of an internal locus of control in which the young person decides for himself or herself what is moral and what is immoral. Almost all psychologists who study the topic of moral development agree that morality by definition must come from within the person, not imposed by religious, political, or social constraints.

Coles' Theory

Robert Coles has spent years studying the moral life of children; rich and poor, black and white, religious and nonreligious. Coles finds that the majority of children and adolescents today have no firm moral code or religious orientation to guide them in the decisions they must make. They receive little instruction or guidance in the home or the school, relying instead on peer influence or what seems to work best in a given situation. Coles firmly believes that in order for moral development to take place, traditional values such as a religious faith and a respect for authority are necessary. Young people must also understand why attitudes of "me first" and "winning at any cost" are unacceptable.

Both affluence and poverty appear to adversely affect moral development. Adolescents with money face the greatest uncertainty of all teenagers when confronted with such questions as to whether it is allright to have an abortion and what to do when pressured to drink at a party. Adolescents from the poorest homes feel the greatest pressure to take drugs, disobey authority, or join a gang.

"Almost 20 percent of the junior and senior high schoolers from the poorest circumstances agreed with the statement: 'Suicide is allright, because a person has a right to do what he wants with himself'" (Coles and Genevie, 1990; p. 46). This is in contrast with just 8 percent of others of the same age who agreed that suicide is all right. However, poor black children in the south who had religious teaching in the home and a social life within the church fared far better than wealthy white children in New England who did not have the advantages of a faith that communicated to them that they are children of God and should seek to follow God's plan for their lives. As Coles (1986) stated in *The Moral Life of Children,* "In home after home I have seen Christ's teachings, Christ's life, connected to the lives of black children by their parents. . . . Such a religious tradition connects with the child's sense of what is important, what matters" (p. 34).

In the fall of 1989 a massive survey was taken of over 5,000 children and adolescents in grades four through twelve throughout the United States asking them a number of questions including, "How do you decide what is right and wrong?" and "What system of values informs your moral decisions?" The survey was sponsored by the Girl Scouts of America, the Lilly Endowment, and the Mott Foundation with Robert Coles designated as the project director. The results showed a wide diversity in the "moral compass" used by young people today. Only 16 percent adhered to some kind of religious authority such as scripture or what the church teaches. Another 20 percent deferred to other authorities such as parents or youth leaders. Twenty-five percent said they would do what they felt was best for everybody, whereas 18 percent said they would do what felt good at the time or made themselves happy. Ten percent used the criterion of whether it would help them improve their situation or get ahead, and the other 11 percent had no rationale to help them decide right from wrong (Coles and Genevie, 1990). Many adults are shocked to find that today's youth do not have the values prevalent a generation or two ago. Yet these same adults are seemingly unaware that their own speech often betrays an emphasis on materialism and self-enhancement. The older generation has not taken the time to communicate to the younger generation the need for a cause greater than oneself. Nor do these older adults show in their own behavior that they adhere to an understanding of morality that transcends personal interests. Youth ministers in a variety of religious contexts need to be aware of the moral problems faced by adolescents today and use the message of faith to help these youngsters deal effectively with their problems.

Suggestions for Helping Adolescents Develop Morally

Help adolescents sort out values that are personal from values that are social.
That moral development takes place within the person rather than being imposed by an outside source does not mean that adolescents do not need help in sorting out values that are relative and personal from values that are fixed and agreed upon by the society. Relative values such as hairstyle or occupation are individualistic, providing freedom of expression. Fixed values such as not

shoplifting or ignoring traffic signals are not a matter of choice, having been determined by societal consensus. Young people have a right to resist interference in adopting personal values; they do not have a right to resist fixed values that are for the good of everyone. If adolescents do refuse to adopt fixed values into their behavioral repertoire, they should at least know what these values are and that deviation may be accompanied by judicial punishment. Youth ministers need to model this ability to differentiate one from the other by accepting choices made by teenagers that reflect individual preferences while not accepting choices that harm others or violate a law. If youth ministers are as judgmental of teenage males wearing earrings as they are of teenagers using drugs, they can hardly expect the young people they lead to discriminate between behaviors one has a right to choose for oneself and behaviors one must accept as a given for the well-being of the larger group.

Many religious communities have their own list of do's and don'ts that become the fixed rules for anyone who is a member. What is included on the lists and how long the lists are, differ from one religious group to another. Young people who match personal values with group values (Kohlberg's conventional thinkers and Erikson's foreclosure types) will not create any problems for themselves or for the youth minister. Other adolescents, however, identify with the religious community and also with groups not religious. Consequently, they are forced to sort out differing expectations, coming to terms with their own sense of morality. These are the adolescents who are most in need of patience and understanding. These are the adolescents who need to think through the consequences of their choices, keeping in mind the well-being of others as well as significance to the self. An attitude of open mindedness on the part of the youth minister and a willingness to discuss moral issues without giving the "right answer" will help adolescents resolve the conflicts they face.

Expose adolescents to the next higher stage of moral reasoning.

A basic tenet of cognitive development theory is that people are naturally drawn to the reasoning of someone at the next higher stage. By discussing moral dilemmas, both real and hypothetical in a group setting, there is a "plus one" model for almost everyone. The adolescent at Stage 2 will be drawn to the reasoning of an adolescent at Stage 3. The adolescent at Stage 3 will see that the reasoning of someone at Stage 4 can solve problems that are unsolvable given his or her own way of thinking. The adolescent at Stage 4 can begin to understand that being a good citizen and a moral person sometimes means looking at changes that need to be made in this world of ours and then setting about to institute those changes (Stage 5). The youth leader or minister can be a "plus one" model for adolescents who are at higher stages, providing the youth leader or minister reasons at a still higher stage. In this way the adult can influence the thinking of adolescents without resorting to indoctrination.

James Leming (1981) reviewed fifty-nine moral education programs; thirty-three using a values clarification approach (which did not appear to be effective), and twenty-six using a cognitive developmental approach (which did appear to hold promise). Of the twenty-six based on moral development stages, fifteen were conducted at the secondary level with eleven of the fifteen reporting statistically significant differences between adolescents enrolled in the programs and a control group of adolescents not enrolled in the programs. Differences held regardless of the socioeconomic status of the students. Leming concluded that "the moral development research indicates that with adolescents there is a reasonable expectation that one will find mean class growth of between 1/7 and 2/3 of a stage in cases where the intervention lasts from 16 to 32 weeks" (p. 160). Methods used in the programs were those described by Kohlberg (1978) as being necessary for stage growth development; namely, exposure to the next higher stage of reasoning, exposure to situations posing problems that the person's current level of reasoning does not solve, and an atmosphere of interchange and dialogue where conflicting moral views are compared in an open manner. Dennis Dirks (1988) writes that the lower than expected scores seen in members of conservative evangelical institutions may be due to the absence of cognitive dissonance and to church leaders asking for acceptance of their ideas rather than encouraging innovative thought. This is in contrast with the parables of Jesus that always produced cognitive disequilibrium, making the hearers question the meaning of his words.

Give adolescents opportunities to help others.

Helping others may range from assisting the neighbor next door to being involved in nonprofit agencies such as hospitals, nursing homes, day-care centers, or shelters for the homeless. Part of the ministry of the religious groups with which teenagers identify is to aid members of the parish or synagogue who are in need. Rather than being sporadic endeavors, these opportunities should be ongoing functions of the religious community. There is no better way to teach the younger generation the values of altruism, compassion, courtesy, generosity, and responsibility than to give them opportunities to help others. Adolescents need to see that they can make a difference in the lives of others, that they can contribute to the neighborhood in a positive way, that they are appreciated and needed and have a vital part in making the world a better place in which to live. Terry Anderson (1988) reports that in 1984 the Atlanta public school system began requiring high-school students to perform seventy-five hours of community service as part of the requirements for a diploma. The results were very positive. Anderson also mentions other programs used throughout the United States including a program in San Marcos, California, in which values were stressed. Educators in San Marcos reported that within three years test scores were up 26 percent for eighth-graders and 29 percent for high-school seniors. There was a 65 percent decrease in drug suspensions and a 90 percent drop in teen pregnancies. The dropout rate was 1.9 percent compared with the state average of 21.2 percent. Programs that are effective in the school can also be effective when used within the context of the church (see chapter nine for more ideas on social action in the church).

Adolescent Sexuality

Adolescents are physically capable of bearing children, but they are neither emotionally nor economically prepared to rear them. In our complex society where adolescence extends for a period of six or more years, young people are expected to put sexual drives on hold while they expend their energies preparing for the adult tasks of a career, financial independence, and social maturity. They must come to terms with their own identity before they are ready for intimacy (Erikson, 1968), and intimacy takes time—lots of time. It means intimacy with oneself, with friends, and finally intimacy with a special person with whom one wishes to be intimate in a way one does not wish to be intimate with anyone else. Erikson believed that this special relationship provides the foundation for marriage and in turn establishes a secure base for the children born of that union. Teenagers simply have not had the time to go through the necessary psychological stages to be good parents. Other psychologists hold that adolescents are not intellectually ready for the difficult decisions that accompany parenthood. "Although the human organism is reproductively mature in early adolescence (ages ten to fifteen), the brain does not reach a fully adult stage of development until the end of the teenager years" (Hamburg and Takanishi, 1989; p. 825).

Teenage Pregnancy

In the light of this psychological and cognitive unpreparedness, the figures on teen pregnancy are startling. Each year more than a million American teenagers become pregnant, four out of five of them unmarried. The proportion of blacks is about twice that of whites. White teens are more apt to have an abortion (47 percent) than black teens (41 percent) and more apt to marry prior to the birth of the baby (35 percent marital births) than blacks (8 percent marital births), resulting in 19 percent of white babies and 51 percent of black babies being born to unwed mothers (Wallis, 1985). The pregnancy rate among teenagers in the United States is more than twice that of Britain, Canada, France, Sweden, or the Netherlands, a fact attributed not to the frequency of the sex act but to the low use of contraceptives among United States teenagers (Adler, Katz, and Jackson, 1985).

The focus of attention is usually on the unwed mother who raises the child, but more recently studies have looked at the teenager father as well. Stengel (1985) reported that teen fathers are often more caring and feel more responsibility than the public image of them would expect. However, low income, bewilderment as to how to care for an infant, and rejection by the teenage mother's family often means teen fathers cannot cope. Their relationship with mother and child is often short in duration. In some families, the cycle of teen pregnancy is repeated time and again, the babies of unwed teens becoming parents in their own right within twelve to sixteen years.

Attitudes toward Premarital Sex

Behaviors cannot be divorced from attitudes, and, although there is not a one-to-one correspondence between what a person thinks and what a person does, thought and action are often related. Between 1969 and 1985 the percentage of Americans who viewed premarital sex as wrong dropped 29 points, from 68 percent in 1969 to 39 percent in 1985. It rose to 46 percent in 1987 perhaps because of the growing concern for sexually transmitted diseases such as herpes and AIDS (*Gallup Report,* 1987, August). In January of 1989, Market Facts, Inc. polled 2,046 teenagers, half male and half female, as to their attitudes on sex, religion, school, family, and future plans. The results were reported in *Seventeen* magazine (Chace, 1989). Forty-four percent of the girls and 54 percent of the boys agreed with the statement, "There's nothing wrong with premarital sex." In another survey, this one conducted in the fall of 1989 by Louis Harris for the Girl Scouts of America and involving 5,000 children in grades four to twelve, "54 percent of boys and 22 percent of girls in junior and senior high school say they'd have sex with someone they loved; 11 percent of boys and 22 percent of girls would 'try to hold off' if they could" (Hellmich, 1990). The *Gallup Report* (1987, August) found older adults and females to be less approving of premarital sex than younger adults and males. Persons over sixty-five years of age and Evangelicals had the highest disapproval rate (70 percent each). Protestants and Catholics were about even in 1969 (70 percent and 72 percent respectively) but by 1987 only 50 percent of Protestants and 39 percent of Catholics disapproved of premarital sex.

It would appear from these figures that the picture in many people's minds of premarital sex being approved by adolescents and young adults but not by parents and religious persons is not accurate. To place "blame" on the adolescent's peer group and not upon the society as a whole is unfair. The world of advertising and television programing communicates that sex is all right for any physically mature person and can be engaged in strictly for pleasure. "In the course of a year the average viewer sees more than 9,000 scenes of suggested sexual intercourse or innuendo on prime-time TV" (Wallis, 1985; p. 81). The large number of couples living together without benefit of marriage is interpreted by adolescents to mean that if others live this way, they can too.

Peer Influence

This is not to say that the peer group does not play a part in influencing teens, for causal observation and research studies show that it does make a difference what friends say and do. By the age of twelve, most children would rather go out with their age-mates than with their parents. At fourteen, they are extremely concerned with appearance, form a sense of identity with the peer group, have a lower opinion of parents, and withdraw emotionally from their parents. By age seventeen they have a better sense of who they are, are more self-reliant, and exhibit greater emotional stability (Hellmich, 1986). The advent to junior and senior high school introduces the adolescent to a larger and more heterogeneous group in terms of beliefs, values, and attitudes. Consequently, adolescents begin to question what they have been taught. Acceptance by friends becomes all important. The adolescent cannot be too different in appearance, speech, and actions in order to gain this acceptance.

Engaging in sex is sometimes viewed by adolescents as a way to increase popularity. Newcomer, Undry, and Cameron (1983) in a study at the junior high level found that teenagers with sexual experience were chosen more often by opposite sex peers as being popular. Sexual experience was also associated with feelings of independence. A self-administered questionnaire was completed by 1,153 adolescents from four public junior high schools in an urban area of Florida regarding their attitudes toward engaging in sex, their best friend's attitude toward engaging in sex, whether they had engaged in intercourse, and whether their best friend had engaged in intercourse. A follow-up study two years later revealed no evidence of same sex or opposite sex best friend influence on blacks or white males in making the transition from virginity to intercourse. White females, by contrast, were more than twice as apt to have intercourse within two years if their best friend had engaged in this activity, whether the friend was male or female (Billy and Udry, 1985).

After reviewing the literature, Woodroof (1985) concluded that peers rather than parents are the reference group exerting the greatest control over adolescent sexual behavior. This is consistent with a Louis Harris survey of 1,000 teens, ages twelve to seventeen in 1986 in which 73 percent of girls and 50 percent of boys said that peer pressure was the main reason for engaging in sexual activity. On the other hand, in the survey reported by Coles and Genevie (1990) only 11 percent of junior and senior high-school students reported feeling "a lot" of pressure to have sex.

Adult Influence

When teens do go to an adult rather than to peers for information about sexuality, parents are more apt to be approached than someone at the church or synagogue. Only 1 percent of 760 students in eight public junior high schools said they would consult a priest, minister, or rabbi, or a lay religious leader or other layperson within the church about sexual matters (*Search Institute Source,* 1989). Only 3 percent of over 5,000 children and adolescents in the survey sponsored by the Girl Scouts of America said they would seek out a member of the clergy for help with a moral problem. This is a relatively small figure considering that 82 percent of this group said they believed in the existence of God, 40 percent prayed daily, and more than a third said they had had a significant religious experience that changed the direction of their lives. This matter of not consulting adults outside the family was dubbed "The Wallpaper Factor" by Jeff Meade (1990). It appears that children and adolescents no longer take traditional authority figures seriously. "When it comes to the truly serious issues of right and wrong in children's lives, teachers and clergy are, much like wallpaper, present—but almost purely decorative" (p. 47).

If, as the research indicates, peers have the greatest influence, parents are second, teachers are third, and religious leaders have the least influence, what part, then, does the youth worker have in deterring the sexual activity of young people? The picture may seem bleak but the youth worker is part of a much larger scene. The whole influence of religion on youth may play a greater role than it would seem. One needs to look at studies comparing religious adolescents and nonreligious adolescents in terms of attitudes and behaviors regarding sexual conduct.

Does Religion Make a Difference?

Many studies have been conducted on this topic but relatively few have been published. There is no way to know if unpublished and published material come to similar conclusions. However, even the published studies show little agreement as to the effect of religion on the sexual behavior of adolescents. McCormick, Izzo, and Folcik (1985) administered a questionnaire to seventy-five male and eighty-eight female high-school students from a rural county of New York that asked them about their personal values and sexual experiences. Very religious students were not more likely to abstain from sexual intercourse than less religious students. Sheppard (1989), in a summary article for *Christian Parenting Today,* stated that "research shows little difference between the sexual behavior of Christian teens and a cross section of American adolescents" (p. 68). This statement is based on a survey conducted during the summer of 1987 with 1,438 young people, ages twelve through eighteen attending eight evangelical denominations. The survey was commissioned by the Josh McDowell Ministry with assistance provided by the Barna Research Group of Glendale, California. By age eighteen, 43 percent of these churched adolescents had experienced sexual intercourse and another 21 percent had engaged in fondling breasts or genitals. Nearly three in ten said they would be more likely to have intercourse if they were positive a pregnancy would not result, and four in ten said that if they intended to marry a person, intercourse with that individual would be acceptable (Sheppard, 1989).

Woodroof's summary of the literature on this topic published during the 1970s and early 1980s came to very different conclusions. Woodroof (1986) found a consistent inverse relationship between the degree of religiosity and the incidence of sexual intercourse. His own study of 477 freshmen attending eight colleges affiliated with the Churches of Christ supported this relationship. Mahoney (1980), likewise, found that adolescents high in religiosity were less likely to engage in sexual behaviors. In other research, Jensen, Newell, and Holman (1990) studied the frequency of sexual intercourse of 423 single students enrolled in family relations classes at Cameron University in Lawton, Oklahoma, and at the University of Wisconsin-Stout. A five-way analysis of variance design included the variables of church attendance, age, state, gender, and attitude toward sexual permissiveness. Attitude toward sexual permissiveness was the only significant predictor although it interacted with church attendance in that non-permissive males and females who attended church had the lowest frequency of sexual behavior, but permissive subjects who also attended church every week had one of the highest frequencies of sexual intercourse.

Attitudes, then, appear time and again to be correlated with adolescent sexual behavior. Religious belief may or may not be related. With older adolescents, however, attitude and belief are not so readily separated. Davids (1982) found religious belief to be important in his study of 298 Jewish students at York University in Toronto. Students who were more involved in religious practice and to whom the Jewish religion was a greater force were less likely to favor premarital sex. In an earlier study with 443 late adolescents at Indiana State University, Clouse (1973) noted a statistically significant difference between religious conservatives and religious liberals in their response to the statement, "Premarital sex is not wrong as long as both people are willing." Students who accepted the basic doctrines of the Christian faith were significantly less apt to agree with the statement. Medora and Woodward (1982) also found significant differences in opinion on premarital sex between religious and nonreligious students enrolled in human development courses at the University of Nebraska-Lincoln.

The lack of agreement as to the role of religion in the conclusions of these studies may be accounted for in a number of ways: the age of adolescents surveyed, the definition of religiosity, the decade in which the study was made, whether sexual behavior or attitude toward sexual behavior is investigated, the content and wording of the questions, the kind of statistics used, and the way in which the study was reported. All of these are factors to be considered. Many more studies need to be made before a definitive conclusion can be reached as to the ways in which religion impacts on the sexual conduct of young people today.

Delaying Premarital Sex

Some religious persons, as has been mentioned, and some not so religious persons believe that intercourse should occur only within the marriage relationship. This is optimal and should be encouraged, but for many adolescents it is not realistic. Given natural biological urges, the use of sex in advertisements, the pleasure accompanying the sex act, the association of sexual activity with being adult, and the expectation within the society that all physically mature persons will engage in sexual behavior, the issue facing concerned citizens today is not so much how to keep adolescents virgins until they marry as it is how to enable them to delay the time at which sexual intimacy begins.

There is some indication that the proportion of older adolescents engaging in sexual activity may be declining. However, sexual activity among younger adolescents, especially those under sixteen years of age appears to be increasing

(Jackson and Hornbeck, 1989). Incidence, of course, increases with age. In the *Seventeen* survey with 2,046 teenagers and young adults, 24 percent of both boys and girls had sex by age fifteen. By age eighteen, 60 percent had sex, and by age twenty-one, 82 percent had. Teenagers lose their virginity, on average, at age sixteen (Chace, 1989). These figures are slightly higher than those given by the National Center for Health Statistics in which 54 percent of young women in 1988, ages fifteen to nineteen, had engaged in intercourse. By contrast, a similar survey six years earlier showed 47 percent of women this age had engaged in intercourse (research finds teenage girls having sex sooner, 1990).

The younger the adolescent, the less apt he or she is to practice birth control. In older teens, there is some indication that condom use is increasing. The National Survey of Adolescent Males compared data gathered in 1979 on 609 seventeen-to nineteen-year-old males with data gathered in 1988 on 742 males of the same age. Condom use increased from 21 percent in 1979 to 58 percent in 1988. The reason for the increase appeared to be related not to the fear of fathering a child but to the fear of getting AIDS (Landers, 1990). It would seem, then, that the younger the teen the greater the risks for having a child and for contracting a sexually transmitted disease (STD). "Adolescents have alarmingly high rates of STDs: Fully one-fourth of all adolescents will be infected with a sexually transmitted disease before graduating from high school. . . . Among young adolescents, rates of gonorrhea, for example, have increased for male teens from 10 per 100,000 in 1966 to 24 per 100,000 in 1985; for female teens rates increased from 18.5 per 100,000 to 73 per 100,000 over the same time period" (Jackson and Hornbeck, 1989; p. 834). It is estimated that 2.5 million teenagers are infected with sexually transmitted diseases each year (Landers, 1988, November). The seeming inability of the young adolescent to think through the consequences of sexual intimacy makes the task of increasing the age at which sexual behavior begins a crucial matter.

Stages of Intimacy and Delaying Premarital Sex

As was mentioned, Erikson (1968) wrote that adolescents are at the stage where they are coming to terms with their own identity. They are not in a position to engage in intimate relationships with others until they can successfully answer the question of who they are. They must be comfortable with their own uniqueness as persons in order to form genuine and lasting friendships with others. Sexual intimacy is the culmination of a singular relationship with one special person and this kind of intimacy in turn provides the security necessary for the children born of that union. Parenting, then, follows intimacy, and intimacy follows identity. If sexual intimacy precedes identity, confusion will result. When a parent leaves the family to "find himself," this regressive behavior is an indication that the natural order for personality development has not run its course.

Late adolescence and early adulthood provide the optimal time for the development of intimacy. Desmond Morris (1971) in *Intimate Behaviour* presents a twelve-step sequence in the course taken by a human love affair. Any speeding up of the steps detracts from the richness and fullness of the bond between lovers. The steps are as follows: 1) *Eye to body*. A head-to-toe glance puts a person on a scale from extremely attractive to extremely repulsive. If the person falls near the attractive end of the continuum, the potential lover goes to the next phase. 2) *Eye to eye*. When eyes meet there is often embarrassment, so the first eye contact is momentary. Rather than staring, the interested party will quickly look away but will establish eye contact again, watching the reaction of the other person. If the response is accompanied by a nod or a slight smile, the next step follows. 3) *Voice to voice*. Small talk begins. Any conversation between strangers allows either person to retreat from further involvement should voice quality, mode of verbalization, or use of vocabulary prove the other to be unattractive.

4) *Hand to hand*. Touching may begin as a handshake or in the form of supporting aid as when the male helps the female into a car or over an obstacle. Prolonged hand-holding or arm-holding signals that intimacy is viewed as desirable by both persons. 5) *Arm to shoulder*. A large portion of the body is in contact with the other person, often with the man's arm around the woman's shoulders. This posture signals an interest midway between close friendship and love. 6) *Arm to waist*. The wrapping of the arm around the waist becomes a more direct statement of intimacy. Furthermore, the hand is now closer to the genital area. 7) *Mouth to mouth*. Kissing on the mouth with a frontal embrace is a major step forward. If prolonged or repeated it may be accompanied by physiological arousal. 8) *Head to head*. This comes as an extension of the mouth-to-mouth stage with hands caressing the face, neck, and hair. 9) *Hand to body*. Hands explore the partner's body. This includes the stroking and fondling of the female's breasts by the male. Further physiological arousal occurs making this the last stage at which it is reasonable that a halt may be called to further advancement of intimacy.

10) *Mouth to breast*. Breast kissing must be done in private because it involves exposure of the female breast. It is the last of the pregenital stages of intimacy. 11) *Hand to genitals*. Manual manipulation of the partner's genitals increases arousal to the point where orgasm may occur for either sex. Lovers who fear pregnancy or have a religious restriction against coitus may use this form of culmination. 12) *Genitals to genitals*. Full copulation tightens the bond of attachment and brings into play the possibility of the irreversible acts of losing one's virginity and of fertilization. Morris (1971) cautions that "this final copulatory action is clearly related to a phase where the earlier intimacies will already have done their job of cementing the bond, so that the pair will want to stay together after the sex drive has been reduced by the consummation of orgasm. If this bonding has failed, the female is liable to find herself pregnant in the absence of a stable family unit" (pp. 78-79).

Donald Joy (1985) in *Bonding: Relationships in the Image of God* applies Desmond Morris' twelve steps to the bond between husband and wife. It begins when a man is ready to leave his father and mother, cleave to his partner, and with her become one flesh (Gen 2:24). The first three steps of eye-to-body, eye-to-eye, and voice-to-voice signal his readiness to become attached to another person. These steps are strictly "no touch" and may occur in rapid succession or take place over a period of months. In any event, he is readying himself to leave his parents. The middle six steps from casual touching to the exploration of the partner's body involves cleaving to her. The relationship will be on a more solid basis if these steps occur slowly over an extended period of time. The last three steps of mouth-to-breast, hand-to-genitals, and genitals-to-genitals makes the two as one flesh, cementing a relationship that can last a lifetime.

Pair-bonding is part of the creation order, the plan of God for Adam and Eve and for all couples that follow. Joy writes that Desmond Morris' twelve steps "correspond, overall, to the sequence laid down in the Judeo-Christian blueprint" (p. 43). Joy considers it a serious matter when parents try to break up their son's or daughter's bonding, putting age and economic concerns above affective and personal ones. He believes early marriage is preferable to advising one's offspring to use birth control measures or to have an abortion. When God joins two people together, no one should put them asunder.

Joy further believes that religious young people who care about God's plan for their lives need to be aware that sexual intimacy outside the marriage relationship goes against the creation order and will make for a weakening of the marriage bond later. Knowing about the steps and engaging in each one in their proper order over a period of time with the last steps reserved for the wedding night will slow the time when sexual intimacy occurs. It also will discourage promiscuous behavior.

As intriguing as this idea is, there is little research to verify or deny Joy's claim that a slowdown of the intermediate steps with the last steps being reserved for marriage is essential for the marriage bond to be strong. The optimal time frame probably differs from one couple to another with a number of personality characteristics coming into play in a good marriage besides that of a willingness to delay gratification. However, there is some evidence to support a slow progression. The worst scenario is forcible rape in which the aggressor goes from step one to step twelve as rapidly as possible leaving out intervening steps in his desire to overpower and exploit the victim. Recreational sex, by comparison, is by mutual consent and gives physical pleasure to both parties, but it is engaged in with the understanding that neither partner has a claim on the other and bonding is not to take place. Cobliner (1988) studied the sexual mores of the contemporary college population and noted that it was not uncommon for sexual involvement between partners of the opposite sex to be "sporadic, episodic, without commitment, and accompanied by a deliberate effort of both partners to suppress tender, romantic feelings and intimacy" (p. 99). Personal interviews showed that these deliberate and premeditated restraints of affection left students vulnerable to two types of psychiatric disturbance, depersonalization and derealization. Rather than sexual union enhancing sociability, it acted as a barrier and inhibitor of "enduring attachment and a sense of continuity" (p. 99). The extent to which this inhibits pair-bonding within marriage at a later time is not known. It would seem that sexual relations with a number of partners might make satisfaction with only one partner less likely after marriage.

Couples who live together without benefit of clergy often have an affection for each other and bonding is present or expected to occur at some time in the future. Some are "testing the waters" to see if they are compatible before a final commitment is made. However, they are less apt to remain married than couples who do not live together prior to marriage (*Medical Aspects of Human Sexuality*, 1990) a fact attributed not so much to their living together as to the fact that they tend to have a less exalted view of what marriage means. If two can share a common bed without being married, then marriage loses much of the meaning it traditionally has been given.

Teenage dating behavior usually begins at step four, hand-to-hand. The interested parties have already checked each other for attractiveness, have established eye contact, and have talked endlessly on the phone. Now physical contact begins with the holding of hands, the linking of arms, and the goodnight kiss. In a two-year study of the sexual behaviors of white and black adolescents, twelve to fifteen years of age at the beginning of the study, Smith and Udry (1985) found that white adolescents were more apt to engage in a predictable series of noncoital behaviors for a period of time prior to their first intercourse experience. The sequence progressed through kissing, necking, heavy petting, and intercourse. Black adolescents, who were more apt to be accepted by peers if they were nonvirgins, tended to go directly from necking to intercourse. Of the young adolescents who were virgins at the onset of the study, 67.9 percent of black males and 30.7 percent of white males were no longer virgins two years later. The same was true for 41.4 percent of black females and 23.8 percent of white females. Smith and Udry indicate that "the role of noncoital sexual behaviors as substitutes or delay mechanisms for coitus needs to be more fully understood" (p. 1203).

Age of Dating and Delaying Premarital Sex

In many cultures, parents have a specific age at which "dating" may begin. This is done for the protection of the child, especially the female child. Parents know that the sooner two teenagers of the opposite sex are alone for extended periods of time, the sooner sexual intimacy will occur. There is good reason to keep teenagers in groups and to provide a chaperon. Miller, McCoy, and Olson (1986) examined the age at which dating began and the sexual attitudes and behaviors of 790 students, aged fourteen to nineteen. Two-thirds were female and over half were Mormons. Mormons have institutionalized age sixteen as the legitimate age to begin dating. Miller, McCoy, and Olson found that the younger a girl began dating the more likely she was to have had sex before graduating from high school. In a larger study by the same researchers with 2,400 teens and reported in *Christian Parenting Today,* 91 percent of girls who began dating at twelve years of age had engaged in sex before graduation. This compared to 53 percent who began dating at age fourteen and 20 percent who began dating at age sixteen (Sheppard, 1989).

Does Sex Education Help?

Literally hundreds of studies have been conducted in an effort to answer this question. There are so many variables in these efforts or programs that no definitive answer can be given. It is necessary to factor out these variables, including the *place* where information is given—home, school, or church; the *age* of the child or adolescent receiving the information—prepubertal, pubertal, or post-pubertal; *who* gives the information—parent, sibling, peers, teachers, minister, youth worker within the church; the character of the person giving the information—poor role model or good role model; and the content of the *information* given—technical details, possible outcomes, birth control, values, responsibility.

William Bennett (1988), head of the Office of National Drug Control Policy in the Bush administration and formerly Education Secretary in the Reagan administration, says that sex education is about character, and that issues of right and wrong should occupy center stage in any sex education course. Children should be taught sexual restraint, that sex is not simply a physical act, and that sex should occur within marriage. Parents and other adults should be welcomed as allies, and the teacher must be a person of good character, speaking his or her convictions and living by them.

Sex Education Programs Encouraging Abstinence

James Dobson (1990) agrees that sex should wait until marriage and has produced a values-based curriculum entitled "Family Values and Sex Education" available from *Focus on the Family.* Another source is *Teen Sexual Behavior: A Leader's Resource of Practical Strategies with Youth* by Linda Berne and Pamela Wild (1988). They, too, believe that "abstinence is the best sexual practice for teenagers in junior high and high school and should be encouraged over any other sexual behavior for the age group" (p. 5). The unit on abstinence includes what it means to be abstinent, that all adults must be   abstinent at times, why "being in love" is a poor standard for sexual intimacy, and avoiding AIDS through abstinence. Role-playing on how to say "no" in a sexually permissive world is also given. This resource book was sponsored by the Association for the Advancement of Health Education and is available from The American Alliance for Health, Physical Education, Recreation and Dance. Another program for youth leaders who believe that abstinence should be encouraged is *Why Wait?* by Josh McDowell and Dick Day (1987). Materials can be obtained from Josh McDowell Ministry and include a film to be shown to youth groups and written information of help to pastors and youth workers. Harold Smith (1987), managing editor of *Christianity Today*, believes that the time has come for churches to provide a moral and spiritual foundation and for Christian parents to insist on "say no" sex education.

If all children and adolescents came from stable, intact families in which traditional parental attitudes were conveyed and expectation for compliance was nonnegotiable, then "just say no" programs might be adequate. And, if all young people cared about God's plan for their lives and considered chastity as part of that plan, then an encouragement of that view would be in order. For the younger adolescent who has not yet engaged in sex, an abstinence program may be the right approach. The best time for training in decision-making skills is before they are needed.

However, a program based on abstinence will be less effective with teens who are already sexually active. These are the young people who are more apt to come from single-parent households, especially if the custodial parent dates (Peterson, 1985). Adolescents with early sexual experience are more apt to be black, come from low socio-economic homes, have little interest in religion, and have parents who are poorly educated (Forste and Heaton, 1988). A preference for heavy metal music is also associated with an attitude favoring premarital sex (Landers, 1988, July). Even so, sexually active youngsters are found in all types of homes. Religious communities who wish to reach these young people may find that an effective sex education program must include information that will minimize the negative consequences of early sexual experience. Youth leaders also must be willing to help teens who are experiencing a crisis resulting from their sexual behaviors. For some adolescents a "just say no" program comes too late and will not meet their needs at the time.

A 1987 Gallup poll noted a sharp increase in Americans' acceptance of sex education in the elementary school with 71 percent expressing support compared with 52 percent expressing support in 1985. As in the past, women, younger adults of both sexes, and persons who attended college were more accepting. Seventy-one percent also favored including discussions about AIDS, and 69 percent said that condom ads should be aired on television (*Gallup Report*, 1987, March). Considering that this is sex education at grades four to eight, it is obvious that many Americans believe that sex education programs must include far more than an encouragement to be abstinent. Many people would prefer that information be given by parents and religious organizations, but if children and teenagers do not receive adequate instruction in the home or in the church, then the schools must accept the responsibility.

Sex Education Programs Encouraging Responsible Decision Making

Adolescents are faced with a number of decisions including choosing friends, dating, physical touching and sex, birth control, pregnancy, and avoiding sexually transmitted diseases. *Take Charge of Your Life* (1988), a workbook for pre-teens and teenagers sponsored by the California State Department of Health Services and used by the Salvation Army deals with these issues. It focuses on building self-esteem and thinking through choices that must be made. Teens may or may not wish to share their answers with others but are encouraged to consider why they feel as they do and to consider the consequences of their decisions. Another resource is *Safe Sex,* a booklet by Verne Becker (1988) distributed by InterVarsity Press that asks such questions as "How can I keep from getting pregnant?" "When is it OK to sleep with someone?" "How can I protect myself from AIDS and other sexually transmitted diseases?" "Am I sufficiently protected legally in case any unfortunate or undesirable results occur from sex with my partner?" Becker makes it clear that *totally* safe sex—physically, emotionally, and spiritually—takes place within "a loving, committed, faithful marriage" (p. 30). This is the Christian view of sexuality and what the Bible teaches. However, many questions are asked by today's young person, and these questions need to be addressed. *Safe Sex* does not provide a program but would be useful to distribute to adolescents within the religious community.

OCTOPUS is the acronym for *O*pen *C*ommunication *R*egarding *T*eenagers *O*r *P*arents *U*nderstanding of *S*exuality," a church-based sex education program for teens and parents. Its purpose is to establish a forum for family discussion within a religious setting, to provide factual information, enhance communication skills, and cultivate decision-making abilities. Nurses, health educators, counselors, ministers, and church members interested in dialogue are to be included, the major aim being that of training parents to be the primary sex educators of their children. The program is flexible depending on those present and the minister's perspective on morality. Once designed, the program is approved by the church's governing body, publicized in the church bulletin, and implemented. It may coincide with "family month" (Jacknik, Isberner, Gumerman, Hayworth, and Braunling-McMorrow, 1984).

The Decision-Making Process Model (Maskay and Juhasz, 1983) provides a framework for parents, counselors, teachers, and others who interact with adolescents having problems and questions related to sexual decisions. It is a seven-step process of identifying the decision to be made, determining why it is needed, identifying alternative choices for action, analyzing the information and hypothesizing about positive and negative consequences, evaluating the desirability of various choices, estimating the practicality of behaviors and deciding on a conclusion for action. For example, a basic decision is whether or not to have sexual intercourse. If the answer is in the affirmative, then this leads to other decisions such as whether to have children, whether to use birth control, if pregnant whether to bear the child or have an abortion, if the child is delivered whether to keep it or give it up for adoption, in either case whether to marry or remain single. Posing such questions shows the adolescent that a chain of decisions may accompany a single sex-related act. Being sexually intimate is not something one does without thinking through the possible ramifications of the behavior.

These programs are only a sampling of the many available for the youth minister within the church or temple. The number and variety are such that it should not be difficult to find one that suits the needs of the young people in the group as well as the orientation of the teacher or counselor in charge. Adolescents are bombarded with so many influences that it is important that religious leaders do their part to reinforce those decisions that are optimal while countering those actions that lead to less fortunate consequences for the teenager and for the society.

A Word of Optimism

It is easy to emphasize adolescents at risk and to forget that there are many adolescents who live chaste lives. Morality is not restricted to past generations. As was noted in the *Seventeen* survey (Chace, 1989) with 2,046 teenagers, 24 percent had sex by age fifteen and 60 percent had sex by age eighteen. That means that 76 percent had *not* engaged in sex at age fifteen and 40 percent were still virgins at age eighteen.

There are other encouraging signs. Adolescents today honor their parents, 82 percent of them saying they owe their parents a lot (Chace, 1989). Teenagers would like to marry in the mid-twenties and they want to have children. Furthermore, although 92 percent recognize that America has problems, they believe that America is basically a good country.

There is an orientation for greater equality between males and females. Most teens say they would vote for a woman president. Girls as well as boys expect to work outside the home. If a man can have a career and a family, a woman can have a career and a family. Four percent of the girls and 1 percent of the fellows want to be full-time homemakers, although 28 percent of the girls said they would prefer not to work when their children are young.

Like every generation that has come before them, today's adolescents expect to make the world a better place. Eighty-five percent believe in God and most say that believing in God helps them have hope for the future (Chace, 1989). Although advancement in morality and sexual responsibility seems to move at a snail's pace in comparison with rapid technological changes, nevertheless if the younger generation sees promise in the future, the older generation would do well to share their optimism. The youth minister within the religious community has the awesome task of helping adolescents realize their desire of making the world a better place, and this is more apt to take place if young people are given the encouragement and support they need. Communicating to them that God cares about each one and has a plan for each life will help adolescents have the purpose and stability needed in a world that lacks meaning and constancy. The challenge is of such magnitude that all who work with teenagers within the church or other religious contexts will find plenty to do to fulfill their role of ministering to today's youth.

REFERENCES

Adler, J., Katz, S., and Jackson, T. (1985, March 25). A teen-pregnancy epidemic. *Newsweek*, p. 90.

Anderson, T. (1988, November 23). Schools plant seeds to cultivate kids with character. *USA Today*, Sec. D., p. 6.

Bandura, A. (1965). Influence of model's reinforcement contingencies on the acquisition of imitative responses. *Journal of Personality and Social Psychology, 1*, 589-595.

Bebeau, M. J., and Brabeck, M. M. (1987). Integrating care and justice issues in professional moral education: A gender perspective. *The Journal of Moral Education, 16*, 189-203.

Becker, V. (1988). *Safe sex*. Downers Grove, Ill.: InterVarsity Press.

Bennett, W. J. (1988). Sex and the education of our children. *Curriculum Review, 27*(3), 7-12.

Berne, L. A., and Wild, P. (1988). *Teen sexual behavior: A leader's resource of practical strategies with youth*. Reston, Va.: American Alliance for Health, Physical Education, Recreation and Dance.

Billy, J. O. G., and Udry, J. R. (1985). The influence of male and female best friends on adolescent sexual behavior. *Adolescence, 20*, 21-32.

Blizard, R. A. (1982). *The relationships between three dimensions of religious belief and moral development* (Doctoral dissertation. California School of Professional Psychology, 1980). *Dissertation Abstracts International, 43*, 271B.

Chace, S. (1989, October). My generation. *Seventeen*, pp. 99-106.

Cistone, D. F. (1980). *Levels of moral reasoning compared with demographic data among teachers, administrators, and pupil personnel employees enrolled in graduate schools* (Doctoral dissertation, University of Southern California, 1980). *Dissertation Abstracts International, 41*, 237A.

Clouse, B. (1973). Attitudes of college students as a function of sex, politics, and religion. *Journal of College Student Personnel, 14*, 260-264.

Clouse, B. (1985a). *Moral development: Perspectives in psychology and Christian belief*. Grand Rapids, Mich.: Baker Book House.

Clouse, B. (1985b). Moral reasoning and Christian faith. *Journal of Psychology and Theology, 13*, 190-198.

Clouse, B. (1986). Church conflict and moral stages: A Kohlbergian interpretation. *Journal of Psychology and Christianity, 5*, 14-19.

Cobliner, W. G. (1988). The exclusion of intimacy in the sexuality of the contemporary college-age population. *Adolescence, 23*, 99-113.

Coles, R. (1986). *The moral life of children*. Boston: Atlantic Monthly Press.

Coles, R., and Genevie, L. (1990, March). The moral life of America's school children. *Teacher Magazine*, pp. 43-49.

Davids, L. (1982). Ethnic identity, religiosity, and youthful deviance: The Toronto computer dating project—1979. *Adolescence, 17*, 673-684.

DiGiacomo, J. J. (1979). Ten years as moral educator in a Catholic high school. In T. C. Hennessy (Ed.), *Value/moral education: Schools and teachers* (pp. 51-71). New York: Paulist Press.

Dirks, D. H. (1988). Moral development in Christian higher education. *Journal of Psychology and Theology, 16*, 324-331.

Dobson, J. C. (1990, April). A promise with a ring to it. *Focus on the Family*, pp. 1-4.

Duska, R., and Whelan, M. (1975). *Moral development: A guide to Piaget and Kohlberg*. New York: Paulist Press.

Duvall, E. M. (1971). *Family development*. Philadelphia: Lippincott.

Erikson, E. H. (1968). *Identity, youth and crisis.* New York: W. W. Norton.

Ernsberger, D. J., and Manaster, G. J. (1981). Moral development, intrinsic/extrinsic religious orientation and denominational teachings. *Genetic Psychology Monographs, 104,* 23-41.

Fodor, E. M. (1972). Delinquency and susceptibility to social influence among adolescents as a function of level of moral development. *Journal of Social Psychology, 86,* 257-260.

Forste, R. T., and Heaton, T. B. (1988). Initiation of sexual activity among female adolescents. *Youth and Society, 19,* 250-268.

Freud, S. (1949). *A general introduction to psychoanalysis* (J. Riviere, Trans.). New York: W. W. Norton. (Original work published 1913)

Gallup Report. (1987, March). Sex education grades 4-8 soars in public acceptance. Report No. 258, p. 19.

Gallup Report. (1987, August). More today than in 1985 say premarital sex is wrong. Report No. 263, p. 20.

Getz, I. (1984). The relation of moral reasoning and religion: A review of the literature. *Counseling and Values, 28,* 94-116.

Gilligan, C. (1982). *In a different voice: Psychological theory and women's development.* Cambridge, Mass.: Harvard University Press.

Godin, A. (1971). Some developmental tasks in Christian education. In M. P. Strommen (Ed.), *Research on religious development.* New York: Hawthorne.

Haan, N., Smith, M. B., and Block, J. (1968). Moral reasoning in young adults: Political-social behavior, family background, and personality correlates. *Journal of Personality and Social Psychology, 10,* 183-201.

Hamburg, D. A., and Takanishi, R. (1989). The critical transition of adolescence. *American Psychologist, 44,* 825-827.

Harris, A. T. (1981). *A study of the relationship between stages of moral development and the religious factors of knowledge, belief and practice in Catholic high school adolescents* (Doctoral dissertation, University of Oregon, 1981). *Dissertation Abstracts International, 42,* 638A.

Havinghurst, R. J. (1953). *Developmental tasks and education.* New York: Longmans, Green.

Hellmich, N. (1986, May 19). Those adolescent years are a turbulent period. *USA Today,* Sec. D, p. 5.

Hellmich, N. (1990, February 1). Cheating, sex and kid's scruples. *USA Today,* Sec. D, p. 1.

Hersch, R. ,Paolitto, D., and Reimer, J. (1979). *Promoting moral growth from Piaget to Kohlberg.* New York: Longman.

Hill, C. I. (1986). A developmental perspective on adolescent "rebellion" in the church. *Journal of Psychology and Theology, 14,* 306-318.

Humanist Manifesto II. (1980). *The Humanist, 40* (5), 5-10.

Jacknik, M., Isberner, F., Gumerman, S., Hayworth, R., and Braunling-McMorrow, D. (1984). OCTOPUS—A church-based sex education program for teens and parents. *Adolescence, 19,* 757-783.

Jackson, A. W., and Hornbeck, D. W. (1989). Educating young adolescents. *American Psychologist, 44,* 831-836.

Jensen, L., Newell, R. J., and Holman, T. (1990). Sexual behavior, church attendance, and permissive beliefs among unmarried young men and women. *Journal for the Scientific Study of Religion, 29:* 113-117.

Joy, D. M. (1983). Kohlberg revisited: A supra-naturalist speaks his mind. In D. M. Joy (Ed.) *Moral development foundations* (pp. 37-62). Nashville, Tenn.: Abingdon Press.

Joy, D. M. (1985). *Bonding: Relationships in the image of God.* Waco, Tex.: Word Books.

Keasey, C. B. (1975). Implicators of cognitive development for moral reasoning. In D. J. DePalma and J. M. Foley (Eds.), *Moral development: Current theory and research* (pp. 39-56). Hillsdale, N.J.: Lawrence Erlbaum.

Kohlberg, L. (1964). Development of moral character and moral ideology. In M. L. Hoffman and L. W. Hoffman (Eds.), *Review of child development research* (Vol. 1, pp. 383-431). New York: Russell Sage Foundation.

Kohlberg, L. (1967). Moral and religious education and the public schools: A developmental view. In T. R. Sizer (Ed.), *Religion and public education* (pp. 164-183). Boston: Houghton Mifflin.

Kohlberg, L. (1973a). Implications of developmental psychology for education: Examples from moral education. *Educational Psychologist, 10,* 2-14.

Kohlberg, L. (1973b). Stages of aging in moral development—some speculations. *The Gerontologist, 13,* 497-502.

Kohlberg, L. (1978). The cognitive-developmental approach to moral education. In P. Scharf (Ed.), *Readings in moral education* (pp. 36-51). Minneapolis: Winston Press.

Kohlberg, L. (1981). *Essays on moral development: The philosophy of moral development.* (Vol. 1). New York: Harper & Row.

Kohlberg, L. (1984). *Essays on moral development: The psychology of moral development.* (Vol. 2). New York: Harper & Row.

Kohlberg, L., Levine, C., and Hewer, A. (1983). *Moral stages: A current formulation and a response to critics.* New York: Karger.

Kohlberg and Simon: An exchange of opinion. (1972). *Learning, 1* (2), 19.

Landers, S. (1988, July). Sex, drugs 'n' rock: Relation not causal. *The American Psychological Monitor,* p. 40.

Landers, S. (1988, November). Survey verifies teen risk-taking. *The American Psychological Monitor,* p. 30.

Landers, S. (1990, April). Sex, condom use up among teenage boys. *The American Psychological Monitor,* p. 25.

Lawrence, J. A. (1979). *The component procedures of moral judgment-making* (Doctoral dissertation, University of Minnesota, 1978). *Dissertation Abstracts International, 40,* 896B.

Leming, J. S. (1981). Curricular effectiveness in moral/values education: A review of research. *Journal of Moral Education, 10,* 147-164.

Lickona, T. (1983). *Raising good children.* New York: Bantam Books.

Mahoney, E. R. (1980). Religiosity and sexual behavior among heterosexual college students. *Journal of Sex Research, 16,* 97-113.

Marcia, J. E. (1967). Ego identity status: Relationship to change in self-esteem, "general maladjustment," and authoritarianism. *Journal of Personality, 35,* 119-133.

Marcia, J. E. (1980). Identity in adolescence. In J. Adelson (Ed.), *Handbook of adolescent psychology* (pp. 159-187). New York: John Wiley.

Maskay, M. H., and Juhasz, A. M. (1983). The decision-making process model: Design and use for adolescent sexual decisions. *Family Relations, 32,* 111-116.

Maslow, A. H. (1970). *Motivation and personality* (2nd ed.). New York: Harper & Row.

McCormick, N., Izzo, A., and Folcik, J. (1985). Adolescents' values, sexuality, and contraception in a rural New York county. *Adolescence, 20,* 385-395.

McDowell, J., and Day, D. (1987). *Why wait? What you need to know about teen sexuality crisis.* San Bernadino, Calif.: Here's Life Publishers.

McGeorge, C. (1976). Some correlates of principled moral thinking in young adults. *Journal of Moral Education, 5,* 265-273.

Meade, J. (1990, March). The wallpaper factor. *Teacher Magazine*, p. 47.

Medical Aspects of Sexuality (1990, January). "Trial marriage" no guarantee of marital success, p. 23.

Medora, N., and Woodward, J. C. (1982). Premarital sexual opinions of undergraduate students at a midwestern university. *Adolescence, 17,* 213-224.

Miller, B. C., McCoy, J. K., and Olson, T. D. (1986). Dating age and stage as correlates of adolescent sexual attitudes and behavior. *Journal of Adolescent Research, 1,* 361-371.

Moore, M. E. (1980). *The differential effect of a church-related college environment and a state college or university environment on the moral development of self-described religious students* (Doctoral Dissertation, University of Virginia, 1979). *Dissertation Abstracts International, 40,* 4901A.

Moran, T. (1988). *Moral development and moral action: A study of youthful offenders* (Doctoral dissertation, University of British Columbia, 1988). *Dissertation Abstracts International, 49,* 3666A.

Morris, D. (1971). *Intimate behaviour.* New York: Random House.

Motet, D. (1978). Kohlberg's theory of moral development and Christian faith. *Journal of Psychology and Theology, 6,* 18-21.

Newcomer, S. F., Udry, J. R., and Cameron, F. (1983). Adolescent sexual behavior and popularity. *Adolescence, 18,* 515-522.

O'Gorman, T. P. (1979). *An investigation of moral judgment and religious knowledge scores of Catholic high school boys from Catholic and public schools* (Doctoral dissertation, Boston College, 1979). *Dissertation Abstracts International, 40,* 3365A.

Orlofsky, J. L., Marcia, J. E., and Lesser, I. M. (1973). Ego identity status and the intimacy vs. isolation crisis of young adulthood. *Journal of Personality and Social Psychology, 27,* 211-219.

Peck, R. F., and Havinghurst, R. J. (1960). *The psychology of character development.* New York: John Wiley & Sons.

Peterson, J. L., et al. (1985). *Starting early: The antecedents of early premarital intercourse.* Educational Resources Information, 36 p.

Piaget, J. (1932). *The moral judgment of the child* (M. Gabain, Trans.). London: K. Paul, Trench, Trubner.

Pressau, J. R. (1977). *I'm saved, you're saved—maybe.* Atlanta: John Knox Press.

Research finds teen-age girls having sex sooner. (1990, February 7). *The Terre Haute Tribune.*

Rest, J. R. (1980). The Defining Issues Test: A survey of research results. In L. Kuhmerker, M. Mentkowski, and V. L. Erickson (Eds.), *Evaluating moral development and evaluating educational programs that have a value dimension* (pp. 113-120). Schenectady, N.Y.: Character Research Press.

Rest, J. R. (1986). *Moral development: Advances in research and theory.* New York: Praeger.

Rogers, C. R. (1978). Some questions and challenges facing a humanistic psychology. In I. D. Welch, G. A. Tate, and F. Richards (Eds.). *Humanistic psychology: A source book* (pp. 41-51). Buffalo, N.Y.: Prometheus Books.

Rothman, G. R. (1980). The relationship between moral judgment and moral behavior. In M. Windmiller, N. Lambert, and E. Turiel (Eds.), *Moral development and socialization* (pp. 107-127). Boston: Allyn & Bacon.

Ruma, E., and Mosher, P. (1967). Relationship between moral judgment and guilt in delinquent boys. *Journal of Abnormal Psychology, 72,* 122-127.

Sanderson, S. K. (1974). *Religion, politics, and morality: An approach to religious and political belief systems and their relation through Kohlberg's cognitive-develop-*

mental theory of moral judgment (Doctoral dissertation, University of Nebraska at Lincoln, 1973). *Dissertation Abstracts International, 34,* 6259B.

Sapp, G. L., and Jones, L. (1986). Religious orientation and moral judgment. *Journal for the Scientific Study of Religion, 25,* 208-214.

Search Institute Source. (1989, July). What influences teenagers' decisions about sex? Vol. IV, Number 3, pp. 1-5.

Sheppard, S. (1989, November/December). The case for chastity: 7 ways to help your teen save sex for marriage. *Christian Parenting Today,* pp. 67-71.

Skinner, B. F. (1978). *Reflections on behaviorism and society.* Englewood Cliffs, N.J.: Prentice Hall.

Smith, E. A., and Udry, J. R. (1985). Coital and non-coital sexual behaviors of white and black adolescents. *American Journal of Public Health, 75,* 1200-1203.

Smith, H. (1987, February). Saying no: Public officials concerned about teen pregnancy try a "new" approach to sex education. *Christianity Today,* pp. 12-13.

Sprinthall, R. C., and Sprinthall, N. A. (1981). *Educational psychology: A developmental approach* (3rd ed.). Reading, Mass.: Addison-Wesley.

Stengel, R. (1985, December 9). The missing-father myth. *Time,* p. 90.

Stoop, D. A. (1980). *The relation between religious education and the process of maturity through the developmental stages of moral judgments* (Doctoral dissertation, University of Southern California, 1979). *Dissertation Abstracts International, 40,* 3912A.

Take charge of your life! (1988). Salvation Army Booth Memorial Center. Santa Cruz, Calif.: Network Publications, 32 p.

Thoma, S. J. (1984). *Estimating gender differences in the comprehension and preference of moral issues.* Unpublished manuscript. Minneapolis: University of Minnesota.

Tryon, G., and Lilienthal, J. (1950). Developmental tasks: I. The concept and its importance. In *Fostering mental health in our schools.* Washington, D.C.: Association for Supervision and Curriculum Development, National Education Association.

Vitz, P. (1983). The Kohlberg phenomenon. *Pastoral Renewal, 7,* 63-68.

Walker, L. J., (1984). Sex differences in the development of moral reasoning: A critical review. *Child Development, 55,* 677-691.

Wallis, G. (1985, December 9). Children having children. *Time,* pp. 78-90.

Watson, J. B. (1931). *Behaviorism.* London: Routledge & Kegan Paul.

Wolterstorff, N. (1980). *Educating for responsible action.* Grand Rapids, Mich.: Eerdmans.

Woodroof, J. T. (1985). Premarital sexual behavior and religious adolescents. *Journal for the Scientific Study of Religion, 24,* 343-366.

Woodroof, J. T. (1986). Reference groups, religiosity, and premarital sexual behavior. *Journal for the Scientific Study of Religion, 25,* 436-460.

Young, R. G. (1981). Values differentiation as stage transition: An expansion of Kohlbergian moral stages. *Journal of Psychology and Theology, 9,* 164-174.

Ziv, A. (1976). Measuring aspects of morality. *Journal of Moral Education, 5,* 189-201.

Chapter Eight

Procedures in the Religious Education of Adolescents

JAMES MICHAEL LEE

"A youth without fire is followed by an old age without experience."

Charles Caleb Colton (1828)

Youth Ministry and Religious Education

Is youth ministry an activity *apart* from religious education or is youth ministry *a part* of religious education?

If youth ministry is *apart* from religious education, then what is it fundamentally a part of? Is youth ministry basically social work? Not really, though there might be elements of social work involved in the discharge of youth ministry. Is youth ministry basically musical activity? Not really, though there might be elements of musical activity involved in the enactment of youth ministry. Is youth ministry basically physical or recreational activity? Not really, though there might be elements of physical and recreational activity involved in the deployment of youth ministry.

Looking closely and carefully at youth ministry, we will discover that youth ministry is essentially *a part* of religious education. After all, education is the broad process by which a person learns something (Lee, 1971, pp. 6-7). The educator, then, is one who deliberatively structures the situation in order to intentionally facilitate the acquisition of a desired learning outcome. Religion is that form of lifestyle which enfleshes the lived relationship which a person enjoys with a transpersonal being. Thus it can be readily appreciated that even though youth ministry does utilize areas such as social work, music, and recreational activity, it does so out of an ecology of religious education and for the purposes of religious education.

Why, then, are so many youth ministers reluctant to see themselves as religious educators? The most probable reason is that many youth ministers erroneously regard religious education as exclusively a school-based process which is narrowly cognitive, recitative, and heavily teacher-directed. This view of religious education is seriously defective—even though there are religious educators who, unfortunately, limit their educational activity to this kind of severely circumscribed pedagogical practices. (Usually these are the religious educators who have not been adequately trained in the art/science of teaching.) Narrowly cognitive, strongly recitative, and heavily teacher-directed teaching procedures represent just a small portion not only of religious education as a whole but also of that segment of religious education conducted in school settings. Other forms of religious education include nonverbal processes, affective procedures, project methods, social laboratory experiences, educationally rooted community service activities, and the like. Furthermore, the environment in which religious education occurs is far wider than formal settings such as the classroom or the church building. To be sure, religious education is conducted in a wide variety of informal settings such as the home, the playground, the street, the soup kitchen, and so forth. As a general rule, the more formal the educational setting, the more tightly structured the facilitational procedure will likely be. Thus, for example, teacher-directed question-answer events tend to occur in a formal educational setting like a classroom, while easygoing banter is a parallel facilitational procedure in an informal educational setting such as a home or a playground.

Regretfully, quite a few religious education speculationists (Moran, 1979), tractarians (Westerhoff, 1970), and practitioners (Schaeffler, 1990) hold an excessively narrow and basically uninformed view of what actually happens and what should happen pedagogically in classrooms. This myopic view possibly results from a lack of adequate knowledge both of professional education literature and what is happening in those classrooms around the nation which are judged to be examples of good teaching. While there are indeed drills, recitations, and other formalized cognitive procedures occurring in effective classroom settings, there are also even more cognitively expansive, affectively suffused, and lifestyle-oriented instructional practices taking place at all school levels and for all school subjects. Indeed, virtually all major world-class modern educational thinkers, persons as disparate as Maria Montessori (1965) and John Dewey (1900) have called for classroom teaching to be holistically experience-centered and to utilize social-laboratory teaching procedures. When one examines the writings of antischooling authors like John Westerhoff (1976), one discovers that virtually all of the educational procedures they advocate are ones which are directly derived from the classroom/school setting.

The key and overriding point of all of this as far as youth ministers are concerned is that sound educational procedures are valid and effective no matter where they are used. These procedures are not valid or effective in the school alone. If an instructional procedure is effective in the school, it will most probably be effective in youth work enacted in an informal setting—*if* the four molar variables involved in every teaching-learning act are adjusted appropriately to the new set of facilitational conditions. There has been a good deal of solid, sophisticated, and useful empirical research done on the intentional facilitation of learning in formal settings such as schools. These research data can be easily extrapolated to facilitational activities in informal settings such as those in which much youth ministry takes place. It would be foolhardy and perilous for youth ministers to ignore such research findings, especially since the data on the intentional facilitation of desired learning outcomes in informal settings is so meager.

Religious education and ministry are in no way opposed or counter to one another. Religious education is a particular form of ministry. There are other major forms of ministry, such as sacramental ministry, liturgical ministry, and so forth. The goals and many of the basic procedures of each form of ministry are distinct. To eradicate the distinctiveness of religious education or liturgical activities or sacramental confection by claiming that these are opposed to ministry or are all basically identical to ministry in general is not only invalid conceptually but also destroys both the specialness and the effectiveness of these particularized forms of ministry. As Aristotle (1949) observed long ago, there is particularization rather than opposition and identity between a genus (ministry) and its specific differences (religious education, pastoral counseling, liturgical facilitation, and so forth). As with all genera, the term ministry, while circumscribed to a large extent, still lacks details. It is the specific difference which supplies the genus with those large and small details which are absolutely necessary for engaging in purposeful human living.

Possibly the most important overall thrust of this chapter is to help youth ministers see themselves foremost as religious educators of youth. Once this general awareness becomes pervasively embedded in the psyche of youth ministers, then these persons will be impelled to gain proficiency in the underlying concepts and facilitational procedures of religious education. Such a dual proficiency is absolutely essential for successful youth ministry. To assist youth ministers gain the pervasive awareness that their work is fundamentally that of religious education, this chapter will henceforth use the term *youth religious educator* rather than youth minister.

To assert that the youth minister is primarily a youth religious educator is to assert that the youth worker deals with religion in an educational way. There are two elements in this task description, namely religion and education.

Religion is essentially different from theology. Religion is a lifestyle, a more or less habitual way of concrete living. Virtually all major theologians from

Edward Schillebeeckx (1967, p. 100), to Paul Tillich (1951, p. 28), to Helmut Thielicke (1977, p. 3) consistently assert that theology is a cognitive science which investigates the workings of God in the world, and derivatively, investigates religion from its own particular intellectual perspective. Religion, on the other hand is holistic, embracing all major domains of human functioning—psychomotor, cognitive, affective, and lifestyle. Theology is cognitive and only cognitive. Hence the youth religious educator, precisely because he/she is a youth *religious* educator and not a youth theological educator, concentrates on educating adolescents for religious outcomes primarily rather than for theological outcomes. The youth religious educator deals with theological material only to the extent that theology contributes to the acquisition of religious outcomes. Consequently, the educational procedures which the youth religious educator uses must span the gamut of all human domains, and not be restricted to cognitive processes.

Education is an art/science. In other words, education is a set of facilitational procedures based on a body of scientific data, laws, and theories (Gage, 1978, pp. 13-24). This scientific base enables education to be optimally effective rather than just a hit-or-miss affair. The enactment of educational procedures is an art—not art in the sense of painting a picture or playing a symphony, but art in the original Latin meaning of performing an action, any action, in a coordinated way. Just as painters root the practice of their art in the scientific data and principles of perspective and coloration, so also do religious educators root the practice of their art in the scientific data and principles of human learning and of effective facilitation. Consequently, every successful religious educator, including the youth religious educator, is at once a procedurist and a procedurologist. A procedurist is one who enacts procedure. A procedurologist is one who is conversant with the scientific data, laws, and theories underlying the effective enactment of procedure. To be a consistently successful procedurist, one must also be a procedurologist. Unfortunately many people tend to disvalue procedure. Specialists in procedure are often denigrated as mere "procedure persons," "methods men," "techniques women." But this mentality is a false and a debilitating one. Surgeons have great prestige. But surgeons are basically procedure persons. If youth religious educators are to become consistently successful, they must not only regard themselves primarily as procedure persons, but prize the incontrovertible fact that at bottom they are indeed procedurists. It is procedure which causes things to happen. Without procedure, the world would be inert and lifeless. In religious terms, procedure is incarnation.

There are three main forms of intentional education, namely instruction, guidance/counseling, and administration. Instruction is the process by and through which learning is caused in an individual in some way. Guidance/counseling is the process by which individuals are assisted in fulfilling their human potential, in negotiating the tasks of personal development, and in solving special personal problems. Administration is the process of directing, controlling, and managing instructional and guidance activities. This chapter will concentrate on instruction. It is primarily concerned with youth religious instruction rather than with either youth religious counseling or with the administration of youth religious education activities.

Instruction is synonymous with teaching. Specialists in instruction often prefer the word instruction to the word teaching because instruction connotes proficiency in procedurology as well as in procedure. The term instruction, then, points to the fact that successful teaching is not just an art, but an art consciously rooted in and flowing from a scientific base. Because of stylistic reasons, I will often use the word teaching in this chapter rather than the word instruction. In such cases, teaching should always be understood as instruction, namely a fusion of the art and the science of teaching.

When reading this chapter, the youth religious educator would do well to avoid the erroneous conclusion that the view of the instructional dynamic set forth in this chapter is excessively complex and out of touch with the realities of youth work. To be sure, the analysis of the instructional dynamic is complex. It is complex because the intentional facilitation of learning is by its very nature complex due to the many intersecting variables which are necessarily involved. Complexity and facilitation go hand-in-hand. There is just no way around this irrefutable fact. Such complexity will seem excessive only to those who view the instructional dynamic in a simplistic or artless fashion. One of the biggest reasons why successful youth ministry is so difficult and so draining is that it is complex. Also, the view of the instructional dynamic presented in this chapter is very much in touch with the reality of every form of educational ministry, including youth religious education. To appreciate the validity of this point, all the youth religious educator has to do is to analyze what does in fact transpire at the basic structural level when he/she is educationally ministering to youth in an effective manner. For example, the Lee model of teaching which will be presented in the following pages was not concocted out of the blue. It is thoroughly empirical in its origins and practical in its effects. The Lee model was devised as a result of both personal analysis of the teaching act in a wide variety of situations and a knowledge of the relevant empirical research studies reported on a broad range of instructional activities worldwide. Youth religious educators can consistently attain the fullness of their special ministry only when they are aware of what transpires foundationally in the enactment of their educational work. Running away from this foundational knowledge, or dismissing it as unimportant, has the same destructive consequences for youth religious education as such self-blinding behaviors have for the fruitful enactment of any human activity.

More often than not, the "methods chapter" in a general youth religious education book amounts to nothing more than a simplistic cookbook listing some specific instructional procedures. Moreover, those specific instructional procedures which are given in such chapters are seldom described in requisite detail, and almost never situated within operable theory or buttressed by the available empirical research as to their effectiveness. Consequently, the "methods" chapter in general youth books is typically superficial, poorly regarded, little read, and minimally effective. In marked contrast, the chapter in this present book eschews the simplistic cookbook enumeration of specific instructional procedures. Instead, it concentrates primarily on equipping the youth religious educator with the basic functions required for successful youth religious instruction. These basic functions are generalizable and so apply to every specific facilitational style, strategy, method, and technique. Conversely, every facilitational style, strategy, method, and technique which is not rooted in and suffused by these basic pervasive functions will be fundamentally ineffective. This chapter will also provide, briefly but adequately, an overview of each of the four basic zones in which all teaching procedures lie. Again, the emphasis will be on foundational processes instead of on a cookbook enumeration. In this way youth religious educators will gain familiarity with basic procedural contours and thrusts so that they can be thereby empowered 1) to deepen or expand, as the case may be, their knowledge of specific facilitational procedures which are supported by applicable theory and empirical research evidence, and 2) to devise new and creative facilitational procedures in each of the basic zones, procedures which, though new and creative, are in one way or another consonant with applicable theory and with the available empirical research evidence.

Basic Functions

The Four Interactive Variables

Religious instruction is not the same as standing in front of a group of youths and talking. Indeed, this is a caricature of the instructional process. In reality, religious instruction is the intentional facilitation of desired learning outcomes whenever, wherever, and however any kind of human interaction takes place directly or indirectly. In any human interaction that is educational there are four major ingredients which are always present, namely, the educator, the learner, the subject matter, and the environment. In every educational situation, each of these four ingredients is somewhat different. It is for this reason that these molar ingredients are called variables because they vary from person to person and from situation to situation.

Because some youth religious educators labor under the false assumption that instruction is limited to teacher talk and to learner passivity in the classroom setting, it is important to briefly delineate the meaning of each of the four molar variables involved in all instructional acts. A *teacher* is one who intentionally facilitates learning in any way, shape, or form. Thus youth religious educators are teaching when they set up a situation in which young people visit the homeless, when they work with adolescents to write letters to state senators to influence legislation, when they interact sensitively with a jilted teenager, when they help adolescents see the application of a biblical text to fair play during a heated athletic contest, and so forth. A *learner* is a person who acquires one or another desired learning outcome. Thus young persons are learners whenever or wherever they are learning something as a result of the religious educator's activity—on the playground, in a classroom, in worship services, on a retreat, on a camping trip, in a mission for homeless women, and so forth. *Subject matter* is that which is taught. It is important to realize that subject matter is far wider than just cognitive subject matter such as biblical understanding or verbal information. Other key subject-matter contents include attitudes, values, appreciations, feelings, conduct, ways to live religiously, and so forth. It is probably fair to assert that in youth religious instruction there is more noncognitive subject-matter content taught/learned than cognitive subject matter. And finally, *environment* is the setting in which the instructional event takes place. In youth religious education, the environment can be extremely varied: on the street, in church, on the playground, in a late-night session in someone's home, over a campfire on a two-day hike, in a classroom, at a drug abuse center, and so on.

The central fact that every religious instruction act is composed of four interactive variables shows that religious instruction is essentially contextual in nature. All four variables operate in a somewhat different fashion depending on the here-and-now interactive context in which they occur. The interactive contextual character of religious instruction is best illustrated in a pictorial model which I devised in 1973 and which over the years has proven to be very useful in understanding the inner dynamic structure of the instructional act (Lee, 1973, pp. 233-236).

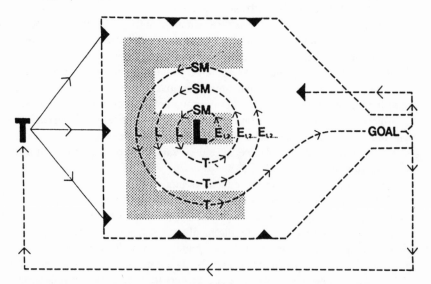

Because youth religious educators work in so many widely varied situations, this model is especially helpful in that it reveals the basic structural dynamics which are always present in every teaching act. In this way youth religious edu-cators are enabled to keep their educational equilibrium amid the swirl of count-less activities with many different persons in a panoply of different settings. This equilibrium brought about by the knowledge of the fundamental dynamic structure of the facilitational act is necessary for the attainment of the objec-tives of a particular instructional event.

In this model, T stands for the teacher—in our case, the youth religious edu-cator. L stands for learner, E for environment, and SM for subject-matter content. The large square circumscribed by dotted lines represents the learning situa-tion. As the diagram indicates, the learning situation converges toward a tight, open-ended funnel, suggesting that the dynamics of the learning situation are tar-geted toward a desired outcome or goal. The diagram also depicts a large shad-ed E which covers the entire learning situation; this shows that the learning sit-uation is an environment and therefore all four independent variables (causative factors) in the learning situation have their locus in the environment. Put anoth-er way, it indicates that everything contained within the large dotted-line square comprises an interactive aspect of the learning situation which is the instruc-tional environment. Learning takes place within an environmental context and is therefore being constantly modified by all the relevant variables inside and out-side it. This awareness of the tremendous importance of the internal and exter-nal environment on the instructional act represents yet another assurance to youth religious educators that the Lee model is eminently useful for their work. Like the theologically oriented religious education speculationists upon whom they claim to draw (Burgess, 1975, pp. 119-120), many classroom-based religious educators pay scant attention to the environment, usually without realizing how such abject neglect seriously hampers the effectiveness of their work. Because classroom religious education is conducted within the same four walls week after week, classroom religious educators can easily come to the false belief that they can ignore the internal and external environments in which they teach. Such disregard for the teaching/learning environment is a major cause of the relative ineffectiveness of much classroom religious education (Hyde, 1990, pp. 297-298). Those youth religious educators whose work is conducted large-ly in informal environments know first-hand the enormous educational impact not only of that environment external to the immediate instructional act, but of the environment in which the act is being conducted here-and-now. There is simply no way in which the youth religious educator can ignore or minimize the environment if this youth religious educator wishes to be successful (Foster, 1982). The Lee model highlights the fact that the internal and external instruc-tional environment is no mere appendage to the instructional act, but is a key and indispensable variable in this act (Dunkin and Biddle, 1974, pp. 41-43; Rapport, 1982, pp. 177-195; Berry, 1980, pp. 83-106; Lowenthal and Prince, 1976, pp. 117-131; Little, 1987, pp. 205-244).

As everyone knows, it is the teacher—in our case, the youth religious educator—who is the key to the effective facilitation of desired learning outcomes. The Lee model of teaching delineates two major functions of the teacher. The T outside the learning situation puts emphasis on the youth religious educator as both the initial and the constant structurer of the learning situation. (A learning situation is not only a set of conditions in which learning takes place; it is also a set of conditions which provides the ecology which is either favorable to learning or which actively promotes the acquisition of desired learning outcomes.) It is the teacher who initially sets up the learning situation either by bringing it into being or by taking an already existing situation and shaping it into an intentional teaching/learning situation. Once this situation is set up and/or shaped, the youth religious educator continually adjusts it so as to promote the attainment of the desired learning outcomes. The T inside the dotted lines indicates that the youth religious educator is also one aspect of the learning environment itself, a variable which dynamically interacts with the other variables in the ongoing instructional act. The environment is therefore structured and controlled by the teacher from both the outside and the inside, as it were.

If the Lee model depicts the teacher as the structurer and facilitator of desired outcomes, it also places the learner at the center of the instructional act. This is where the ongoing circle of learning (not teaching) begins. The cycle of teaching has already begun prior to this time when the youth religious educator selected or adapted, and then structured, a particular environment. This particular instructional environment was selected or adapted, and then structured, by the youth religious educator on the basis of the hypothesis he/she made about which kind of environment, subject-matter content, and teacher variables are most predictive of success with these particular adolescents or group of adolescents.

In terms of learning, the Lee model indicates that it is the learner—his/her present existential self, his/her perceptions, needs, attitudes, and goals—that form the necessary starting point. The circular lines indicate how, in a religious education situation, the learner does in fact learn. Since all learning takes place according to the mode of the learner (Aquinas, 1950; Howe, 1980; Royer and Feldman, 1984), the path delineated in the Lee model is the one which the teaching act must follow if it is to be effective. First, the learner acts as a stimulus to the youth religious educator (teacher), setting in motion the whole teaching/learning process. The teacher responds to this stimulus by modifying his/her instructional behavior according to the nature and kind of learner stimuli he/she receives, e.g., a smile, a frown, a word of disagreement, walking away, and so on. The youth religious educator, as an aspect of the instructional environment, modifies his/her own behavior in such a way as to facilitate the attainment of the desired outcome as a variable lying outside the instructional environment, he/she modifies the entire environment or other parts of the environment, as needed, to facilitate the desired learning outcome. Then the learner, as indicated by the circular dotted lines on the Lee model, interacts with various aspects of this teacher-structured environment. E_1, E_2 . . . are symbols designating particularized aspects of the environment, like, for example, a Bible, a basketball, camping equipment, the size of the group, and so on. (These particular environmental aspects differ from the large shaded-in E. The large E suggests that the youth religious educator, the learners, the subject-matter content, and the particularized environmental factors also constitute larger, more global chunks of the environment with which the learner interacts.) Next, as suggested by the circular dotted lines, the learner interacts with various kinds of subject matter which the youth religious educator has prepared, introduced, or had the young persons introduce. (To reinforce what was stated earlier in this chapter, subject-matter content is not the same thing as the exclusively cognitive, verbal, and product content which unfortunately typifies some religion classes in school settings. Subject-matter content is anything which is being dealt with in the learning situation. In a bullsession around a campfire, the subject-matter content is what is being discussed. In helping out at a shelter for homeless families as part of a religious education project, the subject-matter content might be ladling the soup. And so on.) Proceeding along the circular dotted lines, we see the overall process being continued until it terminates in the attainment of the desired objective or goal. The circular dotted lines shooting into the funnel suggest that the instructional process is an intentional dynamic leading to the attainment of a desired outcome. Each of the four molar variables acts and interacts within the structured learning situation to produce the goal. It will be observed that the goal is open-ended as depicted in the model. This suggests that once it has been attained, the outcome acts as feedback both to the adjusted teacher behavior and to new learner activity. This feedback of the goal to the youth religious educator and to the learner is shown by the dotted lines emanating from the goal. The teaching-learning act is thus a system in which each variable impacts the other (Lines, 1987; pp. 31-67; Bertalanffy, 1968, pp. 208-218).

The Lee model shows in a variety of ways that religious instruction is a highly complex activity. Effective youth religious instruction involves the continual arrangement and rearrangement of all those multitudinous factors and conditions subsumed under each of the four molar variables. Thus those youth religious educators who blithely believe that all they need to know or do is "proclaim the Good News" or to "minister caringly to young persons" or to be "a faith companion on the way" will almost certainly fail. It is not enough, not nearly enough, to want to proclaim or minister or be a companion; one must know the facilitational details involved in proclaiming or ministering or being a companion, then be skilled in actually facilitating these many details. "Proclaiming the Good News," "ministering caringly to young persons," "being a faith companion on the way" are all worthwhile statements, but they are basically amorphous and thus unhelpful to youth religious educators (Lee, 1971, pp. 208-218). These and other forms of ceremonial language (Williamson, 1970, pp. 41-42) are basically unhelpful because they do not tell youth religious educators what to do or how to act while proclaiming the Good News, ministering caringly to young

persons, or being a faith companion on the way. Effective youth religious education, like all effective facilitation, lies in the proper understanding and the
skillful execution of the details—details encased in an overarching vision to be
sure, but unrelenting, nitty-gritty details nonetheless. The Lee model depicts
the cluster of basic details which go to make up the actual facilitation of desired
religious outcomes in young persons. It might be consoling or even ego-build-
ing in the superficial sense for youth religious educators to assure themselves that
they are proclaiming or ministering caringly or accompanying. But if youth
religious educators fail to give unremitting attention to the facilitational dynamics involved in proclaiming or ministering caringly or any other youth ministry
process, their high-sounding self-descriptions will be as hollow as their work is
ineffective. One cannot be a successful youth minister unless one attends to and
enacts the specific facilitational behaviors involved in any teaching-learning
act no matter where or how that act takes place.

Of the many practical consequences which the Lee model directly suggests
to youth religious educators, at least six are so important as to merit inclusion in
this chapter. These six are 1) structuring the learning situation, 2) continuous
awareness of what is happening educationally, 3) antecedent-consequent behavioral chaining, 4) intentionality and directedness, 5) teaching as prediction, and
6) teaching as decision making. Each of these six is integrated with the others not
just in theory but in actual youth religious education practice.

Structuring the Learning Situation

At its most fundamental processive level, youth religious instruction, like
any other form of intentional facilitation of desired learning outcomes, is foremost a matter of structuring the learning situation (Lee, 1970). Indeed, all professionally informed practice is centrally concerned with what Herbert Simon calls
design, namely the process of "changing existing situations into preferred ones"
(1972, p. 44. Also see Schön, p. 55). Neglect of structural design, neglect of
seeing the facilitational act primarily and holistically as structuring the learning
situation, leads to that kind of practice which is "intellectually soft, intuitive, and
cookbooky (Simon, 1972, p. 56). Simon's views are akin to what I term the
"Mr. Fix-It" and cookbook approach to facilitating religious outcomes (Lee,
1973, pp. 35-38). This Mr. Fix-It, cookbook approach to facilitational practice
flows from a combination of an antitheoretical bias toward facilitation (Lee,
1973, pp. 149-205) and what Donald Schön (1983, p. 46) contends is a view of
practice rooted in positivistic epistemology. Every educator, including every
youth religious educator, is primarily a structurer of the learning situation. As a
structurer, the educator is both architect and builder: the architect of the overall
facilitational structure in such a way as to best bring about the desired learning
outcomes, and the on-site builder during construction who puts the architect's
plans concretely into place and modifies these plans as appropriate to most
effectively bring the intent of the plans to realization. More specifically, the

youth religious educator continuously arranges and adjusts both the salience and the configuration of the ever-present molar variables.

As mentioned in the previous sentence, there are four interactive elements involved in the structuring process, namely arrangement, adjustment, salience, and configuration.

First, the youth religious educator *arranges* beforehand the salience and configuration of the four molar variables involved in every instructional act. This arrangement is based on what the youth religious educator predicts will be the most effective apportionment of the molar variables for achieving the desired learning outcomes.

Second, the youth religious educator *adjusts* the salience and configuration of the four molar variables during the concrete enactment of instructional activity. This adjustment takes place as a result of what is actually occurring in the educational event. When, for example, the youth religious educator sees that one aspect of the environment is having an effect different from that which he/she originally predicted, then the educator downplays that aspect while simultaneously bringing another aspect more to the fore.

Third, the youth religious educator keeps in place, maximizes, or minimizes the *salience* of one or more of the molar variables in both the arrangement phase and the adjustment phase of the facilitational activity. Let us say, for example, that a youth religious educator working with African-American adolescents in an innercity playground setting sees a prominent black businessman walking by. Knowing from reading the relevant empirical research (Fairchild, 1971) and from personal experience that many African-American young people tend to prefer immediate rather than delayed gratification, the youth religious educator moves immediately to structure the learning situation in such a way as to teach his/her black adolescents some personalistic outcomes about the importance of delayed gratification in their own lives. The youth religious educator invites the black businessman over to chat with the group for a few minutes. In so doing, the youth religious educator has adjusted the salience of two of the four molar variables, namely the minimization of the conspicuousness of his/her role as facilitator, and the maximization of one aspect of the learners' environment by introducing into that environment a generally admired role model.

Fourth, the youth religious educator arranges and adjusts the overall *configuration* of the structure on the basis of what he/she predicts will occur educationally (arrangement phase) and what actually does occur as a consequence of the enactment of this configuration (adjustment phase). Let us say, for example, that just after the youth religious educator invites the black businessman over to chat with the minority youngsters, he/she predicts that it will be more educationally effective if the environment is changed from the center of the playground to a quiet corner of it. During the conversation between the businessman and the youngsters, the constantly observant youth religious educator notices that several adolescents with particularly low levels of self-discipline seem to be bored and listless. The youth religious educator then suggests to the successful black businessman to set up a meeting with the youth persons in the building which houses the company of which he is founder/president. On the day of the meeting, and in accordance with the suggestion made by the youth religious educator, the black businessman conducts the youngsters on a tour of the building and provides the youths with some hands-on experience with computers and other office machines. The tour is followed by low-key but nonetheless inspirational talk by the businessman about all the sacrifices he made while he was younger in order to achieve his present great success. The youth religious educator had predicted that a configurational change of the four molar variables in this facilitational situation would optimize the possibility that the African-American youngsters would personalize the importance of delayed gratification in their own lives.

Youth religious educators naturally tend to structure the learning situation according to their own facilitational style. Because of a host of factors including their own personalities (Lee 1973, pp. 152-159), the way they themselves were taught (Ball and McDiarmid, 1990), and their own successes and failures as facilitators, youth religious educators typically prefer to use one teaching style or set of styles over others. Notwithstanding, if youth religious educators are going to be facilitators for all seasons, they must learn to incorporate into their teaching style new and different kinds of facilitational procedures. These new procedures will both increase and modify (sometimes significantly) the youth religious educators' own teaching styles and make it more probable that they will be able to structure an increasingly wide array of different learning situations in a host of fresh, creative, and effective ways.

In effectively structuring the learning situation, the youth religious educator has to pay careful attention first to the outcomes which he/she wishes to facilitate (Mays, 1986) and then to each of the four molar variables present in every instructional event. The Lee model clearly shows that 1) all the four molar variables are structured singly and interactively so that they yield the desired outcome, and 2) once having been achieved, the outcome acts as feedback to the other molar variables on how they should be adjusted to meet successively interrelated goals (Lee, 1973, p. 236).

The youth religious educator is an especially important molar variable. The educator's own attitudes and beliefs (Harris, 1981, p. 30; Ryan and Phillips, 1982), the interactive contextual ecology of his/her past and present life (Smith, 1983), his/her age and gender (Lightfoot, 1983; Lowther, Gill, and Coppard, 1985; Ryans, 1960; Krupp, 1986; Spencer, 1986) current family status, i.e. single, married, married with children, divorced, and overall personality structure and valence (Pajak and Blase, 1989) all combine to exert an impact on the way the youth religious educator performs the tasks of ministry. Nonetheless, it is extremely important to note that while the youth religious educator's personality is an important dimension in his/her facilitational activities, still this personality does not produce desired learning outcomes independent of the other three molar variables always present in every educational situation (Lee, 1973, pp. 153-160). Any youth religious educator who believes that his/her personality, however scintillating, is all that is needed to produce the desired results is in for a big shock. What is essential for effective youth ministry is not so much the personality of the youth religious educator but how that educator consciously and purposively places his/her personality at the disposal of the goal to be accomplished. Thus Sandra Hollingsworth's (1989) empirical research study concluded that the most important factor in becoming a successful educator is task awareness, namely, how to understand the way in which persons in an educational situation attain the desired goals. This study found that in order to gain adequate task awareness, the educator has to organize his/her thinking in specific directions in order to structure the molar variables and complex dynamics of the facilitational situation in such a way that the desired outcome is achieved. Even some more mature advocates of the theological approach to ministry (as contrasted with the social-science approach) hold that the structural axis of all ministry is practice—not mindless practice, but practice in which the youth religious educator deliberatively devotes the resources of his/her personality to the accomplishment of a desired goal despite the difficulties involved (Whitehead and Whitehead, 1980, pp. 177-188).

Because the youth religious educator at the deepest processive level is essentially a structurer of the learning situation, he/she is basically a clinical problem solver. Every educational situation presents itself to the thoughtful practitioner as a problem. The problem is this: How does the practitioner structure the molar variables so as to bring about the desired learning outcome? Youth religious education is a form of clinical practice. In clinical practice, problems are not the same as, for example, an arithmetic problem which is unidimensional. In clinical practice, a problem is really a problematic situation, one characterized by a certain degree of uncertainty, indeterminacy, and even disorder flowing necessarily from the interaction of the four molar variables present in that situation (Schön, 1983, pp. 15-16). In every kind of clinical practice, including that of youth religious education, the practitioner is confronted not with problems which operate independently of one another, "but with dynamic situations that consist of complex systems of changing problems that interact with each other (Ackoff, 1979, pp. 93-104). Because all intentional education is essentially a structured learning situation, youth religious educators are not mindless or robotic implementers of some set of prearranged facilitational procedures. Rather, youth religious educators are persons who 1) formulate teaching problems and propose predictive hypotheses about the solution (procedurology) and also 2) enact those facilitational procedures which flow from the above-mentioned formulation and prediction (procedurism) (Lee, 1973, pp. 208-215; Ackoff, 1979, pp. 94, 100). Thus one important empirical research study found that seasoned, expert teachers tend to view a facilitational task in terms of a broad-based problem out of which can be generated specific educational procedures. In contrast, novice, unseasoned educators tend to view a facilitational task in terms of specific procedural solutions primarily (Swanson, O'Connor, and Cooney, 1990).

The focus of youth religious education is, of course, on the adolescent. As the Lee model clearly shows, the learner is the starting point and the continuing axis of all the youth religious educator's endeavors. All of the four molar variables flow together toward the learner at every stage of the learning activity— the nature of the young person, the degree to which the young person is learning, and the goal of the learning activity.

In working with youngsters, therefore, the youth religious educator must always keep in active awareness those characteristics of the learner which inevitably come into play in one way or another in educational activity. For example, adolescents are in the process of forging their own personalities. Ego development is thus a major process and task of all adolescents (Kegan, 1982, pp. 73-110; Loevinger, 1976). But ego development "is costly—for everyone, the developing person and those around him or her. Growth involves a separation from an old system of meaning. In practical terms this can involve both the agony of felt meaninglessness and the repudiation of commitments and investments. To the educator, the first can be experienced as frightening, the second as offensive; both are alienating" (Kegan, 1980, p. 439). Closely tied in with ego development is self-concept, namely the unified set of perceptions which an individual has of self. One empirical research study of the goals of religious education/youth ministry as enunciated by leaders in six major Christian denominations found that these denominations gave high priority to the development of the adolescents' self-concept formation (Hoge et al., 1982). Because the growth of one's self-concept, especially in adolescence, is heavily affected by direct interaction with other persons (Markus and Wurf, 1987, p. 305) as well as by the configuration of one's immediate environment (McGuire, 1984), the adolescent tends to be strongly influenced by his/her own subculture (Poerschke, 1977) and by peer pressure (Vorath and Brendtro, 1985; Berzonsky, 1981, pp. 411-420). Thus the youth religious educator is dealing not only with the way in which the adolescent's self-concept is unfolding from the inside, as it were, but also with the subculture and the peer group in which the adolescent travels. Consequently the youth religious educator has to be attentive both to the young person's environment as well as to the youngster's psychophysiological make-up. In the latter connections, youth religious educators would do well to take into consideration the gender of the adolescent. As Carol Gilligan's (1982, 1988) research suggests, females tend to operate psychologically on an axis of personalistic care whereas males tend to operate on an axis of abstract reasoning. There is empirical research evidence which suggests that there tends to be a significant correlation between self-esteem and religiousness for male adolescents but not for female adolescents (Moore and Stoner, 1977; Potvin, 1977).

Exacerbating the wide variety of developmental difficulties faced by adolescents as a matter of maturation is the fact that to a certain extent contemporary culture creates the phenomenon we call adolescence and youth. Adolescence/youth is as much a cultural construct as it is a psychophysiological phenomenon (Neville, 1982, pp. 81-86). Being a youngster and acting according to what society demands of a youngster is quite different in the United States, Italy, Peru, and China, for example. While subcultures modify the valence and texture of the larger culture's views and expectancies of adolescence, nonetheless it by no means negates the impact of the larger, dominant culture.

In devising general goals and specific concrete facilitational processes, therefore, it is essential that the youth religious educator strongly take into account the adolescent's ego development, self-concept, gender, and cultural milieu. One effective way in which the youth religious educator can do this is to insert his/her whole personality into the educational activity and encourage the young persons to do the same with their own personalities (Dillon, 1977). (As previously noted, however, the injection of the youth religious educator's personality into the instructional dynamic is done in such away as to place the richness of that personality at the service of the desired learning outcomes.) To the youth religious educator's own professional skill in facilitating desired learning outcomes is added his/her personal care and concern for learners. This kind of personal facilitation should be especially appealing to youth religious educators because its exercise is more often than not easier to accomplish in informal settings than in a formal milieu such as the classroom. Another effective way in which the youth religious educator can productively incorporate the characteristics of adolescents into his/her educational work is to treat the youngsters not so much as a group but as individual persons. One review of the pertinent empirical research (Shavelson, 1981) found that when learners are grouped or treated as a group for educational purposes the facilitators tend to think of the group as a group rather than as a individual persons. One consequence of this categorization is that educators working with groups plan and implement their activities on the basis of a group as a group rather than on the basis of individual learners in that group.

Whenever learning is involved, there is always subject-matter content present. This is true whether or not learning takes place in a formal or an informal setting. One of the follies of progressive education (Dewey, 1978, pp. 29-38, 77-83) and of the so-called "religious education as a happening" trend of the 1960s (Coulson, 1968) is in both movements subject-matter content was seriously denigrated and ignored. Because the instructional dynamic is composed of four interactive components each of which depends to a certain extent upon the other for the attainment of the desired outcome, the richer the subject matter, the richer the educational activity, all other molar variables being equal. Subject-matter content should not be narrowly conceived, as for example solely cognitive, solely verbal, and so forth. As has been repeatedly shown throughout this chapter, subject-matter content is far wider than any one single constituent substantive content such as cognition or verbal language (Lee, 1985, pp. 49-50).

In youth religious instruction, the subject-matter content is religion. As was briefly mentioned toward the beginning of this chapter, but which bears frequent repetition, religion is a lifestyle, a way of life. Though religion incorporates cognition and affect, as appropriate, religion is not primarily cognitive or affective. Thus the subject-matter content of youth religious instruction is not theology which is fundamentally a cognitive science (Rahner, 1965, p. 14). The goal of religion is an improved lifestyle, whereas the goal of theology is improved understanding. Because it is inherently cognitive, theology is incapable of directly generating a lifestyle such as religion (Lee, 1982, pp. 100-110; Gutiérrez, 1973, pp. 11-13). Hence in structuring the learning situation, the youth religious educator should try to make sure that the subject-matter content is religious or is related in some way to religion. Theology or other cognitive subject-matter content can of course be dealt with, but only in a manner which plugs into religious material and religiously related goals.

To assert that the subject-matter content of youth religious education is religion does not mean that youth ministry should be churchy or that religion should be dragged into the educational event by the heels. Religion may be focused, as in the sacraments, or diffused, as in helping an elderly person across the street. It often does no real educational service to attempt to convert diffused religion into focused religion. However, it is sometimes helpful for the youth religious educator to show a genuine (not an artificial) connection between a diffused religious subject-matter content such as helping an elderly person across the street and a focused religious content such as the Eucharist (God's gift to us), as the Bible pointedly states (Mt 25:40; 1 Cor 13:2-3).

The fourth molar variable which is structured in one way or another in every learning situation is the environment. There is a considerable amount of empirical research dating back many years which underscores the great power of the environment on the shape, quality, and thrust of learning (Lee, 1973, pp. 65-72). Awareness of the great power of the environment to facilitate desired outcomes has been well-known in the church for centuries, even among those who have not been professionally trained in education. Thus, for example, there has been an enduring emphasis among liturgists and thoughtful pastors on structuring the environment (e.g., the church interior) in such a way that the participants in the worship service will learn a sense and a way of the holy (White, 1980, pp. 76-109; Hatchette, 1976, pp. 10-11; Second Vatican Council, 1963). It is small wonder, then, that an empirical research study comparing expert seasoned educators with novice unseasoned educators found that the expert educators were more likely to rely on environment interventions than were the novices (Swanson, O'Connor, and Cooney, 1990). The environment in and of itself, then, is facilitative. But the environment does not automatically produce learning outcomes (Mazzuca, 1990). The other three molar variables must play an active role if the environment is to enrich the learning event with its potential.

Because every educational event is a dynamic interaction among the four constituent molar variables, as the Lee model clearly shows, the environment affects not only the learner and the subject-matter content but also the youth religious educator together with the way he/she structures and implements an instructional activity. Thus Dona Kagan's (1988) review of the pertinent empirical research studies and analyses concludes that the learning environment exercises a profound influence on the way the educator plans, structures, and actually facilitates the educational event.

In 1975, Harold William Burgess published an important book which concluded that with the exception of the proponents of the social-science approach to religious instruction, religious education thinkers in the twentieth century consistently and abjectly neglected to take the environment into adequate consideration when describing and prescribing religious education activities (Burgess, 1975). Unfortunately, Burgess' conclusion is as true today as when he originally unearthed it. Yet it is essential for every competent practitioner, including the youth religious educator, to be able to effectively structure an educational environment, to be aware of what transpires in this environment during the instructional event, and to be able to alter the variables and factors within that environment so that the desired learning outcome is achieved (Argyris and Schön, 1974, p. 150).

Because the immediate educational environment exerts such a powerful influence on learning, it is essential that the youth religious educator structure it in such a way as to promote the attainment of the desired learning outcomes. The way the adolescent experiences the instructional environment depends in no small measure on how the youth religious educator constructs it (Argyris and Schön, 1974, p. 150). Constructing a learning environment includes, but is not restricted to, space or place or arrangement (Lee, 1973, pp. 65-73; Doyle, 1977; Zeichner and Gore, 1990; Saegert and Winkel, 1990). The learning environment also includes socioemotional climate (Dunkin and Biddle, 1974; Vasguez, 1988, pp. 93-134; Anderson, 1987). Sometimes the youth religious educator can create a physical environment *de novo*, while at other times he/she adapts the already existing environment in such away as to render it optimally promotive of yielding the desired learning outcome.

Structuring the learning environment in such a way that it becomes a productive molar variable is a creative process which is at once exciting and hard work.

Continuous Awareness of What Is Actually Occurring in the Instructional Event

The effectiveness of different instructional events varies because of the way the four molar variables interact during this event. If the youth religious educator wishes to improve the quality and success of his/her activities, then he/she must necessarily be continuously aware of what is actually transpiring during the teaching/learning dynamic—where, as Michael Dunkin and Bruce Biddle (1974,

p. 13) aptly remark, the action is. This awareness is an awareness, not of any of the four molar variables in isolation, but rather of all four molar variables 1) as each acts singly, 2) as each interacts with one or more of the other molar variables, and 3) as all of them interact together as a single holistic dynamic.

Behavioral analysis is the process of carefully and critically examining how the components of an instructional event are actually operating in the three ways mentioned at the conclusion of the previous paragraph. Religious instruction is an art/science (Lee, 1973, pp. 215-221), namely, a process based upon scientifically validated facts, laws, and theories of facilitation (Gage, 1978). Behavioral analysis is the activity in which scientific examination and explanation are brought to bear upon the instructional event in order to shed necessary light on what is actually taking place educationally in this event. The effective youth religious educator is one who is continuously conscious and attentively aware of what is really and truly taking place during the instructional event so that he/she can modify the molar variables in order to most effectively facilitate the desired learning outcomes.

From the intersecting vantage points of philosophy and psychology, behavioral analysis is a form of metacognition. Even before Edmund Husserl's (1962, pp. 91-234; 1970, pp. 335-341) philosophical phenomenology, philosophy had long been regarded as thought reflecting upon itself. In the psychological sector, Flavell (1976, pp. 231-235) conceptualizes metacognition as that intellective activity which refers to one's awareness of one's own cognitive processes and products. The use of metacognitive data and theory is very helpful to youth religious educators in adequately diagnosing the dynamics of the instructional event so that these dynamics can be successfully strengthened or modified (Wong, 1985).

Reflective teaching is the name given to the act of continuous instructional awareness. Donald Cruikshank and Jane Applegate (1981) define reflective teaching as the cognitive process by which an educator thinks about what has happened in the instructional event, why it happened, and what else could have been done to attain the desired learning outcome. John Smyth (1989) sees reflective teaching as proceeding along four sequential steps: 1) describing ("What did I do?"); 2) informing ("What does this mean?"); 3) confronting ("How did I come to do this or be like this?"); and 4) reconstructing ("How might I do things differently?"). Reflective teaching can be regarded as a form of self-questioning by the educator as to what is occurring or what could occur in the teaching/learning dynamic (Wong, 1985).

Many instruments have been devised to assist educators, including youth religious educators, enhance and make continuous their behavioral awareness during the instructional event. Probably the most celebrated and most widely used general type of these instruments is the interaction analysis system. An interaction analysis system is that form of content analysis (Krippendorff, 1980) which records what actually happens behaviorally during the instructional event.

Interaction analysis systems are nonjudgmental in that they simply record more or less what actually transpired rather than evaluate the quality of the teaching which occurred in the event. Interaction analysis systems are also subject-matter free in that they do not record the substantive content that was facilitated, but only the way the facilitation took place in the instructional event. Thus interaction analysis systems can be used with every kind of youth religious education activity in every kind of informal or formal setting. Interaction analysis systems typically are built around categories of particular behaviors which are recorded in such a manner that the interactions among these specific behaviors are made especially manifest. The most famous of the interaction analysis systems for educators, namely that developed by Ned Flanders (1965) contains ten categories of verbal behaviors such as accepting feeling, praising and encouraging, accepting ideas, giving directions, initiation, silence, and so on.

It might be objected that continuous attentive awareness of what is actually taking place during the instructional event will slow down or otherwise interfere with the youth religious educator's ability to effectively deal with the rapid pace of things which occur in the instructional event, especially when the overall structure of this event is loose as often occurs in youth religious instruction conducted in informal settings. This objection is weak, not only because every person's cognitive processes are dazzlingly rapid, but also because the lack of awareness of what is actually happening in the instructional event poses an even greater interference in the youth religious educator's work. Objecting to the exercise of continuous behavioral awareness on the grounds that it impedes the flow of the instructional event begs the question of the respective value of the two competing perspectives of awareness on the one hand and utility on the other hand. The maintenance of continuous awareness basically enhances utility rather than impedes it. And, as Röbert Floden and Margret Buchmann (1990, p. 53) observe, the objection further begs the question because while awareness can and does interrupt the instructional event, such interruption also makes the event more effective by 1) eliminating interactive blockages among the four molar variables and 2) modifying some of the molar variables so as to better facilitate the attainment of the desired learning objectives.

The youth religious educator would do well to focus his/her continuous awareness in such a way that what is being awared is neither too large nor too small. What Lilian Katz and James Raths note about instructional research (1985) also holds true for behavioral awareness, namely, that some facilitational activities are so large that they are too general, too vague, or too ambiguous to be placed into concrete operational terms useful for the youth religious educator. An example of an excessively general object of awareness would be that a youth religious educator notices that the learners like him/her during the course of the instructional dynamic. To be facilitationally useful, this very general construct of liking needs to be broken down so that what is observed are those particular adolescent behaviors which can be construed to indicate the adolescents' liking of him/her. Conversely, the smaller, more specific, and more concrete objects of awareness ought not to be interpreted atomistically but rather deliberately placed into a wider framework so that the specific behaviors are seen holistically and in a pattern. Specific behavioral objects and frequency counts for discrete acts occurring in the instructional event constitute a vital part of the educator's total awareness. However, each part must be awared as a part and then placed into the whole context of the facilitational event if awareness is to be accurate and ultimately effective (Stodolsky, 1984).

Awareness of what is actually occurring in the instructional event does not exist for its own sake. It exists to improve the youth religious educator's ministry. Behavioral awareness, that is to say continuous and systematic behavioral analysis, needs to be organically linked to subsequent behavioral control if it is to eventuate in effective youth religious instruction (Lee, 1973, pp. 279-289). Behavioral control is that process in which the youth religious educator works on the here-and-now enactment of one or more general or specific facilitational procedures in such a manner as to lead to demonstrated improvement of these facilitational procedures. In *The Flow of Religious Instruction* (Lee, 1973, p. 280) I give a pictorial model of how behavioral analysis and behavioral control work together to produce more effective facilitation. Another pictorial model illustrating the flow of behavioral analysis→behavioral control is that developed by Fred Korthagen (1988, p. 37) and which is shown below.

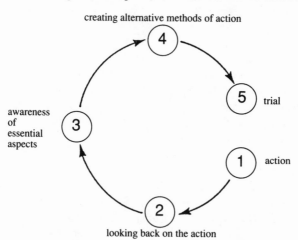

As I emphasize repeatedly throughout this chapter, behavioral awareness is by no means limited to formal settings such as the classroom. Facilitational practice is fundamentally facilitational practice; the setting is only one portion of only one of the four molar variables involved in every instructional event. Thus Kenneth Zeichner (1981-1982, pp. 1-22) states that reflective awareness "which is directed toward the improvement of practice does not necessarily need to

take place within the boundaries of the classroom to have an impact." Let me give
an example of the point made thus far in this paragraph. Years ago, as an unde-
tected observer in an outdoor cafe in the Bahamas, I used the Flanders Interaction
Analysis System to behaviorally analyze what was structurally taking place
during a heated argument between a husband and wife who were sitting at the next
table. The results were quite revealing and pinpointed the structural root of their
quarrel. Behavioral analysis can be used whenever and wherever human interaction takes place, including any and all facilitation events in youth religious education situations.

Antecedent-Consequent Behavioral Chaining

Another important functional focal point for the youth religious educator is
that of antecedent-consequent behavioral chaining (Lee, 1973, pp. 196-197).
This term refers to the dynamic sequence of cause-effect behaviors which occur
in every teaching-learning event regardless of the environment in which that
event occurs. As was shown earlier in this chapter, all teaching occurs as a structured learning situation in which the youth religious educator makes the first
move. The learner then responds in one way or another to the youth religious educator's initiatory move. The learner's move is influenced by the shape, flow,
and content of the educator's previous move. The youth religious educator then
responds to the learner's move. The thrust and texture of the youth religious
educator's response to the learner's response to the educator's initiatory move
is almost totally influenced by the educator's awareness of the degree to which
the learner's response is leading the learner toward the attainment of the desired
learning outcome. The learner then responds to the educator's move, and so it continues.

I have given the term antecedent-consequent behavioral chaining to the
sequence of instructional moves for two reasons. First, all educator and learner
moves are, at bottom, behaviors. A behavior is anything which a human being
does and which can be directly or indirectly observed by someone, including the
person engaging in that behavior. Youth religious instruction, like all other
forms of intentional education, is a series of interactive behaviors. Second, the
behaviors which occur in an instructional event are necessarily chained in an initiatory-response fashion. The youth religious educator makes the initiatory first
move. The adolescent then responds. Precisely because the instructional event
is interactive, the adolescent's response is both a response and an initiation. It is
a response because it is the adolescent's reaction to the educator's prior behavior. It is also an initiation because it causes the youth religious educator to
respond in deliberative fashion to the young person's behavior. The youth religious educator's response in turn becomes an initiatory behavior which itself
invites a response from the adolescent. These initiatory-response behaviors form
a chain of interlocking behaviors, each one dependent upon and linked to the prior
behavior.

Supportive of Lee's earlier conceptualization of teaching as antecedent-consequent behavioral chaining, Christopher Clark and Penelope Peterson (1986) state that the desire to which the learners in an instructional event are actually learning tends to influence their responses to the educator. Furthermore, continue Clark and Peterson, the educator's response to the learners is largely determined by the degree of learning which the learners exhibit in their responses to the educator.

Kathy Carter's (1990) review of some of the pertinent empirical research data suggests that depending on their degree of process sensitivity and expansive experience, educators tend to exhibit three levels of awareness during the ongoing instructional event. At the beginning and lowest level, educators become aware of the facilitational procedures with which they are comfortable. With further experience of the fruitful and expansive variety, many (but by no means all) educators fine-tune these facilitational procedures. The empirical research (Carter, 1990) suggests that educators operating at both of these levels are primarily endeavoring to maintain a coherent framework of facilitation. In so doing, they tend to ignore those learner responses which do not fit within that framework, a framework which more often than not tends to have a rigid cast. At the third and highest level of awareness, educators become attuned to 1) the learners' responses, and 2) the need to reframe both their instructional procedures and their view of the facilitation process as a result of the learners' responses.

Focusing intently and continuously on antecedent-consequent behavioral chaining is one of the quickest and most effective ways in which the youth religious educator can improve the dynamics of his/her ministry. This is especially true for those religious instruction activities carried on in informal settings, settings which often lack some of the inbuilt facilitational valence and explicit intentionality as do many formal settings.

Intentionality

Virtually all religious educationists, regardless of their explicit or implicit theoretical anchorage, argue that religious education activity is necessarily directed toward the attainment of a desired learning outcome. Another way of putting this is to say that all religious instruction is intentional, namely, the deliberative targeting of an educational activity toward a desired outcome.

Who determines the intention of the instructional event? The Lee model suggests that both the youth religious educator and the adolescents share intentionality as appropriate to the subject-matter content, to the environment, and to the goals/objectives of the event. As a general rule it can be said that the more the subject-matter is affective and lifestyle, and the more that the environment is informal and the more the learners are able to productively share in helping to shape the desired learning outcome. Conversely, the more that the subject-matter is cognitive and the more that the environment is formal, the more difficult it is for learners to fruitfully play a significant role in shaping the goals/objectives of the instructional event. Youth religious educators, therefore, have a fine opportunity to involve adolescents directly in formulating the goals/objectives of instructional activity since a great deal of youth religious education is affective and lifestyle and is often conducted in an informal setting.

Intentionality is absolutely necessary if desired learning outcomes are to occur in youth religious education activity. Virtually every major psychological theory ranging from psychoanalysis at one end of the spectrum (Freud, 1924, pp. 224-239) to behaviorism at the other end (Skinner, 1974, pp. 61-63) holds that intentionality is an essential axis and thrust of human beings. Man/woman is a purposive animal, a goal-directed being (Ryan, 1970, pp. 3-85; Irwin, 1971, pp. 3-11). One aim of all religious instruction is to make more effective and more focused the inherent goal-directedness and purposiveness of life and religion.

Intentionality should not be confused with structuring. Intentionality refers to the goals/objectives of an instructional event. Structuring refers to the way in which this event is planned, architected, and enacted. Structuring temporally and causally follows intentionality: its aim and deployment is to bring about the intended outcomes. As the Lee model clearly suggests, the youth religious educator is the primary structurer of the instructional event. This is part and parcel of his/her special competence as an educator. However, if the youth religious educator sees to it that the youngsters participate to a certain degree, as appropriate, in the formulation of the intended goals/objectives of the instructional event, then it is fitting and useful for these youngsters to be involved, as appropriate, in the structuring and enactment of the instructional event. In this regard, it is well to recall that the relevant empirical research suggests that the more a person (including a young person) is involved in an activity, the more that person will tend to learn it, to develop favorable attitudes toward it, and in general to "own" it (Tesser and Shaffer, 1990). Because the youth religious educator possesses procedural competence, he/she is, of course, the primary structurer and enacter. But the young persons can help, as appropriate.

Intentionality is one of the cardinal reasons why religious youth workers should regard themselves as youth religious educators rather than as youth ministers. The word ministry is an amorphous term having no real parameters and therefore having no inbuilt axis of intentionality. The term ministry more often than not tends to be as vacuous as it is inflationary (Boys, 1981, p. 7). The vacuousness of intentionality and the inflation of parameters attendant upon the current usage of the term *ministry* is tellingly brought home in an empirical research study conducted by William McCready (1985). This sociologist of religion found that those Catholic religious educators who identified their work as ministry tended to have unclear goals and unformulated objectives about their work. In marked contrast, those Catholic religious educators who identified their work as education tended to have clear goals and well-formulated objectives about their work.

Youth religious educators should labor assiduously to sharpen the intentionality of their work. One way of doing this is to carefully plan the goals/objectives of the instructional event. Another way is to constantly relate what is actually happening in the instructional event to the original intentions for that event so as to keep the event on course. Yet another way is to gain feedback from the adolescents, from other religious educators, from observational instruments such as interactional analysis systems, and from self-reflection, on the degree to which the instructional event did indeed fulfill the intention for it (Menges, 1977, pp. 105-110).

Prediction

Effective youth religious instruction requires that the educator is usually able to predict which instructional practices will tend to yield specified desired learning outcomes. Prediction is important because without it, youth religious instruction would degenerate into a hit-or-miss affair. As every youth religious educator knows from bitter experience, hit-or-miss results are demoralizing both to the youths and to the religious educator.

The Lee model clearly shows that customary successful prediction flows from the successful arrangement of all the variables in the instructional act and not from just one or two of them (Lee, 1973, pp. 212-215). Successful prediction involves what Donald Schön (1983, p. 40) calls problem setting, namely "the process by which [the practitioner] defines the decision to be made, the ends to be achieved, the means which may be chosen." Problem setting consists in identifying the four molar variables together with the goal/objective and then framing the instructional context in which the youth religious educator will attend to these four variables and the desired goal/objective. Problem setting thus establishes the parameters and the conditions necessary for the exercise of technical expertise which, in our case, consists in the successful facilitation of a desired learning outcome in youth. Technical expertise necessitates problem solving. The youth religious educator views the desired learning objective as a problem which is to be solved by means of structuring the four molar variables in such a way that this objective is successfully attained by adolescents. In order to solve the problem, the youth religious educator makes a hypothesis that facilitational procedure X will be more effective than facilitational procedure Y as he/she deals with a particular subject-matter content with these particular learners in this particular environment.

The youth religious educator's prediction on which specific facilitational procedures to use in a given situation is ultimately based on a combination of three factors: 1) his/her own past experience in facilitational events; 2) his/her knowledge of the relevant empirical research; 3) his/her theory of facilitation.

From past experience, youth religious educators know which facilitational procedures have worked for them and which have not. Youth religious educators know that because of their own personalities (Fuller, 1989) and their own personal lives (Pajak and Blase, 1989), some facilitational styles have in the past proven successful and others unsuccessful for them. (Brown, 1981). But past experience of successful or unsuccessful facilitational procedures considered solely from the perspective of past experience is not a trustworthy guide to the prediction of future facilitational success. Past experience qua past experience is valid for present prediction only when the learning objective and all four molar variables in past facilitational events are sufficiently similar to the learning objectives and to the four molar variables in the present situation.

While past experience can be a helpful guide to present prediction, more helpful still is the research base of the particular facilitational procedure which the youth religious educator predicts will lead to the attainment of the desired objective. Sometimes the youth religious educator's interpretation of his/her past facilitational experience is faulty because of wishful thinking, defense mechanisms, incomplete information, latent ideology, and so forth. At other times the past situation is inapplicable to the present facilitational event. The advantage of relying on empirical research is that this kind of research shows with requisite definitiveness and objectivity whether a particular facilitational procedure will likely be effective or not in a certain kind of situation. All art, including the art of facilitation, rests upon a scientific research base, a base absolutely necessary for adequate prediction (Lee, 1972). Knowledge of the relevant empirical research enables youth religious educators "to base their artistry on something more than hunch, feeling, intuition, unaided insight, or raw experience (Gage, 1985, p. 6). An active, working knowledge of the relevant empirical research requires that the youth religious educator keep abreast of this research. He/she can do this by attending first-rate conferences and especially by reading top-notch books and articles which detail and discuss this research.

While informed past experience is helpful and necessary for successful prediction, and while a working knowledge of the relevant empirical research is even more helpful and more necessary, by far the most helpful and most necessary of all is the continuous and conscious use of theory. It should be underscored that theory is not just reflection. Rather, "a theory is a statement or group of statements organically integrating interrelated concepts, facts, and laws in such a fashion as to offer a comprehensive and systematic view of reality by specifying relations among variables. A theory, then, is a tentative statement which attempts to make molar sense out of the facts from which it is necessarily constructed. Facts simply are: they have no meaning or significance in and of themselves" (Lee, 1982). A theory is not constructed out of thin air; it is fashioned on the basis of facts and the laws governing these facts. A theory has three primary functions, one of which is prediction. Thus a theory enables the youth religious educator to predict which facilitational procedure is likely to work in a given situation. Every youth religious educator operates out of a theory of facilitation. The more reflective the youth religious educator is the more he/she will have an explicit theory of facilitation and the more consciously will he/she radicate prediction and practice in that theory. Youth religious educators who imagine themselves to be exempt from the influence of theory are often the unwitting slaves of some defunct or inefficacious theory (Gergen, 1973). The kind of theory which the youth religious educator wittingly or unwittingly employs before and during the facilitational act can be called "theory-in-use" (Argyris and Schön, 1975, pp. 3-34). Such a theory might be effective or defective. To improve his/her predictive efforts, the youth religious educator would do well to examine the extent to which his/her theory in use is congruent with established and organized theories of facilitation, theories which, because of the high level of their empirical support, possess great predictive power.

Decision Making

Continuous awareness of antecedent-consequent behavioral chaining, of intentionality, of prediction—these and the other basic functions of the youth religious educator already discussed in this chapter all flow into decision making. All teaching, all youth religious instruction, is primarily a process of deciding how/when to structure the learning situation, and how/when to intervene during the educational event so that the desired learning outcome will be achieved. The youth religious educator, then, is foremost a person of action because he/she decides when and how to do something educationally worthwhile in a given situation and then implements this decision in action. The role of constant awareness of what is happening instructionally, of intentionality, of prediction, and so on, is to transform uninformed decision making into informed decision making. This information which the youth religious educator gains from awareness and intentionality and prediction and so on enables him/her to make those instructional decisions which are effective in the here-and-now and which are wise over the long term.

Productive decision making is tied up not only with the basic principles previously discussed in this chapter; it also includes the all-important element of evaluation. Before deciding which general instructional style or particular technique to deploy at a particular moment, the youth religious educator must evaluate the probable effectiveness of enacting this general facilitational style or that particular technique (Lee, 1973, pp. 32-33). As is consistently noted in the educational literature, the whole purpose and thrust of evaluation is to make informed decisions about some aspect of educational activity (Galluzzo and Craig, 1990; Cronbach, 1977). The evaluation which the youth religious educator makes of past (and probable) effectiveness of an instructional procedure should not be only summative but even more importantly, formative (Scriven, 1967, 1981; Bloom, Hastings, and Madaus, 1971, pp. 61-84). The evaluation should be summative in that it assesses the effectiveness of that large or small phase of the completed teaching event, formative in that it seeks to improve the quality and productivity of the youth religious educator's series of present and future instructional interventions. The evaluation should not be simplistic, but should richly include all four molar variables and their subfactors detailed in the Lee model.

Such inclusiveness perforce embraces what Robert Stake (1967) calls the general preexisting conditions antecedent to the instructional event, the transactions during the event, and the outcomes which flow from each general and specific portion of the event. Evaluation in education exists primarily for the purpose of helping the educator decide more effectively and more wisely what to do processively, when to do it, and how to do it. Thus productive decision making, decision making which is not just a seat-of-the-pants (or seat-of-the-skirt) operation, must be informed by evaluation all along the line prior to, during, and after the instructional event.

Basic Zones

There are four basic zones of all instructional procedures, namely the psychomotor, the cognitive, the affective, and the lifestyle. These four basic zones correspond to the four primary domains of human functioning.

Youth religious educators would do well to keep in mind three cardinal points when facilitating the attainment of outcomes in any one or more of these four domains of human functioning. First, the most effective way—and in a foundational sense, the only true effective way—of facilitating outcomes in a specific domain is to so structure the facilitational situation that the learner functions here-and-now along the particular lines and operations of that specific domain. This is the familiar axiom of "learning by doing" which has been advocated by serious and influential thinkers from Aristotle (1980, sec. 11036-11076) to John Dewey (1916, pp. 308-323). For example, if the youth religious educator wishes the adolescents to deepen their trust in God (affective domain), then he/she must so structure the learning situation that the adolescents actually engage in trust behaviors, such as, for example, enacting the methodology of the trust walk (Lee, 1985, p. 113).

Second, each of these domains revolves around one particular functional axis. Thus, for example, the functional axis for the psychomotor domain is physical movement, for the cognitive domain intellectual activity, and so forth. This fact means that the youth religious educator who wishes to facilitate outcomes in one or another of the domains must so structure the situation that the learning experience falls as directly as possible within the parameters of that domain and includes as far as possible salient aspects of the desired domain. To illustrate: an affective outcome cannot be facilitated by using cognitive substantive content or by enacting cognitive facilitational procedures. If the desired learning outcome is affective in nature, the learning situation itself should be primarily affective both substantively and structurally. Cognitive experiences cannot and do not directly yield affective outcomes.

Third, though each domain revolves on its own particular axis, nonetheless the primary domain-axis is intertwined with other domains in concrete here-and-now human activity. This is called holism. In other words, primary functioning in one domain is accompanied by secondary functioning in all other three domains.

These accompaniments are just that, namely accompaniments. Though these accompaniments might influence to a limited extent the intensity and thrust of the primary function which it is accompanying, these influences do not fundamentally alter the basic axis, characteristics, and parameters peculiar to that primary function. Thus, for example, when an adolescent is principally engaged in a cognitive activity such as attempting to understand the reasons why some persons voluntarily choose to be homeless, secondary processes from all the other three domains accompany the youth's cognitive activity, e.g., a passion to help the physically afflicted (affective domain). This passion does not alter the psychological laws or functional axis of the cognitive process of understanding. The accompanying passion might, however, serve as a motivator propelling the youth to deepen his/her understanding in the face of cognitive difficulties and obscurities. In structuring the facilitational situation, therefore, the youth religious educator would do well not to concentrate solely on the primary domain called for by the nature of the desired outcome but should also accord requisite attention to the accompanying domains since these accompaniments can augment or hinder the attainment of the primary domain outcome.

The Two Macrocontents of Youth Religious Instruction

Like all facilitational activities, youth religious instruction has not one but two macrocontents, namely, substantive content and structural content.

Substantive content is the area, affect, problem, behavior, conduct, or other kind of basic "material" which occurs in the learning event. For example, in a group discussion of the morality of abortion, the substantive content of the learning event is abortion. Substantive content is what is typically meant when youth religious educators speak of content (Ng, 1984, p. 57).

Structural content is the way in which the youth religious educator actually facilitates the learning of substantive content. For example, the way in which the youth religious educator introduces the discussion of abortion, the way he/she uses environmental variables before and during the discussion, the way he/she conducts the discussions—these are illustrations of structural content. Structural content is what is usually meant when youth religious educators speak of facilitational procedures or teaching methods (Underwood, 1986).

While youth religious educators, like other kinds of religious educators, tend to devote considerable time, attention, and energy to substantive content, they more often than not tend to neglect or even to denigrate structural content. This is unfortunate because structural content is typically more powerful and more long-lasting in its effect than is substantive content. Indeed, I give the name structural content to teaching procedure to underscore the fact that teaching procedure is itself a co-macrocontent with substantive content (Lee, 1982). The way one teaches is what one teaches. The way one facilitates is what one facilitates. Didier-Jacques Piveteau, one of the most important French religious educationists of the twentieth century whose own professional focus accorded a central place to youth, was fond of asserting that a religious educator can pour tons of biblical material [substantive content] over the heads of learners in such a way [structural content] as to negate the essence of the Bible. Piveteau (1970, p. 111) also remarks that "there is a way of saying 'Good morning, John' which is authentic projection of the long-experienced attitude of God to human beings and which is very biblical"—a structural content. Because structural content is so pervasive, so potent, and so long-lasting, the youth religious educator must value it and pay unremittingly careful attention to it at every state of the facilitational process. The effective facilitation of each of the four major domains of human existence and of human learning requires markedly different forms of structural content. Philosophical analysis, empirical research, and common sense are all quite clear that there is no one facilitational procedure or teaching method which can effectively bring about the desired outcomes for all four domains or even for major sectors within each of those domains (Joyce, Weil, and Wald, 1981).

The Four Domains of Human Functioning

Authentic religious instruction must include a mixture of all four domains if it is to be human, humane, and religious.

The Psychomotor Domain. One taxonomy of the psychomotor domain (Harrow, 1972) lists six major categories of psychomotor activity: 1) reflex movements; 2) basic-fundamental movements such as locomotor movements; 3) perceptual abilities such as body awareness and coordinated abilities; 4) physical abilities such as endurance and agility; 5) skilled movements, namely, adaptive skills; 6) nondiscursive communications such as gestures and posture.

Psychomotor activities are very important in youth religious instruction because adolescence is a period of intense and gradually focused physical growth and exploration in a wide variety of different areas. Because it is a domain of human functioning, psychomotor activity should be dealt with by the religious educator not only as a means to an end, but also as an end in itself. All too frequently youth religious instructional activities utilizing the psychomotor domain seem to be exclusively conducted either to distract youths from their physical development and psychomotor awareness by simply burning off motor energy, or as vehicles for using physical activity as motivators for cognitive tasks. Optimum use of psychomotor activities in youth religious instruction necessitates that these activities also be used just for the sake of physical fulfillment itself, since the physical is part of every youth's divinely bestowed equipment as a person. One gains the impression that there is an ingrained distrust and even fear of both the physical and the empirical lurking deep down in religious educators and educationists. Possibly the reason for this is that American Christian religious educationists and educators, like many American Christians in general, have not shaken off the residues of Manicheanism and Puritanism which tint their worldview considerably. Yet is it crucial to keep in mind that the physical stands

at the center of Christianity by virtue of the Incarnation (Lee, 1985b), and that
the empirical was given by Jesus as both a dimension and a test of the efficacy
of a Christian's apostolic work (Mt 7:16-20; 9:2-8).

One cause of the deep suspicion and even fear which some youth religious educators seem to have of psychomotor domain is sexuality in adolescence. As
Edgar Friedenberg (1964, p. 3) notes, the very term adolescent "has overtones
at once pedantic and erotic, suggestive of primitive fertility rites and the orgies
of ancient antiquity." But sexuality, and all other physical activity, is God-given.
If the youth religious educator does not deal with sexuality and indeed with all
dimensions of the psychomotor domain, the youths will inevitably learn and
explore these dimensions from less healthy sources. Youth religious educators
simply cannot afford to ignore or downplay the psychomotor domain. Not only
is this domain crucial in itself for religious development, but it is also crucial to
the functioning, and therefore to the religious development, of the other domains.
The physiological and psychological research manifest the fact that, for example, cognitive development and physiological activity are deeply intertwined, with
cognitive development dependent upon, to a certain extent, both physiological
development and structure (Siegler, 1989). Psychomotor activity accompanies
and correlates with affective operations as well as cognitive functions (Cacioppo,
Petty, and Geen, 1989).

There are many things which the imaginative and resourceful youth religious educator can do to help utilize the psychomotor domain in and of itself for
religious development. Dance is one of these. A major attraction which dance
holds for young people is that it involves the psychomotor domain in a more or
less aesthetic manner (at least to them). The youth religious educator can suggest
a project in which the youths do social dancing or acrobatic dancing for persons in a retirement home—something which is appealing both to the adolescents
and to the elderly. In this way the youths contribute in a diffused religious manner to their own religious development. In a focused religious manner, the youths
could engage in liturgical dance at a worship service or in denominations where
this might be forbidden, to a group of parents and relatives. (I have always
thought that if the ancient Benedictine tradition has it that a person who sings for
the Lord prays twice, then a person who dances for the Lord prays thrice.)

The youth religious educator should try not to miss opportunities of linking
psychomotor activities with learnings in other domains. For example, when an
adolescent genuflects, the youth religious educator should help the adolescent realize that the physical action of genuflection has three dimensions over and above
being part of the person's overall lifestyle: uniting one's physical corporeal-
ness with God, cognitively assenting to God's sovereignty, and affectively feeling dependence upon God.

Psychomotor activity has always been and will always be an integral part of
youth religious instruction. The psychomotor domain is itself a path to God.
Cognizant of these two major facts, the youth religious educator should try to help

youths grow religiously through the appropriate enactment of their physical-ness.

The Cognitive Domain. The most famous educational taxonomy of the cognitive domain (Bloom, 1956) lists six categories of intellectual activity: 1) knowledge, 2) comprehension, 3) application, 4) analysis, 5) synthesis, and 6) evaluation. Among the many noteworthy aspects of this taxonomy, two are especially relevant for youth religious educators. First, the categories are listed in ascending order. Thus comprehension is a higher-order cognitive activity than knowledge, and so on. Second, the taxonomy structures cognition on the basis of differential intellectual behaviors. Knowledge focuses on cognitive recall. Comprehension focuses on cognitive apprehension. Application focuses on cognitive use. Analysis focuses on cognitive dissection. Synthesis focuses on cognitive integration. Evaluation focuses on cognitive value-judgment.

The above-mentioned taxonomy, almost universally known as the Bloom taxonomy, has important ramifications for the way that youth religious educators facilitate cognitive outcomes. The taxonomy suggests that while knowledge is important, still it ranks at the lowest level of intellectual operation. Thus while the youth religious educator should indeed facilitate knowledge outcomes such as the ability to recall selected doctrines and precepts, he/she should not stop there. It is even more important that the youths comprehend the meaning of the doctrines and precepts, be able to synthesize these doctrines and precepts into a new realm of meaning, be able to integrate these doctrines and precepts into their understanding of daily life, and so forth. One possible cause for so much rejection of religion in youth religious instruction is that the subject-matter content is often based on knowledge rather than on comprehension, application, synthesis, and so forth. As a general rule, higher-order cognitive activities are more challenging and more fun than simple knowledge, and hence more appealing to adolescents.

Another taxonomy of cognitive content gives three levels of intellection, namely knowledge, understanding, and wisdom (Lee, 1985a, pp. 159-161). Knowledge is the simple cognitive grasp of reality. It is information concerning the facts basic to a given reality. Understanding is the grasp of the elementary and penultimate principles of a given reality. Understanding is oriented toward general principles or universals in which particulars participate. Wisdom is the comprehension of the ultimate principles underlying a given reality. Wisdom gives the ultimate why of a given reality. In terms of how cognitive content is learned, it can be said that knowledge can be gained by study. Understanding can only be gained by reflective experience, while wisdom can be acquired only by reflection on the deepest meaning and essence of a given reality as gained from experience.

The taxonomy of cognitive content mentioned in the preceding paragraph suggests that the youth religious educator, while not spurning knowledge, should nonetheless move beyond knowledge to understanding and, if possible, to wisdom. Because much of youth religious education is carried on in informal settings, and because adolescents dearly crave first-hand experiences, the youth religious educator is in a uniquely favored position to teach for understanding and wisdom. Thus the youth religious educator should see to it that adolescents are exposed to as rich and as varied first-hand experiences as possible so that they can acquire understanding and maybe even wisdom. Trips to worship services conducted by different denominations (Lee, 1988), participating in multireligious street processions held on major feast days or civil holidays, visiting sick persons in the hospital—these are the stuff of those experiences from which understanding and wisdom can be extracted. Following the participation in experiences, the youth religious educator should have discussions and other kinds of cognitive sharing with the adolescents either singly or as a group in order to accelerate the acquisition of understanding and possibly even wisdom which can be extracted from these experiences. Experience in and of itself does not yield understanding or wisdom. The youth religious educator must teach deliberatively for these outcomes by engaging the adolescents in deep and relevant cognitive reflection on the meaning of the extensions of these experiences.

A word of caution on the over-reliance on cognitive content is in order. Many denominations have tended to overvalue cognitive content to such an extent that their religious education programs conducted in formal settings have been often exclusively cognitive in character. Worse still, the cognitive content which so many denominational religious education programs sponsor tend to stress knowledge, recall, and factual data to the detriment of synthesis, evaluation, understanding, and wisdom. Small wonder, then, that many denominational religious education programs for youth, especially of the Sunday school and CCD variety, have not been adequately effective, and that as a result many denominations are either shrinking in size or are being sapped in vitality. Cognitive content is important and necessary in youth religious instruction; however its limitations must be recognized. Thus, for example, cognitive content will lead to meaning and to wisdom, but it can never lead to affective outcomes or to lifestyle outcomes. This is important to remember since most classical and contemporary masters of the spiritual life state that affective and lifestyle behaviors are more closely correlated to religion than are cognitive behaviors.

The Affective Domain. As it is understood in education and psychology, the affective domain refers to any kind of content which is characterized by feeling (Lee, 1985a, p. 198). Among the many major kinds of affect, four stand out as particularly important: emotions, attitudes, values, and love.

Emotions are extremely complex—so complex, in fact, that there is no definition of emotion upon which social scientists agree. All do agree, however, that emotion is massive and almost total, which accounts for its great power. Youth religious educators are well aware of the great force of emotion, a force which sweeps aside sound cognitive judgment and good reasoning. Indeed, there are some researchers (Stroufe, 1989) adhering to the organizer theory of psychology who claim that the emerging empirical research suggests that emotion organizes cognition, other affects such as values and attitudes, lifestyle behavior, and ultimately personality.

There has been an unfortunate streak running down the center of the history of Christianity, a streak in which religious education is regretfully a part, of fearing the emotions or even condemning them. Notwithstanding, there exists a great deal of emotion in healthy, mature religion. Conversely, a religion without emotional emphasis is nothing more than sterile rationalism. In deploying facilitational procedures with adolescents, the youth religious educator should endeavor to make sure that there are adequate doses of emotional experiences as part of the overall subject-matter content, as appropriate. These emotions should not be for the sake of acquiring other kinds of content, such as doctrinal content, but for their own sake. Emotional experiences, of course, should not be free floating, but should be integrated, as appropriate, with cognitive content, other kinds of affective content, and lifestyle content. God can often be found in the emotions, and this is a very important point for youth religious educators to remember as they endeavor to facilitate religious subject-matter content (Kelsey, 1977, pp. 125-138).

Attitudes are a second major form of affect. An attitude is an affective, acquired, and relatively permanent disposition or personality-set to respond in a consistent manner toward some physical or mental stimulus. The great power of an attitude is that it pervasively influences and significantly conditions nearly all learning. In this connection it is well worth remembering one of the most frequently quoted passages in all attitude research: "Attitudes will determine for each individual what he will see and hear, what he will think and what he will do" (Allport, 1935, p. 806).

Research study after research study has shown how strongly and how comprehensively attitudes predispose a person to act in one way or another (Lee, 1985a, pp. 216-219). Of particular importance to youth religious educators is that adolescence appears to be one of the three periods in life when a person's deeper attitude structure can be significantly touched (Lee, 1973, pp. 108-111).

The assumption that youth religious educators attempting to facilitate attitude development and change in adolescents are relatively powerless in the face of peer-group influences is not supported by the research. Persons do not automatically introject whatever attitudes their peers happen to hold (Berkowitz, 1964, p. 70). Some attitudes are accepted, while others are rejected. The relevant research indicates that at bottom the basis of attitude acceptance or rejection is the degree to which these new attitudes are consistent with an individual's own initial and foundational attitude configuration. This fact highlights the crucial role of previous attitude formation in the family, especially in the very young years, together with whatever attitudes might have been formed and changed through the youth's past and present religious education experiences.

Attitude formation and change is one of the most important subject-matter contents which the youth religious educator can facilitate. One of the most intensive and extensive shapers of attitude is personal involvement. The more an individual is personally involved with other persons or with a task, the more is that individual's attitude structure amenable to change in one way or another. For example, prejudicial attitudes toward members of another religious or ethnic group can often be modified, removed, or strengthened when the prejudiced youth works productively in the same milieu as persons from other religious or ethnic groups. Hence in seeking to deepen or change attitudes, the youth religious educator would do well to involve adolescents in those kinds of activities which are linked to attitude formation or change.

Value is that affective response to the intrinsic or extrinsic worth of a reality. Values and attitudes are related: values encompass generalities, while attitudes are limited to a fairly specific class of reality. One social scientist who has intensively studied values (Rokeach, 1979) asserts that a value has to do with a preferred goal. As a goal, value becomes an important driving force and axis for all young persons. Adolescents prize values because values are the embodiments of one's major and minor goals. The higher and the more personal the goal, the more the youngster prizes it.

Michael Billig and his associates (1988) suggest that much of an individual's deepest personal soul-searching revolves around value choices, particularly when these choices pose dilemmas between and among competing, deeply felt values. For example, adolescents are often torn between the clashing values of equality and authority, dependence and independence, and so forth.

Because of the importance of values in an era when values seem to be fuzzy and even lost, there has been a host of suggestions on how to teach values to adolescents. One of these procedures is values clarification, a technique designed to help persons identify, sharpen, and make public their own values (Simon, Howe and Kirschenbaum, 1972; Simon and Kirschenbaum, 1973). Another procedure is that of value dilemmas in which youths role-play situations which exhibit opposing values. Role-playing is an especially effective instructional technique for developing and enriching values (and attitudes as well) (Wohlking and Gill, 1980; Shaw et al., 1980). One advantage of role-playing is that it is very amenable of being enacted both in formal and informal settings.

Love is the greatest of all affects. There is no generally agreed-upon definition of love, even though most persons seem to think that they know and feel what love is. Lee (1985a, pp. 238-242) has given seven major characteristics of love as derived from the relevant literature in psychology, philosophy, theology, sociology, history, and world literature. First, love is a set of behaviors. Second, love is learned; it is not instinctive. Third, love is interpersonal, i.e., one can only love other persons, and cannot love inanimate objects. Fourth, love seeks union with the beloved. Fifth, love seeks union with the beloved as the beloved is in himself/herself. Sixth, love features self-giving and self-emptying. Seventh, love is marked by personal freedom, namely the free bestowal of a person and the acceptance of the freedom of the beloved to be whoever he or she wishes to be.

In religious education that is Christian, the centrality of love is pinpointed by the biblical text which states that God is love (1 Jn 4:16), and that the highest form of human and religious behavior is love (Mt 22:34-40). Despite the fact that love is so very central in Christian religious education, almost all significant authors in the field—including Thomas Groome (1980), Gabriel Moran (1981, 1987), and Mary Elizabeth Moore (1983) to name just a few—either totally fail to even mention love or just give it a passing nod. The emphases in these writers seem to be on religious education as power and cognition (two variations on the same theme, one might add).

The most effective way of teaching love to youths is to love them. This does not mean gooeyness, or wallowing in soupy sentimentality, or suffusion in touchy-feely behaviors, or kissy-face kinds of things. Such behaviors are often more associated with attempts to ingratiate oneself into the affections of the youngsters or to unnecessarily coddle or hand-hold them. Love is self-sacrifice with no thought of any return for self. Love is not the same as liking—a youth religious educator might love a particular boy but not like him, for example. The youth religious educator can effectively teach love by caring for the adolescents unconditionally, by going out of his/her way to help adolescents, by doing whatever can be done to help adolescents. Youths are quick to pick up which of their religious educators really care for them and sacrifice for them and which are frauds. Additionally, the youth religious educator can teach love by telling the youngsters stories of persons who truly loved God and sought nothing in return, persons like Mother Teresa or Father Damian of Molokai or Dorothy Day or John Wesley. Youths can also put on plays or little skits depicting the lives and motivations of those persons in yesteryear and today who gave all they had for the love of God. Finally, the youth religious educator can help youths develop and deepen their religious love for other persons by serving in soup kitchens for the poor, by caring for persons in need, by doing volunteer work in hospitals, by teaching illiterate men and women to read, by driving persons without automobiles to church on Sunday, and so forth.

The Lifestyle Domain. Lifestyle content refers to the overall pattern of human activity. Put somewhat more personalistically, lifestyle content consists of the way in which one organizes one's self-system and lives out one's life (Lee, 1985a, pp. 608-609). Lifestyle is the all-inclusive shape and flow of one's overall behavior. Lifestyle not only includes the psychomotor, the cognitive, and the affective areas of human functioning, but also integrates these domains and places them into a new and holistic pattern of human conduct (Lee, 1985a, pp. 608-735).

In the final analysis, lifestyle content is the most important subject-matter content in all religious instruction, including youth religious instruction. Lifestyle is not mindless doing—it is total doing, it is all-embracing conduct, is it holistic behaving with one's body, with one's mind, and with one's heart. Each person's religion is judged by others and by God, not so much on how one knows religiously, or even how much one feels religiously, but on how religious one's lifestyle is.

Of the various facilitational devices which can hasten the acquisition of lifestyle outcomes, three can be mentioned here: simulation, observe-judge-feel-act, and the project. Each of these techniques involves at least two central elements. First, each is experiential, namely the involvement of the adolescent in first-hand activity. Second, each holistically utilizes all four domains (Hendrix and Hendrix, 1975, pp. 16-60).

Simulation is an instructional technique which attempts to replicate as closely as possible the molar variables of the situation which is being imitated (Boocock and Schild, 1968; Thiagarajan and Stolovitch, 1978). Simulation is helpful when it is not possible for youths to experience the original situation. For example, a youth religious educator dealing with at-risk youngsters might wish to set up a simulation activity which replicates as far as possible prison life, so that the adolescents will vicariously experience the brutalizing and dehumanizing effect of incarceration on inmates—and on themselves if they continue their deviant behavior and are eventually sent to prison. Simulation is not role-playing; simulation involves lifestyle behaviors as well as affective behaviors.

The observe-judge-feel-act strategy is drawn from the familiar cell technique (Anderl and Ruth, 1945; Dwyer, 1960). This technique, which drew its inspiration from either neo-Scholasticism (one kind) or from Marxism (another kind)—two highly cognitive systems—featured only observe-judge-act, with no place for affect. My expansion of the cell technique adds the all-important affective element so that this procedure can be truly holistic. Let us say, for example, that a group of youths notice that Sunday church attendance is declining. They decide that they wish to ameliorate this problem. The youth religious educator then suggests that they form one or more cells of about six to eight members apiece. The first task of each cell is to observe the pattern of church attendance, who goes to church, and so forth. Once the observation is completed, the cell members then judge these actions on the basis of the gospels, church tradition, denominational teaching, psychological data on religiousness, and so forth. Third, the cell members then try to feel the problem—feel the attitudes, feel the values, and so forth of persons who go and who do not go to church regularly. Finally, the cell members put a concrete plan of operation into effect whereby they will experientially and holistically act so that church attendance is both increased and deepened.

The project is a facilitational technique which puts into lifestyle practice some idea, feeling, hope, and so on (Kilpatrick, 1918; NSSE, 1934). A project endeavors to systematically construct and implement an activity which involves all domains of human functioning in such a way that the youths learn why, how, when, and what to do by doing it. Let us say, for example, that the young people in a particular religious education group are dissatisfied with the quality, depth, relevance, and zest of the Sunday worship service. They then embark on a liturgical project which creates a youth liturgy which at once combines the soul of the traditional worship service with that special valence, meaningfulness, and depth for youth.

There is a strong sense in which the deployment of every domain in youth religious education should culminate in enriched Christian living, in a religious lifestyle. Youth religious education groups should be truly laboratories for Christian living (Lee, 1985a, pp. 618-626) where ideas, feelings, attitudes, values, love, and lifestyle activities can be tried out and implemented in such a way that each young person can grow closer to God.

Conclusion

Youth is a time of great change—physically, intellectually, affectively, and lifestylistically. As a result, religious education activities for youth can be enormously potent. It is up to the religious educator to maximize this potential.

It is probably true to assert that the weakest link in youth religious education is what should be among its two strongest links, namely facilitational procedure. Without an adequate understanding of and skill in facilitational procedure, youth ministry will flounder. Thus every denomination which sponsors youth religious education activities, and every youth religious educator, should give unremitting and in-depth attention to improving their understanding of and skills in facilitational procedure.

REFERENCES

Ackoff, R. (1979). The future of operational research is past. *Journal of the Operational Research Society, 30* (No. 2), 93-104.

Allport, G. W. (1935). Attitudes. In C. A. Murchison (Ed.), *A handbook of social psychology.* Worcester, Mass: Clark University Press.

Anderl, S., and Ruth, M. (1945). *The technique of the Catholic action cell* (3d ed.). La Crosse, Wis.: St. Rose Convent.

Anderson, L. W. (1987). The classroom environment study. *Comparative Education Review, 31* (Feb), 69-87.

Aquinas, T. (1950). *Expositio in librum beati Dionysii divinis nominibus,* II, 4. C. Pera (Ed.). New York; Turin.

Argyris, C., and Schön, D. (1974). *Theory in practice: Increasing professional effectiveness.* San Francisco: Jossey-Bass.

Aristotle (1980). *Nichomachean ethics,* I, II. W. D. Ross, trans. Oxford: Oxford University Press.

Aristotle (1949). *Posterior analytics, B-13.* W. Ross (Ed.). Oxford: Oxford University Press.

Ball, D. L., and McDiarmid, G. W. (1990). The subject-matter preparation of teachers. In W. R. Houston (Ed.), *Handbook of research in teacher education.* New York: Macmillan.

Berkowitz, L. (1964). *The development of motives and values in the child.* New York: Basic Books.

Berry, J. W. (1980). Cultural ecology and individual behavior. In I. Altman, A. Rapoport, and J. F. Wohwill (Eds.), *Human behavior and environment,* Vol. IV. New York: Plenum.

Berzonsky, M. D. (1981). *Adolescent development.* New York: Macmillan.

Billig, M., et al. (Eds.) (1988). *Ideological dilemmas: A social psychology of everyday thinking.* London: Sage.

Bloom, B. J., et al. (1956). *Taxonomy of educational objectives: Cognitive domain.* New York: McKay.

Bloom, B. S., Hastings, J. T., and Madaus, G. F. (1971). *Handbook of formative and summative evaluation of student learning.* New York: McGraw-Hill.

Boocock, S. S., and Schild, E. O. (Eds.) (1968). *Simulation games in learning.* Beverly Hills, Calif.: Sage.

Boys, M. C. (1981). Introduction. In M. C. Boys (Ed.), *Ministry and education in conversation.* Winona, Minn.: St. Mary's Press.

Brown, C. C. (1981). The relationship between teaching styles, personality, and setting. In B. R. Joyce, C. C. Brown, and L. Peck (Eds.), *Flexibility in teaching.* New York: Lippincott.

Burgess, H. W. (1975). *An invitation to religious education.* Birmingham, Ala.: Religious Education Press.

Cacioppo, J. T., Petty, R. E., and Geen, R. (1989). From the tripartite to the homeostasis model of attitude. In A. R. Pratkanis, S. J. Breckler, and A. G. Greenwald (Eds.), *Attitude structure and function.* Hillsdale, N. J: Erlbaum.

Carter, K. (1990). Teachers' knowledge and learning to teach. In W. R. Houston (Ed.), *Handbook of research in teacher education.* New York: Macmillan.

Clark, C. and Peterson, P. (1986). Teachers' though processes. In M. Whittrock (Ed.), *Handbook of research on teaching,* 3d ed. New York: Macmillan.

Colton, C. C. (1828). *Lacon.* London: Longman.

Coulson, W. R. (1968). Let's go roller-skating for Christ! *Living Light, 5* (Summer), 6-19.

Cronbach, L. J. (1977). Course improvement through evaluation. In A. A. Bellack and H. Kliebard (Eds.), *Curriculum and evaluation.* Berkeley, Calif.: McCutchan.

Cruikshank, D. R., and Applegate, J. H. (1981). Reflective teaching as a strategy for educational growth. *Educational Leadership, 38* (April), 553.

Dewey, J. (1900). *The school and society.* Chicago: University of Chicago Press.

Dewey, J. (1916). *Democracy and education.* New York: Macmillan.

Dewey, J. (1978). *Experience and education.* New York: Macmillan.

Dillon, J. T. (1977). *Personal teaching.* Columbus, Ohio: Merrill.

Doyle, W. (1977). Learning the classroom environment. *Journal of Teacher Education 28* (Nov-Dec), 51-55.

Dunkin, M. J., and Biddle, B. J. (1974). *The study of teaching.* New York: Holt, Rinehart and Winston.

Dwyer, M. D. (1960). *Historical survey of the jocist inquiry method as exemplified in the Youth Christian Student Movement in the United States.* Washington, D. C.: The Catholic University of America Press.

Fairchild, R. W. (1971). Delayed gratification: A psychological and religious analysis. In M. P. Strommen (Ed.), *Research on religious development.* New York: Hawthorn.

Flanders, N. A. (1965). *Interaction analysis in the classroom.* Ann Arbor, Mich: School of Education, University of Michigan.

Flavell, J. H. (1976). Metacognitive aspects of problem solving. In L. B. Resnick (Ed.), *The nature of intelligence.* Hillsdale, N. J.: Erlbaum.

Floden, R. E., and Buchmann, M. (1990). Philosophical inquiry in teacher education. In W. R. Houston (Ed.), *Handbook of research on teacher education.* New York: Macmillan.

Foster, C. R. (1982). *Teaching in the community of faith.* Nashville.: Abingdon.

Freud, S. (1924). *A general introduction to psychoanalysis,* J. Riviere (tr.). New York: Washington Square Press.

Friedenberg, E. Z. (1964). *The vanishing adolescent.* Boston: Beacon.

Fuller, F. F. (1989). Concerns for teachers. *American Educational Research Journal, 26* (Summer), 283-310.

Gage, N. L. (1978). *The scientific base of the art of teaching.* New York: Teachers College Press.

Gage, N. L. (1985). *Hard gains in the soft sciences: The case of pedagogy.* Bloomington, Ind.: Phi Delta Kappa.

Galluzzo, G. R., and Craig, J. R. (1990). Evaluation of preservice teacher education programs. In W. R. Houston (Ed.), *Handbook of research on teacher education.* New York: Macmillan.

Gergen, K. J. (1973). Social psychology as history. *Journal of Personality and Social Psychology, 26* (May), 316.

Gilligan, C. (1982). *In a different voice.* Cambridge, Mass: Harvard University Press.

Gilligan, C. (1988). Exit-voice dilemmas in adolescent development. In C. Gilligan, et al. (Eds.), *Mapping the moral domain: A contribution of women's thinking to psychological theory and education.* Cambridge, Mass: Center for the Study of Gender, Education, and Human Development, Harvard Graduate School of Education.

Groome, T. H. (1980). *Christian religious education.* San Francisco, Calif.: Harper & Row.

Gutiérrez, G. (1973). *Theology of liberation,* trans, C. Inda and J. Eagleson. Maryknoll, N.Y.: Orbis.

Harris, M. (1981). *Portrait of youth ministry.* New York: Paulist.

Harrow, A. J. (1972). *A taxonomy of the psychomotor domain.* New York: McKay.

Hatchette, M. H. (1976). *Santifying life, time and space.* New York: Crossroad.

Hendrix, J., and Hendrix, L. (1975). *Experiential education.* Nashville: Abingdon.

Hoge, D. R. et al. (1982). Desired outcomes of religious education and youth ministry in six denominations. In D. C. Wyckoff and D. Richter (Eds.), *Religious education with youth.* Birmingham, Ala.: Religious Education Press.

Hollingsworth, S. (1989). Prior beliefs and cognitive change in learning to teach. *American Educational Research Journal, 26* (Summer), 160-189.

Howe, M. J. A. (1980). *The psychology of human learning.* New York: Harper & Row.

Husserl, E. (1962). *Ideas,* trans. W. R. B. Gibson. New York: Collier.

Husserl, E. (1970). Philosophy as mankind's self-reflection (supplementary text). In E. Husserl, *The crisis of European sciences and transcendental phenomenology,* trans. D. Carr. Evanston, Ill: Northwestern University Press.

Hyde, K. E. (1990). *Religion in childhood and adolescence.* Birmingham, Ala.: Religious Education Press.

Irwin, F. W. (1971). *Intentional behavior and motivation.* Philadelphia: Lippincott.

Joint Committee on Standards for Educational Evaluation (JCSEE) (1981). *Standards for evaluation of educational programs, projects, and materials.* New York: McGraw-Hill.

Joyce, B. R., Weil, M., and Wald R. (1981). A structure for pluralism in teacher education. In B. R. Joyce, C. C. Brown, and L. Peck (Eds.), *Flexibility in teaching.* New York: Lippincott.

Kagan, D. (1988). Teaching as clinical problem solving. *Review of Educational Research, 58* (Winter), 490-496.

Katz, L. and Raths, J. (1985). A framework for research on teacher education programs. *Journal of Teacher Education, 36* (Nov.-Dec.): 9-15.

Kegan, R. (1980). There the dance is: Religious dimensions of a developmental framework. In C. Brusselmans and J. A. O'Donohoe (co-covenors), *Toward moral and religious maturity.* Morristown, N. J.: Silver Burdett.

Kegan, R. (1982). *The evolving self.* Cambridge: Harvard University Press.

Kelsey, M. (1977). *Can Christians be educated?* Birmingham, Ala.: Religious Education Press.

Kilpatrick, W. H. (1918). The project method. *Teachers College Record, 19* (Sept), 319-335.

Korthagen, F. (1988). The influence of learning orientatios on the development of reflective teaching. In J. Calderhead (Ed.), *Teachers' professional learning.* London: Falmer.

Krippendorff, K. (1980). *Content analysis: An introduction to its methodology.* Beverly Hills, Calif.: Sage.

Krupp, J. A. (1986). Understanding and motivating personnel in the second half of life. Paper presented at the annual convention of the American Educational Research Association, April.

Lee, J. M. (1970). The teaching of religion. In J. M. Lee and P. C. Rooney (Eds.), *Toward a future for religious education.* Dayton, Ohio: Pflaum.

Lee, J. M. (1971). *The shape of religious instruction.* Birmingham, Ala.: Religious Education Press.

Lee, J. M. (1972). Prediction in religious instruction. *Living Light, 9* (Summer), 53-54.

Lee, J. M. (1973). *The flow of religious instruction.* Birmingham, Ala.: Religious Education Press.

Lee, J. M. (1982). The authentic source of religious instruction. In N. H. Thompson (Ed.), *Religious education and theology.* Birmingham, Ala.: Religious Education Press.

Lee, J. M. (1985a). *The content of religious education.* Birmingham, Ala.: Religious Education Press.

Lee, J. M. (1985b). Lifework spirituality and the religious educator. In J. M. Lee (Ed.), *The spirituality of the religious educator.* Birmingham, Ala.: Religious Education Press.

Lee, J. M. (1988). The blessings of religious pluralism. In N. A. Thompson (Ed.), *Religious pluralism and religious education.* Birmingham, Ala.: Religious Education Press.

Lightfoot, S. L. (1983). The lives of teachers. In L. S. Shulman and G. Sykes (Eds.), *Handbook of teaching and policy.* New York: Longman.

Lines, T. A. (1987). *Systemic religious education.* Birmingham, Ala.: Religious Education Press.

Little, B. R. (1987). Personality and environment. In D. Stokols and I. Altman, (Eds.), *Handbook of environmental psychology.* New York: Wiley.

Loevinger, J. (1976). *Ego development.* San Francisco: Jossey-Bass.

Lowenthal, D., and Prince, H. C. (1976). Transcendental experience. In S. Wapner, S. B. Cohen, and B. Kaplan (Eds.), *Experiencing the environment.* New York: Plenum.

Lowther, M. A., Gill, S. J. and Coppard, L. C. (1985). Age and the determinants of teacher job satisfaction. In *Gerontologist, 25* (Oct), 520-525.

Markus, H., and Wurf, E. (1987). The dynamic self-concept. In M. R. Rosenzweig and L. W. Porter (Eds.), *Annual review of psychology,* vol. 38. Palo Alto, Calif.: Annual Reviews.

Mays III, R. H. (1986). Setting, using and maintaining goals in youth ministry. In D. Roadcup (Ed.), *Methods for youth ministry.* Cincinnati, Ohio: Standard.

Mazzuca, S. A. (1990). Effects of the clinical environment on physicians' response to postgraduate medical education. *American Educational Research Journal, 27* (Fall), 473-488.

McCready, W. (1985). Personal conversation, Chicago, April 4.

McGuire, W. J. (1984). Self for the self: Going beyond self-esteem and the reactive self. In R. A. Zucvker, J. Aronoff, and A. I. Rabin (Eds.), *Personality and the prediction of behavior.* Orlando, Fla.: Academic Press.

Menges, R. J. (1977). *The intentional teacher*. Monterey, Calif.: Brooks/Cole.

Montessori, M. (1965). *The Montessori method*, trans. A. B. George. Cambridge, Mass.: Bentley.

Moore, K., and Stoner S. (1977). Adolescent self-respect and religiosity. *Psychological Reports, 41* (August), 55-56.

Moore, M. E. (1983). *Education for continuity and change*. Nashville: Abingdon.

Moran, G. (1979). *Education for adulthood*. New York: Paulist.

Moran, G. (1981). *Interplay*. Winona, Minn.: St. Mary's Press.

Moran, G. (1987). *No ladder to the sky*. San Francisco, Calif.: Harper & Row.

Moran, G. (1989). *Religious education as a second language*. Birmingham, Ala.: Religious Education Press.

National Society for the Study of Education (NSSE) (1934). *The activity movement*, thirty-third yearbook, part 2. Bloomington, Ill.: Public School Publishing.

Neville, G. (1982). Culture, youth, and socialization in American Protestantism. In D. Wyckoff and D. Richter (Eds.), *Religious education ministry with youth*.

Ng, D. (1984). *Developing leaders for youth ministry*. Valley Forge, Pa.: Judson.

Pajak, E., and Blase, J. J. (1989). The impact of teachers' personal lives on professional role enactment. *American Educational Research Journal, 26* (Summer), 283-310.

Piveteau, D.-J. (1970). Biblical pedagogics. In J. M. Lee and P. C. Rooney (Eds.), *Toward a future for religious education*. Dayton, Ohio: Pflaum.

Poerschke, R. E. (1977). Adolescents in the family and subculture. In G. T. Sparkman (Ed.), *Knowing and helping youth*. Nashville: Broadman.

Potvin, R. H. (1977). Adolescent God images. *Review of Religious Research, 29* (September), 43-53.

Rahner, K. (1965). *Theological investigations*, vol. 1 (2d ed.), trans. C. Ernst. Baltimore, Md.: Helicon.

Rapport, A. (1982). *The meaning of the built environment*. Beverly Hills, Calif.: Sage.

Rokeach, M. (1979). *Understanding human values*. New York: Free Press.

Royer, J. M., and Feldman, R. S. (1984). *Educational psychology*. New York: Knopf.

Ryan, T. A. (1970). *Intentional behavior: An approach to human motivation*. New York: Ronald.

Ryan, K., and Phillips, D. H. (1982). Teacher characteristics. In H. E. Mitzell (Ed.), *Encyclopedia of educational research*, vol. IV. New York: Free Press.

Ryans, D. G. (1960). *Characteristics of teachers*. Washington, D.C.: American Council on Education.

Saegert, S. S., and Winkel, G. H. (1990). Environmental psychology. In M. R. Rosenzweig and L. W. Porter (Eds.), *Annual review of psychology*, vol. 41. Palo Alto, Calif.: Annual Reviews.

Schaeffler, J. (1990). The DRE as faith companion. *Living Light, 27* (Fall), 63-65.

Schillebeeckx, E. (1967). *Revelation and theology*, trans. N. D. Smith. New York: Sheed and Ward.

Schön, D. A. (1983). *The reflective practitioner*. New York: Basic Books.

Scriven, M. (1967). The concept of evaluation. In M. W. Apple (Ed.), *Educational evaluation analysis and responsibility*. Berkeley, Calif.: McCutchan.

Scriven, M. (1981). Summative teacher evaluation. In J. Millman (Ed.), *Handbook of teacher evaluation*. Beverly Hills, Calif.: Sage.

Second Vatican Council (1963). The constitution on the sacred liturgy (Dec. 4), V.

Shavelson, R. J. (1981). Research on teachers' pedagogical thoughts, decisions, and behavior. *Review of Educational Research, 51* (Winter), 475.

Shaw, M. E., et al. (1980). *Role playing: A practical manual for group facilitators*. San Diego: University Associates.

Siegler, R. S. (1989). Mechanisms of cognitive development. In M. R. Rosenzweig and

L. W. Porter (Eds.), *Annual review of psychology,* vol. 40. Palo Alto, Calif.: Annual Reviews.

Simon, H. (1972). *The science of the artificial.* Cambridge, Mass.: MIT Press.

Simon, S. B., Howe, L. W., and Kirschenbaum, H. (1972). *Values clarification: A handbook of practical strategies.* New York: Hart.

Simon, S. B., and Kirschenbaum, H. (Eds.) (1973). *Readings in values clarification.* Minneapolis: Winston.

Skinner, B. F. (1974). *About behaviorism.* New York: Vantage.

Smith, J. K. (1983). Quantitative versus qualitative research: an attempt to clarify the issue. In *Educational Researcher, 12* (March) 6-13.

Smyth, J. (1989). Developing and sustaining critical reflection in teacher education. *Journal of Teacher Education, 40* (March-April), 2-9.

Spencer, D. A. (1986). Contemporary women teachers. New York: Longman.

Stake, R. E. (1967). The countenance of educational evaluation. *Teachers College Record, 68* (April), 523-540.

Stodolsky, S. S. (1984). Teacher evaluation: The limits of looking. *Educational Researcher, 13* (Nov), 11-18.

Stroufe, L. A. (1989). The organization of emotional development. In K. R. Scherer and P. Ekman (Eds.), *Approaches to emotions.* Hillsdale, N.J.: Erlbaum.

Swanson, H. L., O'Connor, J. E., and Cooney, J. B. (1990). An information processing analysis of expert and novice teachers' problem solving. *American Educational Research Journal, 27* (Fall), 533-556.

Tesser, A., and Shaffer, D. R. (1990). Attitudes and attitude change. In M. R. Rosenzweig and L. W. Porter (Eds), *Annual review of psychology,* Vol. 41. Palo Alto, Calif.: Annual Reviews.

Thiagarajan, S., and Stolovitch, H. D. (1978). *Instructional simulation games.* Englewood Cliffs, N.J.: Instructional Technology Publications.

Thielicke, H. (1977). *The Evangelical faith,* Vol. 2, trans. and ed. G. W. Bromily. Grand Rapids, Mich.: Eerdmans.

Tillich, P. (1951). *Systematic theology,* Vol. 1. Chicago: University of Chicago Press.

Underwood, J. (1986). Using small groups in youth ministry. In D. Roadcup (Ed.), *Methods in youth ministry.* Cincinnati, Ohio: Standard.

Vasguez, J. A. (1988). Contexts of learning for minority students. *Educational Forum, 52* (Spring), 243-253.

Vorath, H. H., and Brendtro, L. K. (1985). *Positive peer culture.* New York: Aldine.

Westerhoff III, J. H. (1970). *Values for tomorrow's children.* Philadelphia: Pilgrim.

Westerhoff III, J. H. (1976). *Tomorrow's church.* Waco, Tex.: Word.

White, J. F. (1980). *Introduction to Christian worship.* Nashville: Abingdon.

Whitehead, J. D., and Whitehead, E. E. (1980). *Method in ministry.* San Francisco: Harper & Row.

Williamson, W. B. (1970). *Language and concepts in Christian education.* Philadelphia: Westminster.

Wohlking, W., and Gill, P. J. (1980). *Role playing.* Englewood Cliffs, N.J.: Prentice Hall.

Wong, B. Y. L. (1985). Self-questioning instructional research. *Review of Educational Research, 55* (Summer), 229-230.

Zeichner, K. (1981-1982). Reflective teaching and field-based experience in teacher education. *Interchange, 12,* 1-22.

Zeichner, K. M., and Gore, J. M. (1990). Teacher socialization. In W. R. Houson (Ed.), *Handbook of research on teacher education.* New York: Macmillan.

Chapter Nine

Activist Youth Ministry

ANTHONY CAMPOLO AND DONALD RATCLIFF

Social activism has been a consistent concern among teenagers, although the degree of interest and involvement has varied from era to era. In his classic study, *Five Cries of Youth,* Merton Strommen (1974) identified the "cry of outrage" among American youth, the protest against unfair social practices. In his recently updated version of the book, Strommen (1988) cites research that now indicates that this concern has all but evaporated. In the place of social activism is a preoccupation with money, power, and status.

While the late 1970s and 1980s have been marked by an apparent increase in apathy, seen in the decrease in extreme activism and violence on college campuses, it is an overreaction to suggest that social concern is completely missing among adolescents. As Davies has noted (see chapter one), young people are still active in fighting injustice. In fact, there appears to be an increase in social awareness and activism in the late 1980s. This is consistent with the thirty-year cycle of increased public interest which predicts that activism will again peak in the late 1990s as it did in the late 1960s (Schlesinger, 1986). Likewise, Barna (1989) concludes from his study of current trends that people will be more interested in issues of social justice than religious content during the next few years. It has been our observation that church youth in particular are probably more activistic than ever before.

Social activism in this present decade is not, however, the same as that of the 1960s. The predominant issues, particularly among church youth, tend to be more conservative than the social issues of twenty-five years ago. The destruction of life and property are, thankfully, less likely. Mass gatherings of students to protest social inequities are apparently not as common.

257

The use of the word "apparently" in the last sentence is important. To a considerable extent, the perception (or misperception) of activism by youth results from selective media attention. Today large numbers of individuals can protest social injustice, yet they receive minimal attention by the media because demonstrations and protests are not deemed "news" by the major media. There may actually be as many youth participating in productive social concerns today as there ever was, but they may not be getting the attention of the public because of media inattention.

What We Say Versus What We Do

For decades, social scientists have underscored that our opinions and statements have little bearing upon what we really do. In the classic *What We Say/What We Do,* Deutscher (1973) documented this tendency among humans, a fact further supported by many recent studies in social psychology (see Myers, 1990 for an excellent survey of this research).

In *Youthworker* magazine Campolo (1984) emphasizes the importance of a praxis approach in religious education of youth. While this term is often associated with Marxist politics, the concept can be used within any political orientation. Praxis emphasizes the importance of practice, in contrast with mere theory. Praxis refers to the struggle of living, and the subsequent philosophy of life that is articulated. In the process of experiencing social and spiritual events, the individual constructs his or her interpretation of what those events mean; an intellectual ideology or belief system is developed as a result of living out those beliefs. In this respect, praxis has much in common with the philosophy of existentialism, Reality Therapy in psychology, and symbolic interaction theory in the discipline of sociology, but it need not carry any political overtones.

Praxis is opposite traditional Greek philosophy, which emphasizes that knowing precedes doing. Instead, praxis affirms that doing precedes understanding. We are told to be "doers of the Word," the scriptures tell us, that we may become believers in the Word. In contrast, skepticism is more likely to result from disobedience. Pascal noted that "atheism is born in disobedience."

Applied to youth ministry, praxis underscores the need for active involvement, not just listening to preaching; crisis affords the best opportunity for the formation of character. The role of the youth minister, then, is to minimize didacticism and concentrate on changing the lifestyle of youth. Much of the preaching that is considered "religious education" produces youth (and ultimately adults) who imitate the words they have heard but who fail to relate what is understood to everyday life. Changes in attitude *can* occur prior to behavioral results. The constant danger, however, is that religion will be compartmentalized from lifestyle, and faith without action is pointless (see Jas 2:26).

Religious educators of youth need to select courses of action that will produce lasting faith and godly behavior. *Directing the young person's action is more important than directing his or her thinking.* Consequent to the behavioral decision and implementation, the youth minister can help youth develop a rationale for what was accomplished. Thus praxis requires cognitive activity, but it stimulates rationality in the process of obedience to divine mandate. Søren Kierkegaard (Perkins, 1983) noted that Abraham first obeyed God in his willingness to offer Isaac as a sacrifice (Gen 22:1-18), and afterward his theological understanding developed (see Heb 6:13-20). Theology about God becomes secondary to obedience to God. How, then, can we facilitate praxis experiences for youth?

Four Contexts of Youth Ministry

Richard Niebuhr (1956) suggested four ways in which religion can relate to culture. These four approaches have been applied to psychology (Carter and Narramore, 1979), politics (Patterson, 1987), missions (Hesselgrave, 1984), and sociology (Reimer, 1982). First is the "Christ *against* culture" approach in which contemporary culture is perceived as completely contrary to Christianity, and thus the two cannot have any relationship. Culture and religion are considered incompatible; one must affirm faith at the expense of culture. Second, the "Christ *of* culture" perspective elevates society. It sees religion as only another expression of society's values. Religion is little more than secularist views wrapped in holy garb, thus trivializing religious faith. The third approach is "Christ *above* culture." This provides a more optimistic perspective in which religion and culture are each respected, but no ultimate reconciliation is likely. They are "separate but equal" realities. Finally, "Christ *transforms* culture" emphasizes that both religion and culture are valuable, and the individual with religious faith helps to bring about a reconciliation between the two through a building of "the kingdom of God." Faith enhances culture, while culture is dynamically related to faith.

The remainder of this chapter uses this four-fold paradigm as a way of organizing the various approaches to youth ministry. However, as noted by Meier, Minirth, Wichern, and Ratcliff (1991), these four alternatives are not mutually exclusive; it is possible to combine certain aspects of the four options. Most churches probably follow some combination of these perspectives in their ministry to teens. Productive youth leaders practice eclecticism; they make use of the techniques and approaches from each perspective that best serves individual needs. However, they also maintain a priority on producing crises and opportunities for practicing one's faith so that praxis will occur.

Christ *against* Culture

This view, applied to youth ministry, is dominant in many conservative and fundamentalist circles. Religion is assumed to be antithetical to culture, therefore diatribes against culture are regularly pronounced. Personal guilt and piety are emphasized as central to religious faith, combined with a retreatism from active involvement in culture.

There is some validity in this perspective, yet there are implicit dangers as well. One must not forget that Jesus Christ was attacked as not being pious, and his principal opponents were condemned for their false piety. Piety can be godly, but it also can be a pretext for false humility. The latter can too easily lead to a phariseeism that is oblivious to social injustice, as it did in the Bible.

The emphasis upon guilt is all too likely to be dysfunctional in youth groups. Tournier (1958) emphasized the distinction between *false* guilt, where one is made to feel guilty by others, and *genuine* guilt from breaking the laws of God. Religious groups that attempt to use guilt as a motivator are likely to find that young people will avoid those groups, particularly when extreme coercive guilt is used (Myers, 1990). Sapp (1991) documents the ineffectiveness of guilt in motivating compassionate behavior.

As noted by Freud (1961), sometimes guilt-oriented churches have taught youth to ask only those questions the church can answer and to consider other questions irrelevant or silly. Thus the small child's question "Where is God?" becomes the object of ridicule or laughter by adults and peers. This "works" temporarily, but when youth meet those "unimportant" questions being asked by scholarly faculty in the secular university they find their truncated religious faith to be of little value. The church is shocked that the youth asks tough questions, while the young person is frustrated that the church is too lazy to answer such legitimate questions. The "Christ against culture" perspective inadequately prepares youth to face the challenges of the culture.

The retreatism that often accompanies the "Christ against culture" position is a mixed blessing. One can appreciate the Trappist monks of the Middle Ages, and be thankful that they preserved the Bible and other important documents of antiquity, without suggesting that retreatism be the modern norm. Social change is unlikely to result from retreat. Yet periodic withdrawal provides several important functions for Christian youth. It can be a healthy change of pace and a catalyst for insight from reflection. As indicated by Franciscan John Michael Talbot, beautiful music and thoughtful ideas can be the product of retreat. The occasional use of retreat can be a means for significant meditation and worship, important aspects of religious faith for youth. While youth camps could have this as a function, too many camps have the primary function of being entertainment for young people, consistent with Niebuhr's second approach.

Perhaps the greatest positive value of the "Christ against culture" position is the separation of church and culture. One of the functions of the church is to call the culture and its institutions into accountability. This position is likely to draw that line of demarcation clearly, consistent with sect/ecclesia theory (Troeltsch, 1931). As will be seen later in this chapter, the distinction between culture and Christianity can also be a vital part of Niebuhr's fourth option.

Christ *of* Culture

This alternative emphasizes the priority of culture over faith. While most youth leaders may reject this option in theory, it is too commonly practiced in the American culture. The emphasis is upon the youth, not the ministry. Individuals in the local parish or church tend to be more interested in attracting ever growing numbers of youth rather than genuinely transforming those they have into disciples. Instead of developing personal piety or social concern, entertainment such as special singing groups, hayrides, and other recreational activities are the principal functions of the youth group. Youth today are not looking to the church for entertainment, which is readily available elsewhere. They want a church that will place them on mission.

In contrast, celebration is entirely compatible with socially involved youth ministry. Clearly the church is a place to celebrate, as indicated throughout scriptures. But celebration is to occur within the context of social concern, not in place of activism. Celebration is a natural consequence of alleviating injustice, but it can also occur in the middle of supposed failure, as the scriptures document so well (Acts 16:25).

Sociologist Peter Berger (1960) emphasizes that one of the functions of religion is to socialize youth into the dominant values of the culture. Churches too often produce nice, acceptable Americans rather than radicals who follow the extreme values in the Sermon on the Mount. Durkheim (1917) conducted research that clearly indicates that we tend to create our views of God from our social value system; the god worshiped is of our own making (also see Rom 1). Most of us (the authors included) are far too comfortable with the American value system. Perhaps we need to take a second look at what our goals should be in the behavior of our youth. We need to portray spiritual maturity in terms of self-sacrifice exemplified by Mother Teresa, while maintaining an emphasis upon living Christian doctrine.

The "Christ *of* culture" approach is also likely to be found in those churches who have little concern about the specific content of faith. Being a good Christian may be equated with being a good American or simply being a good moral person. While goodness is clearly a Christian virtue, surely religious faith requires greater distinctiveness. Yet churches that have substantive content for adults often capitulate to offering "something for the kids" that will attract youth to an essentially secular function under the auspices of the church. There is an important place for the Boy Scout type functions, but surely these cannot be considered uniquely Christian ministry.

However, in our concern to preserve the religious aspects of ministry, we must be careful not to dichotomize too strongly the sacred and secular. The above comments are not to suggest that recreation must be completely separated from church activities. Instead, the intent is to call into question the preoccupation with essentially recreational activities that occurs in some church youth groups, to the neglect of more important concerns.

Christ *above* Culture

Niebuhr's third perspective affirms both culture and religion, yet keeps them in complete separation. This is certainly an improvement over the exclusive use of either of the first two perspectives. As Reimer (1982) articulates this view, (borrowing a bit from Augustine) there are two kingdoms to which the Christian is responsible: the kingdom of God and the kingdom of man. Thus the individual has a foot in each world, each with its attendant responsibilities.

Many youth should learn to accept responsibility. Many young people avoid the responsibilities of adulthood, delaying that eventuality as long as possible. Indeed the whole phenomenon of adolescence extends well into the twenties (and thirties and forties and . . .) for some individuals. By definition, the adolescent is "not quite" adult (a social creation, not a biological reality, as is well-documented by Kotesky in chapter five). Instead of encouraging irresponsibility through attempts to "find the self" through introspection and self-discovery, the church must help youth create the self through praxis experiences. Helping youth accept responsibility in this world is a legitimate goal for religious educators, although there is the danger of capitulating to societal demands, as emphasized in the previous section.

Accepting responsibilities in the kingdom of God is a worthy goal of religious education. Here the importance of fellowship in a small group context needs to be underscored. While mass gatherings are popular in Christian circles today, they are most likely to be effective if followed up with membership in a small group (see Zimmel in Wolf, 1959, and Davies, 1983). The small group should ideally be no more than twelve plus the leader for maximal solidarity. This small number helps develop community, vital to development of the kingdom of God (see Robert Bellah, 1985, on the importance of community in modern life).

Christian sociologist S. D. Gaede in his book *Belonging* (1985) emphasizes the importance of ritual to the cohesiveness of a group, large or small. While it has been fashionable to disparage ritual and tradition in recent years, they are crucial to the development of group identity.

Long ago Emile Durkheim in *The Elementary Forms of the Religious Life* (1917) noted that ritual performs four functions: it creates social solidarity, enhances commitment, educates so that participants will not forget, and creates psychological peace and well-being. Perhaps the most ritualistic group within Christianity is the Roman Catholic church, and their generally greater loyalty and identity may in part be explained by the degree of ritualism they practice. Those devoted to the Islamic faith are extremely resistant to proselytizing, perhaps due to the extent of their rituals which are infused into daily life (e.g., the requirement of five ritual prayers each day). In similar manner the commitment of Jews to their faith may in part be explained by their reliance upon ritual—even atheistic Jews generally retain their Jewish identity and celebrate their religious holidays.

A careful examination of the scriptures reveals the priority of ritual and tradition in antiquity. It may be that religious faith can be passed on uniquely, and in a holistic manner, through ritual because it requires active involvement concretely, emotionally, and cognitively.

Christ *transforms* Culture

This fourth perspective is deemed by the authors to be the most compatible with the notion of Christian praxis (though praxis is possible to a limited extent with the other three perspectives). Because of the importance of praxis in youth ministry, this fourth perspective will be described in detail.

In considering the transformation of culture, it must be acknowledged that genuine Christianity is at odds with the culture in several respects, as is noted by the "Christ *against* culture" viewpoint. Yet culture is redeemable. An important goal of religious faith is to move culture toward the kingdom of God. While the culmination of the kingdom must await the coming Eschaton, Christians can significantly and positively influence social conditions. The transformation of society is a central task of the church.

The remainder of this chapter will consider specific methods within this fourth perspective proposed by Niebuhr. While the term "activism" will be employed, it should be understood that these methods can be subsumed under the broader category of "Christ *transforming* culture," and that their goal is the development of Christ-like attitudes, theology, and lifestyle through the process of experience and crisis (praxis).

Methods of Activism

Activism can range from a relatively minor commitment, such as writing a letter to a member of Congress, to radical commitment, in which one's entire lifestyle is permanently changed. With such a broad range, everyone can participate at some level, although it might be argued that full discipleship requires a commitment toward the radical end of the scale.

It is important that a church youth group not get involved in a project that lasts forever. Barna (1989) notes that while people in the next few decades are more likely to participate in social justice and community action projects, the emphasis will be upon short-term commitments in this area (the volunteers' literature also supports this, see Wilson, 1976). Choosing a specific task or problem for a given unit of time is more likely to attract young people.

It is important that activism not be dichotomized from more specifically religious activities. There can and should be conversion, spiritual growth, and group fellowship within the context of activism. Yet religious instruction without activism is a failure to fulfill Christ's mandate of compassionate activity (Mt 25:31-41). In addition activism is not unilateral; both the giver and receiver develop spiritually in the process. There is mutuality in growth. Genuine self-sacrifice for others requires a receptivity combined with servanthood.

Political Activism

Several years ago I* ran for the United States House of Representatives. Initially the goal was not to become a Representative but to bring some issues to the attention of the voters in our district. Running against the incumbent with little more than the help of some earnest college students, we hardly dreamed of winning the primary; we simple desired to have our issues heard. To our astonishment we won the primary election and thus faced the general election, for which we were ill-equipped. While the ultimate outcome was not successful (for which I am thankful!), a great deal was learned about the political process.

When I ran for office, my political philosophy was straightforward—there were bad guys in power and the solution was to get more good guys (i.e., me) in power. Over the years I have come to reexamine this simplistic assumption, to which many Christians hold, both those on the political right and left.

Scripturally Jesus had power, but he was most effective in reaching humankind when he surrendered his power and glory and became "one with us." In the realm of politics, the goal should not be to accumulate power and hopefully use that power for Christ. Instead, we should exercise influence without seeking power. As Lord Acton long ago observed, "power tends to corrupt and absolute power corrupts absolutely." We might want to believe that the principle is less the case for Christians, but even a cursory view of church history indicates just the opposite. Power is not our goal because all humanity (including Christians) still have a bent toward evil, even though forgiven by Christ.

Implicit in the democratic system of government is the balance of powers, a concept related to the separation of the prophet, priest, and king in the Old Testament. The powers of even good leaders must be limited because of the inclination toward serving self after accumulating power. The goal of the Christian political activist, then, is not seeking power but influencing existing powers and calling them into accountability.

Short of national or state office-holding, how can Christian youth become involved in politics? There are several levels of involvement.
Letter writing.

Perhaps the easiest form of political activism is to implement a letter writing campaign. A current political issue may demand a distinctively Christian response be communicated to local, state, or national leaders.

A governmental official with about twenty years of experience in Washington,

*The use of the first person refers to the primary author for the remainder of this chapter.

D. C. has been quoted as saying, "If the average member of Congress received as many as half a dozen letters scrawled in pencil on brown wrapping paper, it would be enough to change his or her vote on most issues" (quoted in Cizik, 1984; p. 195). While this may be an exaggeration, the comment does underscore the importance of giving the Representative feedback.

Cizik (1984) outlines several pointers for letter writing campaigns. First, letters tend to be most effective when sent to *your* Representative; other Representatives probably will forward your letters or simply toss them. Second, confine the letter to one topic. Third, write the letter in your own words; mass produced letters have little effect. Fourth, be brief, since long letters are less likely to be read. Keep the content to one page. Fifth, ask the Representative a question that requires a response. This might be a question regarding his or her stand on the issue. Sixth, do not assume the Representative is well-informed on the issue. If you have expert knowledge, it should be shared with the Representative. Seventh, be constructive, courteous, and accurate. Eighth, be timely—letters should arrive well before the upcoming vote on an issue. Ninth, give reasons for your stand on an issue, including any moral aspects involved. Tenth, avoid being a "pen pal" who writes about every issue, but be sure to thank your Representative if he or she votes the way you desire.

Regardless of the response (or nonresponse) you receive from the Representative, a follow-up letter should be sent. This is particularly important if he or she disagrees with your stand. The follow up should be positive, but should clearly state why you disagree with his or her position.

A youth group may choose to write letters to influence important political decisions, but obviously they should not all be sent in one envelope or at the same time. The wording should be different, as noted previously. It is also important to note that a letter writing campaign presumes that the youth group has considered the issue using the Bible and has formulated a distinctively Christian position on the topic.

Some variations on letter writing include the sending of telegrams and making telephone calls to Representatives. These are probably best reserved for those situations when a letter will not arrive in time. Calls to the local office are usually as effective as calling the state capital or Washington office, but it is important to ask for a response from the Representative. Another variation is to circulate petitions, which tend to be much less effective unless you can obtain several hundred (or preferably several thousand) signatures within the voting district. Finally you may elect to write an "open letter" to a Representative, which is a letter printed in the newspaper. Obviously these are measures with which youth groups can participate.

Local politics.

One need not start at the national or state level of politics to be a significant influence. Local politics can be a very exciting form of involvement for young people. Local political structures can be powerfully influenced by a youth group.

This is generally not too difficult to accomplish.

To begin, the youth group should locate the meeting place for the political party at the local precinct level. If the youth group has members aligned with each political party, each participant would work within the context of his or her own party structure. Very often precinct meetings have only a half-dozen attendees, thus the presence of even ten youths will immediately be sensed. The location and dates of meetings can be obtained by calling the local party office. If there is no local party structure (because the other political party always runs unopposed) the youth group can form the local office of the party and thus automatically be in charge.

A basic principle in politics, at any level, is reciprocity: "If I help you out, you will help me out in the future." Thus if a youth group can provide ten warm bodies to hand out literature, the individual running for an election has incurred an indebtedness to the young people. At this point it is important to hold back from taking strong positions on topics; this will come later at the next election. When the candidate runs for reelection, he or she is more likely to consider the opinions of these young, energetic teenagers. The youth group then can carefully cross-examine the candidate in terms of the specific positions on various topics. Should the candidate's views be incompatible with the youth group's perspective, the youth group tells the candidate they cannot support those ideas and that the group must therefore support another candidate. Even when young people are not of voting age, they can carry political clout in local elections! Those who work for the party have the most influence because very few people get involved in the nitty gritty work such as handing out party literature.

As noted previously, such involvement requires that members of the youth group define a Christian view on the current issues. This can be developed between elections through careful Bible study in which the members of the youth group comes to articulate a Christian perspective. While the entire youth group may be involved in selecting key issues and forming a biblical viewpoint, actual political involvement remains voluntary.

A candidate's night.

Another effective approach with local politics is to have a candidate's night at a local church. This will entail the cooperation of several youth groups, who meet to assess local candidates on important issues. Those running for political office should be informed that the youth are trying to decide who to support for the local elections. While most teenagers cannot vote, politicians generally realize that young people significantly influence their parents, particularly when parents are ignorant of local issues and candidates. Politicians also realize that if they do not attend such a symposium, the other side can give its perspective without opposition.

Developing a lobby group.

Lobbyists, particularly at the state level of politics, can carry a great deal of weight. But how can a member of a youth group become an official lobbyist? This varies from state to state, and the local state representative can be contacted for specific details.

One approach is to develop a Christian coalition at the local level. A coalition is a group that represents several other groups. These other groups could be several church youth groups, or even several subdivisions of a single youth group. Through the state representative the Christian coalition can be recognized as an official state lobby group. This generally gives the group special privileges, such as copies of all proposed bills in the state legislature and free access to the state legislative buildings.

When a bill of interest to the Christian coalition is to be debated in committee, the young people who make up the lobby group may come to the committee and speak for their position on the topic. When the time comes for open discussion in the committee, members of the Christian coalition lobby group can biblically legitimate their stand on the issue. In a sense the committee will become a Bible study group! Again, this requires prior preparation in the youth group, preparation that involves detailed Bible study of the topic and a thorough analysis of the related issues. The Bible thus becomes extremely relevant to the issues of the day and perhaps for the first time will become relevant to legislators. It might be noted that if a bill desired by the youth group is not introduced in the legislature, the group can themselves draft such a bill and suggest to the local representative that it be introduced.

Corporate shareholding.

Major corporations carry an enormous amount of political and international influence. Young people can purchase shares in a major company, then attend shareholders meetings (any shareholder can attend such meetings, but few do so). The teenagers can take the floor and speak on injustices that may be perpetuated by the corporation and suggest constructive alternatives. I did this with a major multinational organization, and after many struggles was able to influence the corporation to provide several million dollars in educational benefits to a third world country. But this only occurred after we gave up trying to change the corporation through power, and came to them in weakness, pleading the cause of the helpless. "In our weakness is his strength made perfect" the scriptures tell us. The only way to change people is through crucifixions, not power plays.

Cross-cultural Experiences

One very effective method of social activism is short-term cross-cultural experiences in a third world country. We have found that this kind of experience can change attitudes as much as any other approach.

While existing missionaries on a field may be good initial contacts for such an experience, their agenda is often too limited. Instead, it is important to rub shoulders with the poor and hungry, so young people will go away with a greater understanding of the needs overseas.

For example, one star athlete accompanied us on a third world trip and was awed by the extent of the poverty and conditions. He refused to play in athletics after that because "I just don't have the time." It is a sad commentary on American priorities when we show greater concern for who won the most recent ballgame than we do about helping those who are starving overseas.

One problem with overseas experiences is becoming American voyeurs. While the purpose is to observe the conditions of the needy, this can easily become condescension or pity rather than compassion and empathy. A Jeep filled with well-scrubbed American young people toting expensive cameras and staring at local residents is hardly the kind of testimony desired! It may help the teenagers, but it hurts those who are the victims of misfortune. I have found that I cannot take pictures of poverty—it is too obscene.

On the other hand, work teams to build churches and other buildings are not as desirable. Such teams often keep local people unemployed, thus it would be preferable to send money for nationals to build the buildings than spend funds on airplane tickets to send a work team. It should be noted that a number of writers in this area would disagree with our opinion at this point, believing that the benefits for the young participants outweigh this disadvantage (Bush, 1979; Shaw, 1987; Carney, 1984; Moore, 1982; Borthwick, 1988).

One constructive possibility is for young people to visit colleges and universities in third world countries and talk with students to get the nationals' perspectives on the situation. The InterVarsity organization has particularly been helpful in establishing healthy contacts in higher education contexts.

It is important to prepare young people before you take them overseas. They should not eat in the homes of the poor because of the health dangers, but it is good for them to stay in the homes of the poor. Some orientation to customs, appropriate dress, and language is desirable. One effective approach is to have youths testify in a third-world church, and then find homes for them to stay in rather than a hotel.

It is generally best to send only two or three of the youth group, including a leader or two. If the whole youth group goes, it is not only expensive but the likelihood of voyeurism increases. Two or three teens will return with dozens of stories, and money will remain to fund projects to help the impoverished. The purpose of the visit is not to accomplish a project, but rather to sensitize youth to what is needed, what can be done, and what has been accomplished.

Are we to motivate young people for a lifetime of missionary service? This depends upon what we mean by missions. In recent years there has been a strong movement toward healthy indigenization of missionary work. What this means is that national pastors can often do the evangelism and other church ministry in their home culture more effectively than Americans. Thus what we need today are missionaries that see their primary goal as working with local pastors overseas in a social activism role.

For example one colleague of mine helped the people in a remote area of a country build a canning factory so their produce would not spoil before it arrived at the distant market. Not only did the cannery help local farmers obtain income for their crops, it also provided food for those who purchased the canned goods. Another example is an individual who lived in the rural third world area and grew a small garden. The local teachers observed his methods the first year and the next year grew their own gardens in a similar manner. The third year the students, who had observed how their teachers grew gardens, brought the knowledge to their families who in turn grew gardens. One person thus significantly decreased hunger and suffering in one area of a needy country.

The latter person was self-supporting. This is an important trend in missions today, the development of "tent-maker" missionaries. The idea of being self-supporting was fundamental to missionary work from the beginning—Paul, one of the first missionaries, supported himself through literally making tents. The "tent-makers" today are more likely to be computer specialists, instructors in English as a second language, agriculturalists, business people, and other specialists. A key need in missions at present is the "tent-maker," since they often have access to India, China, and Islamic countries where traditional missionaries are forbidden. "Tentmakers" also allow more church funds to get to the hungry and hurting masses of the world, since they do not drain church finances. Increasingly there is a need for contextualized missionaries, people who will show others how to improve their living conditions as well as preach the gospel side by side with nationals. The goal for such missionaries is to work themselves out of a job.

While not every young person in the church will, or should, become a missionary, it is important for them to catch the vision of this new type of missionary. They need to understand the need for socially activist cross-cultural work that places a strong emphasis upon caring for people's physical and spiritual needs.

One form of missionary work that is very worthwhile (and affordable for every youth Sunday school class) is to support one or more children overseas through child-care agencies. The advantage of this kind of ministry is that if impoverished children can be reached, they are more likely to change their way of life permanently and the cycle of poverty will be broken. Another advantage is the possibility of regular contacts by exchanging letters with the child, personalizing the concern for the needy. One must exercise caution in the choice of such an agency, since some have high administrative costs and little may get to the child as a result. There are, however, many fine agencies such as World Vision and Compassion. Even if one is not willing to surrender one's entire lifestyle for cross-cultural ministry, such an approach provides help for specific individuals in other countries.

Stateside Social Activism

There are many activities in which youth groups can participate. A number of these are outlined in *Ideas for Social Action* (Campolo, 1983), which also includes methods of raising funds for such activities. Here we will survey only a few possibilities in detail.

Innercity ministry.

One does not have to go overseas to be involved in cross-cultural ministry. Demographic trends indicate that the proportion of minorities is growing rapidly, from 14 percent in 1950 to 22 percent in 1987, and estimated to be 30 percent by 2020 (Crews and Cancellier, 1988). Growth rates are especially high for Hispanics and Asians. The newest mission fields are just down the street and across town.

To help young people minister among the most needy of these minorities requires an understanding of cultural differences. Most North Americans have difficulties with enthnocentrism, the tendency to feel one's own culture is better or at least more natural than another culture. Young people may need some instruction in cultural differences, with an emphasis upon appreciation of the positive values of the second culture. Here is an excellent example of how social activism is not without rewards for the giver—cross-cultural ministry for youth helps the young person become less ethnocentric and more of a world Christian. It can foster an appreciation for the rich diversity found in other cultures.

Not only should young people be prepared culturally for ministry, but also they must be spiritually prepared. It is most difficult to give unless one has first received. Yet, consistent with the concept of praxis, many young people who become involved in innercity work report that they grow spiritually while involved in their ministry, perhaps as much or more than before they came. Spiritual growth is also reciprocal.

Bart Campolo, son of the primary author of this chapter, coordinates one such program in the innercity area of Philadelphia. Each year well over a hundred young people give their time without pay, sleeping in church basements or in storefront buildings, to be able to minister to children on the streets. Throughout the summer they learn that the most important values are not making money and living for pleasure, but rather giving of themselves in a sacrificial way. Many other similar programs exist, some of them denominationally affiliated, and others more individual efforts, in which physical, emotional, and spiritual needs can be met through ministry by young people.

Other forms of ministry.

Another example of ministry by youth that can be valuable is participation in organizations such as Habitat for Humanity in Americus, Georgia. This group goes among the poor and helps them build new homes. The organization provides interest-free home loans to the poor and volunteers give of their time in building the low-cost homes. Young people can help with construction, learning useful skills such as carpentry in the process. Again we find reciprocity in helping others. At the time of this writing Habitat for Humanity has built more than 5000 homes in the United States and 28 foreign countries. There are religious work camps that serve a somewhat similar purpose.

Other kinds of ministry are available for church teenagers as well, among migrant workers, the homeless, adults who want to read, and camps for children from innercity areas. Youth groups also could become involved in helping refugees, both financially and in helping them acculturate to the United States. Ministry for the physically and mentally handicapped also is possible. Indian reservations often have churches, schools, and other contexts in which a youth group can help. Peer education for minorities or those who are impoverished can offer a great opportunity for teenagers to help others academically as well as socially and spiritually. Again, this is only a sampling of the possibilities available.

It is crucial that youth come to envision the possibility of shaping a lifestyle of social activism. To take the perspective of the poor and needy is to be like Christ, who strongly identified with the unfortunate and rejected of his day. This may mean going beyond just the perspective of the have-nots to adopting their lifestyle. John Perkins (1982), a black evangelist, has encouraged middle-class Christians to reconsider the accepted American idea of a fine home in the suburbs and suggests that we should give serious thought to living among the poor.

Maximizing the Effectiveness of Social Activism

Proper use of the media and effective storytelling can expedite whatever methods of social activism have been chosen. Several guidelines are important in each of these.

Using the Media.

One factor that is especially crucial is to ensure effective coverage by the press. Before becoming involved in an activity, a press release needs to be produced so that the event will be covered. How can a person develop a press release?

First, use good journalistic style. The first paragraph should tell what will happen, where, when, and other crucial details. Use quotations from identifiable sources, such as the youth group leader or pastor. The first sentence provides the primary thrust of the event, while the remainder gives details.

The press release should be sent to all local newspapers, radio stations, and television stations two weeks prior to the event. One week later someone from the youth group should hand deliver the same press release to each of the above and try to get a commitment of coverage. Generally this is not too difficult to accomplish. Finally the person who personally delivered the press release should contact each facility the day before the event and remind their contact person of the promise of coverage.

Sometimes radio stations will use promotional announcements made by the youth group if they are professionally produced. This may involve little more than obtaining the interest of a local deejay and his spending a few minutes helping the youth group put together an announcement. Radio stations often will play a good thirty-or twenty-second public service announcement several times at no cost.

Effective storytelling.

Storytelling is a very important factor in motivating youth and adults toward social awareness and activism. It is awesome to see the power of a story effectively told to an audience, large or small. A good story can outdo some of the finest audio visuals. In public speaking (or even preaching) when you are about to lose the audience, it is possible to recapture attention through a story. Americans must reaffirm and rediscover the art of good storytelling.

For this reason it may be better for the youth leader to visit Haiti or another impoverished third world country, but instead of just taking slides, write down events that will grab the attention of people. Slides are not passionate, whereas a storyteller can instill feeling. This is partly because a story requires the audience to picture the event for themselves and thus the listeners are more likely to get personally involved in what is being said.

Facts can communicate effectively but too often they can overwhelm the listener with despair rather than give hope. For example, twenty to thirty million people will die in the Sahara region in the next few years, a statistic that is almost unfathomable. On the other hand, I have sometimes told a story of how a mother chose to kill one of her two children because she did not have enough food for both, and only through the death of one could the other survive. That story of one individual carries a much greater impact.

In telling a story it is important to "remember big." This does not mean exaggerating; it means including details that will grab the attention. For example, we had to help choose fifty children out of three hundred who needed an orphanage in Haiti because there was only room and resources for the fifty. During the choosing, it became clear that we were choosing who would live and who would die. Almost all of the 250 not chosen are now dead, yet we can vividly recall their singing "God is so good" as we prepared to leave. They died, not because God is not good, but because *we* are not good. In this story it is obvious that the detail of the children singing is especially effective because it arouses emotions; compassion for others is partly empathic, but it is also emotional.

After telling one's story, it is important to have specific steps that the audience can take immediately. If some tangible, concrete action is not possible, it diminishes the effectiveness of storytelling and the next time they may not respond at all.

It is significant that the gospel came to us in stories, not in theology. Storytelling was dominant in Christ's ministry because he could communicate truth more holistically and tangibly. We can easily forget commands to help others, but who can forget the story of the Good Samaritan?

A key aspect of effective storytelling is to have our hearts broken by the things that break the heart of Jesus. It is not clever techniques but rather intensive, emotional involvement that will communicate. We must feel before we can tell, we must experience before we can articulate that experience. This is the heart of praxis.

The subversive youth minister.

In a sense those who work with church youth are called to be subversives. Generally churches hire youth ministers to help their young people become good citizens and accept the values of society. But the mission of the youth minister is not to help teenagers become adjusted to a fallen and ungodly culture but to help them become genuine Christians who seek to redeem society into the kingdom of God.

Radical commitment to Christ and social activism is not without its costs. Some may misunderstand and disagree with the activisitic stance, probably because they hold exclusively to one of the first three of the four perspectives identified by Niebuhr. Some members of the youth group (sometimes even the majority) may be unwilling to commit themselves to social causes. It can be appropriate to confront such individuals with the demands of scripture in this area. Occasionally those who refuse to do anything constructive in a youth group should be asked to leave. John Wesley, the great eighteenth-century evangelist, once returned from a series of services in the north of England. His brother Charles asked him, "Were many added to the church?" John answered, "None was added, but there was a host of blessed subtractions." Individuals must sometimes be pruned for greater service, the scriptures tell us, and sometimes youth groups need to have unfruitful branches pruned as well.

Conclusion

There is and always has been a need for heroes among young people. This is no less the case in today's materialistic world. Ernest Becker in his book *Denial of Death* (1973) noted that youth are made for heroism, not pleasure. Young people realize they have a dual nature, one side bent toward death, corruption, and decay, and the other side positive and God-like. In heroism there is the possibility of failure and corruption because of the dark side of human nature, but heroism is affirmed when in spite of this possibility they do something that would be a credit to angels, thus affirming the image of God within. The great task of youth ministry is to challenge young people to do something heroic.

Young people who become involved in social activism can become modern heroes who, like the characters in Star Trek, will "boldly go where no one has gone before." Rather then being imaginary characters in a movie or television program, they will be real people helping save the world.

REFERENCES

Barna, G. (1989). *America 2000*. Glendale, Calif.: Barna Research Group.

Becker, E. (1973). *The denial of death*. New York: Free Press.

Bellah, R. (1985). *Habits of the heart*. Berkeley: University of California Press.

Berger, P. (1960). *The noise of solemn assemblies*. Garden City, N.Y.: Doubleday.

Borthwick, P. (1988). *Youth and missions: Expanding your students' worldview*. Wheaton, Ill.: Victor.

Bush, J. C. (1979). *Disaster response*. Scottdale, Pa.: Herald Press.

Campolo, A. (1983). *Ideas for social action*. El Cajon, Calif.: Youth Specialties.

Campolo, A. (1984). Praxis: The revolutionary new principle for crisis counseling. *Youthworker* (Spring), pp. 48-51.

Carney, G. (1984). *Creative urban youth ministry*. Elgin, Ill.: D.C. Cook.

Carter, J. and B. Narramore (1979). *Psychology and Christianity*. Grand Rapids, Mich.: Zondervan.

Cizik, R. (1984). *The high cost of indifference*. Ventura, Calif.: Regal.

Crews, K., and Cancellier, P. (1988). *U.S. Population*. Washington, D.C.: Population Reference Bureau.

Davies, J. (1983). Small groups: Are they really so new? *Christian Education Journal, 2,* 43-52.

Deutscher, I. (1973). *What we say/What we do*. Glenview, Ill.: Scott, Foresman.

Durkheim, E. (1917). *The elementary forms of the religious life*. New York: Free Press.

Freud, S. (1961). *The future of an illusion*. New York: W. W. Norton.

Gaede, S. (1985). *Belonging*. Grand Rapids, Mich.: Zondervan.

Hesselgrave, D. J. (1984). *Counseling cross-culturally*. Grand Rapids, Mich.: Zondervan.

Meier, P., Minirth, F., Wichern, F., and Ratcliff, D. (1991). *Introduction to psychology and counseling* (2nd ed.). Grand Rapids, Mich.: Baker.

Moore, D. (1982). *Youth try the impossible.*Whiteface Woods, Cotton, Minn.: Camping Guideposts.

Myers, D. (1990). *Social psychology* (3rd ed.). New York: McGraw-Hill.

Niebuhr, R. (1956). *Christ and culture*. New York: Harper & Row.

Patterson, J. (1987). Personal correspondence.

Perkins, J. (1982). *With justice for all*. Glendale, Calif.: Regal.

Perkins, R. (1983). *Kierkegaard: Fear and trembling*. Tuscaloosa, Ala.: University of Alabama Press.

Reimer, M. (1982). The study of sociology: An introduction. In S. Grunlan and M. Reimer (Eds.), *Christian perspectives on sociology*. Grand Rapids, Mich.: Zondervan.

Sapp, G. (1991). Psychological foundations of religious compassion. In G. Sapp (Ed.), *Compassion in pastoral ministry*. Birmingham, Ala.: Religious Education Press.

Schlesinger, A. (1986). *Cycles of American history*. Boston: Houghton Mifflin.

Shaw, J. C. (1987). *The workcamp experience*. Loveland, Col.: Group Books.

Strommen, M. (1974). *Five cries of youth*. San Francisco: Harper & Row.

Strommen, M. (1988). *Five cries of youth*. (rev. ed.). San Francisco: Harper & Row.

Tournier, P. (1958). *Guilt and grace*. New York: Harper & Row.

Troeltsch, E. (1932). *The social teaching of the Christian churches*. London: Allen and Unwin.

Wilson, M. (1976). *Effective management of volunteer programs*. Bolder, Col.: Volunteer Management.

Wolf, K. (Ed.). (1959) *The sociology of Georg Simmel*. New York: Free Press.

Chapter Ten

Conducting a Needs Analysis and the Research Process

JAMES F. ENGEL

The focus of this book is developing and executing an effective youth ministry. This objective will not be achieved, however, unless leaders understand teenagers—their hurts, strivings, victories, and struggles as they apply the Word of God to life.

One of the greatest hindrances to youth ministry lies in the fact that far too many teenagers view Christianity as just another part of their life. They are not sufficiently challenged to be involved in religious faith in a growing and vital way. Ways must be found to discover what is behind the "mask" of today's teenagers.

Stephen Olford once commented, "God creates only originals, not carbon copies." The challenge for leaders is to uncover "God's original" in each person to whom we minister. Research can help accomplish this. It is not an end in itself. Rather, it is just one component, albeit a vital one, in Spirit-led planning.

Strategic Planning

A logical, disciplined approach to planning in Christian ministry is not an option—it is a necessity. It is through this process that we cooperate with God as he leads through his Spirit. John R. W. Stott put it well (1976; p. 127):

Some say rather piously that the Holy Spirit is himself the complete and satisfactory solution to the problem of communication, and indeed that when he is present and active, then communication ceases to be a problem. What on

275

earth does such a statement mean? Do we now have liberty to be as obscured, confused, and irrelevant as we like, and the Holy Spirit will make all thing plain? To use the Holy Spirit to rationalize our laziness is nearer blasphemy than piety. Of course *without* the Holy Spirit all our explanations are futile. . . . Trust in the Holy Spirit must not be used as a device to save us the labor of biblical and contemporary studies.

While strategic planning is not a linear process, the stages described in Figure 1 are necessary components (Engel, 1989). Any decision maker in Christian ministry begins with two assets: 1) intuition and analytical ability and 2) experience. One may have a hunch about what should be done in a ministry program, and this hunch is refined and modified by what has been learned in the past. In today's rapidly changing world, however, intuition and experience are increasingly insufficient. Research is a necessary third ingredient.

Figure 1. Stages in the Strategic Planning Process

1. *Evaluate and clarify institutional mission.* Why do we exist? What are the specific outcomes if we are successful in meeting our purpose?
2. *Evaluate present programs against mission.* Are we achieving our purpose?
3. *Discern the factors which bear upon mission and program.* Who is the target audience? What are their motivations and needs, background, and understanding?
4. *Define and prioritize action alternatives.* What are the most promising options? What will happen if we do nothing? Do we need audience research to test proposed options?
5. *Choose, develop, and carry out those options which appear to be best.*
6. *Set specific, measurable objectives.*
7. *Prepare a detailed action plan and monitor outcomes.*

Source: James F. Engel, (1989), *Strategic Planning for Extension Education.*

Research provides the factual basis upon which leaders can find God's unique plan for their ministry. Research provides vital input throughout the planning process, but it is especially helpful at these stages:
1. *Evaluation of programs against mission.* The only way to discover ministry impact on youth is to ask them. This assumes, of course, that specific, measurable objectives are in place, an assumption which all too frequently is erroneous.
2. *Discernment of factors bearing upon mission.* Analysis of the target audience is especially crucial. What is known about adolescents in the church?
3. *Definition and prioritization of action alternatives.* Pretesting of proposed religious education programs is a necessity.

4. *Evaluation of outcomes*. The intent is exactly the same as #1 above. Have we achieved our objectives?

An Overview of the Research Process

Figure 2 describes the steps in the research process (Engel, 1977; also see Alreck and Settle, 1985). All stages will be discussed in this chapter with the exception of sampling design. The reason for this omission is that most users of this manual will undertake a census (i.e., analysis of the totality) of their youth group. If the group is extremely large (say, a regional area or an entire denomination), noncomplex systematic random sampling can easily be used by those without technical training (see Engel, 1977; ch. 4).

Figure 2. Stages in the Research Process

1. Definition of the problem
2. Clarification of research objectives
3. Identification of data requirements
   a. Categories of data needed to solve the problem
   b. Sources of data
4. Determination of data collection procedures
5. Design of the sampling plan
6. Design of the data collection instrument
7. Data collection
8. Tabulation, analysis, and reporting
9. Phasing research into strategy

Problem Definition

In my experience most of the research undertaken in both the secular and Christian worlds is either underutilized or winds up collecting dust on someone's shelf. Such waste is indefensible from any perspective, especially that of Christian stewardship. Therefore, it is necessary from the outset to be clear on three basic issues:
1. Why is the research being undertaken?
2. What is the real problem?
3. How will the data be used in ministry planning?

Some Inadequate Motivations for Conducting Research

When I first entered full-time Christian work nearly twenty years ago, I was among "unreached people" insofar as research and strategic planning. Now, the pendulum has swung radically. Many religious writers and popular speakers cite someone else's data and often do so indiscriminately and inappropriately.

It almost seems as if research is being embraced as a kind of magic key to the ministry promised land. This is not the case at all, and there are some wrong reasons for jumping on the research bandwagon:

1. *Everyone else is doing it.* Research has become an "in thing" for the good reason that many are discovering its value in augmenting intuition and experience. It will become just another passing fad, however, unless it is used in the context of strategic planning.

2. *Justification of current programs without commitment to change.* It has been discouraging to see how many Christian leaders seek research data to confirm their own opinions with no intention of changing programs. While objective data can perform a confirming role, this is the wrong motivation from the start, and the outcome can be contaminated research results. It is essential to recognize this point; *unless one is willing to change current programs to increase ministry effectiveness, research can be more of a hindrance than a help.*

3. *Pressure from the top.* At times, pressure for ministry accountability comes from boards, institutional leadership, or outsiders. While this can be entirely appropriate, it becomes counter productive unless there is complete ownership of the process at every level. When this is not the case, leaders become defensive and even less willing to adapt programs and strategies to meet needs that surface.

4. *Desire to eliminate risk.* There are many in leadership positions who are unwilling to act unless the risk of failure is minimal. Research can lower risk but never eliminates it. Innovation always requires risk taking, because perfect prediction is impossible. In reality, uncertainty is a good thing, because most of us otherwise simply would do it our way.

Research should be undertaken only when leaders are united in their vision that enhanced ministry effectiveness is the guiding objective. It must be recognized that research does not replace intuition and experience. What it can do is to illuminate previously unlit avenues of inquiry and thereby verify or disconfirm preliminary hunches.

Uncovering the Real Problem

Not many years ago I was approached by a minister who was concerned about his youth program. In particular, he felt the need to undertake a survey to find out why so few teenagers were attending the regular Sunday evening worship service. His hunch was that some changes, especially the addition of contemporary music, would reverse the trend.

As we talked it became more and more apparent that the Sunday evening service was only a symptom of a much deeper issue—a general lack of participation by junior high and senior high kids in all church programs. We could have done a survey focusing on the evening service, but this would have missed the point entirely. The problem was redefined, first of all, to call for an evaluation of the spiritual maturity, interests, and felt needs of the church youth and, second to discover the perceived relevance of the entire range of church programs and activities.

This same situation surfaced when a major denomination asked us to undertake a survey to find out how their youth magazine could be improved to attract more readers. They had designed a preliminary questionnaire asking present and potential readers what suggestions they would have. I broadened the focus far beyond the magazine to encompass the more basic issue of the role of various sources and influences (media of all types, friends, parachurch ministries, etc.) in their spiritual growth.

The resulting survey showed that youths simply felt no need for this magazine, no matter how it is changed. Hence, it was discontinued, saving the denomination nearly $100,000 a year.

These two examples underscore the need to move beyond symptoms to the bottomline issues. This requires inquiry into what the real problem might be. Admittedly, this sometimes proves to be illusive, in which case the goal of the research becomes problem clarification and definition.

Here is an example of how we defined the research problem for a large church (the disguised name used here is Midwest Community Chapel):

Midwest Community Chapel has grown rapidly in recent years. With such a large and diverse congregation, it is difficult to assess properly the spiritual needs from one segment of the congregation to another. Therefore, a survey profile of the congregation focusing on their attitudes and needs is appropriate at this point in time.

Clarification of Research Objectives

The next step is to break the problem down into its major components by clarifying the types of information needed. It is necessary to dialog at length with all who will make practical use of the proposed research asking *what information do you feel is necessary to help you to be more effective?* Quite a list can be generated through this process.

Often the decision makers forget that research also requires use of scarce resources. There is a great difference between information which is merely interesting and that which is vitally useful.

It is helpful to use this criterion in whittling an "information wish list" down to its essential elements: for each item of information suggested, *what will you do differently if you have this information?* A suggestion never makes its way onto a research instrument if there is little or no strategic usefulness.

Here is an illustration of a set of research objectives for a nationwide survey designed to uncover ways of coping with declining receptivity and interest in religion among non-Christian students on secular college and university campuses:

1. Identify the needs of students which could serve as the entry points for religion;

2. Assess attitudes and beliefs that will have bearing on receptivity to religion;
3. Obtain information on media preferences to determine how to communicate most effectively with the student population;
4. Obtain other demographic and lifestyle data that will be helpful in reaching youth;
5. Gain insight into the felt needs and influences that played a role in the spiritual decision process of recent converts.
6. Assess the felt needs and interests of Christian students with an eye toward mobilizing them in reaching peers.

Objectives stated in this way provide a clear overall roadmap for the research process. The details in each category are worked out at the next stage.

Identification of Data Requirements

Once the problem is defined it is necessary to specify in detail exactly what information is needed and from which sources.

Categories of Needed Data

Without question, the data requirements of each research situation differ. But four broad categories prove helpful as a starting point in religious education research:

1. *Awareness and understanding:* How much is known and comprehended about the topic(s) under consideration?
2. *Attitudes:* How do those who are being interviewed feel about the topic(s) under consideration?
3. *Motivation and lifestyles:* What motivations and felt needs are likely to affect attitudes and behavior?
4. *Decision-making styles:* How do the research subjects arrive at decisions with respect to the topic(s) under consideration? What are the respective roles of such information sources and influences as family members, friends, and media?

Here the researcher must specify exactly what questions will be on the survey. One or more questions are designed for each research objective. Most surveys, for example, include a felt need assessment. Then the specific categories of felt need must be identified—i.e., overcoming loneliness, finding a better relationship with parents, learning to accept myself, and so on.

All who are stakeholders in the process must continue to be actively involved, and the "usefulness criterion" remains the central consideration. I rarely will compromise much when using this criterion, because experience has shown that data overkill always is an ever-present possibility. Why enhance the possibility of overkill and impair research implementation by including nonactionable findings?

Once this detail is provided for each objective, our research roadmap now is specific and actionable. The resulting document, often referred to as an *overview abstract*, is invaluable in questionnaire design.

Data Sources

Most of the discussion here will focus on surveys which are tailor-made for a given situation (i.e., primary data). Surveys should always take into account which information is available elsewhere (secondary data). More and more relevant published research is available on youth ministry issues; therefore, the library always should be a starting point. At the very least, published research will be useful in hypothesis generation.

Determination of Data Collection Procedures

There are three general categories of research design: 1) observation; 2) descriptive survey; and 3) experiment. In addition there are several types of survey design.

Observation

Observation is the most inexpensive form of research, and there are many occasions when it is the only valid approach. How else can one isolate friendship and interaction patterns and various other types of behavior?

The obvious advantage is that observation can be unobtrusive (Webb et al., 1966)—there is no need to have someone ask questions and thereby incur the potential bias from this source. The disadvantages are equally obvious. First the observer never can be totally free from interpretation bias. Also, knowledge, feelings, needs, and attitudes often cannot be observed and inferred with any precision.

Descriptive Survey

Surveys are structured conversation encompassing more than one person. Surveys are equivalent to a snapshot of reality at a given point in time. Therefore, the survey is limited to description, and causal factors must be inferred rather than actually observed.

Experimental Design

Assume that a new curriculum is being introduced into your youth program. Will it be superior to what you now are using? A descriptive survey of responses to it will not fully answer the question. Therefore, it is necessary to design an experiment in which the researcher manipulates or changes some variables (in this case the new curriculum) while holding all other things constant. This is the essence of experimental design (see Campbell and Stanley, 1966).

An experiment of this type may also use questionnaires. Multiple measurement and controls make it possible to move beyond description into inference of cause and effect.

Types of Surveys

Survey designs fall into five basic categories: 1) personal interview; 2) self-administered interview; 3) telephone interview; 4) direct mail; and 5) focus groups. The pros and cons of each are summarized in Figure 3.

Figure 3. Five Types of Survey Designs, Strengths and Weaknesses

CRITERION	PERSONAL INTERVIEW	SELF-ADMINISTERED INTERVIEW	TELEPHONE INTERVIEW	DIRECT MAIL	FOCUS GROUPS
Ease of data collection	Highly flexible, interviewer can probe, complex scales are possible. Flow can be altered.	No flexibility. Complex scales possible. Opportunity given for detailed answers.	Somewhat flexible, interviewer can probe, complex rating scales not feasible	Inflexible, no opportunity to modify. Complex scales are possible.	Highly flexible, group interaction is a benefit. Little structured data. Great opportunity to probe.
Speed of data collection	Time-consuming in respondent contact and interviewing.	Can be done quickly in group setting.	Very quick and can be done instantaneously with many interviewers.	Very time-consuming—six to eight weeks.	Can be extremely fast, depending upon number of groups.
Geographic coverage	Limited by travel cost.	Unlimited.	Unlimited.	Unlimited—its greatest advantage.	Limited by cost of interviewer travel.
Quantity of data	Not a problem if good relationship is established.	Unlimited.	Decidedly limited and depends on interest.	Not a problem if respondent is interested.	Limited by interviewing time and extent of interaction. Possible to probe deeply.
Accuracy of data	Interviewer can probe, but also can bias answers.	Very good. No interviewer bias.	Usually not an issue if subject is nonthreatening. Otherwise limited.	Very good. Opportunity for careful thought and reflection.	Very good with skilled interviewer. Some group bias possible.
Cost	Most costly.	Inexpensive.	Expensive if paid interviewers are used.	Very low cost per respondent if return rates are high.	Costly if skilled interviewers and incentives are used.

Self-administered questionnaires are commonly used in youth ministry research.* The individual is assured of anonymity and is allowed the opportunity for careful reflection. If the subject is interesting, those interviewed can be quite responsive.

Focus groups can be helpful. For example, a parachurch ministry considered introducing a series of videotapes designed to promote group interaction with high-school aged kids. It was pretested in focus groups and found to be unacceptable, thus preventing a strategic mistake. Usually such groups consist of about ten people, and the interviewer must be a skilled group leader. The opportunity is provided for in-depth analysis of feelings and responses. After interviewing a handful of focus groups it is surprising how much can be learned about a target audience.

---

* One such questionnaire, available as part of a complete survey package for use in local churches, has been developed by Search Institute (Benson and Williams, 1987)-Ed.

On occasion you may consider other methods, but we have found that youth are not likely to return direct mail questionnaires unless the topic is of unusual interest. They enjoy talking on the telephone but may be reluctant to respond freely unless they know the interviewer.

I strongly recommend that someone other than the youth ministry leaders be involved in interviewing and data collection. People open up and respond objectively only if they feel that interviewers are neutral and nonthreatening.

Design of Data Collection Instruments

The starting point in questionnaire design is the statement of objectives and data requirements referred to above as the *overview abstract*. Unless it is precise and clear, the questionnaire will be of little practical value.

Many Christian leaders underestimate the challenge of questionnaire design and feel, often erroneously, that anyone can come up with a usable instrument. Even mature graduate students may find this process to be more difficult than they imagined when they are exposed to professional criteria and expectations.

The greatest difficulty is to minimize the ever-present problem of bias— *those errors and mistakes made in the communication process which cause findings to deviate from objective truth.* Bias never can be eliminated completely because questionnaire design still is more of an art than a science. Yet, there are some commonsense rules which, if followed, will reduce bias to acceptable levels and result in useful research findings.

The Questionnaire Design Process

Questionnaires never can be designed by formula; as with all other forms of communication, creativity is a necessity. There are usually many ways to ask the same question. The best practice is to "let the creative juices flow." The rules of thumb presented here can only serve as rough guidelines.

There is just one indispensable element—pretesting. Every questionnaire should be tried on a minimum of ten people from the target group. Each question is asked as it would be under full-scale field conditions. Time is taken to ask respondents how they comprehend each question. The goal is to determine whether their understanding is the same as yours.

Ask pretest respondents to give suggestions for change, and take their suggestions seriously. Continue pretesting until you have reasonable assurance that there is mutual understanding between sender and receiver. Omission of this stage can be costly. Nothing is more frustrating than high frequencies of nonresponse and answers which go in nonintended directions.

Figure 4 gives a simple diagram of the basic categories of questions. Structure refers to the presence or absence of response alternatives. If response categories are provided, the question is said to be structured; if none are provided the question is unstructured.

Figure 4. Four Variations of Question Design and Structure		
	Structured	Unstructured
Undisguised	1	3
Disguised	2	4

The criterion of disguise, on the other hand, designates the extent to which the purpose of the question is obvious to the respondent. An undisguised question comes right out and asks for the desired information, whereas a disguised question will employ less overt means.

The Unstructured, Undisguised Question (1). Here is an example:

Do you feel that your youth group meeting on Sunday night needs more or less Bible teaching? (check one)
_____ Needs more
_____ Needs less
_____ Neither more nor less
_____ Not sure

This type of question is easy to administer, regardless of interviewing method. Because it is structured, this facilitates computer tabulation without the time-consuming step of classification and interpretation of wide-ranging answers.

One disadvantage of this format is that some may be hesitant to reveal their true opinion, especially if an interviewer is present. Because of this factor, direct questions are best used to acquire nonthreatening information and not values or opinions.

Another disadvantage is that no opportunity is provided to explore the reasons for the answer given. This can be easily remedied by asking for open-ended responses such as "why did you say this?"

The Structured, Disguised Question (2). The advantages of structure often can be retained while minimizing reluctance to reveal true feelings in response to a direct question. Wording can be varied to allow the person being interviewed to respond in terms of a third person as this example demonstrates:

Would you say that most of the other members of your youth group would prefer more or less Bible teaching during your Sunday evening meetings? (check one)
_____ Prefer more
_____ Prefer less
_____ Neither more nor less
_____ No opinion

The assumption of the third-person format is that the answer given will, in reality, reveal the respondent's own opinions. Whether this is the case or not is open to question, but the disguised approach is worthy of consideration.

The Unstructured, Undisguised Question (3). This form is open-ended in that response alternatives are not given and the respondent is allowed to use his or her own words. Our question now might be worded in this way:

What are your feelings about the amount of Bible teaching during your Sunday evening youth group meetings? Would you like more or less or what? Why do you say this?

This free-response format is useful when there is: 1) no advance knowledge about the likely answer categories; 2) likely to be variation in replies from one person to the next; 3) a desire to avoid structuring thinking so as to elicit the respondent's own words; and 4) a need to probe more deeply into underlying motivations and reasons.

One can easily see the disadvantage. Either an interviewer or the respondent (in self-administered settings) must write the answer onto the questionnaire itself. This makes tabulation and analysis much more difficult. Responses must be sorted one-by-one into broader categories so that they can be computer entered or hand tabulated. This is time consuming and subject to the biases of those who are doing the classifying. For these compelling reasons, only a few open-ended questions should be asked.

The Unstructured, Disguised Question (4). This type of question opens the door for almost unlimited creativity and variety. One of the most popular variations is a sentence completion question focusing on third persons. The theory is that some will be more susceptible to revealing their personal feelings as long as they see themselves as answering in someone else's terms. For example,

Most of my friends would say that the length of time devoted to Bible teaching during the Sunday night youth meeting is: _____.

Which Format Is Best? There is general agreement among researchers that structured questions are preferable for computer tabulation, whereas the yield of responses from unstructured approaches is greater. Whether or not some measure of disguise is introduced depends upon the sensitivity of the subject matter and the willingness of those being interviewed to respond openly and honestly. Unstructured questions generally are limited to those areas in which it is necessary to probe further to achieve greater depth and/or clarity of response.

Some Guidelines for Questionnaire Construction

To begin questionnaire construction, here are some suggestions:

1. Immerse yourself in the objectives, making sure that questions are designed

to cover each in a comprehensive manner.

2. Whenever possible, use two questions for major objectives. This provides the opportunity to check response consistencies, and this further insures that answers are valid.

3. Continue to interact and brainstorm with those who will use the data. Do this until everyone endorses the process.

4. Consult previously used questionnaires for ideas—don't reinvent the wheel. I am not suggesting copyright violation, but some researchers, including the author, willingly share what they do and are the beneficiaries from others as well.

Figure 5 provides a summary of criteria which are most often used both to design and evaluate questionnaires. These should be viewed as rules of thumb, not hard and fast principles. If any are violated, however, make sure that you do so in full awareness that problems could be created.

Figure 5. Criteria to Use in Questionnaire Design

1. Are all objectives covered?

2. Does the questionnaire communicate as intended?

    a. Is the order and flow logical?
    b. Are any unfamiliar words used?
    c. Is any of the wording ambiguous?
    d. Are two questions asked in one?
    e. Does the subject matter require several questions rather than one?
    f. Are the response alternatives appropriate?
    g. Are there any leading questions?

Is the Order and Flow Logical? Always remember that a questionnaire is nothing more than structured conversation. One rarely jumps back and forth within a conversation in a disjointed fashion; yet this is commonly done by inexperienced questionnaire writers. If it is necessary to shift gears from one topic to the next (and it usually is), insert transition sentences explaining what is happening.

As a general principle questionnaires flow from the broad and nonthreatening subjects to the more sensitive issues—the so-called "inverted funnel." Therefore, begin with strictly factual items such as number of years in the church and so on. The purpose of the inverted funnel is to establish credibility and rapport with the respondent. As they proceed through the instrument there usually is a growing willingness to tackle the sensitive issues honestly.

A caution must be inserted here, however. Some of the demographic classification information normally conducted on questionnaires can be sensitive and hence should be put at the end. Income and age are good examples. While this is particularly true with adults, it also can be true of teenagers.

Another point to bear in mind is that prior questions can influence the answers to later questions. Consider what might happen if you were to include questions calling for an evaluation of leadership prior to more general questions on the program itself. A real bias could be created.

Are Any Unfamiliar Words Used? "Biblical exegesis?" "Pauline theology?" Such terms are largely unknown to lay people, especially youth, but I have seen worse on some local church questionnaires. As a general rule, keep your wording at the concrete level of life issues. If technical terms must be used, define them specifically. Most youth directors are sensitive to these points, but they are worth stressing nonetheless.

Is Any of the Wording Ambiguous? "How often do you *usually* attend church?" "How *regularly* do you read the Sunday School handouts?" Words such as "usually" and "regularly" are to be avoided. If you must ask questions of this variety, focus on a given time period—the last week, within the past month, and so on.

Are Two Questions Asked in One? "When you attend youth group, do you feel accepted by the others?" What would you conclude if someone answered "no"? Does this mean they do not attend the youth group, or does it mean they are not accepted? These are two questions, of course, and including two in one is a common error.

Does the Subject Matter Require Several Questions? Sometimes questions are worded in this way: "How would you evaluate the last meeting of the youth group when Mr. X spoke?" What criteria should the respondent use? It is far better to ask a series of specific questions. "Was the subject interesting?" "What have you done differently since?"

Are the Response Alternatives Appropriate? Here is a real loser taken from someone else's questionnaire:

> After returning from your two weeks of working in the hospice ministry in the innercity, would you say that your experience was (check one).
> ____ Very enjoyable
> ____ Enjoyable
> ____ Somewhat enjoyable
> ____ Not very enjoyable

Is the degree of enjoyment the appropriate criterion to use in evaluating such ministry? Try focusing on such adjectives as "spiritually challenging," "life changing," and so on.

Are There Any Leading Questions? Here is another loser:
How interested are you in seeing your friends and relatives develop a personal relationship with Jesus Christ?

____ Very interested
____ Interested
____ Somewhat interested
____ Not very interested

How may teens would come right out and say that they are not interested, even if this is the case? The question leaves no choice. Keep your eyes open—questions can become leading in subtle ways.

Measuring Felt Needs

Felt needs must be a key focus of any viable youth ministry, and here are some ways they can be measured. Sometimes general open-ended questions are of great help, especially if they are used prior to structured questions. Here are some which have proved to be especially helpful:

All of us have hopes and dreams. If all barriers were removed right now, what would you most like to see happen in your life in the next few weeks?

If you could change one thing in your life right now, what would that be?

What one thing do you worry about the most?

Sentence completion questions also can be helpful:

I am most satisfied these days when_____

I have the most fun when _____

I get most upset when _____

I will be most successful when _____

Questions of these two types will surface the most important issues, but it usually proves necessary to get more detail. Therefore, I have made considerable use of felt need scales in a variety of contexts. The one appearing in Figure 6 could be a useful model. It was used in a survey of both Christians and non-Christians on secular campuses. You should modify it to delete inappropriate categories and include those needs which are specific to your situation.

When analyzing data of this type, concentrate only on the first response category: "This is an issue which concerns me and I would like help in finding answers." After tabulating the results for your youth group, focus on the top four or five needs which emerge and make these your priority issues. If a person does not use the first response category indicating a desire for help, the need is of lower importance and should not receive your primary focus at this point in time.

General Motivations and Attitudes About Life

There is much to be gained by probing values and lifestyle. This is best done using a scale which encompasses a variety of agree/disagree questions. Known

Figure 6. A Felt Need Scale

Please circle a number following each of these issues indicating the extent to which you have this concern and would like to learn more about possible answers and solutions.

	This issue concerns me and I would like help in finding answers	This issue is of some concern and I have some interest in finding answers	This issue is of no concern to me right now
Getting the right job when I graduate	1	2	3
How to be sure I'm in love	1	2	3
How to get better grades	1	2	3
How to be free from financial worries when I graduate	1	2	3
Overcoming resentment toward my parents	1	2	3
Having consistently good sex	1	2	3
Getting more done in the time I have	1	2	3
How to know whether what the Bible says is true	1	2	3
How to overcome stress of life here on the campus	1	2	3
How to attract the right person to date	1	2	3
Finding out how God relates to everyday life	1	2	3
Finding people who will love and accept me	1	2	3
Getting along with brothers and sisters	1	2	3
Knowing more about life after death	1	2	3

in marketing research as *psychographics*, each item makes a definite statement which, taken by itself, could be leading. The idea, however, is to explore many issues to see which point of view respondents hold. Figure 7 contains some questions which proved to be helpful in the campus research mentioned above.

Figure 7. A Scale Assessing General Attitudes About Life

We would like to know what's important to you. Please read each of the following statements carefully and indicate the extent to which you agree or disagree with each by circling the number in the appropriate column. Try to avoid checking "I don't know." Your answers are completely anonymous

	Strongly agree	Agree	Somewhat agree	Somewhat disagree	Disagree	Strongly disagree	Don't know
I feel a definite sense of purpose in my life	1	2	3	4	5	6	7
I feel guilty when I go against my own standards	1	2	3	4	5	6	7
I feel I don't fit in at this church	1	2	3	4	5	6	7
My parents push me too hard to get good grades and be successful	1	2	3	4	5	6	7
I'm pretty satisfied with my life the way it is right now	1	2	3	4	5	6	7
I find it difficult to live up to my own standards as a Christian	1	2	3	4	5	6	7
My parents generally respect my opinion	1	2	3	4	5	6	7
I have a pretty clear basis for determining right from wrong	1	2	3	4	5	6	7
I am feeling guilty for the mess I have made of my life	1	2	3	4	5	6	7
It seems as if other kids in the church think it's unspiritual to have a personal struggle	1	2	3	4	5	6	7
There are no absolutes—what is right or wrong is up to the individual	1	2	3	4	5	6	7
Attending morning worship service has little meaning for me	1	2	3	4	5	6	7
My spiritual life is up and down and not consistent	1	2	3	4	5	6	7
I often wonder what will happen to me when I die	1	2	3	4	5	6	7

It is largely a matter of personal preference how many response positions there are on the scale. I like to use at least six so that people can respond on the extremes if they wish. When data of this type are analyzed, we always begin by looking for a pattern of agreement or disagreement. Focus especially on the agree/disagree responses and largely disregard the "somewhat" categories.

Notice the question in Figure 7 which states, "I am feeling guilty for the mess I have made of my life." In the survey referred to here, only 56 percent disagreed, and 31 percent agreed. This means that nearly a third in the youth group was undergoing a sense of crisis. As a result, the curricular agenda was set for the next semester.

If the number surveyed is small, it may be necessary to collapse the two extreme categories and use only three alternatives: 1) agree; 2) neither agree nor disagree (combining the two "somewhat" categories); and 3) disagree. This is because many will avoid the extremes. Look for a pattern across responses. You will get a sense of the spiritual health and identify some of the most sensitive issues if you include questions of this type.

Measures of Spiritual Maturity

This is a difficult area to measure. How can one recognize a mature Christian? What values, beliefs, and behaviors will be evidenced without crossing into the arena of legalism? Unless we are very clear in this respect, measurement is impossible.

While no one has definitive answers, here are some aspects of spirituality which can be measured using any of the above questionnaire formats:
1. Individual prayer life and devotions both alone and with others.
2. Knowledge and application of spiritual truth to diverse life problems.
3. Participation in relevant phases of church life.
4. A commitment to sharing one's faith with others.
5. Meaningful involvement (*koinonia*) with other Christians.

Questions under these headings can be quite specific. For example, is a kid experiencing *koinonia* or not? Questions can center on loneliness, perceptions of whether there are people who care, and so on. Devotional life can be assessed by asking questions about the number of days in the past week in which he or she read the Bible, amount of time spent in prayer, etc.

Program Evaluation

The agree/disagree format also can be used to evaluate youth programs. Be sure to include questions which cover the full range of opinion on the most relevant dimensions. Another approach is to use paired adjectives, allowing respondents to check all that apply.

Here are a few examples:

____ Out-of-date	____ Narrow	____ Second rate
____ Boring	____ Relevant	____ Dull
____ Fun	____ Helpful	____ Not for me

Classification Information

It is necessary to get descriptive information such as age, number of brothers and sisters, Christian background, year in school, sex, and so on. This provides a demographic description of the group and is useful in cross-classification analysis. The purpose of this is to isolate differences between subgroups (more on this later).

Data Collection

At times personal interviewers will be used. While space does not permit a detailed analysis, it is sufficient simply to note that the role of the interviewer is to find out *what* people think, not *change* what they think. This means that everything must be done to be completely neutral and nondirectional at all times. This should come naturally to those who are skilled in group processes. For more detail, see Engel (1977), ch. 7.

Data Tabulation and Analysis

In today's world, all but the simplest surveys should be computer data processed. Data processing and statistical packages are widely available for PCs and are well within the technical grasp of any reader. Hand tabulation is tedious and prone to error.

When analyzing scaled data such as that in Figure 7, one always should look, first of all, for the median. This is calculated by totaling the percentage response from each answer category until the total reaches or exceeds 50 percent. This tells you the general direction of the responses.

Take, for example, the first question in Figure 7: "I feel a definite sense of purpose in life." The respondent circles a number between 1 and 6 indicating the extent of agreement and circles 7 if he or she does not know. Assume the data come out like this:

Strongly agree						Don't know
18.3%	32.7%	19.2%	8.8%	14.9%	4.1%	3.0%
____	____	____	____	____	____	____

The median falls in the "agree" category (i.e., 18.3 percent + 32.7 percent). The conclusion is that the majority of those who were interviewed feel they have a definite sense of purpose in life.

You always should focus on the first two "agreement" categories and the last two "disagreement" categories while largely disregarding those who fall in the middle. See what pattern emerges from which you will draw your conclusions. To refresh your memory, I suggest using the same approach with felt need data (Figure 6) and focusing on the percentages of those who check the first category indicating a strong felt need and desire for change.

It usually is necessary to undertake a cross-classification analysis. Cross classification refers to breaking down the responses given by everyone into sub-groupings such as age categories, year in school, or degree of exposure to Christianity. This is done because groups often are heterogeneous, and there may be a variety of traits that will be overlooked unless subgroups are distinguished. When this is the case, major clues and insights will be lost if cross classification is not undertaken.

Figure 8 gives an example of a simplified cross-classification table in which magazine readership (the dependent variable) is cross classified by age (the independent variable). Notice that readership varies sharply from one age category to the next. With those under fifteen, magazine D is the most preferred (35 percent) closely followed by magazine A (30 percent). Those aged fifteen to eighteen, however, strongly prefer magazine B (68 percent), while D emerged on top in the over-eighteen age bracket (43 percent).

Figure 8. Christian Magazine Readership Cross Classified by Age

MAGAZINE	AGE CATEGORY					
	Under 15		15-18		Over 18	
	No.	%	No.	%	No.	%
A	60	30%	28	10%	34	22%
B	40	20	170	63	21	13
C	30	15	40	15	70	43
D	70	35	31	12	38	22
Total	200	100%	269	100%	163	100%

It is customary to undertake statistical analysis to assess whether or not differences this large could occur by chance. The most common statistical test for this purpose is chi square analysis (see Engel 1977; pp. 134-137). This is always done by computer, and the outcome is a score which indicates the probability that chance alone is the explanation. When we can reject chance (this certainly would be the case with Figure 8), then we can say that data are *statistically significant*. When this is not the case, then the table is rejected and not analyzed further.

While statistics at times may seem confusing and unnecessary, it is important to recognize that this type of analysis is part of the standard repertoire of reputable researchers. Cross-classification data should be statistically analyzed so the findings will not be misleading. There are standard computer programs that do this in a "user friendly" manner.

Phasing Research into Strategy

If research is to be used by those who are working together in ministry, it is necessary that all be involved in analysis and interpretation. The goal is to *build ownership*. This is a creative process, because there usually will be many strategic options.

The only caution is to go slow—be a *change agent*. A series of small steps will do more than one gigantic step in most situations. There also is wisdom in testing your program changes before cementing them in place. Research rarely answers every question, thus small-scale testing is a virtual necessity. As a result, *research is an ongoing process*.

Conclusion

A short chapter such as this can only give a few basic principles and will not equip one to be a researcher. Nevertheless, experience has shown that research largely is a matter of common sense channeled by the types of guidelines given here. Research, in the final analysis, is as much an attitude as a set of methods—it is *an enlightened listening ear*. When viewed this way, anyone can be a researcher, regardless of background and training. Start by asking pertinent questions from the point of view of how programs can be changed or adapted to bring about greater effectiveness.

There is wisdom in consulting someone who is a trained researcher. Take the first steps in research design yourself and seek qualified input. Courses on this subject are commonplace in many disciplines, and one does not have to look far to find help.

There is no magic formula for success, but research undertaken in the context of strategic planning is a valuable way to find the mind of Christ and provide a catalytic impetus for change.

REFERENCES

Alreck, L., and Settle, R. B. (1985). *The survey research handbook*. Homewood, Ill.: Irwin.

Benson, P. L., and Williams, D. L. (1987). *Determining needs in your youth ministry*. Loveland, Colo.: Group Books.

Campbell, D. T., and Stanley, J. C. (1966). *Experimental and quasi-experimental designs for research*. Chicago: Rand McNally.

Engel, J. F. (1989). *Strategic planning for extension education*. Wheaton, Ill.: ACCESS.

Engel, J. F. (1977). *How can I get them to listen?* Grand Rapids, Mich.: Zondervan. This book is scheduled to be revised for publication in 1991.

Stott, J. R. W. (1976). *Christian mission in the world*. Downers Grove, Ill.: InterVarsity Press.

Webb, E. J., Campbell, D. T., Schwartz, R. D., and Sechrest, L. (1966), *Unobtrusive measures: Nonreactive research in the social sciences*. Chicago: Rand McNally.

CONTRIBUTORS

JERRY ALDRIDGE teaches in the School of Education at the University of Alabama at Birmingham. Previous teaching experiences include first and fourth grades, special education, and college level at Livingston University, Samford University, and Furman University. He has a doctoral degree in special education as well as masters degrees in special education and early childhood education, and an educational specialist degree in special education with a concentration in school psychometry. Dr. Aldridge has written a text for the National Education Association on early elementary classrooms, three instructors manuals for developmental psychology textbooks, chapters in two books on exceptionality, and more than twenty articles in professional journals. He is also a popular conference speaker and consultant.

ANTHONY CAMPOLO is Chairman of the Sociology Department at Eastern College. He is a well-known speaker and author. His numerous books include *A Reasonable Faith, Partly Right,* and *Growing Up in America: A Sociology of Youth Ministry.* He has authored many articles for scholarly sociology journals, but is also known for his practical involvements overseas. He attended the Franklin Institute as a teenager. He has also been a candidate for the United States House of Representatives, a television talk show host, a pastor, and Vice President of the American Baptist Convention. Dr. Campolo is founder and President of the Evangelical Association for the Promotion of Education, as well as Executive Director of Youth Guidance of Southeastern Pennsylvania.

BONNIDELL CLOUSE is Professor of Educational and School Psychology at Indiana State University. She possesses an MA in psychology from Boston University and a PhD in educational psychology from Indiana University. She is author of *Moral Development: Perspectives in Psychology and Christian Belief* and co-editor of *Women in Ministry: Four Views.* She has also contributed numerous articles to professional and religious journals. Dr. Clouse is actively involved in the Brethren Church where her husband serves as minister.

JAMES DAVIES is Director of the Doctor of Ministry program at Canadian Theological Seminary, as well as Associate Professor of Christian Education. He received a masters degree from Trinity Evangelical Divinity School and has an EdD from the University of Georgia. He was a successful youth minister for a number of years, and is a popular speaker at churches in Canada and the United States. He has been published in a number of professional journals.

JAMES F. ENGEL is currently the Distinguished Professor of Marketing, Research, and Strategy in the MBA/MS Program in Economic Development at Eastern College, as well as serving as Director of the Leadership Development Institute at Eastern. For eighteen years he was on the faculty of Wheaton College, where he pioneered the application of marketing concepts to Christian ministry. Among his many books and articles are *What's Gone Wrong With the Harvest* and *Contemporary Christian Communications,* as well as being senior author of two standard texts *Consumer Behavior* (now in a sixth edition) and *Promotional Strategy* (in a seventh edition). Dr. Engel has been a consultant for over 200 Christian organizations in sixty countries. He was the founder and first president of the Association of Consumer Research, and has taught at the University of Illinois, the University of Michigan, and Ohio State University. His MS and PhD degrees are in business from the University of Illinois.

KENNETH HYDE is a retired educator living in Hull, England. He has a Bachelor of Divinity degree from the University of London and a PhD in education from the University of Birmingham. He has taught at nearly every level of education, and most recently was the senior advisor for religious education with the Inner London Education Authority. He has had extensive involvement in curriculum development and teacher training for religious education in both church and public school contexts. He was also Chief Examiner for public examinations in religious studies for many years. His many scholarly writings include *Religious Learning in Adolescence, Religion and Slow Learners,* and his recent American release *Religion in Childhood and Adolescence.*

RONALD L. KOTESKEY is Professor of Psychology at Asbury College in Kentucky. He received MA and PhD degrees in experimental psychology from Wayne State University, but has spent most of his career in scholarly analysis of psychology from a Christian perspective and studying the development of adolescence. The author of more than fifty articles in professional journals, his best-known books include *Understanding Adolescence, The Loved Triangle: Sex, Dating, and Love,* and *General Psychology for Christian Counselors.*

JAMES MICHAEL LEE is Professor of Education at the University of Alabama at Birmingham, and publisher of Religious Education Press. He acquired a doctoral degree at Columbia University. He taught at the University of Notre Dame for fifteen years. In addition to writing numerous chapters in scholarly books, he is acknowledged as the leading proponent of the social-science theory of religious education. Perhaps his finest work to date is *The Content of Religious Education*, the final volume of his massive trilogy documenting how research in the social sciences is the only adequate foundation for teaching religious education. He has lectured widely in the United States, Canada, and Europe.

BLAKE NEFF is the Director of the School of Communication at Toccoa Falls College. He possesses an MDiv degree from Asbury Theological Seminary and a PhD in interpersonal and public communication from Bowling Green State University. He also pastors a United Methodist Church. He is a popular speaker and has conducted numerous family enrichment seminars. He was a visiting lecturer at Winebrenner Theological Seminary, and served on the editorial advisory board of Roxbury Publishing Company. Neff coauthored a chapter in the forthcoming *Handbook of Children's Religious Education*.

DONALD RATCLIFF is Assistant Professor of Psychology and Sociology at Toccoa Falls College, and has an MA from Michigan State University and an EdS from the University of Georgia, both in educational psychology. He has published numerous articles on psychology and sociology in scholarly journals. He is the author of *Using Psychology in the Church*, a coauthor of *Introduction to Psychology and Counseling*, and editor of both *Handbook of Preschool Religious Education* and *Handbook of Children's Religious Education*.

GARY L. SAPP is Professor of Counseling, Human Services, and Foundations at the University of Alabama at Birmingham. He acquired an MA degree at the University of Kentucky in counseling, and an EdD degree in educational psychology and psychology at the University of Tennessee. He has served as the director of the UAB educational clinic, was the acting director of the school psychology program at Moorhead State University, and has taught at the University of Tennessee, Chulalongkorn University (Thailand), and the University of North Carolina. He edited *A Handbook of Moral Development, Perspectives in Educational Psychology*, and *Compassion in Pastoral Ministry*. He has also authored more than seventy book chapters, articles in professional journals, and scholarly papers. He attends a Southern Baptist church.

Index of Names

Index of Subjects

Related Books of Interest From Religious Education Press

RELIGION IN CHILDHOOD AND ADOLESCENCE
by Kenneth E. Hyde

This comprehensive book gives the findings of virtually every English language research study on this topic. Complete data on youth's and children's religious attitudes, religious beliefs, religious lifestyle, religious development, religious experience, religious thinking, religious opinions, and much more.
529 pages   ISBN 0-89135-076-4

RELIGIOUS EDUCATION MINISTRY WITH YOUTH
edited by D. Campbell Wyckoff and Don Richter

One of the most widely used and most influential of all youth ministry books. Provides the background, spirit, research, and description of leadership skills necessary for effective youth religious education. Aims at empowering youth to become a positive force for Christian leadership.
257 pages   ISBN 0-89135-030-6

INTERGENERATION RELIGIOUS EDUCATION
by James W. White

An all-inclusive examination of the entire area of intergenerational religious education. Provides the four essential ingredients for effective intergenerational religious education, namely theory, research, overall models, and concrete suggestions. An excellent volume to broaden youth religious education by infusing it with the intergenerational element.
290 pages   ISBN 0-89135-067-5

THE SHAPE OF RELIGIOUS INSTRUCTION
by James Michael Lee

The first volume in Lee's monumental trilogy on religious education. This volume presents the rationale for the existence of religious instruction as a social-scientific field in its own right and not as a branch of theology. This volume is quite possibly one of the five most influential books written on religious education in the twentieth century.
330 pages   ISBN 0-89135-002-0

THE FLOW OF RELIGIOUS INSTRUCTION
by James Michael Lee

The second volume in Lee's monumental trilogy on religious education. This volume deals with the structural content of religious instruction, namely, the form and manner of successful religion teaching in all settings. This volume is quite possibly the finest book on how to teach religion written since the end of World War II.
379 pages   ISBN 0-89135-003-9

THE CONTENT OF RELIGIOUS INSTRUCTION
by James Michael Lee

The third volume in Lee's monumental trilogy on religious education. This volume deals with the substantive content of religious instruction, namely, the various kinds of molar substantive kinds of religious outcomes which take place in every kind of religious instruction act. This volume is quite possibly the most comprehensive book ever written on the content of religious education.
814 pages   ISBN 0-89135-050-0

TEACHING CHRISTIAN VALUES
by Lucie W. Barber

A fine resource to help youth ministers effectively teach values to adolescents. Part I is a review of the literature on values. Part II offers many research-based suggestions on how to teach values successfully. Part III delineates how values are formed and how values develop. Part IV identifies seven cardinal Christian values and gives a program to teach them effectively.
250 pages   ISBN 0-89135-041-4

USING MEDIA IN RELIGIOUS EDUCATION
by Ronald A. Sarno

Adolescents are shaped by media. Their consciousness is a media consciousness, not a print consciousness. Hence media is *the* central way of effectively minis-

tering religiously to youth. This comprehensive volume provides virtually everything the youth minister needs to know about understanding and using media. It
gives both the nature and structure of media communication and also a wealth
of practical tested suggestions on how to appreciate and use media effectively.
300 pages   ISBN 0-89135-058-6

LONELINESS AND SPIRITUAL GROWTH
by Samual M. Natale

Many adolescents are lonely, and thus an important task of the youth minister is
to help the adolescent use loneliness as a means for spiritual growth. This book
examines the main forms of loneliness and the eight major theories which explain
the nature and structure of loneliness. It shows how the youth minister can help
lonely adolescents.
171 pages   ISBN 0-89135-055-1

BIBLICAL THEMES IN RELIGIOUS EDUCATION
edited by Joseph S. Marino

The Bible is a central and indispensable element in all youth ministry which is
genuinely Christian. The first two chapters of this volume give basic guidelines
for effectively using the Bible in religious education activity. The remaining
chapters relate central biblical themes to religion teaching. These themes are
faith, prayer, justice, discovery of God, disciplieship, sin, and reconciliation—
all key biblical themes in the religious education of youth.
294 pages   ISBN 0-89135-038-1

CAN CHRISTIANS BE EDUCATED?
by Morton Kelsey

This is Kelsey's only book specifically on religious education. It uses Jungian psychology to illuminate the psycho-spiritual dynamics of teaching learners of all
ages to pray more purely, to love more deeply, to use their emotions more wisely, and to come to Christian wholeness more completely.
154 pages   ISBN 0-89135-008-X

LEADERSHIP IN RELIGIOUS EDUCATION
by David Arthur Bickimer

A valuable resource for persons directing youth ministry programs. Blends
vision, theory, models, and nuts-and-bolts. The core of the book is the Prehensive
Leadership Model which insures the preservation of leadership vision and wholeness while engaging in nitty-gritty practice.
278 pages   ISBN 0-89135-073-X